SUETONIUS

VOLUME II

WITH AN ENGLISH TRANSLATION BY

J. C. ROLFE

HARVARD UNIVERSITY PRESS
CAMBRIDGE, MASSACHUSETTS
LONDON, ENGLAND

ISBN 0–674–99565–1

Typeset in ZephGreek and ZephText
by Chiron, Inc, North Chelmsford, Massachusetts.
Printed in Great Britain by St Edmundsbury Press Ltd,
Bury St Edmunds, Suffolk, on acid-free paper.
Bound by Hunter & Foulis Ltd, Edinburgh, Scotland.

CONTENTS

NOTE TO SECOND EDITION

As in the first volume of this revised edition of Suetonius, Donna W. Hurley has corrected and selectively updated the translation and notes of the Lives of the Caesars. I have revised the Lives of Illustrious Men to take account of recent work, particularly that of Robert A. Kaster.

G.P.G.

LIVES OF THE CAESARS

LIBER V

DIVUS CLAUDIUS

I. Patrem Claudi Caesaris Drusum, olim Decimum
mox Neronem praenomine, Livia, cum Augusto gravida
nupsisset, intra mensem tertium peperit, fuitque suspicio
ex vitrico per adulterii consuetudinem procreatum. Statim certe vulgatus est versus:

τοῖς εὐτυχοῦσι καὶ τρίμηνα παιδία.

2   Is Drusus in quaesturae praeturaeque honore dux
Raetici, deinde Germanici belli Oceanum septemtri-
onalem primus Romanorum ducum navigavit transque
Rhenum fossas navi et immensi operis effecit, quae nunc
adhuc Drusinae vocantur. Hostem etiam frequenter
caesum ac penitus in intimas solitudines actum non
prius destitit insequi, quam species barbarae mulieris
humana amplior victorem tendere ultra sermone Latino
3 prohibuisset. Quas ob res ovandi ius et triumphalia
ornamenta percepit; ac post praeturam confestim inito

---

^a In 38 B.C.   ^b See *Aug.* lxii. 2.
^c In 15 B.C.   ^d In 12 B.C.
^e The *fossae Drusinae* connected the Rhine with what was
the Zuider Zee and furnished a passage to the North Sea.

BOOK V

THE DEIFIED CLAUDIUS

I. The father of Claudius Caesar, Drusus, who at first had the forename Decimus and later that of Nero, was born of Livia[a] within three months after her marriage to Augustus[b] (for she was with child at the time) and there was a suspicion that he was begotten by his stepfather in adulterous intercourse. Certain it is that this verse at once became current:

> Three-month children are born to the blessed.

This Drusus, while holding the offices of quaestor and praetor, was in charge of the war in Raetia and later of that in Germany.[c] He was the first of Roman generals to sail the northern Ocean, and beyond the Rhine with prodigious labour he constructed the huge canal[d] which to this very day is called by his name.[e] Even after he had defeated the enemy in many battles and driven them far into the wilds of the interior, he did not cease his pursuit until the apparition of a barbarian woman of greater than human size, speaking in the Latin tongue, forbade him to push his victory further. For these exploits he received the honour of an ovation[f] with the triumphal regalia;

[f] See *Aug.* xxii.

consulatu atque expeditione repetita supremum diem
morbo obiit in aestivis castris, quae ex eo Scelerata sunt
appellata. Corpus eius per municipiorum coloniarumque
primores suscipientibus obviis scribarum decuriis ad
urbem devectum sepultumque est in campo Martio.
Ceterum exercitus honorarium ei tumulum excitavit,
circa quem deinceps stato die quotannis miles decurreret
Galliarumque civitates publice supplicarent. Praeterea
senatus inter alia complura marmoreum arcum cum
tropaeis via Appia decrevit et Germanici cognomen ipsi
4 posterisque eius. Fuisse autem creditur non minus glo-
riosi quam civilis animi; nam ex hoste super victorias
opima quoque spolia captasse summoque saepius discrimine duces Germanorum tota acie insectatus; nec dissimulasse umquam pristinum se rei p. statum, quandoque
posset, restituturum. Unde existimo nonnullos tradere
ausos, suspectum eum Augusto revocatumque ex provin-
5 cia et quia cunctaretur, interceptum veneno. Quod equidem magis ne praetermitterem rettuli, quam quia verum
aut veri simile putem, cum Augustus tanto opere et vivum

---

^a In 9 B.C.

^b Cf. *Tib.* vii. 3.

^c The reference is probably to the *scribae quaestorii*, the
quaestor's clerks, who were the most important of the attendants
upon the magistrates. They formed a guild composed of six
decuriae, or divisions of ten, presided over by six officers called
sex primi curatorum.

^d A *decursus* or *decursio*. Dio, 56. 42, describes the one
about the funeral pyre of Augustus. After running around it in
full armour, the soldiers cast into the fire the military prizes
which they had received from the emperor; cf. *Jul.* lxxxiv. 4.

and immediately after his praetorship he became consul and resumed his campaign, but died in his summer camp,[a] which for that reason was given the name of "Accursed." The body was carried by the leading men of the free towns and colonies to Rome,[b] where it was met and received by the decuries of scribes,[c] and buried in the campus Martius. But the army reared a monument in his honour, about which the soldiers should make a ceremonial run[d] each year thereafter on a stated day, which the cities of Gaul were to observe with prayers and sacrifices. The senate, in addition to many other honours, voted him a marble arch adorned with trophies on the Appian Way, and the surname Germanicus for himself and his descendants. It is the general belief that he was as eager for glory as he was democratic[e] by nature; for in addition to victories over the enemy he greatly desired to win the "noble trophies,"[f] often pursuing the leaders of the Germans all over the field at great personal risk; and he made no secret of his intention of restoring the old-time form of government, whenever he should have the power. It is because of this, I think, that some have made bold to write that he was an object of suspicion to Augustus; that the emperor recalled him from his province, and when he did not obey at once, took him off by poison. This I have mentioned, rather not to pass it by, than that I think it true or even probable; for as a matter of fact Augustus loved him so dearly while he lived that he

[e] See note on *Tib.* xxvi. 1.

[f] The *spolia opima* were the armour of the leader of the enemy, taken from him in hand-to-hand combat by a Roman general.

dilexerit, ut coheredem semper filiis instituerit, sicut quondam in senatu professus est, et defunctum ita pro contione laudaverit, ut deos precatus sit, similes ei Caesares suos facerent sibique tam honestum quandoque exitum darent quam illi dedissent. Nec contentus elogium tumulo eius versibus a se compositis insculpsisse, etiam vitae memoriam prosa oratione composuit.

6   Ex Antonia minore complures quidem liberos tulit, verum tres omnino reliquit: Germanicum, Livillam, Claudium.

II. Claudius natus est Iullo[1] Antonio Fabio Africano coss. Kal. Aug. Luguduni eo ipso die quo primum ara ibi Augusto dedicata est, appellatusque Tiberius Claudius Drusus. Mox fratre maiore in Iuliam familiam adoptato Germanici cognomen assumpsit. Infans autem relictus a patre ac per omne fere pueritiae atque adulescentiae tempus variis et tenacibus morbis conflictatus est, adeo ut animo simul et corpore hebetato ne progressa quidem aetate ulli publico privatoque muneri habilis existimare-

2   tur. Diu atque etiam post tutelam receptam alieni arbitrii et sub paedagogo fuit; quem barbarum et olim superiumentarium ex industria sibi appositum, ut se quibuscumque de causis quam saevissime coerceret, ipse quodam libello conqueritur. Ob hanc eandem valitudinem et gladiatorio munere, quod simul cum fratre

---

[1] Iullo, *Ihm*; Iulio, Ω; Iulo, *Pulmann*.

---

[a] C. and L. Caesar; see *Tib.* xxiii and Index.

[b] On August 1, 10 B.C.

[c] That is, the age at which one was ordinarily freed from tutelage. The usual formula is *in suam tutelam venire*, Cic. *De Orat.* i. 39. 180.

always named him joint-heir along with his sons, as he once declared in the senate; and when he was dead, he eulogized him warmly before the people, praying the gods to make his Caesars[a] like Drusus, and to grant him, when his time came, as glorious a death as they had given that hero. And not content with carving a laudatory inscription on his tomb in verses of his own composition, Augustus also wrote a memoir of his life in prose.

Drusus had several children by the younger Antonia, but was survived by only three, Germanicus, Livilla, and Claudius.

II. Claudius was born[b] at Lugdunum on the Kalends of August in the consulship of Iullus Antonius and Fabius Africanus, the very day when an altar was first dedicated to Augustus in that town, and he received the name of Tiberius Claudius Drusus. Later, on the adoption of his elder brother into the Julian family, he took the surname Germanicus. He lost his father when he was still an infant, and throughout almost the whole course of his childhood and youth he suffered so severely from various obstinate disorders that the vigour of both his mind and his body was dulled, and even when he reached the proper age he was not thought capable of any public or private business. For a long time, even after he reached the age of independence,[c] he was in a state of pupillage and under a guardian, of whom he himself makes complaint in a book of his, saying that he was a barbarian and a former chief of muleteers, put in charge of him for the express purpose of punishing him with all possible severity for any cause whatever. It was also because of his weak

7

memoriae patris edebat, palliolatus novo more praesedit; et togae virilis die circa mediam noctem sine sollemni officio lectica in Capitolium latus est.

III. Disciplinis tamen liberalibus ab aetate prima non mediocrem operam dedit ac saepe experimenta cuiusque etiam publicavit. Verum ne sic quidem quicquam dignitatis assequi aut spem de se commodiorem in posterum facere potuit.

2 Mater Antonia portentum eum hominis dictitabat, nec absolutum a natura, sed tantum incohatum; ac si quem socordiae argueret, stultiorem aiebat filio suo Claudio. Avia Augusta pro despectissimo semper habuit, non affari nisi rarissime, non monere nisi acerbo et brevi scripto aut per internuntios solita. Soror Livilla cum audisset quandoque imperaturum, tam iniquam et tam indignam sortem p. R. palam et clare detestata est. Nam avunculus maior Augustus quid de eo in utramque partem opinatus sit, quo certius cognoscatur, capita ex ipsius epistulis posui.

IV. "Collocutus sum cum Tiberio, ut mandasti, mea Livia, quid nepoti tuo Tiberio faciendum esset ludis Martialibus. Consentit autem uterque nostrum, semel nobis esse statuendum, quod consilium in illo sequamur. Nam si est artius, ut ita dicam, holocleros, quid est quod dubitemus, quin per eosdem articulos et gradus pro-

---

[a] Of relatives and friends. [b] The future emperor.

[c] Claudius. [d] Perhaps those celebrated by Augustus in A.D. 12 in honour of Mars Ultor.

[e] The two Greek words, ἄρτιος and ὁλόκληρος, mean "complete," "perfect of one's kind"; the meaning therefore is "if he have his five senses."

health that contrary to all precedent he wore a cloak when he presided at the gladiatorial games which he and his brother gave in honour of their father; and on the day when he assumed the gown of manhood he was taken in a litter to the Capitol about midnight without the usual escort.[a]

III. Yet he gave no slight attention to liberal studies from his earliest youth, and even published frequent specimens of his attainments in each line. But even so he could not attain any public position or inspire more favourable hopes of his future.

His mother Antonia often called him "a monster of a man, not finished but merely begun by Dame Nature"; and if she accused anyone of dullness, she used to say that he was "a bigger fool than her son Claudius." His grandmother Augusta always treated him with the utmost contempt, very rarely speaking to him; and when she admonished him, she did so in short, harsh letters, or through messengers. When his sister Livilla heard that he would one day be emperor, she openly and loudly prayed that the Roman people might be spared so cruel and undeserved a fortune. Finally to make it clearer what opinions, favourable and otherwise, his great uncle Augustus had of him, I have appended extracts from his own letters:

IV. "I have talked with Tiberius,[b] my dear Livia, as you requested, with regard to what is to be done with your grandson Tiberius[c] at the games of Mars.[d] Now we are both agreed that we must decide once for all what plan we are to adopt in his case. For if he be sound [e] and so to say complete,[e] what reason have we for doubting that he ought to be advanced through the same grades

2 ducendus sit, per quos frater eius productus sit? Sin autem ἠλαττῶσθαι[1] sentimus eum et βεβλάφθαι καὶ εἰς τὴν τοῦ σώματος καὶ εἰς τὴν τῆς ψυχῆς[2] ἀρτιότητα, praebenda materia deridendi et illum et nos non est hominibus τὰ τοιαῦτα σκώπτειν καὶ μυκτηρίζειν εἰωθόσιν.[3] Nam semper aestuabimus, si de singulis articulis temporum deliberabimus, μὴ προϋποκειμένου

3 ἡμῖν posse arbitremur eum gerere honores necne. In praesentia tamen quibus de rebus consulis, curare eum ludis Martialibus triclinium sacerdotum non displicet nobis, si est passurus se ab Silvani filio homine sibi affini admoneri, ne quid faciat quod conspici et derideri possit. Spectare eum circenses ex pulvinari non placet nobis; expositus enim in fronte prima spectaculorum conspicietur. In Albanum montem ire eum non placet nobis aut esse Romae Latinarum diebus. Cur enim non praeficitur

4 urbi, si potest sequi fratrem suum in montem? Habes nostras, mea Livia, sententias, quibus placet semel de tota re aliquid constitui, ne semper inter spem et metum fluctuemur. Licebit autem, si voles, Antoniae quoque nostrae des hanc partem epistulae huius legendam." Rursus alteris litteris:

5 "Tiberium adulescentem ego vero, dum tu aberis, cotidie invitabo ad cenam, ne solus cenet cum suo Sulpicio et Athenodoro. Qui vellem diligentius et minus μετεώρως deligeret sibi aliquem, cuius motum et habitum et incessum imitaretur. Misellus ἀτυχεῖ· nam ἐν τοῖς σπουδαί-

[1] ἠλαττῶσθαι, *Beroaldus;* ελαττωσθαι *and* ελαττωσεαι, *mss.*
[2] ψυχῆς, *first Roman editions;* ψχης, *mss.*
[3] εἰωθόσιν, *Roman editions;* εηιωθοσιν, *most of the mss.*

[a] See note on *Aug.* xlv. 1.

and steps through which his brother has been advanced? But if we realize that he is wanting and defective in soundness of body and mind, we must not furnish the means of ridiculing both him and us to a public which is wont to scoff at and deride such things. Surely we shall always be in a stew, if we deliberate about each separate occasion and do not make up our minds in advance whether we think he can hold public offices or not. However, as to the matters about which you ask my present advice, I do not object to his having charge of the banquet of the priests at the games of Mars, if he will allow himself to be advised by his kinsman the son of Silvanus, so as not to do anything to make himself conspicuous or ridiculous. That he should view the games in the Circus from the imperial box[a] does not meet with my approval; for he will be conspicuous if exposed to full view in the front of the auditorium. I am opposed to his going to the Alban Mount or being in Rome on the days of the Latin festival; for why should he not be made prefect of the city, if he is able to attend his brother to the Mount? You have my views, my dear Livia, to wit that I desire that something be decided once for all about the whole matter, to save us from constantly wavering between hope and fear. Moreover, you may, if you wish, give this part of my letter to our kinswoman Antonia also to read." Again in another letter:

"I certainly shall invite the young Tiberius to dinner every day during your absence, to keep him from dining alone with his friends Sulpicius and Athenodorus. I do wish that he would choose more carefully and in a less scatter-brained fashion someone to imitate in his movements, bearing, and gait. The poor fellow is unlucky; for

οις, ubi non aberravit eius animus, satis apparet ἡ τῆς ψυχῆς αὐτοῦ εὐγένεια." Item tertiis litteris:

6   "Tiberium nepotem tuum placere mihi declamantem potuisse, peream nisi, mea Livia, admiror. Nam qui tam ἀσαφῶς loquatur, qui possit cum declamat σαφῶς dicere quae dicenda sunt, non video."

7   Nec dubium est, quid post haec Augustus constituerit, et[1] reliquerit eum nullo praeter auguralis sacerdotii honore impertitum ac ne heredem quidem nisi inter tertios ac paene extraneos e[2] parte sexta nuncuparet, legato quoque[3] non amplius quam octingentorum sestertiorum prosecutus.

V. Tiberius patruus petenti honores consularia ornamenta detulit; sed instantius legitimos flagitanti id solum codicillis rescripsit, quadraginta aureos in Saturnalia et Sigillaria[4] misisse ei. Tunc demum abiecta spe dignitatis ad otium concessit, modo in hortis et suburbana domo, modo in Campaniae secessu delitescens, atque ex contubernio sordidissimorum hominum super veterem segnitiae notam ebrietatis quoque et aleae infamiam subiit, cum interim, quanquam hoc modo agenti, numquam aut officium hominum aut reverentia publice defuit.

---

[1] et, mss.; ut, Smilda; cum, Bentley.
[2] e, second Roman edition; ne, Ω.
[3] legato quoque, Ernesti; legatoque, mss.; legato, Torrentius.
[4] sigillaria, L[3]ς; sigillari, Ω.

---

[a] See note on Jul. lxxxiii. 2; the heirs in the third degree had little or no prospect of receiving their inheritance.

[b] December 21 and 22, an extension of the Saturnalia, when it was customary to make presents of little images of various kinds (sigilla); also the name of a quarter or street in Rome, see chap. xvi. 4; Nero, xxviii. 2.

in important matters, where his mind does not wander, the nobility of his character is apparent enough." Also in a third letter:

"Confound me, dear Livia, if I am not surprised that your grandson Tiberius could please me with his declaiming. How in the world anyone who is so unclear in his conversation can speak with clearness and propriety when he declaims, is more than I can see."

There is no doubt at all what Augustus later decided, and that he left him invested with no office other than the augural priesthood, not even naming him as one of his heirs, save in the third degree[a] and to a sixth part of his estate, among those who were all but strangers; while the legacy that he left him was not more than eight hundred thousand sesterces.

V. His paternal uncle Tiberius gave him the consular regalia, when he asked for office; but when he urgently requested the actual position, Tiberius merely replied by a note in these words: "I have sent you forty gold-pieces for the Saturnalia and the Sigillaria."[b] Then at last Claudius abandoned all hope of advancement and gave himself up to idleness, living in obscurity now in his house and gardens in the suburbs, and sometimes at a villa in Campania; moreover from his intimacy with the lowest of men he incurred the reproach of drunkenness and gambling, in addition to his former reputation for dullness. Yet all this time, despite his conduct, he never lacked attention from individuals or respect from the public.

VI. Equester ordo bis patronum eum perferendae pro se legationis elegit, semel cum deportandum Romam corpus Augusti umeris suis ab consulibus exposceret,[1] iterum cum oppressum Seianum apud eosdem gratularetur; quin et spectaculis advenienti assurgere et lacernas[2] 2 deponere solebat. Senatus quoque, ut ad numerum sodalium Augustalium sorte ductorum extra ordinem adiceretur, censuit et mox ut domus ei, quam incendio amiserat, publica impensa restitueretur, dicendaeque inter consulares sententiae ius esset. Quod decretum abolitum est, excusante Tiberio imbecillitatem eius ac damnum liberalitate sua resarsurum pollicente. Qui tamen moriens et in tertiis heredibus eum ex parte tertia nuncupatum, legato etiam circa sestertium vicies prosecutus, commendavit insuper exercitibus ac senatui populoque R. inter ceteras necessitudines nominatim.

VII. Sub Gaio demum fratris filio secundam existimationem circa initia imperii omnibus lenociniis colligente honores auspicatus consulatum gessit una per duos menses, evenitque ut primitus ingredienti cum fascibus Forum praetervolans aquila dexteriore umero consideret. Sortitus est et de altero consulatu in quartum annum; praeseditque nonnumquam spectaculis in Gai vicem, adclamante populo: "Feliciter" partim "patruo imperatoris" partim "Germanici fratri!"

[1] exposceret, ⟨; exposceretur, *Casaubon*; exposcerent, *mss.*
[2] lacernas, $\Pi^2 T$; *the other mss. have* lucernas.

---

[a] Founded by Tiberius for the worship of the Deified Augustus.   [b] Of his house.

[c] Gaius appointed a number of consuls at once, who drew lots for the year when they were to hold the office.

VI. The equestrian order twice chose him as their patron, to head a deputation on their behalf: once when they asked from the consuls the privilege of carrying the body of Augustus to Rome on their shoulders, and again when they offered them their congratulations on the downfall of Sejanus. They even used to rise when he appeared at the public shows and put off their cloaks. The senate too voted that he be made a special member of the priests of Augustus,[a] who were usually chosen by lot; when he later lost his house by fire, that it should be rebuilt at the public expense, and that he should have the honour of giving his opinion among the consulars. This second decree was however repealed, since Tiberius urged Claudius' infirmity as a reason, and promised that he would make the loss[b] good through his own generosity. Yet when Tiberius died, he named Claudius only among his heirs in the third degree, to a third part of his estate, although he gave him in addition a legacy of about two million sesterces, and expressly commended him besides to the armies and to the senate and people of Rome with the rest of his kinsfolk.

VII. It was only under his nephew Gaius, who in the early part of his reign tried to gain popularity by every device, that he at last began his official career, holding the consulship as his colleague for two months; and it chanced that as he entered the Forum for the first time with the fasces, an eagle that was flying by lit upon his shoulder. He was also allotted a second consulship, to be held four years later,[c] and several times he presided at the shows in place of Gaius, and was greeted by the people now with "Success to the emperor's uncle!" and now with "All hail to the brother of Germanicus!"

VIII. Nec eo minus contumeliis obnoxius vixit. Nam et si paulo serius ad praedictam cenae horam occurrisset, non nisi aegre et circuito demum triclinio recipiebatur, et quotiens post cibum addormisceret, quod ei fere accidebat, olearum aut palmularum ossibus incessebatur, interdum ferula flagrove velut per ludum excitabatur a copreis. Solebant et manibus stertentis socci induci, ut repente expergefactus faciem sibimet confricaret.

IX. Sed ne discriminibus quidem caruit. Primum in ipso consulatu, quod Neronis et Drusi fratrum Caesaris statuas segnius locandas ponendasque curasset, paene honore summotus est; deinde extraneo vel etiam domesticorum aliquo deferente assidue varieque inquietatus. Cum vero detecta esset Lepidi et Gaetulici coniuratio, missus in Germaniam inter legatos ad gratulandum etiam vitae periculum adiit, indignante ac fremente Gaio patruum potissimum ad se missum quasi ad puerum regendum, adeo ut non defuerint, qui traderent praecipitatum quoque in flumen, sic ut vestitus advenerat. Atque ex eo numquam non in senatu novissimus consularium sententiam dixit, ignominiae causa post omnis interrogatus. Etiam cognitio falsi testamenti recepta est, in quo et ipse signaverat. Postremo sestertium octogies pro introitu novi sacerdotii coactus impendere, ad eas rei familiaris angustias decidit, ut cum obligatam aerario

---

[a] See *Calig.* viii. 1 and xxiv. 3.

[b] The meeting was at Lugdunum; the river the Rhône or the Saône.

[c] See *Calig.* xxii. 3.

VIII. But all this did not save him from constant insults; for if he came to dinner a little after the appointed time, he took his place with difficulty and only after making the round of the dining-room. Whenever he went to sleep after dinner, which was a habit of his, he was pelted with the stones of olives and dates, and sometimes he was awakened by the jesters with a whip or cane, in pretended sport. They used also to put slippers on his hands as he lay snoring, so that when he was suddenly aroused he might rub his face with them.

IX. But he was exposed also to actual dangers. First in his very consulship, when he was all but deposed, because he had been somewhat slow in contracting for and setting up the statues of Nero and Drusus, the emperor's brothers. Afterwards he was continually harassed by all kinds of accusations, brought against him by strangers or even by the members of his household. Finally, when the conspiracy of Lepidus and Gaetulicus[a] was detected and he was sent to Germany as one of the envoys to congratulate the emperor, he was really in peril of his life, since Gaius raged and fumed because his uncle of all men had been sent to him, as if to a child in need of a guardian. So great, indeed, was his wrath that some have written that Claudius was even thrown into the river[b] clothes and all, just as he had come. Moreover, from that time on he always gave his opinion in the senate last among the consulars, having the question put to him after all the rest by way of humiliation. A case involving the forgery of a will was even admitted, in which Claudius himself was one of the signers. At last he was forced to pay eight million sesterces to enter a new priesthood,[c] which reduced him to such straitened circumstances that he was unable to meet

17

fidem liberare non posset, in vacuum lege praediatoria venalis pependerit sub edicto praefectorum.

X. Per haec ac talia maxima aetatis parte transacta quinquagesimo anno imperium cepit quantumvis mirabili casu. Exclusus inter ceteros ab insidiatoribus Gai, cum quasi secretum eo desiderante[1] turbam submoverent, in diaetam, cui nomen est Hermaeum, recesserat; neque multo post rumore caedis exterritus prorepsit ad solarium proximum interque praetenta foribus vela se abdidit.

2 Latentem discurrens forte gregarius miles, animadversis pedibus, studio[2] sciscitandi quisnam esset, adgnovit[3] extractumque et prae metu ad genua sibi accidentem imperatorem salutavit. Hinc ad alios commilitones fluctuantis nec quicquam adhuc quam frementis perduxit. Ab his lecticae impositus et, quia sui diffugerant, vicissim succollantibus in castra delatus est tristis ac trepidus, miserante obvia turba quasi ad poenam raperetur insons.

3 Receptus intra vallum inter excubias militum pernoctavit, aliquanto minore spe quam fiducia. Nam consules cum senatu et cohortibus urbanis Forum Capitoliumque occupaverant asserturi communem libertatem; accitusque et

---

[1] desiderante, Ʈ; *the other mss. have* desideranti.

[2] studio, *G; the other mss. have* e studio (ex, *T*).

[3] adgnovit] agnovit, *T⁥; the other mss. have* adcognovit.

---

[a] He had borrowed money from the public treasury for his entrance fee into the new priesthood, and pledged his estates as security.

[b] That is, the prefects of the treasury, chosen from the praetors and ex-praetors (see *Aug.* xxxvi). Claudius later restored the charge of the treasury to the quaestors (see chap. xxiv. 2).

18

the obligation incurred to the treasury;[a] whereupon by edict of the prefects[b] his property was advertised for sale to meet the deficiency,[c] in accordance with the law regulating confiscations.

X. Having spent the greater part of his life under these and like circumstances, he became emperor in his fiftieth year[d] by a remarkable freak of fortune. When the assassins of Gaius shut out the crowd under pretence that the emperor wished to be alone, Claudius was ousted with the rest and withdrew to an apartment called the Hermaeum; and a little later, in great terror at the news of the murder, he stole away to a balcony hard by and hid among the curtains which hung before the door. As he cowered there, a common soldier, who was prowling about at random, saw his feet, and intending to ask who he was, pulled him out and recognized him; and when Claudius fell at his feet in terror, he hailed him as emperor. Then he took him to the rest of his comrades, who were as yet in a condition of uncertainty and purposeless rage. These placed him in a litter, took turns in carrying it, since his own bearers had made off, and bore him to the Camp in a state of despair and terror, while the throng that met him pitied him, as an innocent man who was being hurried off to execution. Received within the rampart, he spent the night among the sentries with much less hope than confidence;[e] for the consuls with the senate and the city cohorts had taken possession of the Forum and the Capitol, resolved on maintaining the

[c] *in vacuum*; the meaning is uncertain. It perhaps means that the advertisement was merely a matter of form, though none the less humiliating.   [d] In A.D. 41.   [e] "Hope" of becoming emperor; "confidence" that he had escaped death.

ipse per tr. pl. in curiam ad suadenda quae viderentur, vi
4 se et necessitate teneri respondit. Verum postero die et
senatu segniore in exsequendis conatibus per taedium ac
dissensionem diversa censentium et multitudine, quae
circumstabat, unum rectorem iam et nominatim
exposcente, armatos[1] pro contione iurare in nomen suum
passus est promisitque singulis quina dena sestertia,
primus Caesarum fidem militis etiam praemio pigneratus.

XI. Imperio stabilito nihil antiquius duxit quam id
biduum, quo de mutando rei p. statu haesitatum erat,[a]
memoriae eximere. Omnium itaque factorum dicto-
rumque in eo veniam et oblivionem in perpetuum sanxit
ac praestitit, tribunis modo ac centurionibus paucis e
coniuratorum in Gaium numero interemptis, exempli
simul causa et quod suam quoque caedem depoposcisse
2 cognoverat. Conversus hinc ad officia pietatis ius iurandum neque sanctius sibi neque crebrius instituit quam
per Augustum. Aviae Liviae divinos honores et circensi
pompa currum elephantorum Augustino similem decer-
nenda curavit; parentibus inferias publicas, et hoc
amplius patri circenses annuos natali die, matri carpen-
tum, quo per Circum duceretur,[b] et cognomen Augustae
ab viva[2] recusatum. At in fratris memoriam[3][c] per omnem
occasionem celebratam comoediam quoque Graecam

---

[1] armatos, ΠQ; *the other mss. have* armatus.

[2] viva, *Lipsius*; avia, Ω.

[3] At in fratris memoriam, *suggested by Ihm*; a fratris memoria, *MGX*; ad fratris memoriam, Τ.

---

[a] By restoring the republic.

[b] For carrying her image; see *Calig.* xv. 1, and cf. *Tib.* li. 2.

[c] Germanicus.

public liberty.[a] When he too was summoned to the House by the tribunes of the commons, to give his advice on the situation, he sent word that "he was detained by force and compulsion." But the next day, since the senate was dilatory in putting through its plans because of the tiresome bickering of those who held divergent views, while the populace, who stood about the hall, called for one ruler and expressly named Claudius, he allowed the armed assembly of the soldiers to swear allegiance to him, and promised each man fifteen thousand sesterces; being the first of the Caesars who resorted to bribery to secure the fidelity of the troops.

XI. As soon as his power was firmly established, he considered it of foremost importance to obliterate the memory of the two days when men had thought of changing the form of government. Accordingly he made a decree that all that had been done and said during that period should be pardoned and forever forgotten; he kept his word too, save only that a few of the tribunes and centurions who had conspired against Gaius were put to death, both to make an example of them and because he knew that they had also demanded his own death. Then turning to the duties of family loyalty, he adopted as his most sacred and frequent oath "By Augustus." He had divine honours voted his grandmother Livia and a chariot drawn by elephants in the procession at the Circus,[b] like that of Augustus; also public offerings to the shades of his parents and in addition annual games in the Circus on his father's birthday and for his mother a carriage to bear her image through the Circus and the surname of Augusta, which she had declined during her lifetime. In memory of his brother,[c] whom he took every opportunity of

Neapolitano certamine docuit ac de sententia iudicum
3 coronavit. Ne Marcum quidem Antonium inhonoratum
ac sine grata mentione transmisit, testatus quondam per
edictum, tanto impensius petere se ut natalem patris
Drusi celebrarent, quod idem esset et avi sui Antoni.
Tiberio marmoreum arcum iuxta Pompei theatrum,
decretum quidem olim a senatu verum omissum, peregit.
Gai quoque etsi acta omnia rescidit, diem tamen necis,
quamvis exordium principatus sui, vetuit inter festos
referri.

XII. At in semet augendo parcus atque civilis
praenomine Imperatoris abstinuit, nimios honores
recusavit, sponsalia filiae natalemque geniti nepotis silentio ac tantum domestica religione transegit. Neminem
exsulum nisi ex senatus auctoritate restituit. Ut sibi in
curiam praefectum praetori tribunosque militum secum
inducere liceret utque rata essent quae procuratores sui
2 in iudicando statuerent, precario exegit. Ius nundinarum
in privata praedia a consulibus petit. Cognitionibus magistratuum ut unus e consiliariis frequenter interfuit; eosdem spectacula edentis surgens et ipse cum cetera turba
voce ac manu veneratus est. Tribunis plebis adeuntibus
se pro tribunali excusavit, quod propter angustias non
posset audire eos nisi stantes.

---

[a] See *Aug.* xcviii. 5. The comedy was doubtless written by
Germanicus; see *Calig.* iii. 2.

[b] See *Jul.* lxxvi. 1.

honouring, he brought out a Greek comedy in the contest
at Naples[a] and awarded it the crown in accordance with
the decision of the judges. He did not leave even Mark
Antony unhonoured or without grateful mention, declaring once in a proclamation that he requested the more
earnestly that the birthday of his father Drusus be celebrated because it was the same as that of his grandfather
Antony. He completed the marble arch to Tiberius near
Pompey's theatre, which had been voted some time
before by the senate, but left unfinished. Even in the case
of Gaius, while he annulled all his acts, yet he would not
allow the day of his death to be added to the festivals,
although it was also the beginning of his own reign.

XII. But in adding to his own dignity he was modest
and unassuming, refraining from taking the forename
Imperator,[b] refusing excessive honours, and passing over
the betrothal of his daughter and the birthday of a grandson in silence and with merely private ceremonies. He
recalled no one from exile except with the approval of the
senate. He obtained from the members as a favour the
privilege of bringing into the House with him the prefect
of the praetorian guard and the tribunes of the soldiers,
and the ratification of the judicial acts of his agents in the
provinces. He asked the consuls for permission to hold
fairs on his private estates. He often appeared as one of
the advisers at cases tried before the magistrates; and
when they gave games, he also arose with the rest of the
audience and showed his respect by acclamations and
applause. When the tribunes of the commons appeared
before him as he sat upon the tribunal, he apologised to
them because for lack of room he could not hear them
unless they stood up.

3   Quare in brevi spatio tantum amoris favorisque colle-
git, ut cum profectum eum Ostiam perisse ex insidiis nuntiatum esset, magna consternatione populus et militem
quasi proditorem et senatum quasi parricidam diris exse-
crationibus incessere non ante destiterit, quam unus
atque alter et mox plures a magistratibus in rostra producti salvum et appropinquare confirmarent.

XIII. Nec tamen expers insidiarum usque quaque
permansit, sed et a[1] singulis et per factionem et denique
civili bello infestatus est. E plebe homo nocte media
iuxta cubiculum eius cum pugione deprehensus est;
reperti et equestris ordinis duo in publico cum dolone ac
venatorio cultro praestolantes, alter ut egressum theatro,
alter ut sacrificantem apud Martis aedem adoreretur.

2   Conspiraverunt autem ad res novas Gallus Asinius et
Statilius Corvinus, Pollionis ac Messalae oratorum
nepotes, assumptis compluribus libertis ipsius atque
servis. Bellum civile movit Furius Camillus Scribonianus
Delmatiae legatus; verum intra quintum diem oppressus
est legionibus, quae sacramentum mutaverant, in paenitentiam religione conversis, postquam denuntiato ad
novum imperatorem itinere casu quodam ac divinitus
neque aquila ornari neque signa convelli moverique
potuerunt.

XIV. Consulatus super pristinum quattuor gessit; ex
quibus duos primos iunctim, sequentis per intervallum

---

[1] sed et a, Υ; etaeta, *M*; et a, *GX*.

---

[a] With garlands and perfumes; cf. note on *Tib.* xlviii. 2.

[b] See note on *Jul.* lxii. It was considered a bad omen if it was
difficult to pull the standards from the ground.

By such conduct he won so much love and devotion in a short time that, when it was reported that he had been waylaid and killed on a journey to Ostia, the people were horror stricken and with dreadful execrations continued to assail the soldiers as traitors, and the senate as murderers, until finally one or two men, and later several, were brought forward upon the rostra by the magistrates and assured the people that Claudius was safe and on his way to the city.

XIII. Yet he did not remain throughout without experience of treachery, but he was attacked by individuals, by a conspiracy, and finally by a civil war. A man of the commons was caught near his bed-chamber in the middle of the night, dagger in hand; and two members of the equestrian order were found lying in wait for him in public places, one ready to attack him with a sword-cane as he came out of the theatre, the other with a hunting knife as he was sacrificing in the temple of Mars. Asinius Gallus and Statilius Corvinus, grandsons of the orators Pollio and Messala, conspired to overthrow him, aided by a number of his own freedmen and slaves. The civil war was set on foot by Furius Camillus Scribonianus, governor of Dalmatia; but his rebellion was put down within five days, since the legions which had changed their allegiance were turned from their purpose by superstitious fear; for when the order was given to march to their new commander, by some providential chance the eagles could not be adorned[a] nor the standards pulled up and moved.[b]

XIV. He held four consulships[c] in addition to his original one. Of these the first two were in successive years,

[c] In A.D. 42, 43, 47, and 51.

quarto quemque anno, semenstrem novissimum, bimenstris ceteros, tertium autem novo circa principem exemplo in locum demortui suffectus. Ius et consul et extra honorem laboriosissime dixit, etiam suis suorumque diebus sollemnibus, nonnumquam festis quoque antiquitus et religiosis. Nec semper praescripta legum secutus duritiam lenitatemve multarum ex bono et aequo, perinde ut adficeretur, moderatus est; nam et iis, qui apud privatos iudices plus petendo formula excidissent, restituit actiones et in maiore fraude convictos legitimam poenam supergressus ad bestias condemnavit.

XV. In cognoscendo autem ac decernendo mira varietate animi fuit, modo circumspectus et sagax, interdum inconsultus ac praeceps, nonnumquam frivolus amentique similis. Cum decurias rerum actu expungeret, eum, qui dissimulata vacatione quam beneficio liberorum habebat responderat, ut cupidum iudicandi dimisit; alium interpellatum ab adversariis de propria lite negantemque cognitionis rem sed ordinarii iuris esse, agere causam confestim apud se coegit, proprio negotio documentum daturum, quam aequus iudex in alieno negotio futurus esset. Feminam non agnoscentem filium suum dubia utrimque argumentorum fide ad confessionem compulit

2

---

[a] Before his own tribunal.

[b] More literally "the decuries for court duty," to distinguish them from the decuries of knights, scribes, etc.

[c] That is, he enjoyed the privileges of the *ius trium liberorum*, one of which was freedom from jury duty.

while the other two followed at intervals of four years each, the last for six months, the others for two; and in his third he was substituted for one of the consuls who had died, a thing which was without precedent in the case of an emperor. He administered justice most conscientiously both as consul and when out of office, even on his own anniversaries and those of his family, and sometimes even on festivals of ancient date and days of ill-omen. He did not always follow the letter of the laws, but modified their severity or lenity in many cases according to his own notions of equity and justice; for he allowed a new trial to those who had lost their cases before private judges by demanding more than the law prescribed, while, overstepping the lawful penalty, he condemned to the wild beasts those who were convicted of especially heinous crimes.

XV. But in hearing and deciding cases[a] he showed strange inconsistency of temper, for he was now careful and shrewd, sometimes hasty and inconsiderate, occasionally silly and like a crazy man. In revising the lists of the divisions of jurors[b] he disqualified a man who had presented himself without mentioning that he was immune because of the number of his children,[c] on the ground that he had a passion for jury-duty. Another, who was challenged by his opponents about a suit of his own, said that it did not come before Caesar's tribunal, but the ordinary courts; whereupon Claudius compelled him at once to bring the case before him, saying that the man would show in a case affecting his own interests how just a juror he would be in the affairs of others. When a woman refused to recognise her son, and the evidence on both sides was conflicting, he forced her to admit the truth by

27

indicto matrimonio iuvenis. Absentibus secundum prae-
sentes facillime dabat, nullo dilectu culpane quis an[1] aliqua necessitate cessasset. Proclamante quodam praeci-
dendas falsario manus, carnificem statim acciri cum
machaera mensaque lanionia flagitavit. Peregrinitatis
reum orta inter advocatos levi contentione, togatumne an
palliatum dicere causam oporteret, quasi aequitatem
integram ostentans, mutare habitum saepius et prout
accusaretur defendereturve, iussit. De quodam etiam
negotio ita ex tabella pronuntiasse creditur, secundum
eos se sentire, qui vera proposuissent. Propter quae
usque eo eviluit, ut passim ac propalam contemptui esset.
Excusans quidam testem e provincia ab eo vocatum
negavit praesto esse posse dissimulata diu causa; ac post
longas demum interrogationes: "Mortuus est," inquit,
"puto, licuit." Alius gratias agens quod reum defendi
pateretur, adiecit: "Et tamen fieri solet." Illud quoque a
maioribus natu audiebam, adeo causidicos patientia eius
solitos abuti, ut discedentem e tribunali non solum voce
revocarent, sed et lacinia togae retenta, interdum pede
apprehenso detinerent. Ac ne cui haec mira sint, litigatori Graeculo vox in altercatione excidit: καὶ σὺ γέρων

---

[1] an, *Stephanus*; in, Ω.

---

[a] Cf. Dio, 60. 28.
[b] Only a Roman citizen had the right to wear the toga.

ordering her to marry the young man. Whenever one party to a suit was absent, he was prone to decide in favour of the one who was present, without considering whether his opponent had failed to appear through his own fault or from a necessary cause.[a] On a man's being convicted of forgery, some one cried out that his hands ought to be cut off; whereupon Claudius insisted that an executioner be summoned at once with knife and block. In a case involving citizenship a fruitless dispute arose among the advocates as to whether the defendant ought to make his appearance in the toga[b] or in a Greek mantle, and the emperor, with the idea of showing absolute impartiality, made him change his garb several times, according as he was accused or defended. In one case he is credited with having rendered the following decision, which he had actually written out beforehand: "I decide in favour of those who have told the truth." By such acts as these he so discredited himself that he was held in general and open contempt. One man, in making excuses for a witness that the emperor had summoned from one of the provinces, said that he could not appear, but for a long time would give no reason; at last, after a long series of questions, he said: "He's dead; I think the excuse is a lawful one." Another in thanking the emperor for allowing him to defend his client added "After all, it is usual." I myself used to hear older men say that the pleaders took such advantage of his good-nature, that they would not only call him back when he left the tribunal, but would catch hold of the fringe of his robe, and sometimes of his foot, and thus detain him. To prevent any surprise at this, I may add that a common Greek litigant let slip this remark in a hot debate: "You are both an old man and a

εἶ καὶ μωρός. Equitem quidem Romanum obscaenitatis in feminas reum, sed falso et ab impotentibus inimicis conficto crimine, satis constat, cum scorta meritoria citari adversus se et audiri pro testimonio videret, graphium et libellos, quos tenebat in manu, ita cum magna stultitiae et saevitiae exprobratione iecisse in faciem eius, ut genam non leviter perstrinxerit.

XVI. Gessit et censuram intermissam diu post Plancum Paulumque censores,[a] sed hanc quoque inaequabiliter varioque et animo et eventu. Recognitione equitum iuvenem probri plenum, sed quem pater probatissimum sibi affirmabat, sine ignominia dimisit, habere dicens censorem suum; alium corruptelis adulteriisque famosum nihil amplius quam monuit, ut aut parcius aetatulae indulgeret aut certe cautius; addiditque: "Quare enim ego scio, quam amicam habeas?" Et cum orantibus familiaribus dempsisset cuidam appositam notam: "Litura tamen," inquit, "exstet." Splendidum virum Graeciaeque provinciae principem, verum Latini sermonis ignarum, non modo albo iudicum erasit, sed in peregrinitatem redegit. Nec quemquam nisi sua voce, utcumque quis posset, ac sine patrono rationem vitae passus est reddere. Notavitque[d] multos, et quosdam inopinantis et ex causa novi generis, quod se inscio ac sine commeatu Italia excessissent; quendam vero et quod comes regis in

2

---

[a] In A.D. 48.

[b] In 22 B.C.

[c] On these see *Aug.* xxxix.

[d] By affixing the *nota*, or mark of disgrace, to their names on the census-list.

fool." All the world knows that a Roman knight who was tried for improper conduct towards women, but on a false charge trumped up by unscrupulous enemies, seeing common prostitutes called as witnesses against him and their testimony admitted, hurled the stylus and tablets which he held in his hand into the emperor's face with such force as to cut his cheek badly, at the same time loudly reviling his cruelty and stupidity.

XVI. He also assumed the censorship,[a] which had long been discontinued, ever since the term of Plancus and Paulus,[b] but in this office too he was variable, and both his theory and his practice were inconsistent. In his review of the knights he let off a young man of evil character, whose father said that he was perfectly satisfied with him, without any public censure,[c] saying "He has a censor of his own." Another who was notorious for corruption and adultery he merely admonished to be more restrained in his indulgence, or at any rate more circumspect, adding, "For why should I know what mistress you keep?" When he had removed the mark of censure affixed to one man's name, yielding to the entreaties of the latter's friends, he said: "But let the erasure be seen." He not only struck from the list of jurors a man of high birth, a leading citizen of the province of Greece, because he did not know Latin, but even deprived him of the rights of citizenship; and he would not allow anyone to render an account of his life save in his own words, as well as he could, without the help of an advocate. And he degraded[d] many, some contrary to their expectation and on the novel charge that they had left Italy without consulting him and obtaining leave of absence; one man merely because he had been companion to a king in his

31

provincia fuisset, referens maiorum temporibus Rabirio
Postumo Ptolemaeum Alexandriam crediti servandi causa
3 secuto crimen maiestatis apud iudices motum. Plures
notare conatus, magna inquisitorum neglegentia sed suo
maiore dedecore, innoxios fere repperit, quibuscumque
caelibatum aut orbitatem aut egestatem obiceret, mari-
tos, patres, opulentos se probantibus; eo quidem, qui
sibimet vim ferro intulisse arguebatur, inlaesum corpus
4 veste deposita ostentante. Fuerunt et illa in censura eius
notabilia, quod essedum argenteum sumptuose fabrica-
tum ac venale ad Sigillaria redimi concidique coram
imperavit; quodque uno die XX edicta proposuit, inter
quae duo, quorum altero admonebat, ut uberi vinearum
proventu bene dolia picarentur; altero, nihil aeque facere
ad viperae morsum quam taxi arboris sucum.

XVII. Expeditionem unam omnino suscepit eamque
modicam. Cum decretis sibi a senatu ornamentis triumphalibus leviorem maiestati principali[1] titulum arbitraretur velletque iusti triumphi decus, unde adquireret
Britanniam potissimum elegit, neque temptatam ulli post
Divum Iulium et tunc tumultuantem ob non redditos
2 transfugas. Huc cum ab Ostia navigaret, vehementi circio
bis paene demersus est, prope Liguriam iuxtaque
Stoechadas[2] insulas. Quare a Massilia Gesoriacum us-

[1] principali, ς; principalem, Ω.
[2] Stoechadas, ς; Stochadas, Ω.

[a] Referring to the street or quarter; see note on chap. v.
[b] Suetonius is vague. Dio, 60. 19, says that one Bericus, who
had been expelled from the island during a revolution, persuaded Claudius to send troops there.

province, citing the case of Rabirius Postumus, who in
bygone days had been tried for treason because he had
followed Ptolemy to Alexandria, to recover a loan. When
he attempted to degrade still more, he found them in
most cases blameless; for owing to the great carelessness
of his agents, but to his own greater shame, those whom
he accused of celibacy, childlessness, or lack of means
proved that they were married, or fathers, or well-to-do.
In fact, one man, who was charged with having stabbed
himself, stripped off his clothing and showed a body without a scar. Other noteworthy acts of his censorship were
the following: he had a silver chariot of costly workmanship, which was offered for sale in the Sigillaria,[a] bought
and cut to pieces in his presence; in one single day he
made twenty proclamations, including these two: "As the
yield of the vineyards is bountiful, the wine jars should be
well pitched"; and "Nothing is so effective a cure for
snake-bite as the juice of the yew tree."

XVII. He made but one campaign and that of little
importance. When the senate voted him the triumphal
regalia, thinking the honour beneath the imperial dignity
and desiring the glory of a legitimate triumph, he chose
Britain as the best place for gaining it, a land that had
been attempted by no one since the Deified Julius and
was just at that time in a state of rebellion because of the
refusal to return certain deserters.[b] On the voyage
thither from Ostia he was nearly cast away twice in furi-
ous north-westers, off Liguria and near the Stoechades
islands. Therefore he made the journey from Massilia all

que pedestri itinere confecto inde transmisit ac sine ullo proelio aut sanguine intra paucissimos dies parte insulae in deditionem recepta, sexto quam profectus erat mense 3 Romam rediit triumphavitque maximo apparatu. Ad cuius spectaculum commeare in urbem non solum praesidibus provinciarum permisit, verum etiam exsulibus quibusdam; atque inter hostilia spolia navalem coronam fastigio Palatinae domus iuxta civicam fixit, traiecti et quasi domiti Oceani insigne. Currum eius Messalina uxor carpento secuta est; secuti et triumphalia ornamenta eodem bello adepti, sed ceteri pedibus et in praetexta, M.[1] Crassus Frugi equo phalerato et in veste palmata, quod eum honorem iteraverat.

XVIII. Urbis annonaeque curam sollicitissime semper egit. Cum Aemiliana pertinacius arderent, in diribitorio duabus noctibus mansit ac deficiente militum ac familiarum turba auxilio plebem per magistratus ex omnibus vicis convocavit ac positis ante se cum pecunia fiscis ad subveniendum hortatus est, repraesentans pro opera dig-2 nam cuique mercedem. Artiore autem annona ob assiduas sterilitates detentus quondam medio Foro a turba conviciisque et simul fragminibus panis ita infestatus, ut aegre nec nisi postico evadere in Palatium valuerit, nihil non excogitavit[2] ad invehendos etiam tempore hiberno

---

[1] praetexta M., G; praetextam, M; pretexta, X; eodem ... palmata, omitted by Υ.   [2] excogitavit, TϚ; the other mss. have ex eo cogitavit; ex eo agitavit, Bentley.

---

[a] In A.D. 43.   [b] A suburb of Rome, lying north of the city, outside the Servian wall.

[c] A large building in the campus Martius, where the votes cast in the elections were sorted and counted; according to Dio, 55. 8, the largest building ever covered by a single roof.

the way to Gesoriacum by land, crossed from there, and without any battle or bloodshed received the submission[a] of a part of the island within a few days, returned to Rome within six months after leaving the city, and celebrated a triumph of great splendour. To witness the sight he allowed not only the governors of the provinces to come to Rome, but even some of the exiles; and among the tokens of his victory he set a naval crown on the gable of the Palace beside the civic crown, as a sign that he had crossed and, as it were, subdued the Ocean. His wife Messalina followed his chariot in a carriage, as did also those who had won the triumphal regalia in the same war; the rest marched on foot in purple-bordered togas, except Marcus Crassus Frugi, who rode a caparisoned horse and wore a tunic embroidered with palms, because he was receiving the honour for the second time.

XVIII. He always gave scrupulous attention to the care of the city and the supply of grain. On the occasion of a stubborn fire in the Aemiliana[b] he remained in the Diribitorium[c] for two nights, and when a body of soldiers and of his own slaves could not give sufficient help, he summoned the commons from all parts of the city through the magistrates, and placing bags full of money before them, urged them to the rescue, paying each man on the spot a suitable reward for his services. When there was a scarcity of grain because of long-continued droughts, he was once stopped in the middle of the Forum by a mob and so pelted with abuse and at the same time with pieces of bread, that he was barely able to make his escape to the Palace by a back door; and after this experience he resorted to every possible means to bring

35

commeatus. Nam et negotiatoribus certa lucra proposuit suscepto in se damno, si cui quid per tempestates accidisset, et naves mercaturae causa fabricantibus magna commoda constituit pro condicione cuiusque: (XIX.) civi[1] vacationem legis Papiae Poppaeae, Latino ius Quiritium, feminis ius IIII liberorum; quae constituta hodieque servantur.

XX. Opera magna potius et necessaria[2] quam multa perfecit, sed vel praecipua: ductum aquarum a Gaio incohatum, item emissarium Fucini lacus portumque Ostiensem, quanquam sciret ex iis alterum ab Augusto precantibus assidue Marsis negatum, alterum a Divo Iulio saepius destinatum ac propter difficultatem omissum. Claudiae aquae gelidos et uberes fontes, quorum alteri Caeruleo, alteri Curtio et Albudigno nomen est, simulque rivum Anienis novi lapideo opere in urbem perduxit divisitque in plurimos et ornatissimos lacus. Fucinum adgressus est non minus compendii spe quam gloriae, cum quidam privato sumptu emissuros se repromitterent, si sibi siccati agri concederentur. Per tria autem passuum[3] milia partim effosso[4] monte partim exciso canalem absolvit aegre et post undecim annos, quamvis continuis XXX hominum milibus sine intermissione ope-

2

---

[1] civi, *Turnebus*; civis, Ω; civibus, ς.

[2] magna potius et necessaria, *suggested by Ihm*; magna potius quam n., *mss. The second* quam *is omitted by* Π[1]Q.

[3] passus, *MGL.*

[4] effosso, Sς; exfossa, *M*; *the other mss. have* exfosso *except T*, *which omits* effosso monte partim; ecfosso, *Roth.*

---

[a] Passed in A.D. 9, after the failure of Augustus' law *de maritandis ordinibus*; see *Aug.* xxxiv.

[b] See note on *Aug.* xlvii.

grain to Rome, even in the winter season. To the merchants he held out the certainty of profit by assuming the expense of any loss that they might suffer from storms, and offered to those who would build merchant ships large bounties, adapted to the condition of each: (XIX.) to a citizen exemption from the *lex Papia Poppaea*;[a] to a Latin[b] the rights of Roman citizenship; to women the privileges allowed the mothers of four children.[c] And all these provisions are in force today.

XX. The public works which he completed were great and essential rather than numerous; they were in particular the following: an aqueduct begun by Gaius; also the outlet of Lake Fucinus and the harbour at Ostia, although in the case of the last two he knew that Augustus had refused the former to the Marsians in spite of their frequent requests, and that the latter had often been thought of by the Deified Julius, but given up because of its difficulty. He brought to the city on stone arches the cool and abundant founts of the Claudian aqueduct, one of which is called Caeruleus and the other Curtius and Albudignus, and at the same time the spring of the new Anio, distributing them into many beautifully ornamented pools. He made the attempt on the Fucine Lake as much in the hope of gain as of glory, inasmuch as there were some who agreed to drain it at their own cost, provided the land that was uncovered be given to them. He finished the outlet, which was three miles in length, partly by levelling and partly by tunnelling a mountain, a work of great difficulty and requiring eleven years, although he had thirty thousand men at work all the time without

[c] These were numerous and varied; cf. Dio, 55. 2.

3   rantibus. Portum Ostiae exstruxit circumducto dextra sinistraque brachio et ad introitum profundo iam solo[1] mole obiecta; quam quo stabilius fundaret, navem ante demersit, qua magnus obeliscus ex Aegypto fuerat advectus, congestisque pilis superposuit altissimam turrem in exemplum Alexandrini Phari, ut ad nocturnos ignes cursum navigia dirigerent.

XXI. Congiaria populo saepius distribuit. Spectacula quoque complura et magnifica edidit, non usitata modo ac solitis locis, sed et commenticia et ex antiquitate repetita, et ubi praeterea nemo ante eum. Ludos dedicationis Pompeiani theatri, quod ambustum restituerat, e tribunali posito in orchestra commisit, cum prius apud superiores aedes supplicasset perque mediam caveam

2   sedentibus ac silentibus cunctis descendisset. Fecit et saeculares, quasi anticipatos ab Augusto nec legitimo tempori reservatos, quamvis ipse in historiis suis prodat, intermissos eos Augustum multo post diligentissime annorum ratione subducta in ordinem redegisse. Quare vox praeconis irrisa est invitantis more sollemni ad ludos, quos nec spectasset quisquam nec spectaturus esset, cum superessent adhuc qui spectaverant, et quidam histrionum producti olim tunc quoque producerentur. Cir-

---

[1] salo, *Stephanus.*

---

[a] This had been brought by Gaius from Heliopolis and set up in the *spina* of his circus, near the Vatican hill. It now stands before the cathedral of St. Peter. The great ship in which it was transported to Rome from Alexandria is described by Pliny, *N.H.* 16. 201.   [b] Pompey placed the temple of Venus Victrix at the top of his theatre, so that the seats of the auditorium formed an approach to it. There were also shrines of Honos, Virtus and Felicitas. See Pliny, *N.H.* 8. 20.

interruption. He constructed the harbour at Ostia by building curving breakwaters on the right and left, while before the entrance he placed a mole in deep water. To give this mole a firmer foundation, he first sank the ship in which the great obelisk[a] had been brought from Egypt, and then securing it by piles, built upon it a very lofty tower after the model of the Pharos at Alexandria, to be lighted at night and guide the course of ships.

XXI. He very often distributed largesses to the people. He also gave several splendid shows, not merely the usual ones in the customary places, but some of a new kind and some revived from ancient times, and in places where no one had ever given them before. He opened the games at the dedication of Pompey's theatre, which he had restored when it was damaged by a fire, from a raised seat in the orchestra, after first offering sacrifice at the temples[b] in the upper part of the auditorium and coming down through the tiers of seats while all sat in silence. He also celebrated secular games,[c] alleging that they had been given too early by Augustus and not reserved for the regular time; although he himself writes in his own History that when they had been discontinued for a long time, Augustus restored them to their proper place after a very careful calculation of the intervals. Therefore the herald's proclamation was greeted with laughter, when he invited the people in the usual formula to games "which no one had ever seen or would ever see again"; for some were still living who had seen them before, and some actors who had appeared at the former performance appeared at that time as well. He often gave

[c] See *Aug.* xxxi. 4.

censes frequenter etiam in Vaticano commisit, non-
3 numquam interiecta per quinos missus venatione. Circo
vero Maximo marmoreis carceribus auratisque metis,
quae utraque et tofina ac lignea antea fuerant, exculto
propria senatoribus constituit loca promiscue spectare
solitis; ac super quadrigarum certamina Troiae lusum
exhibuit et Africanas, conficiente turma equitum praetorianorum, ducibus tribunis ipsoque praefecto; praeterea
Thessalos equites, qui feros tauros per spatia circi agunt
insiliuntque defessos et ad terram cornibus detrahunt.
4   Gladiatoria munera plurifariam[1] ac multiplicia
exhibuit: anniversarium in castris praetorianis sine venatione apparatuque, iustum atque legitimum in Saeptis;
ibidem extraordinarium et breve dierumque paucorum,
quodque appellare coepit "sportulam," quia primum
daturus edixerat,[2] velut ad subitam condictamque cenu-
5 lam invitare se populum. Nec ullo spectaculi genere
communior aut remissior erat, adeo ut oblatos victoribus
aureos prolata sinistra pariter cum vulgo voce digitisque
numeraret ac saepe hortando rogandoque ad hilaritatem
homines provocaret, dominos identidem appellans, im-

---

[1] plurifariam, *R⊊*; plurifaria, Ω (multifaria, *G*).
[2] daturus edixerat, *Basle ed. of* 1533; daturum se dixerat, Ω
(dixerant, *Υ*).

---

[a] Built by Gaius; see note on chap. xx. 3.

[b] The *carceres* were compartments closed by barriers, one for
each chariot. They were probably twelve in number and were so
arranged as to be at an equal distance from the starting point of
the race. When the race began, the barriers were removed. The
metae, or "goals," were three conical pillars at each end of the
spina, or low wall which ran down the middle of the arena, about
which the chariots had to run a given number of times, usually

games in the Vatican Circus[a] also, at times with a beast-baiting after every five races. But the Great Circus he adorned with barriers of marble and gilded goals,[b] whereas before they had been of tufa and wood, and assigned special seats to the senators, who had been in the habit of viewing the games with the rest of the people. In addition to the chariot races he exhibited the game called Troy and also panthers, which were hunted down by a squadron of the praetorian cavalry under the lead of the tribunes and the prefect himself; likewise Thessalian horseman, who drive wild bulls all over the arena, leaping upon them when they are tired out and throwing them to the ground by the horns.

He gave many gladiatorial shows and in many places: one in yearly celebration of his accession, in the Praetorian Camp without wild beasts and fine equipment, and one in the Saepta of the regular and usual kind; another in the same place not in the regular list, short and lasting but a few days, to which he was the first to apply the name of *sportula*,[c] because before giving it for the first time he made proclamation that he invited the people "as it were to an extempore meal, hastily prepared." Now there was no form of entertainment at which he was more familiar and free, even thrusting out his left hand,[d] as the commons did, and counting aloud on his fingers the gold pieces which were paid to the victors; and ever and anon he would address the audience, and invite and urge them to merriment, calling them "masters" from time to time,

seven; see *Dom.* iv. 3.   [c] See note on *Aug.* lxxiv.

[d] Instead of keeping it covered with his toga, an undignified performance for an emperor.

mixtis interdum frigidis et arcessitis iocis; qualis est ut cum Palumbum postulantibus daturum se promisit, si captus esset. Illud plane quantumvis salubriter et in tempore: cum essedario, pro quo quattuor fili deprecabantur, magno omnium favore indulsisset rudem, tabulam ilico misit admonens populum, quanto opere liberos suscipere deberet, quos videret et gladiatori praesidio gratiaeque esse. Edidit et in Martio campo expugnationem direptionemque oppidi ad imaginem bellicam et deditionem Britanniae regum praeseditque paludatus. Quin et emissurus Fucinum lacum naumachiam ante commisit. Sed cum proclamantibus naumachiariis: "Have imperator, morituri te salutant!" respondisset: "Aut non,"[1] neque post hanc vocem quasi venia data quisquam dimicare vellet, diu cunctatus an omnes igni ferroque absumeret, tandem e sede sua prosiluit ac per ambitum lacus non sine foeda vacillatione[2] discurrens partim minando partim adhortando ad pugnam compulit. Hoc spectaculo classis Sicula et Rhodia concurrerunt, duodenarum triremium singulae, exciente[3] bucina Tritone argenteo, qui e medio lacu per machinam emerserat.

XXII. Quaedam circa caerimonias civilemque et militarem more, item circa omnium ordinum statum domi

---

[1] aut non] avete vos, ς.

[2] vacillatione, ς; bacillatione, Ω.

[3] exciente, ΠR; *the other mss. have* eiciente (eitiente, *G*).

---

[a] "The Dove," nickname of a gladiator.

[b] The symbol of discharge; cf. Hor. *Epist.* 1. 1. 2.

[c] See note on *Calig.* xxxv. 3.

[d] About to die; one of Claudius's feeble jokes, which the combatants pretended to understand as meaning that they need not risk their lives in battle.   [e] See chap. xxx below.

and interspersing feeble and far-fetched jokes. For example, when they called for Palumbus[a] he promised that they should have him, "if he could be caught." The following, however, was both exceedingly timely and salutary; when he had granted the wooden sword[b] to an *essedarius*,[c] for whose discharge four sons begged, and the act was received with loud and general applause, he at once circulated a note, pointing out to the people how greatly they ought to desire children, since they saw that they brought favour and protection even to a gladiator. He gave representations in the Campus Martius of the storming and sacking of a town in the manner of real warfare, as well as of the surrender of the kings of the Britons, and presided clad in a general's cloak. Even when he was on the point of letting out the water from Lake Fucinus he gave a sham sea-fight first. But when the combatants cried out: "Hail, emperor, they who are about to die salute thee," he replied, "Or not,"[d] and after that all of them refused to fight, maintaining that they had been pardoned. Upon this he hesitated for some time about destroying them all with fire and sword, but at last leaping from his throne and running along the edge of the lake with his ridiculous tottering gait,[e] he induced them to fight, partly by threats and partly by promises. At this performance a Sicilian and a Rhodian fleet engaged, each numbering twelve triremes, and the signal was sounded on a horn by a silver Triton, which was raised from the middle of the lake by a mechanical device.

XXII. Touching religious ceremonies and civil and military customs, as well as the condition of all classes at home and abroad, he corrected various abuses, revived

forisque aut correxit aut exoleta revocavit aut etiam nova
instituit. In cooptandis per collegia sacerdotibus neminem nisi iuratus nominavit; observavitque sedulo, ut
quotiens terra in urbe movisset, ferias advocata contione
praetor indiceret, utque dira ave[1] in Capitolio visa obse-
cratio haberetur, eamque ipse iure maximi pontificis pro
rostris populo praeiret summotaque operariorum servo-
rumque turba.

XXIII. Rerum actum divisum antea in hibernos aes-
tivosque menses coniunxit. Iuris dictionem de fidei com-
missis quotannis et tantum in urbe delegari magistratibus
solitam in perpetuum atque etiam per provincias potestatibus demandavit. Capiti Papiae Poppaeae legis a
Tiberio Caesare, quasi sexagenarii generare non possent,
2 addito obrogavit. Sanxit ut pupillis extra ordinem tutores
a consulibus darentur, utque ii, quibus a magistratibus
provinciae interdicerentur, urbe quoque et Italia sum-
moverentur. Ipse quosdam novo exemplo relegavit, ut
ultra lapidem tertium vetaret egredi ab urbe.

De maiore negotio acturus in curia medius inter con-
sulum sellas tribuniciove[2] subsellio sedebat. Commeatus
a senatu peti solitos benefici sui fecit.

[1] ave, *Roth* (avi, *Turnebus*); aut, *MGLP*; aut in urbe aut, $\Upsilon'O$.
[2] tribuniciove, *Mommsen*; sella vel tribunicio, *Smilda*; tribunicio, *mss.*

---

[a] That those whom he had selected were worthy of the
honour.

[b] See *Galba* xiv. 3, from which it appears that Claudius made
the summer and autumn seasons continuous, and did away with
the winter term.

[c] The *relegatio* was a milder form of exile, without loss of citizenship or confiscation of property, but in this case the offenders

some old customs or even established new ones. In admitting priests into the various colleges he never named anyone until he had first taken oath,[a] and he scrupulously observed the custom of having the praetor call an assembly and proclaim a holiday, whenever there was an earthquake within the city; as well as that of offering up a supplication whenever a bird of ill-omen was seen on the Capitol. This last he himself conducted in his capacity of chief priest, first reciting the form of words to the people from the rostra, after all day laborers and slaves had been ordered to withdraw.

XXIII. The season for holding court, formerly divided into a winter and a summer term, he made continuous.[b] Jurisdiction in cases of trust, which it had been usual to assign each year and only to magistrates in the city, he delegated for all time and extended to the governors of the provinces. He annulled a clause added to the *lex Papia Poppaea* by Tiberius, implying that men of sixty could not beget children. He made a law that guardians might be appointed for orphans by the consuls, contrary to the usual procedure, and that those who were banished from a province by its magistrates should also be debarred from the city and from Italy. He himself imposed upon some a new kind of punishment,[c] by forbidding them to go more than three miles outside the city.

When about to conduct business of special importance in the House, he took his seat between the two consuls or on the tribunes' bench. He reserved to himself the granting of permission to travel, which had formerly been requested of the senate.

were not banished, but confined to the city and its immediate vicinity.

XXIV. Ornamenta consularia etiam procuratoribus ducenariis indulsit. Senatoriam dignitatem recusantibus equestrem quoque ademit. Latum clavum, quamvis initio affirmasset non lecturum se senatorem nisi civis R. abnepotem, etiam libertini filio tribuit, sed sub condicione si prius ab equite R. adoptatus esset; ac sic quoque reprehensionem verens, et Appium Caecum censorem, generis sui proauctorem, libertinorum filios in senatum adlegisse docuit, ignarus temporibus Appi et deinceps aliquamdiu libertinos dictos non ipsos, qui manu emitteren-

2 tur, sed ingenuos ex his procreatos. Collegio quaestorum pro stratura viarum gladiatorium munus iniunxit detractaque Ostiensi et Gallica provincia curam aerari Saturni reddidit, quam medio tempore praetores aut, uti nunc, praetura functi sustinuerant.

3 Triumphalia ornamenta Silano, filiae suae sponso, nondum puberi dedit, maioribus vero natu tam multis tamque facile, ut epistula communi[1] legionum nomine exstiterit petentium, ut legatis consularibus simul cum exercitu et triumphalia darentur, ne causam belli quoquo modo quaererent. Aulo Plautio etiam ovationem decrevit ingressoque urbem obviam progressus et in Capitolium

---

[1] communi, *Basle ed. of* 1533 (ς?); communis, Ω.

---

[a] The *procuratores* were the emperor's agents, who performed various administrative duties throughout the empire. They were members of the equestrian order and were ranked on the basis of their annual stipend as *trecenarii, ducenarii, centenarii,* and *sexagenarii,* receiving respectively 300,000, 200,000, 100,000, and 60,000 sesterces.

[b] A common reason for this was the desire to engage in business, which senators were not allowed to do.

XXIV. He gave the consular regalia even to the second grade of stewards.[a] If any refused senatorial rank,[b] he took from them that of knight also. Though he had declared at the beginning of his reign that he would choose no one as a senator who did not have a Roman citizen for a great-great-grandfather, he gave the broad stripe even to a freedman's son, but only on condition that he should first be adopted by a Roman knight. Even then, fearful of criticism, he declared that the censor Appius Caecus, the ancient founder of his family, had chosen the sons of freedmen into the senate; but he did not know that in the days of Appius and for some time afterwards the term *libertini* designated, not those who were themselves manumitted, but their freeborn sons. He obliged the college of quaestors to give a gladiatorial show in place of paving the roads; then depriving them of their official duties at Ostia and in Gaul, he restored to them the charge of the treasury of Saturn,[c] which had in the meantime been administered by praetors, or by ex-praetors, as in our time.

He gave the triumphal regalia to Silanus, his daughter's affianced husband, who was still a boy, and conferred them on older men so often and so readily, that a joint petition was circulated in the name of the legions,[d] praying that those emblems be given the consular governors at the same time as their armies, to prevent their seeking all sorts of pretexts for war. To Aulus Plautius he also granted an ovation, going out to meet him when he

[c] The state treasury, located in the temple of Saturn in the Forum; cf. *Aug.* xxxvi.   [d] According to Tac., *Ann.* 11. 20, this was done by the legions in Germany.

47

eunti et inde rursus reverténti latus texit. Gabinio Secundo Cauchis gente Germanica superatis cognomen Cauchi[1] usurpare concessit.

XXV. Equestris militias ita ordinavit, ut post cohortem alam, post alam tribunatum legionis daret; stipendiaque instituit et imaginariae militiae genus, quod vocatur "supra numerum," quo absentes et titulo tenus fungerentur. Milites domus senatorias salutandi causa ingredi etiam patrum decreto prohibuit. Libertinos, qui se pro equitibus R. agerent, publicavit, ingratos et de quibus patroni quererentur revocavit in servitutem advocatisque eorum negavit se adversus libertos ipsorum ius dicturum. 2 Cum quidam aegra et adfecta mancipia in insulam Aesculapi taedio medendi exponerent, omnes qui exponerentur liberos esse sanxit, nec redire in dicionem domini, si convaluissent; quod si quis necare quem mallet quam exponere, caedis crimine teneri. Viatores ne per Italiae oppida nisi aut pedibus aut sella aut lectica transirent, monuit edicto. Puteolis et Ostiae singulas cohortes ad arcendos incendiorum casus collocavit.

3 Peregrinae condicionis homines vetuit usurpare Romana nomina dum taxat gentilicia. Civitatem R. usur-

---

[1] Cauchi, *suggested by Ihm*; Cauchius, *mss.*

---

[a] That is, if their own freedmen proved ungrateful and they wished to bring suit against them.

[b] In the Tiber at Rome, so called from its temple of Aesculapius.

[c] That is, the gentile names such as Claudius, Cornelius, etc.; apparently forenames (Gaius, Lucius, and the like) and surnames (Lentulus, Nasica) might be assumed, although a foreigner often retained his native name as a surname.

entered the city, and walking on his left as he went to the Capitol and returned again. He allowed Gabinius Secundus to assume the surname of Cauchius because of his conquest of the Cauchi, a German nation.

XXV. He rearranged the military career of the knights, assigning a division of cavalry after a cohort, and next the tribunate of a legion. He also instituted a series of military positions and a kind of fictitious service, which is called "supernumerary" and could be performed *in absentia* and in name only. He even had the Fathers pass a decree forbidding soldiers to enter the houses of senators to pay their respects. He confiscated the property of those freedmen who passed as Roman knights, and reduced to slavery again such as were ungrateful and a cause of complaint to their patrons, declaring to their advocates that he would not entertain a suit against their own freedmen.[a] When certain men were exposing their sick and worn out slaves on the Island of Aesculapius[b] because of the trouble of treating them, Claudius decreed that all such slaves were free, and that if they recovered, they should not return to the control of their master; but if anyone preferred to kill such a slave rather than to abandon him, he was liable to the charge of murder. He provided by an edict that travellers should not pass through the towns of Italy except on foot, or in a chair or litter. He stationed a cohort at Puteoli and one at Ostia, to guard against the danger of fires.

He forbade men of foreign birth to use the Roman names so far as those of the clans[c] were concerned. Those who usurped the privileges of Roman citizenship

49

pantes in campo Esquilino[1] securi percussit. Provincias
Achaiam et Macedoniam, quas Tiberius ad curam suam
transtulerat, senatui reddidit. Lyciis ob exitiabiles inter se
discordias libertatem ademit, Rhodiis ob paenitentiam
veterum delictorum reddidit. Iliensibus quasi Romanae
gentis auctoribus tributa in perpetuum remisit recitata
vetere epistula Graeca senatus populique R. Seleuco regi
amicitiam et societatem ita demum pollicentis, si consan-
guineos suos Ilienses ab omni onere immunes praestitis-
4   set. Iudaeos impulsore Chresto assidue tumultuantis
Roma expulit. Germanorum legatis in orchestra sedere
permisit, simplicitate eorum et fiducia commotus, quod
in popularia deducti, cum animadvertissent Parthos et
Armenios sedentis in senatu, ad eadem loca sponte
transierant, nihilo deteriorem virtutem aut condicionem
5   suam praedicantes. Druidarum[2] religionem apud Gallos
dirae immanitatis et tantum civibus sub Augusto interdic-
tam penitus abolevit; contra sacra Eleusinia etiam transferre ex Attica Romam conatus est, templumque in Sicilia
Veneris Erycinae vetustate conlapsum ut ex aerario pop.
R. reficeretur, auctor fuit. Cum regibus foedus in Foro

[1] Esquilino, *GQT; the other mss. have* Esquilinio.
[2] Druidarum, *N⊊;* Driadarum, Ω.

---

[a] The part of the Esquiline hill on both sides of the Servian
wall; occupied in part by the Gardens of Maecenas; see Hor.
Serm. 1. 8. The place of execution seems to have been outside
the Porta Esquilina.

[b] Another form of Christus; see Tert. *Apol.* 3 (at the end). It
is uncertain whether Suetonius is referring to the beginning of
the Christian cult in Rome or to some Jew of that name. Tacitus,
Ann. 15. 44, uses the correct form, Christus, and states that he
was executed in the reign of Tiberius.

he executed in the Esquiline field.[a] He restored to the
senate the provinces of Achaia and Macedonia, which
Tiberius had taken into his own charge. He deprived the
Lycians of their independence because of deadly intes-
tine feuds, and restored theirs to the Rhodians, since they
had given up their former faults. He allowed the people
of Ilium perpetual exemption from tribute, on the ground
that they were the founders of the Roman race, reading
an ancient letter of the senate and people of Rome written in Greek to king Seleucus, in which they promised
him their friendship and alliance only on condition that
he should keep their kinsfolk of Ilium free from every
burden. Since the Jews constantly made disturbances at
the instigation of Chrestus,[b] he expelled them from
Rome. He allowed the envoys of the Germans to sit in
the orchestra, led by their naïve self-confidence; for when
they had been taken to the seats occupied by the common
people and saw the Parthian and Armenian envoys sitting
with the senate, they moved of their own accord to the
same part of the theatre, protesting that their merits and
rank were no whit inferior. He utterly abolished the cruel
and inhuman religion of the Druids among the Gauls,
which under Augustus had merely been prohibited to
Roman citizens; on the other hand he even attempted to
transfer the Eleusinian rites from Attica to Rome, and
had the temple of Venus Erycina in Sicily, which had
fallen to ruin through age, restored at the expense of the
treasury of the Roman people. He struck his treaties with
foreign princes in the Forum, sacrificing a pig and recit-

icit[1] porca caesa ac vetere fetialium praefatione adhibita. Sed et haec et cetera totumque adeo ex parte magna principatum non tam suo quam uxorum libertorumque arbitrio administravit, talis ubique plerumque, qualem esse eum aut expediret illis aut liberet.

XXVI. Sponsas admodum adulescens duas habuit: Aemiliam Lepidam Augusti proneptem, item Liviam Medullinam, cui et cognomen Camillae erat, e genere antiquo dictatoris Camilli. Priorem, quod parentes eius Augustum offenderant, virginem adhuc repudiavit, posteriorem ipso die, qui erat nuptiis destinatus, ex valitudine

2 amisit. Uxores deinde duxit Plautiam Urgulanillam[2] triumphali et mox Aeliam Paetinam consulari patre. Cum utraque divortium fecit, sed cum Paetina ex levibus offensis, cum Urgulanilla[3] ob libidinum probra et homicidii suspicionem. Post has Valeriam Messalinam, Barbati Messalae consobrini sui filiam, in matrimonium accepit. Quam cum comperisset super cetera flagitia atque dedecora C. Silio etiam nupsisse dote inter auspices consignata, supplicio adfecit confirmavitque pro contione apud praetorianos, quatenus sibi matrimonia male cederent, permansurum se in caelibatu, ac nisi permansisset,

3 non recusaturum confodi manibus ipsorum. Nec durare valuit quin de condicionibus continuo tractaret, etiam de Paetinae, quam olim exegerat, deque Lolliae Paulinae, quae C. Caesari nupta fuerat. Verum inlecebris Agrippinae, Germanici fratris sui filiae, per ius osculi et blandi-

---

[1] icit, *Sabellicus*; iecit, Ω. [2] Urgulanilla, *M; the other mss.*
have Ergulanilla (erc-, *GΠQ*). [3] Ergulanilla, Ω (erc-, *GΠQ*).

---

[a] Whose responsibilities had included rites for declaring war and making treaties; see Livy 1. 24.

ing the ancient formula of the fetial priests.[a] But these and other acts, and in fact almost the whole conduct of his reign, were dictated not so much by his own judgment as that of his wives and freedmen, since he nearly always acted in accordance with their interests and desires.

XXVI. He was betrothed twice at an early age: to Aemilia Lepida, great-granddaughter of Augustus, and to Livia Medullina, who also had the surname of Camilla and was descended from the ancient family of Camillus the dictator. He put away the former before their marriage, because her parents had offended Augustus; the latter was taken ill and died on the very day which had been set for the wedding. He then married Plautia Urgulanilla, whose father had been honoured with a triumph, and later Aelia Paetina, daughter of an ex-consul. He divorced both these, Paetina for trivial offences, but Urgulanilla because of scandalous lewdness and the suspicion of murder. Then he married Valeria Messalina, daughter of his cousin Messala Barbatus. But when he learned that besides other shameful and wicked deeds she had actually married Gaius Silius, and that a formal contract had been signed in the presence of witnesses, he put her to death and declared before the assembled praetorian guard that inasmuch as his marriages did not turn out well, he would remain a widower, and if he did not keep his word, he would not refuse death at their hands. Yet he could not refrain from at once planning another match, even with Paetina, whom he had formerly discarded, and with Lollia Paulina, who had been the wife of Gaius Caesar. But his affections were ensnared by the wiles of Agrippina, daughter of his brother Germanicus, aided by the right of exchanging kisses and the opportuni-

tiarum occasiones pellectus in amorem, subornavit proximo senatu qui censerent, cogendum se ad ducendum
eam uxorem, quasi rei p. maxime interesset, dandamque
ceteris veniam talium coniugiorum, quae ad id tempus
incesta habebantur. Ac vix uno interposito die confecit
nuptias, non repertis qui sequerentur exemplum, excepto
libertino quodam et altero primipilari, cuius nuptiarum
officium et ipse cum Agrippina celebravit.

XXVII. Liberos ex tribus uxoribus tulit: ex Urgulanilla[1] Drusum et Claudiam, ex Paetina Antoniam, ex
Messalina Octaviam et quem primo Germanicum, mox
Britannicum cognominavit. Drusum prope iam[2] puberem amisit piro per lusum in sublime iactato et hiatu oris
excepto strangulatum, cum ei ante paucos dies filiam
Seiani despondisset. Quo magis miror fuisse qui tradunt
rent fraude a Seiano necatum. Claudiam ex liberto suo
Botere conceptam, quamvis ante quintum mensem divor-
tii natam alique coeptam, exponi tamen ad matris ianuam
et nudam iussit abici. Antoniam Cn. Pompeio Magno,
deinde Fausto Sullae, nobilissimis iuvenibus, Octaviam
Neroni privigno suo collocavit, Silano ante desponsam.
Britannicum vicesimo imperii die inque secundo consulatu, natum sibi parvulum etiam tum, et militi pro contione manibus suis gestans et plebi per spectacula gremio

2

[1] Erculanilla, Ω (herc-, *L*; erg-, *ST*).
[2] prope iam, *Bentley*; prope tum, *Bücheler*; Pompeis impuberem, *Lipsius*; pompeium, *mss.*

---

[a] In A.D. 20.   [b] Of Claudius from Urgulanilla.
[c] Either Suetonius is in error here, or the text is corrupt,
since Claudius' second consulship did not begin until 42, and he
began to reign Jan. 25, 41.

ties for endearments offered by their relationship; and at the next meeting of the senate he induced some of the members to propose that he be compelled to marry Agrippina, on the ground that it was for the interest of the State; also that others be allowed to contract similar marriages, which up to that time had been regarded as incestuous. And he married her with hardly a single day's delay; but none were found to follow his example save a freedman and a chief centurion, whose marriage ceremony he himself attended with Agrippina.

XXVII. He had children by three of his wives: by Urgulanilla, Drusus, and Claudia; by Paetina, Antonia; by Messalina, Octavia and a son, at first called Germanicus and later Britannicus. He lost Drusus just before he came to manhood, for he was choked by a pear which he had thrown in the air in play and caught in his open mouth. A few days before this he had betrothed him to the daughter of Sejanus, which makes me wonder all the more that some say that the boy was treacherously slain by Sejanus. Claudia was the offspring of his freedman Boter, and although she was born[a] within five months after the divorce[b] and he had begun to rear her, yet he ordered her to be cast out naked at her mother's door and disowned. He gave Antonia in marriage to Gnaeus Pompeius Magnus, and later to Faustus Sulla, both young men of high birth, and Octavia to his stepson Nero, after she had previously been betrothed to Silanus. Britannicus was born on the twenty-second day of his reign and in his second consulship.[c] When he was still very small, Claudius would often take him in his arms and commend him to the assembled soldiers, and to the people at the games, holding him in his lap or in his outstretched

aut ante se retinens assidue commendabat faustisque
ominibus[1] cum adclamantium turba prosequebatur. E
generis Neronem adoptavit, Pompeium atque Silanum
non recusavit modo, sed et interemit.

XXVIII. Libertorum praecipue suspexit Posiden
spadonem, quem etiam Britannico triumpho inter mi-
litares viros hasta pura donavit; nec minus Felicem, quem
cohortibus et alis provinciaeque Iudaeae praeposuit,
trium reginarum maritum; et Harpocran, cui lectica per
urbem vehendi spectaculaque publice edendi ius tribuit;
ac super hos Polybium ab studiis, qui saepe inter duos
consules ambulabat; sed ante omnis Narcissum ab epistulis et Pallantem a rationibus, quos decreto quoque senatus non praemiis modo ingentibus, sed et quaestoriis
praetoriisque ornamentis honorari libens passus est;
tantum praeterea adquirere et rapere, ut querente eo
quondam de fisci exiguitate non absurde dictum sit, abun-
daturum, si a duobus libertis in consortium reciperetur.

XXIX. His, ut dixi, uxoribusque addictus, non
principem,[2] sed ministrum egit, compendio cuiusque
horum vel etiam studio aut libidine honores exercitus
impunitates supplicia largitus est, et quidem insciens
plerumque et ignarus. Ac ne singillatim minora quoque

[1] ominibus, ς; omnibus, Ω.
[2] *The mss. have* se *after* principem.

---

[a] A common military prize.   [b] Only two of these are
known, both named Drusilla. One was the daughter of Juba II,
king of Mauretania, and the other of Herod Agrippa I, of Judaea;
the latter was previously married to Azizus, king of Emesa.
[c] Otherwise restricted to knights.   [d] Chap. xxv. 5.

hands, and he would wish him happy auspices, joined by the applauding throng. Of his sons-in-law he adopted Nero; Pompeius and Silanus he not only declined to adopt, but even put to death.

XXVIII. Of his freedmen he had special regard for the eunuch Posides, whom he even presented with the headless spear[a] at his British triumph, along with those who had served as soldiers. He was equally fond of Felix, giving him the command of cohorts and of troops of horse, as well as of the province of Judaea; and he became the husband of three queens.[b] Also of Harpocras, to whom he granted the privilege of riding through the city in a litter and of giving public entertainments.[c] Still higher was his regard for Polybius, his literary adviser, who often walked between the two consuls. But most of all he was devoted to his secretary Narcissus and his treasurer Pallas, and he gladly allowed them to be honoured in addition by a decree of the senate, not only with immense gifts, but even with the insignia of quaestors and praetors. Besides this he permitted them to amass such wealth by plunder, that when he once complained of the low state of his funds, the witty answer was made that he would have enough and to spare, if he were taken into partnership by his two freedmen.

XXIX. Wholly under the control of these and of his wives, as I have said,[d] he played the part, not of a prince, but of a servant, lavishing honours, the command of armies, pardons or punishments, according to the interests of each of them, or even their wish or whim; and that too for the most part in ignorance and blindly. Not to go into details about less important matters (such as revok-

enumerem, revocatas liberalitates eius, iudicia rescissa, suppositos aut etiam palam immutatos datorum officiorum codicillos: Appium Silanum consocerum suum Iuliasque, alteram Drusi, alteram Germanici filiam, crimine incerto nec defensione ulla data occidit, item Cn. Pompeium maioris filiae virum et L. Silanum minoris

2 sponsum. Ex quibus Pompeius in concubitu dilecti adulescentuli confossus est, Silanus abdicare se praetura ante IIII. Kal. Ian. morique initio anni coactus die ipso Claudi et Agrippinae nuptiarum. In quinque et triginta senatores trecentosque amplius equites R. tanta facilitate animadvertit, ut, cum de nece consularis viri renuntiante centurione factum esse quod imperasset, negaret quicquam se imperasse, nihilo minus rem comprobaret, affirmantibus libertis officio milites functos, quod ad ultionem

3 imperatoris ultro procucurrissent. Nam illud omnem fidem excesserit quod nuptiis, quas Messalina cum adultero Silio fecerat, tabellas dotis et ipse consignaverit, inductus, quasi de industria simularentur ad avertendum transferendumque periculum, quod imminere ipsi per quaedam ostenta portenderetur.

XXX. Auctoritas dignitasque formae non defuit ei, verum stanti vel sedenti ac praecipue quiescenti, nam et prolixo nec exili corpore erat et specie canitieque pulchra, opimis cervicibus; ceterum et ingredientem destituebant poplites minus firmi, et remisse quid vel serio agentem

ing his grants, rescinding his decisions, substituting false letters patent, or even openly changing those which he had issued), he put to death his father-in-law Appius Silanus and the two Julias, daughters of Drusus and Germanicus, on an unsupported charge and giving them no opportunity for defence; also Gnaeus Pompeius, the husband of his elder daughter, and Lucius Silanus who was betrothed to his younger one. Of these Pompey was stabbed in the embraces of a favourite youth, while Silanus was compelled to abdicate his praetorship four days before the Kalends of January and to take his own life at the beginning of the year, the very day of the marriage of Claudius and Agrippina. He inflicted the death penalty on thirty-five senators and more than three hundred Roman knights with such easy indifference, that when a centurion in reporting the death of an ex-consul said that his order had been carried out, he replied that he had given no order; but he nevertheless approved the act, since his freedmen declared that the soldiers had done their duty in hastening to avenge their emperor without instructions. But it is beyond all belief that at the marriage which Messalina had contracted with her paramour Silius he signed the contract for the dowry with his own hand, being induced to do so on the ground that the marriage was a feigned one, designed to avert and turn upon another a danger which was inferred from certain portents to threaten the emperor himself.

XXX. He possessed majesty and dignity of appearance, but only when he was standing still or sitting, and especially when he was lying down; for he was tall but not slender, with an attractive face, becoming white hair, and a full neck. But when he walked, his weak knees gave way under him and he had many disagreeable traits both in his

multa dehonestabant: risus indecens, ira turpior spumante rictu, umentibus naribus, praeterea linguae titubantia caputque cum semper tum in quantulocumque actu vel maxime tremulum.

XXXI. Valitudine sicut olim gravi, ita princeps prospera usus est excepto stomachi dolore, quo se correptum etiam de consciscenda morte cogitasse dixit.

XXXII. Convivia agitavit et ampla et assidua ac fere patentissimis locis, ut plerumque sesceni simul discumberent. Convivatus est et super emissarium Fucini lacus ac paene summersus, cum emissa impetu aqua redundasset. Adhibebat omni cenae et liberos suos cum pueris puellisque nobilibus, qui[1] more veteri ad fulcra lectorum sedentes vescerentur. Convivae, qui pridie scyphum aureum subripuisse existimabatur, revocato in diem posterum calicem fictilem apposuit. Dicitur etiam meditatus edictum, quo veniam daret flatum crepitumque ventris in convivio emittendi, cum periclitatum quendam prae pudore ex continentia repperisset.

XXXIII. Cibi vinique quocumque et tempore et loco appetentissimus, cognoscens quondam in Augusti foro ictusque nidore prandii, quod in proxima Martis aede Saliis apparabatur, deserto tribunali ascendit ad sacerdotes unaque decubuit. Nec temere umquam triclinio

---

[1] qui, Υ'Ο; ut, δ; *the other mss. omit the word, except G, which has* ut *after* veteri.

---

[a] The *fulcra* were the ends of the couches on which the pillows were placed.

[b] Cf. *Aug.* lxiv. 3.

[c] Their feasts were proverbial for luxury; see Hor. *Odes*, i. 37. 2.

lighter moments and when he was engaged in business; his laughter was unseemly and his anger still more disgusting, for he would foam at the mouth and trickle at the nose; he stammered besides and his head was very shaky at all times, but especially when he made the least exertion.

XXXI. Though previously his health was bad, it was excellent while he was emperor except for attacks of heartburn, which he said all but drove him to suicide.

XXXII. He gave frequent and grand dinner parties, as a rule in spacious places, where six hundred guests were often entertained at one time. He even gave a banquet close to the outlet of the Fucine Lake and was well-nigh drowned, when the water was let out with a rush and deluged the place. He always invited his own children to dinner along with the sons and daughters of distinguished men, having them sit at the end[a] of the couches as they ate, after the old time custom.[b] When a guest was suspected of having stolen a golden bowl the day before, he invited him again the next day, but set before him an earthenware cup. He is even said to have thought of an edict allowing the privilege of breaking wind quietly or noisily at table, having learned of a man who ran some risk by restraining himself through modesty.

XXXIII. He was eager for food and drink at all times and in all places. Once when he was holding court in the forum of Augustus and had caught the savour of a meal which was preparing for the Salii[c] in the temple of Mars hard by, he left the tribunal, went up where the priests were, and took his place at their table. He hardly ever left the dining-room until he was stuffed and soaked; then he

abscessit nisi distentus ac madens, et ut statim supino ac per somnum hianti pinna in os inderetur ad exonerandum

2 stomachum. Somni brevissimi erat, nam ante mediam noctem plerumque vigilabat, ut tamen interdiu[1] nonnumquam in iure dicendo obdormisceret vixque ab advocatis de industria vocem augentibus excitaretur. Libidinis in feminas profusissimae, marum omnino expers. Aleam studiosissime lusit, de cuius arte librum quoque emisit, solitus etiam in gestatione ludere, ita essedo alveoque adaptatis ne lusus confunderetur.

XXXIV. Saevum et sanguinarium natura fuisse, magnis minimisque apparuit rebus. Tormenta quaestionum poenasque parricidarum repraesentabat exigebatque coram. Cum spectare antiqui moris supplicium Tiburi concupisset et deligatis ad palum noxiis carnifex deesset, accitum ab urbe vesperam usque opperiri perseveravit. Quocumque gladiatorio munere, vel suo vel alieno, etiam forte prolapsos iugulari iubebat, maxime retiarios, ut

2 exspirantium facies videret. Cum par quoddam mutuis ictibus concidisset, cultellos sibi parvulos ex utroque ferro in usum fieri sine mora iussit. Bestiariis meridianisque adeo delectabatur, ut et prima luce ad spectaculum descenderet et meridie dimisso ad prandium populo per-

---

[1] interdiu, ς; interdum, Ω.

[a] See *Aug.* xxxiii. 1.

[b] See Livy, i. 26. 6; *Nero*, xlix. 2; *Dom.* xi. 2–3.

[c] Their faces were not covered by helmets; see Index, s.v. *retiarius*.

[d] According to Pliny, *N.H.* 28. 34, game killed with a knife with which a man had been slain was a specific for epilepsy.

went to sleep at once, lying on his back with his mouth open, and a feather was put down his throat to relieve his stomach. He slept but little at a time, for he was usually awake before midnight; but he would sometimes drop off in the daytime while holding court and could hardly be roused when the advocates raised their voices for the purpose. He was immoderate in his passion for women, but wholly disinterested in male partners. He was greatly devoted to gaming, even publishing a book on the art, and he actually used to play while driving, having the board so fitted to his carriage as to prevent his game from being disturbed.

XXXIV. That he was of a cruel and bloodthirsty disposition was shown in matters great and small. He always exacted examination by torture and the punishment of parricides[a] at once and in his presence. When he was at Tibur and wished to see an execution in the ancient fashion,[b] no executioner could be found after the criminals were bound to the stake. Whereupon he sent to fetch one from the city and continued to wait for him until nightfall. At any gladiatorial show, either his own or another's, he gave orders that even those who fell accidentally should be slain, in particular the net-fighters,[c] so that he could watch their faces as they died. When a pair of gladiators had fallen by mutually inflicted wounds, he at once had some little knives made from both their swords for his use.[d] He took such pleasure in the combats with wild beasts and of those that fought at noonday,[e] that he would go down to the arena at daybreak and after dis-

[e] Those who fought during the midday interval, perhaps the *paegniarii*; see note on *Calig.* xxvi. 5.

sederet praeterque destinatos etiam levi subitaque de
causa quosdam committeret, de fabrorum quoque ac
ministrorum atque id genus numero, si automatum vel
pegma vel quid tale aliud parum cessisset. Induxit et
unum ex nomenculatoribus suis, sic ut erat togatus.

XXXV. Sed nihil aeque quam timidus ac diffidens fuit.
Primis imperii diebus quanquam, ut diximus, iactator
civilitatis, neque convivia inire ausus est nisi ut specula-
tores cum lanceis circumstarent militesque vice ministrorum fungerentur, neque aegrum quemquam visitavit
nisi explorato prius cubiculo culcitisque et stragulis
praetemptatis et excussis. Reliquo autem tempore saluta-
toribus scrutatores semper apposuit, et quidem omnibus
et acerbissimos. Sero enim ac vix remisit, ne feminae
praetextatique pueri et puellae contrectarentur et ne
cuius comiti aut librario calamariae et graphiariae thecae
adimerentur. Motu civili cum eum Camillus, non dubi-
tans etiam citra bellum posse terreri, contumeliosa et
minaci et contumaci epistula cedere imperio iuberet
vitamque otiosam in privata re agere, dubitavit adhibitis
principibus viris an optemperaret.

XXXVI. Quasdam insidias temere delatas adeo
expavit, ut deponere imperium temptaverit. Quodam, ut
supra rettuli, cum ferro circa sacrificantem se depre-

---

[a] A structure with several movable stories, for show pieces
and other stage effects; see Juv. 4. 122.

[b] See note on *Aug.* xix. 1.

[c] Chap. xii.

[d] Chap. xiii.

missing the people for luncheon at midday, he would keep his seat and in addition to the appointed combatants, he would for trivial and hasty reasons match others, even of the carpenters, the assistants, and men of that class, if any automatic device, or pageant,[a] or anything else of the kind, had not worked well. He even forced one of his pages[b] to enter the arena just as he was, in his toga.

XXXV. But there was nothing for which he was so notorious as timidity and suspicion. Although in the early days of his reign, as we have said,[c] he made a display of simplicity, he never ventured to go to a banquet without being surrounded by guards with lances and having his soldiers wait upon him in place of the servants; and he never visited a man who was ill without having the patient's room examined beforehand and his pillows and bed-clothing felt over and shaken out. Afterwards he even subjected those who came to pay their morning calls to search, sparing none the strictest examination. Indeed, it was not until late, and then reluctantly, that he gave up having women and young boys and girls grossly mishandled, and the cases for pens and styles taken from every man's attendant or scribe. When Camillus began his revolution, he felt sure that Claudius could be intimidated without resorting to war; and in fact when he ordered the emperor in an insulting, threatening, and impudent letter to give up his throne and betake himself to a life of privacy and retirement, Claudius called together the leading men and asked their advice about complying.

XXXVI. He was so terror-stricken by unfounded reports of conspiracies that he had tried to abdicate. When, as I have mentioned before,[d] a man with a dagger

henso, senatum per praecones propere convocavit lacrimisque et vociferatione miseratus est condicionem suam, cui nihil tuti usquam esset, ac diu publico abstinuit. Messalinae quoque amorem flagrantissimum non tam indignitate contumeliarum quam periculi metu abiecit, cum adultero Silio adquiri imperium credidisset; quo tempore foedum in modum trepidus ad castra confugit, nihil tota via quam essetne sibi salvum imperium requirens.

XXXVII. Nulla adeo suspicio, nullus auctor tam levis exstitit, a quo non mediocri scrupulo iniecto ad cavendum ulciscendumque compelleretur. Unus ex litigatoribus seducto in salutatione affirmavit, vidisse se per quietem occidi eum a quodam; dein paulo post, quasi percussorem agnosceret, libellum tradentem adversarium suum demonstravit; confestimque is pro deprenso ad poenam raptus est. Pari modo oppressum ferunt Appium Silanum; quem cum Messalina et Narcissus conspirassent perdere, divisis partibus alter ante lucem similis attonito patroni cubiculum inrupit, affirmans somniasse se vim ei ab Appio inlatam; altera in admirationem formata sibi quoque eandem speciem aliquot iam noctibus obversari rettulit; nec multo post ex composito inrumpere Appius nuntiatus, cui pridie ad id temporis ut adesset praeceptum erat, quasi plane repraesentaretur somnii fides,

---

[a] Of the praetorian guard, in the north-eastern part of the city; see x.2.

was caught near him as he was sacrificing, he summoned the senate in haste by criers and loudly and tearfully bewailed his lot, saying that there was no safety for him anywhere; and for a long time he would not appear in public. His ardent love for Messalina too was cooled, not so much by her unseemly and insulting conduct, as through fear of danger, since he believed that her paramour Silius aspired to the throne. On that occasion he made a shameful and cowardly flight to the camp,[a] doing nothing all the way but ask whether his throne was secure.

XXXVII. No suspicion was too trivial, nor the inspirer of it too insignificant, to drive him on to precaution and vengeance, once a slight uneasiness entered his mind. One of two parties to a suit, when he made his morning call, took Claudius aside, and said that he had dreamed that he was murdered by someone; then a little later pretending to recognize the assassin, he pointed out his opponent, as he was handing in his petition. The latter was immediately seized, as if caught red-handed, and hurried off to execution. It was in a similar way, they say, that Appius Silanus met his downfall. When Messalina and Narcissus had put their heads together to destroy him, they agreed on their parts and the latter rushed into his patron's bed-chamber before daybreak in pretended consternation, declaring that he had dreamed that Appius had made an attack on the emperor. Then Messalina, with assumed surprise, declared that she had had the same dream for several successive nights. A little later, as had been arranged, Appius, who had received orders the day before to come at that time, was reported to be forcing his way in, and as if this were proof positive of the

arcessi statim ac mori iussus est. Nec dubitavit postero die Claudius ordinem rei gestae perferre ad senatum ac liberto gratias agere, quod pro salute sua etiam dormiens excubaret.

XXXVIII. Irae atque iracundiae conscius sibi, utramque excusavit edicto distinxitque, pollicitus alteram quidem brevem et innoxiam, alteram non iniustam fore. Ostiensibus, quia sibi subeunti Tiberim scaphas obviam non miserint, graviter correptis eaque cum invidia, ut in ordinem se coactum conscriberet, repente tantum non 2 satis facientis modo veniam[1] dedit. Quosdam in publico parum tempestive adeuntis manu sua reppulit. Item scribam quaestorium itemque praetura functum senatorem inauditos et innoxios relegavit, quod ille adversus privatum se intemperantius affuisset, hic in aedilitate inquilinos praediorum suorum contra vetitum cocta vendentes multasset vilicumque intervenientem flagellasset. Qua de causa etiam coercitionem popinarum aedilibus ademit.

3 Ac ne stultitiam quidem suam reticuit simulatamque a se ex industria sub Gaio, quod aliter evasurus perventurusque ad susceptam stationem non fuerit, quibusdam oratiunculis testatus est; nec tamen[2] persuasit, cum intra breve tempus liber editus sit, cui index erat μωρῶν

[1] modo veniam, ς; veniam modo, Ω.
[2] tamen, *J. F. Gronov*; ante, Ω (autem, Π[1]).

---

[a] Narcissus.   [b] See note on chap. xxiii. 2.

[c] See *Tib.* xxxiv. 1. Claudius apparently allowed greater freedom. The restrictions were renewed by Nero (see *Nero*, xvi. 2), and according to Dio, 60. 6, Claudius himself (later?) issued an edict forbidding the sale of dressed meats and hot water, as well as abolishing the drinking-booths.

truth of the dream, his immediate accusation and death were ordered. And Claudius did not hesitate to recount the whole affair to the senate next day and to thank the freedman[a] for watching over his emperor's safety even in his sleep.

XXXVIII. He was conscious of his tendency to wrath and resentment and excused both in an edict; he also drew a distinction between them, promising that the former would be short and harmless and the latter not without cause. After sharply rebuking the people of Ostia, because they had sent no boats to meet him when he entered the Tiber, and in such bitter terms that he wrote that they had reduced him to the rank of a commoner, he suddenly forgave them and all but apologised. He repulsed with his own hand men who approached him in public at unseasonable times. He also banished[b] a quaestor's clerk without a hearing, as well as a senator of praetorian rank, although they were blameless: the former for going too far in pleading a suit against him before he became emperor; the latter, because, when aedile, he had fined the tenants of Claudius' estates for violating the law forbidding the selling of cooked victuals, and had whipped his bailiff when he remonstrated. And with the same motive he took from the aediles the regulation of the cook-shops.[c]

He did not even keep quiet about his own stupidity, but in certain brief speeches he declared that he had purposely feigned it under Gaius, because otherwise he could not have escaped alive and attained his present station. But he convinced no one, and within a short time a book was published, the title of which was "The Elevation

ἐπανάστασις, argumentum autem stultitiam neminem fingere.

XXXIX. Inter cetera in eo mirati sunt homines et oblivionem et inconsiderantiam, vel ut Graece dicam, μετεωρίαν et ἀβλεψίαν. Occisa Messalina, paulo post quam in triclinio decubuit, cur domina non veniret requisiit. Multos ex iis, quos capite damnaverat, postero statim die et in consilium et ad aleae lusum admoneri iussit et, quasi morarentur, ut somniculosos per nuntium increpuit.

2 Ducturus contra fas Agrippinam uxorem, non cessavit omni oratione filiam et alumnam et in gremio suo natam atque educatam praedicare. Adsciturus in nomen Neronem, quasi parum reprehenderetur, quod adulto iam filio privignum adoptaret, identidem divulgavit neminem umquam per adoptionem familiae Claudiae insertum.

XL. Sermonis vero rerumque tantam saepe neglegentiam ostendit, ut nec quis nec inter quos, quove tempore ac loco verba faceret, scire aut cogitare existimaretur. Cum de laniis ac vinariis ageretur, exclamavit in curia: "Rogo vos, quis potest sine offula vivere?" Descripsitque[1] abundantiam veterum tabernarum, unde solitus

2 esset vinum olim et ipse petere. De quaesturae[2] quodam candidato inter causas suffragationis suae posuit, quod pater eius frigidam aegro sibi tempestive dedisset. Inducta teste in senatu: "Haec," inquit, "matris meae liberta et ornatrix fuit, sed me patronum semper existimavit; hoc ideo dixi, quod quidam sunt adhuc in domo

---

[1] descripsitque, *Torrentius*; descripsit, *mss.*
[2] quaesturae, ⊊ (*Beroaldus*); questore, Ω.

of Fools" and its thesis, that no one feigned folly.

XXXIX. Among other things men have marvelled at his absent-mindedness and blindness, or to use the Greek terms, his μετεωρία and ἀβλεψία. When he had put Messalina to death, he asked shortly after taking his place at the table why the empress did not come. He caused many of those whom he had condemned to death to be summoned the very next day to consult with him or game with him, and sent a messenger to upbraid them for sleepy-heads when they delayed to appear. When he was planning his unlawful marriage with Agrippina, in every speech that he made he constantly called her his daughter and nursling, born and brought up in his arms. Just before his adoption of Nero, as if it were not bad enough to adopt a stepson when he had a grown-up son of his own, he publicly declared more than once that no one had ever been taken into the Claudian family by adoption.

XL. In short, he often showed such heedlessness in word and act that one would suppose that he did not know or care to whom, with whom, when, or where he was speaking. When a debate was going on about the butchers and vintners, he cried out in the House: "Now, pray, who can live without a snack?" and then went on to describe the abundance of the old taverns to which he himself used to go for wine in earlier days. He gave as one of his reasons for supporting a candidate for the quaestorship, that the man's father had once given him cold water when he was ill and needed it. Once when a witness had been brought before the senate, he said: "This woman was my mother's freedwoman and personal maid, but she always regarded me as her patron; I mention this because there are still some in my household

71

3   mea, qui me patronum non putant." Sed et pro tribunali
Ostiensibus quiddam publice orantibus cum excanduisset, nihil habere se vociferatus est, quare eos demereatur;
si quem alium, et se liberum esse. Nam illa eius cotidiana
et plane omnium horarum et momentorum erant: "Quid,
ego tibi Telegenium videor?" et: "λάλει¹ καὶ μὴ θίγγανε"
multaque talia etiam privatis deformia, nedum principi,
neque infacundo neque indocto, immo etiam pertinaciter
liberalibus studiis dedito.

    XLI. Historiam in adulescentia hortante T. Livio,
Sulpicio vero Flavo etiam adiuvante, scribere adgressus
est. Et cum primum frequenti auditorio commisisset,
aegre perlegit refrigeratus saepe a semet ipso. Nam cum
initio recitationis defractis compluribus subselliis obesitate cuiusdam risus exortus esset, ne sedato quidem
tumultu temperare potuit, quin ex intervallo subinde facti
2 reminisceretur cachinnosque revocaret. In principatu
quoque et scripsit plurimum et assidue recitavit per lec-
torem. Initium autem sumpsit historiae post caedem
Caesaris dictatoris, sed² transiit ad inferiora tempora
coepitque a pace civili, cum sentiret neque libere neque
vere sibi de superioribus tradendi potestatem relictam,
correptus saepe et a matre et ab avia. Prioris materiae
duo volumina, posterioris unum et quadraginta reliquit.
3 Composuit et de vita sua octo volumina, magis inepte

---

¹ λάλει, *Turnebus*; λαλι, *mss.*
² sed et, *mss.*; *Müller struck out* sed, *Torrentius* et.

ᵃ Obviously some man proverbial for his folly; but nothing is
known about him.
ᵇ The famous historian.
ᶜ Because he stammered; see chap. xxx.

now who do not look on me as patron." When the people of Ostia made a public petition to him, he flew into a rage on the very tribunal and bawled out that he had no reason for obliging them; that he was surely free if anyone was. In fact every day, and almost every hour and minute, he would make such remarks as these; "What! do you take me for a Telegenius?"[a] "Scold me, but hands off!" and many others of the same kind which would be unbecoming even in private citizens, not to mention a prince who lacked neither eloquence nor culture, but on the contrary constantly devoted himself to liberal pursuits.

XLI. He began to write a history in his youth with the encouragement of Titus Livius[b] and the direct help of Sulpicius Flavus. But when he gave his first reading to a large audience, he had difficulty in finishing, since he more than once threw cold water on his own performance. For at the beginning of the reading the breaking down of several benches by a fat man raised a laugh, and even after the disturbance was quieted, Claudius could not keep from recalling the incident and renewing his guffaws. Even while he was emperor he wrote a good deal and gave constant recitals through a professional reader.[c] He began his history with the death of the dictator Caesar, but passed to a later period and took a fresh start at the end of the civil war, realising that he was not allowed to give a frank or true account of the earlier times, since he was often taken to task both by his mother and his grandmother.[d] He left two books of the earlier history, but forty-one of the later. He also composed an autobiography in eight books, lacking rather in good taste

[d] His grandmother Octavia was the widow, and his mother Antonia the daughter, of Mark Antony.

quam ineleganter; item Ciceronis defensionem adversus Asini Galli libros satis eruditam. Novas etiam commentus est litteras tres ac numero veterum quasi maxime necessarias addidit; de quarum ratione cum privatus adhuc volumen edidisset, mox princeps non difficulter optinuit ut in usu quoque promiscuo essent. Exstat talis scriptura in plerisque libris ac diurnis titulisque operum.

XLII. Nec minore cura Graeca studia secutus est, amorem praestantiamque linguae occasione omni professus. Cuidam barbaro Graece ac Latine disserenti: "Cum utroque," inquit, "sermone nostro sis paratus"; et in commendanda patribus conscriptis Achaia, gratam sibi provinciam ait communium studiorum commercio; ac saepe in senatu legatis perpetua oratione respondit. Multum vero pro tribunali etiam Homericis locutus est versibus. Quotiens quidem hostem vel insidiatorem ultus esset, excubitori tribuno signum de more poscenti non temere aliud dedit quam

$$\text{ἄνδρ' ἀπαμύνασθαι, ὅτε τις πρότερος χαλεπήνῃ.}^1$$

2   Denique et Graecas scripsit historias, Tyrrhenicon viginti, Carchedoniacon octo. Quarum causa veteri Alexandriae Musio additum ex ipsius nomine novum;[2]

---

[1] ανδραεπ, Ω; χαλεπήνῃ, *Torrentius*; χαλεπελινει, M.

[2] novum, *added by Drechsler*; *Roth suggested* Claudieum *after* Musio.

---

[a] These were ⊢, to represent the sound between *u* and *i* in *maximus, maximus,* etc.; ⊃, for the sound of *bs* as *ps*; ⊢ for consonant *u*.

[b] See *Jul.* xx. 1.

[c] *i.e.* in Greek; cf. *Tib.* lxxi.

than in style, as well as a defence of Cicero against the writings of Asinius Gallus, a work of no little learning. Besides this he invented three new letters and added them to the alphabet, maintaining that they were greatly needed;[a] he published a book on their theory when he was still in private life, and when he became emperor had no difficulty in bringing about their general use. These characters may still be seen in numerous books, in the daily gazette,[b] and in inscriptions on public buildings.

XLII. He gave no less attention to Greek studies, taking every occasion to declare his regard for that language and its superiority. To a foreigner who held forth both in Greek and in Latin he said: "Since you are ready with both our tongues"; and in commending Achaia to the senators he declared that it was a province dear to him through the association of kindred studies; while he often replied to Greek envoys in the senate in a set speech.[c] Indeed he quoted many Homeric lines from the tribunal, and whenever he had punished an enemy or a conspirator, he commonly gave the tribune of the guard[d] this verse when he asked for the usual watchword:

Ward off stoutly the man whosoever is first to
    assail you.[e]

Finally, he even wrote historical works in Greek, twenty books of Etruscan history and eight of Carthaginian. Because of these works there was added to the old Museum at Alexandria a new one called after his

[d] Referring to the cohort on guard at the Palace; cf. chap. x.
[e] *Iliad*, 24. 369; *Odyss.* 21. 133.

institutumque ut quotannis in altero Tyrrhenicon libri, in altero Carchedoniacon diebus statutis velut in auditorio recitarentur toti a singulis per vices.

XLIII. Sub exitu vitae signa quaedam nec obscura paenitentis de matrimonio Agrippinae deque Neronis adoptione dederat, siquidem commemorantibus libertis ac laudantibus cognitionem, qua pridie quandam adulterii ream condemnarat, sibi quoque in fatis esse iactavit omnia impudica, sed non impunita matrimonia; et subinde obvium sibi Britannicum artius complexus hortatus est, ut cresceret rationemque a se omnium factorum acciperet; Graeca insuper voce prosecutus: ὁ τρώσας ἰάσεται. Cumque impubi teneroque adhuc, quando statura permitteret, togam dare destinasset, adiecit: "Ut tandem populus R. verum Caesarem habeat."

XLIV. Non multoque post testamentum etiam conscripsit ac signis omnium magistratuum obsignavit. Prius igitur quam ultra progrederetur, praeventus est ab Agrippina, quam praeter haec conscientia quoque nec minus delatores multorum criminum arguebant.

2   Et veneno quidem occisum convenit; ubi autem et per quem dato, discrepat. Quidam tradunt epulanti in arce cum sacerdotibus per Halotum spadonem praegustatorem; alii domestico convivio per ipsam Agrippinam, quae boletum medicatum avidissimo ciborum talium optulerat. Etiam de subsequentibus diversa fama est.

---

[a] A proverbial expression, derived from the story of Telephus, who when wounded by Achilles was told by the oracle that he could be cured only by the one who dealt the blow. Achilles cured him by applying rust from his spear to the wound.

[b] That is, a legitimate heir to the throne.

name, and it was provided that in the one his Etruscan History should be read each year from beginning to end, and in the other his Carthaginian, by various readers in turn, in the manner of public recitations.

XLIII. Towards the end of his life he had shown some plain signs of repentance for his marriage with Agrippina and his adoption of Nero; for when his freedmen expressed their approval of a trial in which he had the day before condemned a woman for adultery, he declared that it had been his destiny also to have wives who were all unchaste, but not unpunished; and shortly afterwards meeting Britannicus, he hugged him close and urged him to grow up and receive from his father an account of all that he had done, adding in Greek, "He who dealt the wound will heal it."[a] When he expressed his intention of giving Britannicus the gown of manhood, since his stature justified it though he was still young and immature, he added: "That the Roman people may at last have a genuine Caesar."[b]

XLIV. Not long afterwards he also made his will and sealed it with the seals of all the magistrates. But before he could go any farther, he was cut short by Agrippina, who was being accused besides of many other crimes both by her own conscience and by informers.

That Claudius was poisoned is the general belief, but when it was done and by whom is disputed. Some say that it was his taster, the eunuch Halotus, as he was banqueting on the Citadel[c] with the priests; others that at a family dinner Agrippina served the drug to him with her own hand in mushrooms, a dish of which he was extravagantly fond. Reports also differ as to what followed.

[c] The northern spur of the Capitoline Hill.

3 Multi statim hausto veneno obmutuisse aiunt excrucia-
tumque doloribus nocte tota defecisse prope lucem.
Nonnulli inter initia consopitum, deinde cibo affluente
evomuisse omnia, repetitumque toxico, incertum pultine
addito, cum velut exhaustum refici cibo oporteret, an
immisso per clystera,[1] ut quasi abundantia laboranti
etiam hoc genere egestionis subveniretur.

XLV. Mors eius celata est, donec circa successorem
omnia ordinarentur. Itaque et quasi pro aegro adhuc vota
suscepta sunt et inducti per simulationem comoedi, qui
velut desiderantem oblectarent. Excessit III. Id. Octob.
Asinio Marcello Acilio Aviola coss. sexagesimo quarto
aetatis, imperii quarto decimo anno, funeratusque est
sollemni principum pompa et in numerum deorum rela-
tus; quem honorem a Nerone destitutum abolitumque
recepit mox per Vespasianum.

XLVI. Praesagia mortis eius praecipua fuerunt: exortus crinitae stellae, quam cometen vocant,[2] tactumque de
caelo monumentum Drusi patris, et quod eodem anno ex
omnium magistratuum genere plerique mortem obierant.
Sed nec ipse ignorasse aut dissimulasse ultima vitae suae
tempora videtur, aliquot quidem argumentis. Nam et
cum consules designaret, neminem ultra mensem quo
obiit designavit, et in senatu, cui novissime interfuit, multum ad concordiam liberos suos cohortatus, utriusque
aetatem suppliciter patribus commendavit, et in ultima

[1] clystera, ς; clysteram, *MX* (clystere, *T*); clysterum, *G*;
clysterem, Υ.
[2] quam ... vocant: *probably a gloss; cf. Jul.* lxxxviii.

---

[a] On October 13, A.D. 54.

Many say that as soon as he swallowed the poison he became speechless, and after suffering excruciating pain all night, died just before dawn. Some say that he first fell into a stupor, then vomited up the whole contents of his overloaded stomach, and was given a second dose, perhaps in a gruel, under pretence that he must be refreshed with food after his exhaustion, or administered in a syringe, as if he were suffering from a surfeit and required relief by that form of evacuation as well.

XLV. His death was kept quiet until all the arrangements were made about the succession. Accordingly vows were offered for his safety, as if he were still ill, and the farce was kept up by bringing in comic actors, under pretence that he had asked to be entertained in that way. He died on the third day before the Ides of October[a] in the consulship of Asinius Marcellus and Acilius Aviola, in the sixty-fourth year of his age and the fourteenth of his reign. He was buried with regal pomp and enrolled among the gods, an honour neglected and finally annulled by Nero, but later restored to him by Vespasian.

XLVI. The principal omens of his death were the following: the rise of a long-haired star, commonly called a comet; the striking of his father Drusus' tomb by lightning; and the fact that many magistrates of all ranks had died that same year. There are besides some indications that he himself was not unaware of his approaching end, and that he made no secret of it; for when he was appointing the consuls, he made no appointment beyond the month when he died, and on his last appearance in the senate, after earnestly exhorting his children to harmony, he begged the members to watch over the tender years of both; and in his last sitting on the tribunal he

cognitione pro tribunali accessisse ad finem mortalitatis, quanquam abominantibus qui audiebant, semel atque iterum pronuntiavit.

declared more than once that he had reached the end of a mortal career, although all who heard him prayed that the omen might be averted.[a]

[a] The formula was *"Di meliora (duint)!"* "May the Gods grant better things," *i.e.* "the Gods forbid!"

LIBER VI

NERO

I. Ex gente Domitia duae familiae claruerunt, Calvi-
norum et Ahenobarborum. Ahenobarbi auctorem origi-
nis itemque cognominis habent L. Domitium, cui rure
quondam revertenti iuvenes gemini augustiore forma ex
occursu imperasse traduntur, nuntiaret senatui ac populo
victoriam, de qua incertum adhuc erat; atque in fidem
maiestatis adeo permulsisse malas, ut e nigro rutilum
aerique adsimilem capillum redderent. Quod insigne
mansit et in posteris eius, ac magna pars rutila barba
2 fuerunt. Functi autem consulatibus septem, triumpho
censuraque duplici et inter patricios adlecti perseveraverunt omnes in eodem cognomine. Ac ne praenomina
quidem ulla praeterquam Gnaei et Luci usurparunt;
eaque ipsa notabili varietate, modo continuantes unum
quodque per trinas personas, modo alternantes per singulas. Nam primum secundumque ac tertium Ahenobarborum Lucios, sequentis rursus tres ex ordine Gnaeos
accepimus, reliquos non nisi vicissim tum Lucios tum

---

[a] The youths were Castor and Pollux, and the victory that
at Lake Regillus, in 498 B.C., according to the traditional
chronology.   [b] In 261, 122, 96, 94, 54, and 32 B.C. and A.D. 32.
     [c] In 122 B.C.

BOOK VI

NERO

I. Of the Domitian family two branches have acquired distinction, the Calvini and the Ahenobarbi. The latter have as the founder of their race and the origin of their surname Lucius Domitius, to whom, as he was returning from the country, there once appeared twin youths of more than mortal majesty, so it is said, and bade him carry to the senate and people the news of a victory,[a] which was as yet unknown. And as a token of their divinity it is said that they stroked his cheeks and turned his black beard to a ruddy hue, like that of bronze. This sign was perpetuated in his descendants, a great part of whom had red beards. After they had attained seven consulships,[b] a triumph,[c] and two censorships,[d] and were enrolled among the patricians, they all continued to use the same surname. They confined their forenames to Gnaeus and Lucius, and used even these with a noteworthy variation, now conferring each one on three members of the family in succession, and now giving them to individual members in turn. Thus the first, second, and third of the Ahenobarbi, we are told, were called Lucius, the next three in order Gnaeus, while all those that followed were called in turn first Lucius and then Gnaeus. It seems to

[d] In 115 and 92 B.C.

Gnaeos. Pluris e familia cognosci referre arbitror, quo facilius appareat ita degenerasse a suorum virtutibus Nero, ut tamen vitia cuiusque quasi tradita et ingenita rettulerit.

II. Ut igitur paulo altius repetam, atavus eius Cn. Domitius in tribunatu pontificibus offensior, quod alium quam se in patris sui locum cooptassent, ius sacerdotum subrogandorum a collegiis ad populum transtulit; at in consulatu Allobrogibus Arvernisque superatis elephanto per provinciam vectus est turba militum quasi inter

2 sollemnia triumphi prosequente. In hunc dixit Licinius Crassus orator non esse mirandum, quod aeneam barbam haberet, cui os ferreum, cor plumbeum esset. Huius filius praetor C. Caesarem abeuntem consulatu, quem adversus auspicia legesque gessisse existimabatur, ad disquisitionem senatus vocavit; mox consul imperatorem ab exercitibus Gallicis retrahere temptavit successorque ei per factionem nominatus principio civilis belli ad

3 Corfinium captus est. Unde dimissus Massiliensis obsidione laborantis cum adventu suo confirmasset, repente destituit acieque demum Pharsalica occubuit; vir neque satis constans et ingenio truci in desperatione rerum mortem timore appetitam ita expavit, ut haustum

---

[a] In 122 B.C.

[b] Suetonius is in error here; it was the father of the tribune who defeated the Allobroges.

[c] *Os* has about the force of "cheek" in colloquial English.

[d] In 54 B.C.

[e] See *Jul.* xxxiv. 1.

me worth while to give an account of several members of this family, to show more clearly that though Nero degenerated from the good qualities of his ancestors, he yet reproduced the vices of each of them, as if transmitted to him by natural inheritance.

II. To begin then somewhat far back, his great-grandfather's grandfather, Gnaeus Domitius, when tribune of the commons, was enraged at the pontiffs for choosing another than himself in his father's place among them, and transferred the right of filling vacancies in the priesthoods from the colleges themselves to the people. Then having vanquished the Allobroges and the Arverni in his consulship,[a] he rode through the province on an elephant, attended by a throng of soldiers, in a kind of triumphal procession.[b] He it was of whom the orator Licinius Crassus said that it was not surprising that he had a brazen beard, since he had a face[c] of iron and a heart of lead. His son, who was praetor at the time, summoned Gaius Caesar to an investigation before the senate at the close of his consulship, because it was thought that his administration had been in violation of the auspices and the laws. Afterwards in his own consulship he tried to deprive Caesar of the command of the armies in Gaul,[d] and being named Caesar's successor by his party, was taken prisoner at Corfinium at the beginning of the civil war.[e] Granted his freedom, he at first gave courage by his presence to the people of Massilia, who were hard pressed by their besiegers, but suddenly abandoned them and at last fell in the battle at Pharsalus. He was a man of no great resolution, though he had a violent temper, and when he once attempted to kill himself in a fit of despair and terror, he so shrank from the thought of death that he

venenum paenitentia evomuerit medicumque manu-
miserit, quod sibi prudens ac sciens minus noxium tem-
perasset. Consultante autem Cn. Pompeio de mediis ac
neutram partem sequentibus solus censuit hostium
numero habendos.

III. Reliquit filium omnibus gentis suae procul dubio
praeferendum. Is inter conscios Caesarianae necis
quamquam insons damnatus lege Pedia, cum ad Cassium
Brutumque se propinqua sibi cognatione iunctos contulisset, post utriusque interitum classem olim commis-
sam retinuit, auxit etiam, nec nisi partibus ubique profli-
gatis M. Antonio sponte et ingentis meriti loco tradidit.
2 Solusque omnium ex iis, qui pari lege damnati erant,
restitutus in patriam amplissimos honores percucurrit; ac
subinde redintegrata dissensione civili, eidem Antonio
legatus, delatam sibi summam imperii ab iis, quos
Cleopatrae pudebat, neque suscipere neque recusare
fidenter propter subitam valitudinem ausus, transiit ad
Augustum et in diebus paucis obiit, nonnulla et ipse
infamia aspersus. Nam Antonius eum desiderio amicae
Serviliae Naidis transfugisse iactavit.

IV. Ex hoc Domitius nascitur, quem emptorem familiae pecuniaeque in testamento Augusti fuisse mox vulgo
notatum est, non minus aurigandi arte in adulescentia

ᵃ Proposed by Q. Pedius, Caesar's colleague in the consulship; see Index.   ᵇ The Pedian law.   ᶜ In 31 B.C.

ᵈ That is, as his executor. The maker of a will chose a man to
whom he made a symbolic sale (*per aes et librum*; see *Aug.* lxiv.
1) of all his goods in the presence of witnesses. The purchaser
then made the designated payments to the heirs and legatees.

changed his mind and vomited up the poison, conferring freedom on his physician, since, knowing his master, he had purposely given him what was not a fatal dose. When Gnaeus Pompeius brought forward the question of the treatment of those who were neutral and sided with neither party, he alone was for regarding them as hostile.

III. He left a son, who was beyond all question better than the rest of the family. He was condemned to death by the Pedian law[a] among those implicated in Caesar's death, though he was guiltless, and accordingly joined Brutus and Cassius, who were his near relatives. After the death of both leaders he retained the fleet of which he had previously been made commander, and even added to it, and it was not until his party had been everywhere routed that he surrendered it to Mark Antony, of his own free will and as if it were a great favour. He too was the only one of those who were condemned by that same law[b] who was allowed to return to his native land, where he successively held all the highest offices. When the civil strife was subsequently renewed, and he was appointed one of Antony's lieutenants, he did not venture, owing to a sudden attack of illness, to accept the chief command when it was offered him by those who were ashamed of Cleopatra, nor yet positively to decline it; but he went over to Augustus and a few days later died.[c] Even he did not escape with an unblemished reputation, for Antony openly declared that he had changed sides from desire for the company of his mistress, Servilia Nais.

IV. He was the father of the Domitius who was later well known from being named in Augustus' will as the purchaser of his goods and chattels,[d] a man no less famous in his youth for his skill in driving than he was

clarus quam deinde ornamentis triumphalibus ex Germanico bello. Verum arrogans, profusus, immitis censorem L. Plancum via sibi decedere aedilis coegit; praeturae consulatusque honore equites R. matronasque ad agendum mimum produxit in scaenam. Venationes et in Circo et in omnibus urbis regionibus dedit, munus etiam gladiatorium, sed tanta saevitia, ut necesse fuerit Augusto clam frustra monitum edicto coercere.

V. Ex Antonia maiore patrem Neronis procreavit omni parte vitae detestabilem, siquidem comes ad Orientem C. Caesaris iuvenis, occiso liberto suo, quod potare quantum iubebatur recusarat, dimissus e cohorte amicorum nihilo modestius vixit; sed et in viae Appiae vico repente puerum citatis iumentis haud ignarus obtrivit et Romae medio Foro cuidam equiti R. liberius iurganti oculum

2 eruit; perfidiae vero tantae, ut non modo argentarios pretiis rerum coemptarum, sed et in praetura mercede palmarum aurigarios fraudaverit, notatus ob haec et sororis ioco,[1] querentibus dominis factionum repraesentanda praemia in posterum sanxit. Maiestatis quoque et adulteriorum incestique cum sorore Lepida sub excessu Tiberi reus, mutatione temporum evasit decessitque

[1] ioco, ς; loco, Ω; *Some assume a lacuna after* ioco, *which is filled in various ways*: quae, *Casaubon*; qui, *Ursinus, Oudendorp*; et Tiberi edicto qui, *Bücheler.*

[a] *Aug.* lxiv and lxv.

[b] Cf. *Aug.* xxvii. 4, *Nero* xxvi. 2, and the frequent allusions to gouging out eyes in comedy.

[c] And paid for through the bankers; cf. *perscriptum fuisset, Jul.* xlii. 2.   [d] Domitia.

[e] In his capacity as praetor; this was adding insult to injury, since the edict did not affect the present case.

later for winning the insignia of a triumph in the war in
Germany. But he was haughty, extravagant, and cruel,
and when he was only an aedile, forced the censor Lucius
Plancus to make way for him on the street. While holding
the offices of praetor and consul, he brought Roman
knights and matrons on the stage to act a farce. He gave
beast-baitings both in the Circus and in all the regions of
the city; also a gladiatorial show, but with such inhuman
cruelty that Augustus, after his private warning was disregarded, was forced to restrain him by an edict.

V. He had by the elder Antonia a son Domitius who
became the father of Nero, a man hateful in every walk of
life; for when he had gone to the East on the staff of the
young Gaius Caesar,[a] he slew one of his own freedmen for
refusing to drink as much as he was ordered, and when he
was in consequence dismissed from the number of Gaius'
friends, he lived not a whit less lawlessly. On the contrary,
in a village on the Appian Way, suddenly whipping up his
team, he purposely ran over and killed a boy; and right in
the Roman Forum he gouged out the eye[b] of a Roman
knight for being too outspoken in chiding him. He was
moreover so dishonest that he not only cheated some
bankers of the prices of wares which he had bought,[c] but
in his praetorship he even defrauded the victors in the
chariot races of the amount of their prizes. When for this
reason he was held up to scorn by the jests of his own
sister,[d] and the managers of the troupes made complaint,
he issued an edict[e] that the prizes should thereafter be
paid on the spot. Just before the death of Tiberius he was
also charged with treason, as well as with acts of adultery
and with incest with his sister Lepida, but escaped owing
to the change of rulers and died of dropsy at Pyrgi, after

Pyrgis morbo aquae intercutis, sublato filio Nerone ex Agrippina Germanico genita.

VI. Nero natus est Anti[1] post VIIII. mensem quam Tiberius excessit, XVIII. Kal. Ian. tantum quod exoriente sole, paene ut radiis prius quam terra contingeretur. De genitura eius statim multa et formidulosa multis coniectantibus praesagio fuit etiam Domiti patris vox, inter gratulationes amicorum negantis quicquam ex se et Agrippina nisi detestabile et malo publico nasci potuisse.

2 Eiusdem futurae infelicitatis signum evidens die lustrico exstitit; nam C. Caesar, rogante sorore ut infanti quod vellet nomen daret, intuens Claudium patruum suum, a quo mox principe Nero adoptatus est, eius se dixit dare, neque ipse serio sed per iocum et aspernante Agrippina, quod tum Claudius inter ludibria aulae erat.

3 Trimulus patrem amisit; cuius ex parte tertia heres, ne hanc quidem integram cepit correptis per coheredem Gaium universis bonis. Et subinde matre etiam relegata paene inops atque egens apud amitam Lepidam nutritus est sub duobus paedagogis saltatore atque tonsore. Verum Claudio imperium adepto non solum paternas opes reciperavit, sed et Crispi Passieni vitrici sui hereditate ditatus est.

4 Gratia quidem et potentia revocatae restitutaeque matris usque eo floruit, ut emanaret in vulgus missos a Messalina uxore Claudi, qui eum meridi-

---

[1] Anti, *Roth*; Antii, *Turnebus and P in the margin*; ante, Ω.

---

[a] See note on *Tib*. vii. 2. [b] On December 15, A.D. 37.

[c] See note on *Tib*. vii. 2 and cf. *Aug*. v.

[d] Boys on the ninth day after birth, and girls on the eighth, were purified by a sacrifice and given a name; the ceremony was called *lustratio*.

acknowledging[a] Nero son of Agrippina, the daughter of Germanicus.

VI. Nero was born at Antium[b] nine months after the death of Tiberius, on the eighteenth day before the Kalends of January, just as the sun rose, so that he was touched by its rays almost before he could be laid upon the ground.[c] Many people at once made many direful predictions from his horoscope, and a remark of his father Domitius was also regarded as an omen; for while receiving the congratulations of his friends, he said that "nothing that was not abominable and a public bane could be born of Agrippina and himself." Another manifest indication of Nero's future unhappiness occurred on the day of his purification;[d] for when Gaius Caesar was asked by his sister to give the child whatever name he liked, he looked at his uncle Claudius, who later became emperor and adopted Nero, and said that he gave him his name. This he did, not seriously, but in jest, and Agrippina scorned the proposal, because at that time Claudius was one of the laughing-stocks of the court.

At the age of three he lost his father, being left heir to a third of his estate; but even this he did not receive in full, since his fellow heir Gaius seized all the property. Then his mother was banished too, and he was brought up at the house of his aunt Lepida almost in actual want, under two tutors, a dancer and a barber. But when Claudius became emperor, Nero not only recovered his father's property, but was also enriched by an inheritance from his stepfather, Passienus Crispus. When his mother was recalled from banishment and reinstated, he became so prominent through her influence that it leaked out that Messalina, wife of Claudius, had sent emissaries to

antem, quasi Britannici aemulum, strangularent. Additum fabulae eosdem[1] dracone e pulvino se proferente conterritos refugisse. Quae fabula exorta est deprensis in lecto eius circum cervicalia serpentis exuviis; quas tamen aureae armillae ex voluntate matris inclusas dextro brachio gestavit aliquamdiu ac taedio tandem maternae memoriae abiecit rursusque extremis suis rebus frustra requisiit.

VII. Tener adhuc necdum matura pueritia circensibus ludis Troiam constantissime favorabiliterque lusit. Undecimo aetatis anno a Claudio adoptatus est Annaeoque Senecae iam tunc senatori in disciplinam traditus. Ferunt Senecam proxima nocte visum sibi per quietem C. Caesari praecipere, et fidem somnio Nero brevi fecit prodita immanitate naturae quibus primum potuit experimentis. Namque Britannicum fratrem, quod se post adoptionem Ahenobarbum ex consuetudine salutasset, ut subditivum apud patrem arguere conatus est. Amitam autem Lepidam ream testimonio coram afflixit gratificans matri, a qua rea premebatur.

2   Deductus in Forum tiro populo congiarium, militi donativum proposuit indictaque decursione praetorianis scutum sua manu praetulit; exin patri gratias in senatu egit. Apud eundem consulem pro Bononiensibus Latine,

[1] ad *before* eosdem, *MLP*; at, *G*; et, *Υ*; *OST omit.*

[a] That is, as if the story had a better foundation, and the serpent had really saved his life through divine agency.

[b] So the mss., but it should be the twelfth (*Lipsius*) or thirteenth (*Oudendorp*).   [c] In A.D. 50.

[d] That is, his adoptive father Claudius.

[e] On the *decursio* see note *d* on *Claud.* i. 3.

strangle him as he was taking his noon-day nap, regarding him as a rival of Britannicus. An addition to this bit of gossip is that the would-be assassins were frightened away by a snake which darted out from under his pillow. The only foundation for this tale was that there was found in his bed near the pillow the slough of a serpent; but nevertheless[a] at his mother's desire he had the skin enclosed in a golden bracelet, and wore it for a long time on his right arm. But when at last the memory of his mother grew hateful to him, he threw it away, and afterwards in the time of his extremity sought it again in vain.

VII. While he was still a young, half-grown boy he took part in the game of Troy at a performance in the Circus with great self-possession and success. In the eleventh[b] year of his age he was adopted by Claudius[c] and consigned to the training of Annaeus Seneca, who was then already a senator. They say that on the following night Seneca dreamed that he was teaching Gaius Caesar, and Nero soon proved the dream prophetic by revealing the cruelty of his disposition at the earliest possible opportunity. For merely because his brother Britannicus had, after his adoption, greeted him as usual as Ahenobarbus, he tried to convince his father[d] that Britannicus was a changeling. Also when his aunt Lepida was accused, he publicly gave testimony against her, to gratify his mother, who was using every effort to ruin Lepida.

At his formal introduction into public life he announced a largess to the people and a gift of money to the soldiers, ordered a drill[e] of the praetorians and headed them shield in hand, and thereafter returned thanks to his father in the senate. In the latter's consulship he pleaded the cause of the people of Bononia

pro Rhodiis atque Iliensibus Graece verba fecit. Auspicatus est et iuris dictionem praefectus urbi sacro Latinarum, celeberrimis patronis non tralaticias, ut assolet, et
brevis, sed maximas plurimasque postulationes certatim
ingerentibus, quamvis interdictum a Claudio esset. Nec
multo post duxit uxorem Octaviam ediditque pro Claudi
salute circenses et venationem.

VIII. Septemdecim natus annos, ut de Claudio palam
factum est, inter horam sextam septimamque processit ad
excubitores, cum ob totius diei diritatem non aliud auspi-
candi tempus accommodatius videretur; proque Palati
gradibus imperator consalutatus lectica in castra et inde
raptim appellatis militibus in curiam delatus est disces-
sitque iam vesperi, ex immensis, quibus cumulabatur,
honoribus tantum patris patriae nomine recusato propter
aetatem.

IX. Orsus hinc a pietatis ostentatione Claudium appa-
ratissimo funere elatum laudavit et[1] consecravit. Memoriae Domiti patris honores maximos habuit. Matri summam omnium rerum privatarum publicarumque permisit. Primo etiam imperii die signum excubanti tribuno
dedit "optimam matrem" ac deinceps eiusdem saepe lectica per publicum simul vectus est. Antium coloniam
deduxit ascriptis veteranis e praetorio additisque per
domicilii translationem ditissimis primipilarium; ubi et

---

[1] et, Ϛ; *not found in the earlier mss.; the Roman* editiones
principes *have* consecravitque.

---

[a] In A.D. 54.
[b] See *Claud.* x and note *d* on *Claud.* xlii. 1.
[c] Cf. Tac. *Ann.* 12. 68.
[d] In A.D. 61.

before him in Latin, and of those of Rhodes and Ilium in Greek. His first appearance as judge was when he was prefect of the city during the Latin Festival, when the most celebrated pleaders vied with one another in bringing before him, not trifling and brief cases according to the usual custom, but many of the highest importance, though this had been forbidden by Claudius. Shortly afterwards he took Octavia to wife and gave games and a beast-baiting in the Circus, that health might be vouchsafed Claudius.

VIII. When the death of Claudius[a] was made public, Nero, who was seventeen years old, went forth to the watch[b] between the sixth and seventh hour, since no earlier time for the formal beginning of his reign seemed suitable because of bad omens throughout the day.[c] Hailed emperor on the steps of the Palace, he was carried in a litter to the praetorian camp, and after a brief address to the soldiers was taken from there to the House, which he did not leave until evening, of the unbounded honours that were heaped upon him refusing but one, the title of father of his country, and that because of his youth.

IX. Then beginning with a display of filial piety, he gave Claudius a magnificent funeral, spoke his eulogy, and deified him. He paid the highest honours to the memory of his father Domitius. He left to his mother the management of all public and private business. Indeed, on the first day of his rule he gave to the tribune on guard the watchword "The Best of Mothers," and afterwards he often rode with her through the streets in her litter. He established[d] a colony at Antium, enrolling the veterans of the praetorian guard and joining with them the wealthiest of the chief centurions, whom he compelled to change

portum operis sumptuosissimi fecit.

X. Atque ut certiorem adhuc indolem ostenderet, ex Augusti praescripto imperaturum se professus, neque liberalitatis neque clementiae, ne comitatis quidem exhibendae ullam occasionem omisit.[1] Graviora vectigalia aut abolevit aut minuit. Praemia delatorum Papiae legis ad quartas redegit. Divisis populo viritim quadringenis nummis senatorum nobilissimo cuique, sed a re familiari destituto annua salaria et quibusdam quingena constituit, item praetorianis cohortibus frumentum menstruum gratuitum. Et cum de supplicio cuiusdam capite damnati ut ex more subscriberet admoneretur: "Quam vellem," inquit, "nescire litteras." Omnis ordines subinde ac memoriter salutavit. Agenti senatui gratias respondit: "Cum meruero." Ad campestres exercitationes suas admisit et plebem declamavitque saepius publice; recitavit et carmina, non modo domi sed et in theatro, tanta universorum laetitia, ut ob recitationem supplicatio decreta sit eaque pars carminum aureis litteris Iovi Capitolino dicata.

XI. Spectaculorum plurima et varia genera edidit: iuvenales, circenses, scaenicos ludos, gladiatorium munus. Iuvenalibus senes quoque consulares anusque matronas recepit ad lusum. Circensibus loca equiti

---

[1] omisit, *RL*^{2}*S*^{2}*TN* (obm-, *T*); emisit, Ω.

---

[a] See *Claud.* xix.   [b] Cf. *Vesp.* xvii.

[c] Cf. *Aug.* liii. 3, *nullo submonente.*   [d] An honour previously conferred only on generals after a great victory; cf. *Jul.* xxiv. 3, at the end.   [e] That is, the part which he had read.

[f] In commemoration of the first shaving of his beard; see chap. xii. 4, below.

their residence; and he also made a harbour there at great expense.

X. To make his good intentions still more evident, he declared that he would rule according to the principles of Augustus, and he let slip no opportunity for acts of generosity and mercy, or even for displaying his affability. The more oppressive sources of revenue he either abolished or moderated. He reduced the rewards paid to informers against violators of the Papian law[a] to one fourth of the former amount. He distributed four hundred sesterces to each man of the people, and granted to the most distinguished of the senators who were without means an annual salary,[b] to some as much as five hundred thousand sesterces; and to the praetorian cohorts he gave a monthly allowance of grain free of cost. When he was asked according to custom to sign the warrant for the execution of a man who had been condemned to death, he said: "How I wish I had never learned to write!" He greeted men of all orders off-hand and from memory.[c] When the senate returned thanks to him, he replied, "When I shall have deserved them." He admitted even the commons to witness his exercises in the Campus, and often declaimed in public. He read his poems too, not only at home but in the theatre as well, so greatly to the delight of all that a thanksgiving[d] was voted because of his recital, while that part[e] of his poems was inscribed in letters of gold and dedicated to Jupiter of the Capitol.

XI. He gave many entertainments of different kinds: the *Juvenales*,[f] chariot races in the Circus, stage-plays, and a gladiatorial show. At the first mentioned he had even old men of consular rank and aged matrons take part. For the games in the Circus he assigned places to

secreta a ceteris tribuit commisitque etiam camelorum
2 quadrigas. Ludis, quos pro aeternitate imperii susceptos
appellari "maximos" voluit, ex utroque ordine et sexu
plerique ludicras partes sustinuerunt; notissimus eques
R. elephanto supersidens per catadromum[1] decucurrit;
inducta Afrani togata, quae Incendium inscribitur,[2] con-
cessumque ut scaenici ardentis domus supellectilem
diriperent ac sibi haberent; sparsa et populo missilia
omnium rerum per omnes dies: singula cotidie milia
avium[3] cuiusque generis, multiplex penus, tesserae fru-
mentariae, vestis, aurum, argentum, gemmae, margari-
tae, tabulae pictae, mancipia, iumenta atque etiam man-
suetae ferae, novissime naves, insulae, agri.

XII. Hos ludos spectavit e proscaeni fastigio.
Munere, quod in amphitheatro ligneo regione Martii
campi intra anni spatium fabricato dedit, neminem
occidit, ne noxiorum quidem. Exhibuit autem ad ferrum
etiam quadringentos senatores sescentosque equites
Romanos et quosdam fortunae atque existimationis inte-
grae, ex isdem ordinibus confectores quoque ferarum et
varia harenae ministeria. Exhibuit et naumachiam
marina aqua innantibus beluis; item pyrrichas quasdam e
numero epheborum, quibus post editam operam diplo-
2 mata civitatis Romanae singulis optulit. Inter pyrri-

---

[1] catadromum, ς; gatadromum, Ω.   [2] inscribitur, *Erasmus*; scribitur, Ω.   [3] avium, Gς; aulum, Ω; aurum, ς.

---

[a] This had previously been done only at the theatre (see note
on *Jul.* xxxix. 2); senators were first given special seats at the Circus by Claudius; see *Claud.* xxi. 3.   [b] A tight-rope, sloping
downwards across the arena; cf. *Galba*, vi. 1.   [c] In A.D. 58.

[d] The musicians, machinists, etc.; cf. *Claud.* xxxiv. 2.

the knights apart from the rest,[a] and even matched chariots drawn by four camels. At the plays which he gave for the "Eternity of the Empire," which by his order were called the *Ludi Maximi*, parts were taken by several men and women of both the orders; a well known Roman knight mounted an elephant and rode down a rope;[b] a Roman play of Afranius, too, was staged, entitled "The Fire," and the actors were allowed to carry off the furniture of the burning house and keep it. Every day all kinds of presents were thrown to the people; these included a thousand birds of every kind each day, various kinds of food, tickets for grain, clothing, gold, silver, precious stones, pearls, paintings, slaves, beasts of burden, and even trained wild animals; finally, ships, blocks of houses, and farms.

XII. These plays he viewed from the top of the proscenium. At the gladiatorial show, which he gave in a wooden amphitheatre, erected in the district of the Campus Martius within the space of a single year,[c] he had no one put to death, not even criminals. But he compelled four hundred senators and six hundred Roman knights, some of whom were well to do and of unblemished reputation, to fight in the arena. Even those who fought with the wild beasts and performed the various services in the arena[d] were of the same orders. He also exhibited a naval battle in salt water with sea monsters swimming about in it; besides pyrrhic dances[e] by some Greek youths,[f] handing each of them certificates of Roman citizenship at the close of his performance. The pyrrhic dances repre-

[e] Cf. *Jul.* xxxix. 1. Originally war dances, their scope was extended to pantomime of all kinds, as appears from what follows. [f] See note on *Aug.* xcviii. 3.

charum argumenta taurus Pasiphaam ligneo iuvencae simulacro abditam iniit, ut multi spectantium crediderunt; Icarus primo statim conatu iuxta cubiculum eius decidit ipsumque cruore respersit. Nam perraro praesidere, ceterum accubans, parvis primum foraminibus, deinde toto podio adaperto spectare consueverat.

3　Instituit et quinquennale certamen primus omnium Romae more Graeco triplex, musicum gymnicum equestre, quod appellavit Neronia; dedicatisque thermis atque gymnasio senatui quoque et equiti oleum praebuit. Magistros toto[1] certamini praeposuit consulares sorte, sede praetorum. Deinde in orchestram senatumque descendit et orationis quidem carminisque Latini coronam, de qua honestissimus quisque contenderat, ipsorum consensu concessam sibi recepit, citharae autem a iudicibus ad se delatam adoravit ferrique ad Augusti statuam 4　iussit. Gymnico, quod in Saeptis edebat, inter buthysiae apparatum barbam primam posuit conditamque in auream pyxidem et pretiosissimis margaritis adornatam Capitolio consecravit. Ad athletarum spectaculum invitavit et virgines Vestales, quia Olympiae quoque Cereris sacerdotibus spectare conceditur.

---

[1] toto, Ω; toti, ς; *cf. Caes. B.G.* 7. 89; *Prop.* 3. 11. 57, *etc.*

---

[a] The *podium* in the amphitheatre was a raised platform close to the arena, on which the imperial family, the curule magistrates, and the Vestal virgins sat on curule chairs. Nero reclined there on a couch.

[b] In A.D. 60.

[c] In the broad sense, including poetry and oratory.

[d] The baths, the *Thermae Neronianae*, were in the Campus

sented various scenes. In one a bull mounted Pasiphae, who was concealed in a wooden image of a heifer; at least many of the spectators thought so. Icarus at his very first attempt fell close by the imperial couch and bespattered the emperor with his blood; for Nero very seldom presided at the games, but used to view them while reclining on a couch, at first through small openings, and then with the entire balcony[a] uncovered.

He was likewise the first to establish[b] at Rome a quinquennial contest in three parts, after the Greek fashion, that is in music,[c] gymnastics, and riding, which he called the *Neronia*; at the same time he dedicated his baths and gymnasium,[d] supplying every member of the senatorial and equestrian orders with oil. To preside over[e] the whole contest he appointed ex-consuls, chosen by lot, who occupied the seats of the praetors. Then he went down into the orchestra among the senators and accepted the prize for Latin oratory and verse, for which all the most eminent men had contended but which was given to him with their unanimous consent; but when that for lyre-playing was also offered him by the judges, he knelt before it and ordered that it be laid at the feet of Augustus' statue. At the gymnastic contest, which he gave in the Saepta, he shaved his first beard to the accompaniment of a splendid sacrifice of bullocks, put it in a golden box adorned with pearls of great price, and dedicated it in the Capitol. He invited the Vestal virgins also to witness the contests of the athletes,[f] because at Olympia the priestesses of Ceres were allowed the same privilege.

Martius, near the Pantheon. The gymnasium, the first permanent building of the kind at Rome, was attached to the baths.

   [e] And to act as judges.   [f] Cf. *Aug.* xliv. 3.

XIII. Non immerito inter spectacula ab eo edita et Tiridatis in urbem introitum rettulerim. Quem Armeniae regem magnis pollicitationibus sollicitatum, cum destinato per edictum die ostensurus populo propter nubilum distulisset, produxit quo opportunissime potuit, dispositis circa Fori templa armatis cohortibus, curuli residens apud rostra triumphantis habitu inter signa militaria atque vexilla. Et primo per devexum pulpitum subeuntem admisit ad genua adlevatumque dextra exosculatus est, dein precanti tiara deducta[1] diadema inposuit, verba supplicis interpretata praetorio viro multitudini pronuntiante; perductum inde in theatrum ac rursus supplicantem iuxta se latere dextro conlocavit. Ob quae imperator consalutatus, laurea in Capitolium lata, Ianum geminum clausit, tamquam nullo[2] residuo bello.

XIV. Consulatus quattuor gessit: primum bimenstrem, secundum et novissimum semenstres, tertium quadrimenstrem; medios duos continuavit, reliquos inter annua spatia variavit.

XV. In iuris dictione postulatoribus nisi sequenti die ac per libellos non temere respondit. Cognoscendi morem eum tenuit, ut continuis actionibus omissis

2

---

[1] tiara deducta, ς; diariam deductam, Ω.
[2] tamquam nullo, *Faernus and Lipsius*; tam nullo quam, Ω.

[a] Of Pompey.
[b] See note on *Aug.* xiii. 2.
[c] This was usual only when a triumph was celebrated.
[d] See note on *Aug.* xxii.
[e] In A.D. 55, 57, 58, and 60.
[f] He assumed a fifth consulship in 68; see chap. xliii. 2.

XIII. I may fairly include among his shows the entrance of Tiridates into the city. He was a king of Armenia, whom Nero induced by great promises to come to Rome; and since he was prevented by bad weather from exhibiting him to the people on the day appointed by proclamation, he produced him at the first favourable opportunity, with the praetorian cohorts drawn up in full armour about the temples in the Forum, while he himself sat in a curule chair on the rostra in the attire of a triumphing general, surrounded by military ensigns and standards. As the king approached along a sloping platform, the emperor at first let him fall at his feet, but raised him with his right hand and kissed him. Then, while the king made supplication, Nero took the turban from his head and replaced it with a diadem, while a man of praetorian rank translated the words of the suppliant and proclaimed them to the throng. From there the king was taken to the theatre,[a] and when he had again done obeisance, Nero gave him a seat at his right hand. Because of all this Nero was hailed as Imperator,[b] and after depositing a laurel wreath in the Capitol,[c] he closed the two doors of the temple of Janus,[d] as a sign that no war was left anywhere.

XIV. He held four consulships,[e] the first for two months, the second and the last for six months each, the third for four months. The second and third were in successive years, while a year intervened between these and each of the others.[f]

XV. In the administration of justice he was reluctant to render a decision to those who presented cases, except on the following day and in writing. The procedure was, instead of continuous pleadings, to have each point pre-

singillatim quaeque per vices ageret.[1] Quotiens autem ad consultandum secederet, neque in commune quicquam neque propalam deliberabat, sed et conscriptas ab uno quoque sententias tacitus ac secreto legens, quod ipsi libuisset perinde atque pluribus idem videretur pronuntiabat.

2   In curiam libertinorum filios diu non admisit; admissis a prioribus principibus honores denegavit. Candidatos, qui supra numerum essent, in solacium dilationis ac morae legionibus praeposuit. Consulatum in senos plerumque menses dedit. Defunctoque circa Kal. Ian. altero e consulibus neminem substituit improbans exemplum vetus Canini Rebili uno die consulis. Triumphalia ornamenta etiam quaestoriae dignitatis et nonnullis ex equestri ordine tribuit nec utique de causa militari. De quibusdam rebus orationes ad senatum missas praeterito quaestoris officio per consulem plerumque recitabat.

XVI. Formam aedificiorum urbis novam excogitavit et ut ante insulas ac domos porticus essent, de quarum[2] solariis incendia arcerentur; easque sumptu suo exstruxit. Destinarat etiam Ostia tenus moenia promovere atque inde fossa mare veteri urbi inducere.

2   Multa sub eo et animadversa severe et coercita nec minus instituta: adhibitus sumptibus modus; publicae

---

[1] ageret, Υ'; *omitted by MGLP*; quaereret, *Bücheler*.
[2] quarum, ΠΩ; quorum, Ω.

[a] See *Jul.* lxxvi. 2, where, however, the man's name is not mentioned.

[b] See *Aug.* lxv. 2.

[c] This was undoubtedly after the great fire; see chap. xxxviii.

sented separately by the parties in turn. Furthermore, whenever he withdrew for consultation, he did not discuss any matter with all his advisers in a body, but had each of them give his opinion in written form; these he read silently and in private and then gave a verdict according to his own inclination, as if it were the view of the majority.

For a long time he would not admit the sons of freedmen to the senate and he refused office to those who had been admitted by his predecessors. Candidates who were in excess of the number of vacancies received the command of a legion as compensation for the postponement and delay. He commonly appointed consuls for a period of six months. When one of them died just before the Kalends of January, he appointed no one in his place, expressing his disapproval of the old-time case of Caninius Rebilus, the twenty-four hour consul.[a] He conferred the triumphal regalia even on men of the rank of quaestor, as well as on some of the knights, and sometimes for other than military services. As regards the speeches which he sent to the senate on various matters, he passed over the quaestors, whose duty it was to read them,[b] and usually had them presented by one of the consuls.

XVI. He devised a new form for the buildings of the city and in front of the houses and apartments he erected porches, from the flat roofs of which fires could be fought;[c] and these he put up at his own cost. He had also planned to extend the walls as far as Ostia and to bring the sea from there to Rome by a canal.

During his reign many abuses were severely punished and put down, and no fewer new laws were made: a limit

cenae ad sportulas redactae; interdictum ne quid in popinis cocti praeter legumina aut holera veniret, cum antea nullum non obsonii genus proponeretur; afflicti suppliciis Christiani, genus hominum superstitionis novae ac maleficae; vetiti quadrigariorum lusus, quibus inveterata licentia passim vagantibus fallere ac furari per iocum ius erat; pantomimorum factiones cum ipsis simul relegatae.

XVII. Adversus falsarios tunc primum repertum, ne tabulae nisi pertusae ac ter lino per foramina traiecto obsignarentur; cautum ut testamentis primae duae cerae testatorum modo nomine inscripto vacuae signaturis ostenderentur, ac ne qui alieni testamenti scriptor legatum sibi ascriberet; item ut litigatores pro patrociniis certam iustamque mercedem, pro subsellis nullam omnino darent praebente aerario gratuita; utque rerum actu ab aerario causae ad Forum ac reciperatores transferrentur et ut omnes appellationes a iudicibus ad senatum fierent.

---

[a] Various attempts had however been made to check this form of luxury; see note on *Claud.* xxxviii. 2.

[b] Because of their disorderly conduct; see chap. xxvi. 2, and Tac. *Ann.* 13. 25.

[c] The tablets consisted of three leaves, two of which were bound together and sealed. The contract was written twice, on the open leaf and on the closed ones. In cases of dispute the seals were broken in the presence of the signers and the two versions compared.

[d] As witnesses. The testator afterwards wrote the names of the heirs on these leaves.

[e] The Cincian law of 204 B.C. forbade fees. Augustus renewed the law in 17 B.C. (Dio, 54. 18). Claudius limited fees to 10,000 sesterces (Tac. *Ann.* 11. 5–6). The senate again abolished

was set to expenditures; the public banquets were confined to a distribution of food; the sale of any kind of cooked viands in the taverns was forbidden, with the exception of pulse and vegetables, whereas before every sort of dainty was exposed for sale.[a] Punishment was inflicted on the Christians, a class of men given to a new and mischievous superstition. He put an end to the diversions of the chariot drivers, who from immunity of long standing claimed the right of ranging at large and amusing themselves by cheating and robbing the people. The pantomimic actors and their partisans were banished from the city.[b]

XVII. It was in his reign that a protection against forgers was first devised, by having no tablets signed that were not bored with holes through which a cord was thrice passed.[c] In the case of wills it was provided that the first two leaves should be presented to the signatories[d] with only the name of the testator written upon them, and that no one who wrote a will for another should put down a legacy for himself; further, that clients should pay a fixed and reasonable fee for the services of their advocates,[e] but nothing at all for benches, which were to be furnished free of charge by the public treasury; finally as regarded the pleading of cases, that those connected with the treasury should be transferred to the Forum[f] and a board of arbiters, and that any appeal from the juries should be made to the senate.

fees at the beginning of Nero's reign (Tac. *Ann.* 13. 5), but Nero apparently revived the law of Claudius, with a provision against the addition of "costs."

[f] Instead of coming before the prefects of the treasury; cf. *Claud.* ix. 2.

XVIII. Augendi propagandique imperii neque voluntate ulla neque spe motus umquam, etiam ex Britannia deducere exercitum cogitavit, nec nisi verecundia, ne obtrectare parentis gloriae videretur, destitit. Ponti modo regnum concedente Polemone, item Alpium defuncto Cottio in provinciae formam redegit.

XIX. Peregrinationes duas omnino suscepit, Alexandrinam et Achaicam; sed Alexandrina ipso profectionis die destitit turbatus religione simul ac periculo. Nam cum circumitis templis in aede Vestae resedisset, consurgenti ei primum lacinia obhaesit, dein tanta oborta caligo
2 est, ut dispicere[1] non posset. In Achaia Isthmum perfodere adgressus praetorianos pro contione ad incohandum opus cohortatus est tubaque signo dato primus rastello humum effodit et corbulae congestam umeris extulit. Parabat et ad Caspias portas expeditionem conscripta ex Italicis senum pedum tironibus nova legione, quam Magni Alexandri phalanga appellabat.
3 Haec partim nulla reprehensione, partim etiam non mediocri laude digna in unum contuli, ut secernerem a probris ac sceleribus eius, de quibus dehinc dicam.

XX. Inter ceteras disciplinas pueritiae tempore imbutus et musica, statim ut imperium adeptus est, Terpnum citharoedum vigentem tunc praeter alios arcessiit

---

[1] dispicere, ς; despicere, Ω.

---

[a] That is, his adoptive father Claudius.
[b] Of Corinth; cf. *Jul.* xliv. 3, *Cal.* xxi.
[c] Roman measure; a little under 5 ft. 10 in. English.

XVIII. So far from being actuated by any wish or hope of increasing or extending the empire, he even thought of withdrawing the army from Britain and changed his purpose only because he was ashamed to seem to belittle the glory of his father.[a] He increased the provinces only by the realm of Pontus, when it was given up by Polemon, and that of Cottius in the Alps on the latter's death.

XIX. He planned but two foreign tours, to Alexandria and Achaia; and he gave up the former on the very day when he was to have started, disturbed by a threatening portent. For as he was making the round of the temples and had sat down in the shrine of Vesta, first the fringe of his garment caught when he attempted to get up, and then such darkness overspread his eyes that he could see nothing. In Achaia he attempted to cut through the Isthmus[b] and called together the praetorians and urged them to begin the work; then at a signal given on a trumpet he was first to break ground with a mattock and to carry off a basketful of earth upon his shoulders. He also prepared for an expedition to the Caspian Gates, after enrolling a new legion of raw recruits of Italian birth, each six feet tall,[c] which he called the "phalanx of Alexander the Great."

I have brought together these acts of his, some of which are beyond criticism, while others are even deserving of no slight praise, to separate them from his shameful and criminal deeds, of which I shall proceed now to give an account.

XX. Having gained some knowledge of music in addition to the rest of his early education, as soon as he became emperor he sent for Terpnus, the greatest master of the lyre in those days, and after listening to him sing

diebusque continuis post cenam canenti in multam
noctem assidens paulatim et ipse meditari exercerique
coepit neque eorum quicquam omittere, quae generis
eius artifices vel conservandae vocis causa vel augendae
factitarent; sed et plumbeam chartam supinus pectore
sustinere et clystere vomituque purgari et abstinere
pomis cibisque officientibus; donec blandiente profectu,
quamquam exiguae vocis et fuscae, prodire in scaenam
concupiit, subinde inter familiares Graecum proverbium

2 iactans occultae musicae nullum esse respectum. Et
prodit Neapoli[1] primum ac ne concusso quidem repente
motu terrae theatro ante cantare destitit, quam incohatum absolveret nomon. Ibidem saepius et per complures
cantavit dies; sumpto etiam ad reficiendam vocem brevi
tempore, impatiens secreti a balineis in theatrum transiit
mediaque in orchestra frequente populo epulatus, si
paulum subbibisset, aliquid se sufferti[2] tinniturum

3 Graeco sermone promisit. Captus autem modulatis
Alexandrinorum laudationibus, qui de novo commeatu
Neapolim confluxerant, plures Alexandria evocavit.
Neque eo segnius adulescentulos equestris ordinis et
quinque amplius milia e plebe robustissimae iuventutis
undique elegit, qui divisi in factiones plausuum genera
condiscerent—bombos et imbrices et testas vocabant—

---

[1] Neapoli, ΠQ; *the other mss. have* Neapolim.
[2] sufferti, *first Venetian ed.*; sufferi, MG; *the other mss. have*
sufferri.

---

[a] Cf. *Gell.* 13. 31. 3.   [b] It collapsed in consequence, but
not until the audience had dispersed; see Tac. *Ann.* 15. 34.

[c] Literally, "full-packed," *i.e.* full of sound, sonorous.

[d] The first seems to have derived its name from the sound,
which was like the humming of bees, the second and third from

110

after dinner for many successive days until late at night, he little by little began to practise himself, neglecting none of the exercises which artists of that kind are in the habit of following, to preserve or strengthen their voices. For he used to lie upon his back and hold a leaden plate on his chest, purge himself by the syringe and by vomiting, and deny himself fruits and all foods injurious to the voice. Finally encouraged by his progress, although his voice was weak and husky, he began to long to appear on the stage, and every now and then in the presence of his intimate friends he would quote a Greek proverb meaning "Hidden music counts for nothing."[a] And he made his début at Naples, where he did not cease singing until he had finished the number which he had begun, even though the theatre was shaken by a sudden earthquake shock.[b] In the same city he sang frequently and for several successive days. Even when he took a short time to rest his voice, he could not keep out of sight but went to the theatre after bathing and dined in the orchestra with the people all about him, promising them in Greek that, when he had wetted his whistle a bit, he would ring out something good and loud.[c] He was greatly taken too with the rhythmic applause of some Alexandrians, who had flocked to Naples from a fleet that had lately arrived, and summoned more men from Alexandria. Not content with that, he selected some young men of the order of knights and more than five thousand sturdy young commoners, to be divided into groups and learn the Alexandrian styles of applause (they called them "the bees," "the roof-tiles," and "the bricks"),[d] and to ply them vigorously whenever

clapping with the hands rounded or hollowed, like roof-tiles, or flat, like bricks or flat tiles.

111

operamque navarent cantanti sibi, insignes pinguissima
coma et excellentissimo cultu, puris[1] ac sine anulo
laevis,[2] quorum duces quadringena milia sestertia[3] mere-
bant.

XXI. Cum magni aestimaret cantare etiam Romae,
Neroneum agona ante praestitutam diem revocavit flagi-
tantibusque cunctis caelestem vocem respondit quidem
in hortis se copiam volentibus facturum, sed adiuvante
vulgi preces etiam statione militum, quae tunc excubabat,
repraesentaturum se pollicitus est libens; ac sine mora
nomen suum in albo profitentium citharoedorum iussit
ascribi sorticulaque in urnam cum ceteris demissa intravit
ordine suo, simul praefecti praetorii citharam sustinentes,
2 post tribuni militum iuxtaque amicorum intimi. Utque
constitit, peracto principio, Niobam[4] se cantaturum per
Cluvium Rufum consularem pronuntiavit et in horam
fere decimam perseveravit coronamque eam et reliquam
certaminis partem in annum sequentem distulit, ut
saepius canendi occasio esset. Quod cum tardum videretur, non cessavit identidem se publicare. Dubitavit etiam
an privatis spectaculis operam inter scaenicos daret quo-
3 dam praetorum sestertium decies offerente. Tragoedias
quoque cantavit personatus heroum deorumque, item

[1] puris, P^2 (*Bentley*); pueris, $MX\delta$; pueri, $G\Upsilon$.

[2] laevis, *G, and P in a later hand*; laeviis, *M*; levis, Υ.

[3] sestertia, Ω; sestertium *is commonly read.*

[4] Niobā, *G*; Nioban, $M\Upsilon$; Niobem, *X*.

[a] See chap. xii. 3.

[b] Probably asking for the favourable attention of the audience; cf. Dio, 61. 20 and chap. xxiii. 3.

[c] That is, those given by the magistrates; under the Empire

he sang. These men were noticeable for their thick hair and fine apparel; their left hands were bare and without rings, and the leaders were paid four hundred thousand sesterces each.

XXI. Considering it of great importance to appear in Rome as well, he repeated the contest of the Neronia[a] before the appointed time, and when there was a general call for his "divine voice," he replied that if any wished to hear him, he would favour them in the gardens; but when the guard of soldiers which was then on duty seconded the entreaties of the people, he gladly agreed to appear at once. So without delay he had his name added to the list of the lyre-players who entered the contest, and casting his own lot into the urn with the rest, he came forward in his turn, attended by the prefects of the Guard carrying his lyre, and followed by the tribunes of the soldiers and his intimate friends. Having taken his place and finished his preliminary speech,[b] he announced through the ex-consul Cluvius Rufus that "he would sing Niobe"; and he kept at it until late in the afternoon, putting off the award of the prize for that event and postponing the rest of the contest to the next year, to have an excuse for singing oftener. But since even that seemed too long to wait, he did not cease to appear in public from time to time. He even thought of taking part in private performances[c] among the professional actors, when one of the praetors offered him a million sesterces. He also put on the mask and sang tragedies representing gods and heroes and even heroines and goddesses, having the masks fashioned

all but the emperor were *privati*, regardless of their official positions.

heroidum ac dearum, personis effectis ad similitudinem
oris sui et feminae, prout quamque diligeret. Inter cetera
cantavit Canacen parturientem, Oresten matricidam,
Oedipodem[1] excaecatum, Herculem insanum. In qua
fabula fama est tirunculum militem positum ad custodiam
aditus, cum eum ornari ac vinciri catenis, sicut argumentum postulabat, videret, accurrisse ferendae opis gratia.

XXII. Equorum studio vel praecipue ab ineunte
aetate flagravit plurimusque illi sermo, quanquam vetare-
tur, de circensibus erat; et quondam tractum prasinum[2]
agitatorem inter condiscipulos querens, obiurgante paedagogo, de Hectore se loqui ementitus est. Sed cum inter
initia imperii eburneis quadrigis cotidie in abaco luderet,
ad omnis etiam minimos circenses e secessu commeabat,
primo clam, deinde propalam, ut nemini dubium esset eo
die utique affuturum. Neque dissimulabat velle se palmarum numerum ampliari; quare spectaculum multipli-
catis missibus in serum protrahebatur, ne dominis quidem iam factionum dignantibus nisi ad totius diei cursum
greges ducere. Mox et ipse aurigare atque etiam spectari
saepius voluit positoque in hortis inter servitia et sordidam plebem rudimento universorum se oculis in Circo
Maximo praebuit, aliquo liberto mittente mappam unde
magistratus solent.

Nec contentus harum artium experimenta Romae

---

[1] ẹdipodē, *G*; *the other mss. have* Oedipoden.
[2] prasinum, ϛ; prasim, *LST*; prasū, *P*; prasiniū, *G*.

---

[a] By his guardian and teachers.
[b] See note on *Calig.* lv. 2.
[c] The signal for the start.

at Rome, he went to Achaia, as I have said,[a] influenced especially by the following consideration. The cities in which it was the custom to hold contests in music had adopted the rule of sending all the lyric prizes to him. These he received with the greatest delight, not only giving audience before all others to the envoys who brought them, but even inviting them to his private table. When some of them begged him to sing after dinner and greeted his performance with extravagant applause, he declared that "the Greeks were the only ones who had an ear for music and that they alone were worthy of his efforts." So he took ship without delay and immediately on arriving at Cassiope made a preliminary appearance as a singer at the altar of Jupiter Cassius, and then went the round of all the contests.[b]

XXIII. To make this possible, he gave orders that even those which were widely separated in time should be brought together in a single year, so that some had even to be given twice, and he introduced a musical competition at Olympia also, contrary to custom. To avoid being distracted or hindered in any way while busy with these contests, he replied to his freedman Helius, who reminded him that the affairs of the city required his presence, in these words: "However much it may be your advice and your wish that I should return speedily, yet you ought rather to counsel me and to hope that I may return worthy of Nero."

While he was singing no one was allowed to leave the theatre even for the most urgent reasons. And so it is said that some women gave birth to children there, while many who were worn out with listening and applauding, secretly leaped from the wall,[c] since the gates at the

117

oppidorum portis aut furtim desiluisse de muro aut morte
simulata funere elati. Quam autem trepide anxieque cer-
taverit, quanta adversariorum aemulatione, quo metu
iudicum, vix credi potest. Adversarios, quasi plane condicionis eiusdem, observare, captare, infamare secreto,
nonnumquam ex occursu maledictis incessere ac, si qui
3   arte praecellerent, conrumpere etiam solebat. Iudices
autem prius quam inciperet reverentissime adloquebatur,
omnia se facienda fecisse, sed eventum in manu esse Fortunae; illos ut sapientis et doctos viros fortuita debere
excludere; atque, ut auderet hortantibus, aequiore animo
recedebat, ac ne sic quidem sine sollicitudine, taciturni-
tatem pudoremque quorundam pro tristitia et malignitate
arguens suspectosque sibi dicens.

XXIV. In certando vero ita legi oboediebat, ut
numquam exscreare ausus sudorem quoque frontis brachio detergeret; atque etiam in tragico quodam actu, cum
elapsum baculum cito resumpsisset, pavidus et metuens
ne ob delictum certamine summoveretur, non aliter confirmatus est quam adiurante hypocrita non animadversum
id inter exsultationes succlamationesque populi. Victorem autem se ipse pronuntiabat; qua de causa et prae-
conio ubique contendit. Ac ne cuius alterius hieroni-

---

a *Oppida*, the term applied to the towers and other structures
at the entrance to the Circus, seems to be used here of the corresponding part of the theatre.

b The use of a handkerchief was not allowed; see also Tac.
Ann. 16. 4.

c The *hypocrites* (*hypocrita*) made the gestures and accompanied the tragic actor on the flute, as he spoke his lines.

d The heralds for the great festivals were selected by com-
petiton among the rival candidates.

entrance[a] were closed, or feigned death and were carried out as if for burial. The trepidation and anxiety with which he took part in the contests, his keen rivalry of his opponents and his awe of the judges, can hardly be credited. As if his rivals were of quite the same station as himself, he used to show respect to them and try to gain their favour, while he slandered them behind their backs, sometimes assailed them with abuse when he met them, and even bribed those who were especially proficient. Before beginning, he would address the judges in the most deferential terms, saying that he had done all that could be done, but the issue was in the hands of Fortune; they however, being men of wisdom and experience, ought to exclude what was fortuitous. When they bade him take heart, he withdrew with greater confidence, but not even then without anxiety, interpreting the silence and modesty of some as sullenness and ill-nature, and declaring that he had his suspicions of them.

XXIV. In competition he observed the rules most scrupulously, never daring to clear his throat and even wiping the sweat from his brow with his arm.[b] Once indeed, during the performance of a tragedy, when he had dropped his sceptre but quickly recovered it, he was terribly afraid that he might be excluded from the competition because of his slip, and his confidence was restored only when his accompanist[c] swore that it had passed unnoticed amid the delight and applause of the people. When the victory was won, he made the announcement himself; and for that reason he always took part in the contests of the heralds.[d] To obliterate the memory of all

carum memoria aut vestigium exstaret usquam, subverti et unco trahi abicique in latrinas omnium statuas et imagines imperavit.

2 Aurigavit quoque plurifariam, Olympiis vero etiam decemiugem, quamvis id ipsum in rege Mithradate[1] carmine quodam suo reprehendisset; sed excussus curru ac rursus repositus, cum perdurare non posset, destitit ante decursum; neque eo setius coronatus est. Decedens deinde provinciam universam libertate donavit simulque iudices civitate Romana et pecunia grandi. Quae beneficia e medio stadio Isthmiorum die sua ipse voce pronuntiavit.

XXV. Reversus e Graecia Neapolim, quod in ea primum artem protulerat, albis equis introiit disiecta parte muri, ut mos hieronicarum est; simili modo Antium, inde Albanum, inde Romam; sed et Romam eo curru, quo Augustus olim triumphaverat, et in veste purpurea distinctaque stellis aureis chlamyde coronamque capite gerens Olympiacam, dextra manu Pythiam, praeeunte pompa ceterarum cum titulis, ubi et quos quo cantionum quove fabularum argumento vicisset; sequentibus currum ovantium ritu plausoribus, Augustianos militesque se

2 triumphi eius clamitantibus. Dehinc diruto Circi Maximi

---

[1] Mithradate, *M*; *the other mss. have* Mithridate *or* Mitridate.

---

[a] The Greek term *hieronices*, "victor in the sacred games," indicates the religious nature of the festivals.

[b] That is, with local self-government, not with actual independence.

[c] See chap. xx. 3.

other victors in the games[a] and leave no trace of them, their statues and busts were all thrown down by his order, dragged off with hooks, and cast into privies.

He also drove a chariot in many places, at Olympia even a ten-horse team, although in one of his own poems he had criticised Mithridates for just that thing. But after he had been thrown from the car and put back in it, he was unable to hold out and gave up before the end of the course; but he received the crown just the same. On his departure he presented the entire province with freedom[b] and at the same time gave the judges Roman citizenship and a large sum of money. These favours he announced in person on the day of the Isthmian Games, standing in the middle of the stadium.

XXV. Returning from Greece, since it was at Naples that he had made his first appearance, he entered that city with white horses through a part of the wall which had been thrown down, as is customary with victors in the sacred games. In like manner he entered Antium, then Albanum, and finally Rome; but at Rome he rode in the chariot which Augustus had used in his triumphs in days gone by, and wore a purple robe and a Greek cloak adorned with stars of gold, bearing on his head the Olympic crown and in his right hand the Pythian, while the rest were carried before him with inscriptions telling where he had won them and against what competitors, and giving the titles of the songs or the subject of the plays. His car was followed by his claque[c] as by the escort of a triumphal procession, who shouted that they were the attendants of Augustus and the soldiers of his triumph. Then through the arch of the Circus Maximus,

121

arcu per Velabrum Forumque Palatium et Apollinem petit. Incedenti passim victimae caesae sparso per vias identidem croco ingestaeque aves ac lemnisci et bellaria. Sacras coronas in cubiculis circum lectos posuit, item statuas suas citharoedico habitu, qua nota etiam num-

3 mum percussit. Ac post haec tantum afuit a remittendo laxandoque studio, ut conservandae vocis gratia neque milites umquam, nisi absens aut alio verba pronuntiante, appellaret neque quicquam serio iocove egerit, nisi astante phonasco, qui moneret parceret arteriis ac suda-rium ad os applicaret; multisque vel amicitiam suam optulerit vel simultatem indixerit, prout quisque se magis parciusve laudasset.

XXVI. Petulantiam, libidinem, luxuriam, avaritiam, crudelitatem sensim quidem primo et occulte et velut iuvenili errore exercuit, sed ut tunc quoque dubium ne-mini foret naturae illa vitia, non aetatis esse. Post crepus-culum statim adrepto pilleo vel galero popinas inibat cir-cumque vicos vagabatur ludibundus nec sine pernicie tamen, siquidem redeuntis a cena verberare ac repug-nantes vulnerare cloacisque demergere assuerat, tabernas etiam effringere et expilare; quintana domi constituta, ubi

---

^a To make more room for the procession, which passed through the Circus (Dio, 63. 20). The reference is probably to the gateway at the eastern end, through which the procession entered and passed out again, after marching around the *spina* (see note on *Claud.* xxi. 3). Suetonius mentions only the exit from the Circus. In his time the gateway was formed by the Arch of Vespasian and Titus, erected by Domitian in A.D. 81.

^b That is, song-birds, as a compliment to Nero's voice; the other offerings were also typical of his art and his triumph.

^c Cf. *Aug.* lxxxiv. 2.   ^d *Quintana* is really the market of

which was thrown down,[a] he made his way across the Velabrum and the Forum to the Palatine and the temple of Apollo. All along the route victims were slain, the streets were sprinkled from time to time with perfume, while birds,[b] ribbons, and sweetmeats were showered upon him. He placed the sacred crowns in his bedchambers around his couches, as well as statues representing him the guise of a lyre-player; and he had a coin too struck with the same device. So far from neglecting or relaxing his practice of the art after this, he never addressed the soldiers except by letter or in a speech delivered by another, to save his voice; and he never did anything for amusement or in earnest without an elocutionist[c] by his side, to warn him to spare his vocal organs and hold a handkerchief to his mouth. To many men he offered his friendship or announced his hostility, according as they had applauded him lavishly or grudgingly.

XXVI. Although at first his acts of wantonness, lust, extravagance, avarice and cruelty were gradual and secret, and might be condoned as follies of youth, yet even then their nature was such that no one doubted that they were defects of his character and not due to his time of life. No sooner was twilight over than he would catch up a cap or a wig and go to the taverns or range about the streets playing pranks, which however were very far from harmless; for he used to beat men as they came home from dinner, stabbing any who resisted him and throwing them into the sewers. He would even break into shops and rob them, setting up a market[d] in the Palace, where

a camp, named from the *Quintana via*, one of the streets of a Roman camp, on which the market was regularly placed.

partae et ad licitationem dividendae praedae pretium
2 absumeretur. Ac saepe in eius modi rixis oculorum et
vitae periculum adiit, a quodam laticlavio, cuius uxorem
adtrectaverat, prope ad necem caesus. Quare numquam
postea publico se illud horae sine tribunis commisit
procul et occulte subsequentibus. Interdiu quoque clam
gestatoria sella delatus in theatrum seditionibus pantomimorum e parte proscaeni superiore signifer simul
ac spectator aderat; et cum ad manus ventum esset
lapidibusque et subselliorum fragminibus decerneretur,
multa et ipse iecit in populum atque etiam praetoris caput
consauciavit.

XXVII. Paulatim vero invalescentibus vitiis iocularia
et latebras omisit nullaque dissimulandi cura ad maiora
2 palam erupit. Epulas a medio die ad mediam noctem
protrahebat, refotus saepius calidis piscinis ac tempore
aestivo nivatis; cenitabatque nonnumquam et in publico,
naumachia praeclusa vel Martio campo vel Circo Maximo, inter scortorum totius urbis et ambubaiarum minis-
3 teria. Quotiens Ostiam Tiberi deflueret aut Baianum
sinum praeternavigaret, dispositae per litora et ripas
deversoriae tabernae parabantur insignes ganea[1] et
matronarum institorio copas imitantium atque hinc inde
hortantium ut appelleret. Indicebat et familiaribus cenas,

---

[1] ganea, *Salmasius*; ganeae, *mss.*

[a] See note on chap. v. 1.
[b] Julius Montanus; see Tac. *Ann.* 13. 25.
[c] And their bands of partisans; see chap. xvi. 2.
[d] Made for sea-fights; see *Aug.* xliii. 1; *Tib.* lxxii. 1.

he divided the booty which he took, sold it at auction, and then squandered the proceeds. In the strife which resulted he often ran the risk of losing his eyes[a] or even his life, for he was beaten almost to death by a man of the senatorial order,[b] whose wife he had maltreated. Warned by this, he never afterwards ventured to appear in public at that hour without having tribunes follow him at a distance and unobserved. Even in the daytime he would be carried privately to the theatre in a sedan chair, and from the upper part of the proscenium would watch the brawls of the pantomimic actors[c] and egg them on; and when they came to blows and fought with stones and broken benches, he himself threw many missiles at the people and even broke a praetor's head.

XXVII. Little by little, however, as his vices grew stronger, he dropped jesting and secrecy and with no attempt at disguise openly broke out into worse crime. He prolonged his revels from midday to midnight, often livening himself by a warm plunge, or, if it were summer, into water cooled with snow. Sometimes too he closed the inlets and banqueted in public in the great tank,[d] in the Campus Martius, or in the Circus Maximus, waited on by harlots and dancing girls from all over the city. Whenever he drifted down the Tiber to Ostia, or sailed about the Gulf of Baiae, booths were set up at intervals along the banks and shores, fitted out for debauchery, while noble women played the role of cheap entertainers available for a price, and from every hand solicited him to come ashore. He also levied dinners on his friends, one of whom spent four million sesterces for a banquet at

quorum uni mitellita quadragies sestertium constitit, alteri pluris aliquanto rosaria.

XXVIII. Super ingenuorum paedagogia et nuptarum concubinatus Vestali virgini Rubriae vim intulit. Acten libertam paulum afuit quin iusto sibi matrimonio coniungeret, summissis consularibus viris qui regio genere ortam peierarent. Puerum Sporum exsectis testibus etiam in muliebrem naturam transfigurare conatus cum dote et flammeo per sollemnia[1] nuptiarum celeberrimo officio deductum ad se pro uxore habuit; exstatque cuiusdam non inscitus iocus bene agi potuisse cum rebus humanis, si Domitius pater talem habuisset uxorem. 2 Hunc Sporum, Augustarum ornamentis excultum lecticaque vectum, et circa conventus mercatusque Graeciae ac mox Romae circa Sigillaria comitatus est identidem exosculans. Nam matris concubitum appetisse et ab[2] obtrectatoribus eius, ne ferox atque impotens mulier et hoc genere gratiae praevaleret, deterritum nemo dubitavit, utique postquam meretricem, quam fama erat Agrippinae simillimam, inter concubinas recepit. Olim etiam quotiens lectica cum matre veheretur, libidinatum inceste ac maculis vestis proditum affirmant.

XXIX. Suam quidem pudicitiam usque adeo prostituit, ut contaminatis paene omnibus membris novissime quasi genus lusus excogitaret, quo ferae pelle contectus emitteretur e cavea virorumque ac feminarum ad sti-

---

[1] sollemnia, ς; sollemne, *Turnebus*; sollemni, Ω.

[2] ab, Qς; ad, Π (*struck out by a later hand*); *the other mss. omit the word.*

---

[a] With *mitellita* and *rosaria* we may supply *cena*; the former means a banquet at which silken turbans were a distinguishing feature.

which turbans were distributed, and another a considerably larger sum for a rose dinner.[a]

XXVIII. Besides abusing freeborn boys and seducing married women, he debauched the vestal virgin Rubria. The freedwoman Acte he all but made his lawful wife, after bribing some ex-consuls to perjure themselves by swearing that she was of royal birth. He castrated the boy Sporus and actually tried to make a woman of him; and he married him with all the usual ceremonies, including a dowry and a bridal veil, took him to his house attended by a great throng, and treated him as his wife. And the witty jest that someone made is still current, that it would have been well for the world if Nero's father Domitius had had that kind of wife. This Sporus, decked out with the finery of the empresses and riding in a litter, he took with him to the assizes and marts of Greece, and later at Rome through the Street of the Images,[b] fondly kissing him from time to time. That he even desired a sexual relationship with his own mother, and was kept from it by her enemies, who feared that such a relationship might give the reckless and insolent woman too great influence, was notorious, especially after he added to his concubines a courtesan who was said to look very like Agrippina. Even before that, so they say, whenever he rode in a litter with his mother, he had incestuous relations with her, which were betrayed by the stains on his clothing.

XXIX. He so prostituted his own chastity that after defiling almost every part of his body, he at last devised a kind of game, in which, covered with the skin of some wild animal, he was let loose from a cage and attacked the private parts of men and women, who were bound

[b] Cf. *Claud.* xvi. 4.

pitem deligatorum inguina invaderet et, cum affatim desaevisset, conficeretur a Doryphoro liberto; cui etiam, sicut ipsi Sporus, ita ipse denupsit, voces quoque et heiulatus vim patientium virginum imitatus. Ex nonnullis comperi persuasissimum habuisse eum neminem hominem pudicum aut ulla corporis parte purum esse, verum plerosque dissimulare vitium et callide optegere; ideoque professis apud se obscaenitatem cetera quoque concessisse delicta.

XXX. Divitiarum et pecuniae fructum non alium putabat quam profusionem, sordidos ac deparcos esse quibus impensarum ratio constaret, praelautos vereque magnificos qui abuterentur ac perderent. Laudabat mirabaturque avunculum Gaium nullo magis nomine, quam quod ingentis a Tiberio relictas opes in brevi spatio
2 prodegisset. Quare nec largiendi nec absumendi modum tenuit. In Tiridatem, quod vix credibile videatur, octingena nummum milia diurna erogavit abeuntique super sestertium milies contulit. Menecraten citharoedum et Spiculum[1] murmillonem triumphalium virorum patrimoniis aedibusque donavit. Cercopithecum Panerotem faeneratorem et urbanis rusticisque praediis locupletatum
3 tum prope regio extulit funere. Nullam vestem bis induit. Quadringenis in punctum sestertiis aleam lusit. Piscatus est rete aurato[2] et purpura coccoque funibus nexis. Numquam minus mille carrucis fecisse iter traditur, soleis

---

[1] Spiculum, *Beroaldus*; speculum, Ω.   [2] rete aurato, Υ; veste aurato, *M*; *the other mss. have* veste aurata.

---

[a] Used in a double sense.   [b] That is, could balance the account of their expenditures.   [c] See chap. xiii.   [d] That is, for each pip of the winning throw.

to stakes, and when he had sated his mad lust, was finished off[a] by his freedman Doryphorus; for he was even married to this man in the same way that he himself had taken Sporus, going so far as to imitate the cries and lamentations of a maiden being deflowered. I have heard from some men that it was his unshaken conviction that no man was chaste or pure in any part of his body, but that most of them concealed their vices and cleverly drew a veil over them; and that therefore he pardoned all other faults in those who confessed to him their lewdness.

XXX. He thought that there was no other way of enjoying riches and money than by riotous extravagance, declaring that only stingy and niggardly fellows kept a correct account of what they spent,[b] while fine and genuinely magnificent gentlemen wasted and squandered. Nothing in his uncle Gaius so excited his envy and admiration as the fact that he had in so short a time run through the vast wealth which Tiberius had left him. Accordingly he made presents and wasted money without stint. On Tiridates,[c] though it would seem hardly within belief, he spent eight hundred thousand sesterces a day, and on his departure presented him with more than a hundred millions. He gave the lyre-player Menecrates and the gladiator Spiculus properties and residences equal to those of men who had celebrated triumphs. He enriched the monkey-faced usurer Paneros with estates in the country and in the city and had him buried with almost regal splendour. He never wore the same garment twice. He played at dice for four hundred thousand sesterces a point.[d] He fished with a golden net drawn by cords woven of purple and scarlet threads. It is said that he never made a journey with less than a thousand carriages, his mules shod with

129

mularum argenteis, canusinatis mulionibus, armillata phalerataque Mazacum[1] turba atque cursorum.

XXXI. Non in alia re tamen damnosior quam in aedificando domum a Palatio Esquilias usque fecit, quam primo transitoriam, mox incendio absumptam restitutamque auream nominavit. De cuius spatio atque cultu suffecerit haec rettulisse. Vestibulum eius fuit, in quo colossus CXX pedum staret ipsius effigie; tanta laxitas, ut porticus triplices miliarias haberet; item stagnum maris instar, circumsaeptum aedificiis ad urbium speciem; rura insuper arvis atque vinetis et pascuis silvisque varia, cum

2 multitudine omnis generis pecudum ac ferarum. In ceteris partibus cuncta auro lita, distincta gemmis unionumque conchis erant; cenationes laqueatae tabulis eburneis versatilibus, ut flores, fistulatis, ut unguenta desuper spargerentur; praecipua cenationum rotunda, quae perpetuo diebus ac noctibus vice mundi circumageretur; balineae marinis et albulis fluentes aquis. Eius modi domum cum absolutam dedicaret, hactenus comprobavit, ut se diceret quasi hominem tandem habitare coepisse.

3 Praeterea incohabat piscinam a Miseno ad Avernum lacum contectam porticibusque conclusam, quo quidquid

---

[1] falerataque Mazacum, *Salmasius* (Mazycum, *Roth*); phalerata (phalera, *G*) cimazacum, *GXR*; falerata cimazacum, *M*.

---

[a] Celebrated horsemen of Mauretania.

[b] See note on *Aug.* xxv. 3.

[c] That is, with three parallel rows of columns.

[d] One may compare Hadrian's villa at Tibur (Tivoli) with its Canopus, its Vale of Tempe, and the like.

silver and their drivers clad in wool of Canusium, attended by a train of Mazaces[a] and couriers with bracelets and trappings.[b]

XXXI. There was nothing however in which he was more ruinously prodigal than in building. He made a palace extending all the way from the Palatine to the Esquiline, which at first he called the House of Passage, but when it was burned shortly after its completion and rebuilt, the Golden House. Its size and splendour will be sufficiently indicated by the following details. Its vestibule was large enough to contain a colossal statue of the emperor a hundred and twenty feet high; and it was so extensive that it had a triple colonnade[c] a mile long. There was a pond too, like a sea, surrounded with buildings to represent cities,[d] besides tracts of country, varied by tilled fields, vineyards, pastures and woods, with great numbers of wild and domestic animals. In the rest of the house all parts were overlaid with gold and adorned with gems and mother-of-pearl. There were dining-rooms with fretted ceilings of ivory, whose panels could turn and shower down flowers and were fitted with pipes for sprinkling the guests with perfumes. The main banquet hall was circular and constantly revolved day and night, like the heavens.[e] He had baths supplied with sea water and sulphur water. When the edifice was finished in this style and he dedicated it, he deigned to say nothing more in the way of approval than that he was at last beginning to be housed like a human being.

He also began a pool, extending from Misenum to the lake of Avernus, roofed over and enclosed in colonnades,

[e] Suetonius' brevity is here inexact; it was evidently the spherical ceiling which revolved.

totis Baiis calidarum aquarum esset converteretur; fossam ab Averno Ostiam usque, ut navibus nec tamen mari iretur, longitudinis per centum sexaginta milia, latitudinis, qua contrariae quinqueremes commearent. Quorum operum perficiendorum gratia quod ubique esset custodiae in Italiam deportari, etiam scelere convictos non nisi ad opus damnari praeceperat.

4   Ad hunc impendiorum furorem, super fiduciam imperii, etiam spe quadam repentina immensarum et reconditarum opum impulsus est ex indicio equitis R. pro comperto pollicentis thesauros antiquissimae gazae, quos Dido regina fugiens Tyro secum extulisset, esse in Africa vastissimis specubus abditos ac posse erui parvula molientium opera.

XXXII. Verum ut spes fefellit, destitutus atque ita iam exhaustus et egens ut stipendia quoque militum et commoda veteranorum protrahi ac differri necesse esset, calumniis rapinisque intendit animum.

2   Ante omnia instituit, ut e libertorum defunctorum bonis pro semisse dextans ei cogeretur, qui sine probabili causa eo nomine essent, quo fuissent ullae familiae quas ipse contingeret; deinde, ut ingratorum in principem testamenta ad fiscum pertinerent, ac ne impune esset studiosis iuris, qui scripsissent vel dictassent ea; tunc ut lege maiestatis facta dictaque omnia, quibus modo delator non

---

[a] That is, had left him nothing in their wills, or an insufficient amount.

into which he planned to turn all the hot springs in every part of Baiae; a canal from Avernus all the way to Ostia, to enable the journey to be made by ship yet not by sea; its length was to be a hundred and sixty miles and its breadth sufficient to allow ships with five banks of oars to pass each other. For the execution of these projects he had given orders that the prisoners all over the empire should be transported to Italy, and that those who were convicted even of capital crimes should be punished in no other way than by sentence to this work.

He was led to such mad extravagance, in addition to his confidence in the resources of the empire, by the hope of a vast hidden treasure, suddenly inspired by the assurance of a Roman knight, who declared positively that the enormous wealth which queen Dido had taken with her of old in her flight from Tyre was hidden away in huge caves in Africa and could be recovered with but trifling labour.

XXXII. When this hope proved false, he resorted to false accusations and robbery, being at the end of his resources and so utterly impoverished that he was obliged to postpone and defer even the pay of the soldiers and the rewards due to the veterans.

First of all he made a law, that instead of one-half, five-sixths of the property of deceased freedmen should be made over to him, if without good and sufficient reason they bore the name of any family with which he himself was connected; further, that the estates of those who were ungrateful to their emperor[a] should belong to the privy purse, and that the advocates who had written or dictated such wills should not go unpunished. Finally, that any word or deed on which an informer could base an action

3 deesset, tenerentur. Revocavit et praemia coronarum, quae umquam sibi civitates in certaminibus detulissent. Et cum interdixisset usum amethystini ac Tyrii coloris summisissetque qui nundinarum die pauculas uncias venderet, praeclusit cunctos negotiatores. Quin etiam inter canendum animadversam matronam in spectaculis vetita purpura cultam demonstrasse procuratoribus suis dicitur detractamque ilico non veste modo sed et bonis

4 exuit. Nulli delegavit officium ut non adiceret: "Scis quid mihi opus sit," et: "Hoc agamus, ne quis quicquam habeat." Ultimo templis compluribus dona detraxit simulacraque ex auro vel argento fabricata conflavit, in iis Penatium deorum, quae mox Galba restituit.

XXXIII. Parricidia et caedes a Claudio exorsus est; cuius necis etsi non auctor, at conscius fuit, neque dissimulanter, ut qui boletos, in quo cibi genere venenum is acceperat, quasi deorum cibum posthac proverbio Graeco conlaudare sit solitus. Certe omnibus rerum verborumque contumeliis mortuum insectatus est, modo stultitiae modo saevitiae arguens; nam et morari eum desisse inter homines producta prima syllaba iocabatur multaque decreta et constituta, ut insipientis atque deliri, pro irritis habuit; denique bustum eius consaepiri nisi humili levique maceria[1] neglexit.

----

[1] maceria, *Gutherius*; materia, Ω.

----

[a] See chap. xxiv. 2.   [b] Of course confiscating their property.
[c] According to Dio, 60. 35 (at the end) the saying was original with Nero; but as Dio calls it "a remark not unworthy of record," it perhaps became proverbial among the Greeks.   [d] But cf. chap. ix.   [e] The pun on *morari*, "to linger, remain" and *mōrari*, "to play the fool," seems untranslatable.

should be liable to the law against lese-majesty. He demanded the return of the rewards[a] which he had given in recognition of the prizes conferred on him by any city in any competition. Having forbidden the use of amethyst-colored or Tyrian purple dyes, he secretly sent a man to sell a few ounces on a market day and then closed the shops of all the dealers.[b] It is even said that when he saw a matron in the audience at one of his recitals clad in the forbidden colour he pointed her out to his agents, who dragged her out and stripped her on the spot, not only of her garment, but also of her property. He never appointed anyone to an office without adding: "You know what my needs are," and "Let us see to it that no one possess anything." At last he stripped many temples of their gifts and melted down the images of gold and silver, including those of the Penates, which however Galba soon afterwards restored.

XXXIII. He began his career of parricide and murder with Claudius, for even if he was not the instigator of the emperor's death, he was at least privy to it, as he openly admitted; for he used afterwards to laud mushrooms, the vehicle in which the poison was administered to Claudius, as "the food of the gods," as the Greek proverb has it.[c] At any rate, after Claudius' death he vented on him every kind of insult, in act and word,[d] charging him now with folly and now with cruelty; for it was a favourite joke of his to say that Claudius had ceased "to play the fool"[e] among mortals, lengthening the first syllable of the word *morari*, and he disregarded many of his decrees and acts as the work of a madman and a dotard. Finally, he neglected to enclose the place where his body was burned except with a low and mean wall.

2   Britannicum non minus aemulatione vocis, quae illi
iucundior suppetebat, quam metu ne quandoque apud
hominum gratiam paterna memoria praevaleret, veneno
adgressus est. Quod acceptum a quadam Lucusta, vene-
nariorum indice, cum opinione tardius cederet ventre
modo Britannici moto, accersitam mulierem sua manu
verberavit arguens pro veneno remedium dedisse; excu-
santique minus datum ad occultandam facinoris invidiam:
"Sane," inquit, "legem Iuliam timeo," coegitque se coram
in cubiculo quam posset velocissimum ac praesentaneum
3   coquere. Deinde in haedo expertus, postquam is quinque
horas protraxit, iterum ac saepius recoctum porcello
obiecit; quo statim exanimato inferri in triclinium darique
cenanti secum Britannico imperavit. Et cum ille ad primum gustum concidisset, comitiali morbo ex consuetudine correptum apud convivas ementitus postero die
raptim inter maximos imbres tralaticio extulit funere.
Lucustae pro navata opera impunitatem praediaque
ampla, sed et discipulos dedit.

     XXXIV. Matrem facta dictaque sua exquirentem acer-
bius et corrigentem hactenus primo gravabatur, ut invidia
identidem oneraret quasi cessurus imperio Rhodumque
abiturus, mox et honore omni et potestate privavit abduc-

---

[a] In his account of this event, *Ann.* 13. 15–16, Tacitus calls
her Locusta.

[b] Against assassination (*De sicariis*), including poisoning,
passed by Sulla and renewed by Julius Caesar.

[c] For her past offences; see Tac. *Ann.* 12. 66.

[d] See Juv. i. 71 f.

He attempted the life of Britannicus by poison, not less from jealousy of his voice (for it was more agreeable than his own) than from fear that he might sometime win a higher place than himself in the people's regard because of the memory of his father. He procured the potion from an archpoisoner, one Lucusta, and when the effect was slower than he anticipated, merely loosening Britannicus' bowels, he called the woman to him and flogged her with his own hand, charging that she had administered a medicine instead of a poison; and when she said in excuse that she had given a smaller dose to shield him from the odium of the crime, he replied: "It's likely that I am afraid of the Julian law[b];" and he forced her to mix as swift and instant a potion as she knew how in his own room before his very eyes. Then he tried it on a kid, and as the animal lingered for five hours, had the mixture steeped again and again and threw some of it before a pig. The beast instantly fell dead, whereupon he ordered that the poison be taken to the dining-room and given to Britannicus. The boy dropped dead at the very first taste, but Nero lied to his guests and declared that he was seized with the falling sickness, to which he was subject, and the next day had him hastily and unceremoniously buried in a pouring rain. He rewarded Lucusta for her eminent services with a full pardon[c] and large estates in the country, and actually sent her pupils.[d]

XXXIV. His mother offended him by too strict surveillance and criticism of his words and acts, but at first he confined his resentment to frequent endeavours to bring upon her a burden of unpopularity by pretending that he would abdicate the throne and go off to Rhodes. Then depriving her of all her honours and of her guard of

LIVES OF THE CAESARS, VI

taque militum et Germanorum statione contubernio quoque ac Palatio expulit; neque in divexanda quicquam pensi habuit, summissis qui et Romae morantem litibus et in secessu quiescentem per convicia et iocos terra marique praetervehentes inquietarent. Verum minis eius ac violentia territus perdere statuit; et cum ter veneno temptasset sentiretque antidotis praemunitam, lacunaria, quae noctu super dormientem laxata machina deciderent, paravit. Hoc consilio per conscios parum celato solutilem navem, cuius vel naufragio vel camarae[1] ruina periret, commentus est atque ita reconciliatione simulata iucundissimis litteris Baias evocavit ad sollemnia Quinquatruum[2] simul celebranda; datoque negotio trierarchis, qui liburnicam qua advecta erat velut fortuito concursu confringerent, protraxit convivium repetentique Baulos in locum corrupti navigii machinosum illud optulit, hilare prosecutus atque in digressu papillas quoque exosculatus. Reliquum temporis cum magna trepidatione vigilavit opperiens coeptorum exitum. Sed ut diversa omnia nandoque evasisse eam comperit, inops consilii L. Agermum libertum eius salvam et incolumem cum gaudio nuntiantem, abiecto clam iuxta pugione ut percussorem sibi subornatum arripi constringique iussit, matrem occidi,

[1] camare, ML; the other mss. have camerae or camere.
[2] Quinquatruum] Quinquatrum, MLϒ; Quinquatrium, GPT.

[a] The inventor was his freedman Anicetus; Tac. Ann. 14. 3.
[b] See Aug. lxxi. 3.
[c] Given by the future emperor Otho; see Otho, iii. 1.

Roman and German soldiers, he even forbade her to live with him and drove her from the Palace. After that he passed all bounds in harrying her, bribing men to annoy her with lawsuits while she remained in the city, and after she had retired to the country, to pass her house by land and sea and break her rest with abuse and mockery. At last terrified by her violence and threats, he determined to have her life, and after thrice attempting it by poison and finding that she had made herself immune by antidotes, he tampered with the ceiling of her bedroom, contriving a mechanical device for loosening its panels and dropping them upon her while she slept. When this leaked out through some of those connected with the plot, he devised a collapsible boat,[a] to destroy her by shipwreck or by the falling in of its cabin. Then he pretended a reconciliation and invited her in a most cordial letter to come to Baiae and celebrate the feast of Minerva[b] with him. On her arrival, instructing his captains to wreck the galley in which she had come, by running into it as if by accident, he detained her at a banquet,[c] and when she would return to Bauli, offered her his contrivance in place of the craft which had been damaged, escorting her to it in high spirits and even kissing her breasts as they parted. The rest of the night he passed sleepless in intense anxiety, awaiting the outcome of his design. On learning that everything had gone wrong and that she had escaped by swimming, driven to desperation he secretly had a dagger thrown down beside her freedman Lucius Agermus, when he joyfully brought word that she was safe and sound, and then ordered that the freedman be seized and bound, on the charge of being hired to kill the emperor; that his mother be put to death, and the pretence made

quasi deprehensum crimen voluntaria morte vitasset.
4 Adduntur his atrociora nec incertis auctoribus: ad
visendum interfectae cadaver accurrisse, contrectasse
membra, alia vituperasse, alia laudasse, sitique interim
oborta bibisse. Neque tamen conscientiam sceleris,
quanquam et militum et senatus populique gratulationi-
bus confirmaretur, aut statim aut umquam postea ferre
potuit, saepe confessus exagitari se materna specie ver-
beribusque Furiarum ac taedis ardentibus. Quin et facto
per Magos sacro evocare Manes et exorare temptavit.
Peregrinatione quidem Graeciae et Eleusinis sacris, quorum initiatione impii et scelerati voce praeconis sum-
moventur, interesse non ausus est.
5 Iunxit parricidio matris amitae necem. Quam cum ex
duritie alvi cubantem visitaret, et illa tractans lanuginem
eius, ut assolet, iam grandis natu per blanditias forte dixis-
set: "Simul hanc excepero, mori volo," conversus ad proximos confestim se positurum velut irridens ait, prae-
cepitque medicis ut largius purgarent aegram; necdum
defunctae bona invasit suppresso testamento, ne quid
abscederet.

XXXV. Uxores praeter Octaviam duas postea duxit,
Poppaeam[1] Sabinam quaestorio patre natam et equiti R.
antea nuptam, deinde Statiliam Messalinam Tauri bis

---

[1] Poppaeam, *Sabellicus*; Pompeiam, Ω.

[a] Tacitus tells us that some denied this; *Ann.* 14. 9.

[b] Domitia, not Domitia Lepida the aunt with whom he had
lived; vi. 3.

[c] That is, "when I see you arrived at man's estate." The first
shaving of the beard by a young Roman was a symbolic act.
According to Tac. *Ann.* 14. 15, and Dio, 61. 19, Nero first shaved

that she had escaped the consequences of her detected guilt by suicide. Trustworthy authorities[a] add still more gruesome details: that he hurried off to view the corpse, handled her limbs, criticising some and commending others, and that becoming thirsty meanwhile, he took a drink. Yet he could not either then or ever afterwards endure the stings of conscience, though soldiers, senate and people tried to hearten him with their congratulations; for he often owned that he was hounded by his mother's ghost and by the whips and blazing torches of the Furies. He even had rites performed by the Magi, in the effort to summon her shade and entreat it for forgiveness. Moreover, in his journey through Greece he did not venture to take part in the Eleusinian mysteries, since at the beginning the godless and wicked are warned by the herald's proclamation to go hence.

To matricide he added the murder of his aunt.[b] When he once visited her as she was confined to her bed from constipation, and she, as old ladies will, stroking his downy beard (for he was already well grown) happened to say fondly: "As soon as I receive this,[c] I shall gladly die," he turned to those with him and said as if in jest: "I'll take it off at once." Then he bade the doctors purge the sick woman too aggressively and seized her property before she was cold, suppressing her will, that nothing might escape him.

XXXV. Besides Octavia he later took two wives, Poppaea Sabina, daughter of an ex-quaestor and previously married to a Roman knight, and then Statilia Messalina,

his beard in A.D. 59 at the age of twenty-one and commemorated the event by establishing the Juvenalia (chap. xi. 1).

consulis ac triumphalis abneptem. Qua ut poteretur,
virum eius Atticum Vestinum consulem in honore ipso
trucidavit. Octaviae consuetudinem cito aspernatus, cor-
ripientibus amicis sufficere illi debere respondit uxoria

2 ornamenta. Eandem mox saepe frustra strangulare meditatus dimisit ut sterilem, sed improbante divortium
populo nec parcente conviciis, etiam relegavit, denique
occidit sub crimine adulteriorum adeo inpudenti falso-
que, ut in quaestione pernegantibus cunctis Anicetum
paedagogum suum indicem subiecerit, qui fingeret et[1]

3 dolo stupratam a se fateretur. Poppaeam[2] duodecimo die
post divortium Octaviae in matrimonium acceptam dilexit
unice; et tamen ipsam quoque ictu calcis occidit, quod se
ex aurigatione sero reversum gravida et aegra conviciis
incesserat. Ex hac filiam tulit Claudiam Augustam
amisitque admodum infantem.

4 Nullum adeo necessitudinis genus est, quod non
scelere perculerit. Antoniam Claudi filiam, recusantem
post Poppaeae mortem nuptias suas, quasi molitricem
novarum rerum interemit; similiter ceteros[3] aut affinitate
aliqua sibi aut propinquitate coniunctos; in quibus Aulum
Plautium iuvenem, quem cum ante mortem per vim con-
spurcasset: "Eat nunc," inquit, "mater mea et succes-

[1] fingeret et, *X*; fingeret, *MG*; Υ *omits both words.*
[2] Pompeiam, Ω; Poppeiam, *Q.*
[3] *The earlier mss. except* ρ *have* inter *before* ceteros;
interemit *or* item, ς; intercepit, *Polak.*

[a] A brutal pun. Just as the consular *insignia* or *ornamenta*
were given in place of the regular office (see *Claud.* v), and the
triumphal *insignia* in place of a triumph, so Octavia ought to be
content with being the emperor's wife in name only.

daughter of the great-granddaughter of Taurus, who had been twice consul and awarded a triumph. To possess the latter he slew her husband Atticus Vestinus while he held the office of consul. He soon grew tired of living with Octavia, and when his friends took him to task, replied that "she ought to be content with the insignia of wifehood."[a] Presently after several vain attempts to strangle her, he divorced her on the ground of barrenness, and when the people took it ill and openly reproached him, he banished her besides; and finally he had her put to death on a charge of adultery that was so shameless and unfounded that, when all who were put to the torture maintained her innocence, he bribed his former preceptor Anicetus[b] to make a pretended confession that he had raped her by a stratagem. He dearly loved Poppaea, whom he married twelve days after his divorce from Octavia, yet he caused her death too by kicking her when she was pregnant and ill, because she had scolded him for coming home late from the races. By her he had a daughter, Claudia Augusta, but lost her when she was still an infant.

Indeed there is no kind of relationship that he did not violate in his career of crime. He put to death Antonia, daughter of Claudius,[c] for refusing to marry him after Poppaea's death, charging her with an attempt at revolution; and he treated in the same way all others who were in any way connected with him by blood or by marriage. Among these was the young Aulus Plautius, whom he forcibly molested before his death, saying "Let my

[b] Anicetus was at the time prefect of the praetorian fleet at Misenum; see Tac. *Ann.* 14. 62.   [c] See *Claud.* xxvii. 1.

sorem meum osculetur," iactans dilectum ab ea et ad
5 spem imperii impulsum. Privignum Rufrium Crispinum
Poppaea natum, impuberem adhuc, quia ferebatur duca-
tus et imperia ludere, mergendum mari,. dum piscaretur,
servis ipsius demandavit. Tuscum nutricis filium relegavit, quod in procuratione Aegypti balineis in adventum
suum exstructis lavisset. Senecam praeceptorem ad
necem compulit, quamvis saepe commeatum petenti
bonisque cedenti persancte iurasset suspectum se frustra
periturumque potius quam nociturum ei. Burro praefecto remedium ad fauces pollicitus toxicum misit. Libertos divites et senes, olim adoptionis mox dominationis
suae fautores atque rectores, veneno partim cibis partim
potionibus indito intercepit.

XXXVI. Nec minore saevitia foris et in exteros grassa-
tus est. Stella crinita, quae summis potestatibus exitium
portendere vulgo putatur, per continuas noctes oriri
coeperat. Anxius ea re, ut ex Balbillo astrologo didicit,
solere reges talia ostenta caede aliqua illustri expiare
atque a semet in capita procerum depellere, nobilissimo
cuique exitium destinavit; enimvero multo magis et quasi
per iustam causam duabus coniurationibus provulgatis,
quarum prior maiorque Pisoniana Romae, posterior Vini-
2 ciana Beneventi conflata atque detecta est. Coniurati e

---

[a] Seneca's speech and Nero's reply are preserved by Tacitus
(*Ann.* 14. 53–56).

[b] Pallas and Doryphorus; see Tac. *Ann.* 14. 65.

[c] Tacitus mentions two comets, one in 60 and the other in 64;
see *Ann.* 14. 22; 15. 47.

[d] In A.D. 65.

mother come now and kiss my successor," openly charging that Agrippina had loved Plautius and that this had roused him to hopes of the throne. Rufrius Crispinus, a mere boy, his stepson and the child of Poppaea, he ordered to be drowned in the sea by the child's own slaves while he was fishing, because it was said that he used to play at being a general and an emperor. He banished his nurse's son Tuscus, because when procurator in Egypt, he had bathed in some baths which were built for a visit of Nero's. He drove his tutor Seneca to suicide, although when the old man often pleaded to be allowed to retire and offered to give up his estates,[a] he had sworn most solemnly that he did wrong to suspect him and that he would rather die than harm him. He sent poison to Burrus, prefect of the Guard, in place of a throat medicine which he had promised him. The old and wealthy freedmen who had helped him first to his adoption and later to the throne, and aided him by their advice,[b] he killed by poison, administered partly in their food and partly in their drink.

XXXVI. Those outside his family he assailed with no less cruelty. It chanced that a comet[c] had begun to appear on several successive nights, a thing which is commonly believed to portend the death of great rulers. Worried by this, and learning from the astrologer Balbillus that kings usually averted such omens by the death of some distinguished man, thus turning them from themselves upon the heads of the nobles, he resolved on the death of all the eminent men of the State; but the more firmly, and with some semblance of justice, after the discovery of two conspiracies. The earlier and more dangerous of these was that of Piso at Rome;[d] the other was set on foot by Vinicius at Beneventum and detected there.

vinculis triplicium catenarum dixere causam, cum quidam ultro crimen faterentur, nonnulli etiam imputarent,
tamquam aliter illi non possent nisi morte succurrere
dedecorato flagitiis omnibus. Damnatorum liberi urbe
pulsi enectique veneno aut fame; constat quosdam cum
paedagogis et capsariis uno prandio pariter necatos, alios
diurnum victum prohibitos quaerere.

XXXVII. Nullus posthac adhibitus dilectus aut modus
interimendi quoscumque libuisset quacumque de causa.
Sed ne de pluribus referam, Salvidieno Orfito obiectum
est quod tabernas tres de domo sua circa Forum civitatibus ad stationem locasset, Cassio Longino iuris consulto
ac luminibus orbato, quod in vetere gentili[1] stemmate C.
Cassi percussoris Caesaris imagines retinuisset, Paeto

2 Thraseae tristior et paedagogi vultus. Mori iussis non
amplius quam horarum spatium dabat; ac ne quid morae
interveniret, medicos admovebat qui cunctantes continuo
curarent; ita enim vocabatur[2] venas mortis gratia
incidere. Creditur etiam polyphago cuidam Aegypti
generis crudam carnem et quidquid daretur mandere
assueto, concupisse vivos homines laniandos absumen-

3 dosque obicere. Elatus inflatusque tantis velut successi-
bus negavit quemquam principum scisse quid sibi liceret,

[1] gentili, $S^2\delta\varsigma$; gentilis, *MGX*; gentis, Υ.
[2] vocabatur, *M*Υ; iocabatur, *G*; vocabat, *X*.

---

[a] As Dio says (62. 24) "they desired at the same time to be rid
of these evils *and to give Nero his release from them.*" Death was
the only remedy for one as far gone in wickedness; hence in
attempting to apply this remedy, they were doing him a favour.
Cf. also Tac. *Ann.* 15. 68.

[b] The *capsarii* carried the children's books and writing materials in a box (*capsa*).

The conspirators made their defence in triple sets of fetters, some voluntarily admitting their guilt, some even making a favour of it, saying that there was no way except by death that they could help a man disgraced by every kind of wickedness.[a] The children of those who were condemned were banished or put to death by poison or starvation; a number are known to have been slain all together at a single meal along with their preceptors and attendants,[b] while others were prevented from earning their daily bread.

XXXVII. After this he showed neither discrimination nor moderation in putting to death whomsoever he pleased on any pretext whatever. To mention but a few instances, Salvidienus Orfitus was charged with having let to certain states as headquarters three shops which formed part of his house near the Forum; Cassius Longinus, a blind jurist, with retaining in the old family tree of his house the mask of Gaius Cassius, the assassin of Julius Caesar; Paetus Thrasea with having a sullen mien, like that of a preceptor. To those who were bidden to die he never granted more than a few hours' respite, and to avoid any delay, he brought physicians who were at once to "attend to" such as lingered; for that was the term he used for killing them by opening their veins. It is even believed that it was his wish to throw living men to be torn to pieces and devoured by a monster[c] of Egyptian birth, who would crunch raw flesh and anything else that was given him. Transported and puffed up with such successes, as he considered them, he boasted that no prince had ever known what power he really had, and he often

[c] The Greek word means "a glutton," or something stronger.

multasque nec dubias significationes saepe iecit, ne reliquis quidem se parsurum senatoribus, eumque ordinem sublaturum quandoque e re p. ac provincias et exercitus equiti R. ac libertis permissurum. Certe neque adveniens neque proficiscens quemquam osculo impertiit ac ne resalutatione quidem;[a] et in auspicando opere Isthmi[1] magna frequentia clare ut sibi ac populo R. bene res verteret optavit dissimulata senatus mentione.

XXXVIII. Sed nec populo aut moenibus patriae pepercit. Dicente quodam in sermone communi:

ἐμοῦ θανόντος γαῖα μειχθήτω πυρί,[b]

"Immo," inquit, "ἐμοῦ ζῶντος," planeque ita fecit. Nam quasi offensus deformitate veterum aedificiorum et angustiis flexurisque vicorum, incendit urbem tam palam, ut plerique consulares cubicularios eius cum stuppa taedaque in praediis suis deprehensos non attigerint, et quaedam horrea circa domum Auream, quorum spatium maxime desiderabat, ut bellicis machinis labefacta atque inflammata sint, quod saxeo muro constructa erant. Per sex dies septemque noctes ea clade saevitum est ad monumentorum bustorumque deversoria[2] plebe compulsa. Tunc praeter immensum numerum insularum[d] domus

2

---

[1] Isthmii, Π[2]R; *the greater number of the mss. have* Sthmii.
[2] deversoria] diversoria, Ω.

---

[a] Such a salutation was usual; see Plin. *Paneg.* xxiii.
[b] A line put by Dio, 58. 23, into the mouth of Tiberius. It is believed to be from the *Bellerophon*, a lost play of Euripides.
[c] But cf. Tac. *Ann.* 15. 38.   [d] *Insulae* here refers to blocks of houses, or tenements, in which rooms were rented to the poorer classes; *domus* to detached houses or mansions.

threw out unmistakable hints that he would not spare even those of the senate who survived, but would one day blot out the whole order from the State and hand over the rule of the provinces and the command of the armies to the Roman knights and to his freedmen. Certain it is that neither on beginning a journey nor on returning did he kiss any member[a] or even return his greeting; and at the formal opening of the work at the Isthmus the prayer which he uttered in a loud voice before a great throng was, that the event might result favourably "for himself and the people of Rome," thus suppressing any mention of the senate.

XXXVIII. But he showed no greater mercy to the people or the walls of his capital. When someone in a general conversation said:

"When I am dead, be earth consumed by fire,"[b]

he rejoined "Nay, rather while I live," and his action was wholly in accord. For under cover of displeasure at the ugliness of the old buildings and the narrow, crooked streets, he set fire to the city[c] so openly that several ex-consuls did not venture to lay hands on his chamberlains although they caught them on their estates with tow and firebrands, while some granaries near the Golden House, whose room he particularly desired, were demolished by engines of war and then set on fire, because their walls were of stone. For six days and seven nights destruction raged, while the people were driven for shelter to monuments and tombs. At that time, besides an immense number of dwellings,[d] the houses of leaders of old were

priscorum ducum arserunt hostilibus adhuc spoliis adornatae deorumque aedes ab regibus ac deinde Punicis et
Gallicis bellis votae dedicataeque, et quidquid visendum
atque memorabile ex antiquitate duraverat. Hoc incendium e turre Maecenatiana prospectans laetusque "flammae," ut aiebat, "pulchritudine" Halosin Ilii in illo suo

3   scaenico habitu decantavit. Ac ne non hinc quoque quantum posset praedae et manubiarum invaderet, pollicitus
cadaverum et ruderum gratuitam egestionem nemini ad
reliquias rerum suarum adire permisit; conlationibusque
non receptis modo verum et efflagitatis provincias privatorumque census prope exhausit.

XXXIX. Accesserunt tantis ex principe malis probrisque quaedam et fortuita: pestilentia unius autumni,
quo triginta funerum milia in rationem Libitinae
venerunt; clades Britannica, qua duo praecipua oppida
magna civium sociorumque caede direpta sunt; ignominia
ad Orientem legionibus in Armenia sub iugum missis
aegreque Syria retenta. Mirum et vel praecipue notabile
inter haec fuerit nihil eum patientius quam maledicta et
convicia hominum tulisse, neque in ullos leniorem quam

2   qui se dictis aut carminibus lacessissent exstitisse. Multa
Graece Latineque proscripta aut vulgata sunt, sicut illa:

---

     [a] A tower connected with the house and gardens of Maecenas
on the Esquiline; see Hor. *Odes*, 3. 29. 10, *molem propinquam
nubibus arduis*. It was probably connected with the Palatine by
the *domus transitoria*; see chap. xxi. 2 and Tac. *Ann.* 15. 39,
whose account, as well as that of Dio, 62. 18, differs from that of
Suetonius.   [b] Probably a composition of his own; cf. Juv. 8.
221 and *Vitell.* xi. 2.
     [c] Venus Libitina, in whose temple funeral outfits and a register of deaths were kept; cf. Hor. *Serm.* 2. 6. 19.

burned, still adorned with trophies of victory, and the temples of the gods vowed and dedicated by the kings and later in the Punic and Gallic wars, and whatever else interesting and noteworthy had survived from antiquity. Viewing the conflagration from the tower of Maecenas[a] and exulting, as he said, in "the beauty of the flames," he sang the whole of the "Sack of Ilium,"[b] in his regular stage costume. Furthermore, to gain from this calamity too all the spoil and booty possible, while promising the removal of the debris and dead bodies free of cost he allowed no one to approach the ruins of his own property; and from the contributions which he not only received, but even demanded, he nearly bankrupted the provinces and exhausted the resources of individuals.

XXXIX. To all the disasters and abuses thus caused by the prince there were added certain accidents of fortune; a plague which in a single autumn entered thirty thousand deaths in the accounts of Libitina;[c] a disaster in Britain, where two important towns were sacked[d] and great numbers of citizens and allies were butchered; a shameful defeat in the Orient, in consequence of which the legions in Armenia were sent under the yoke and Syria was all but lost. It is surprising and of special note that all this time he bore nothing with more patience than the curses and abuse of the people, and was particularly lenient towards those who assailed him with gibes and lampoons. Of these many were posted or circulated both in Greek and Latin, for example the following:

[d] Camulodunum (Colchester) and Verulamium (St. Albans); according to Xiphilinus (62. 1; Loeb ed. of Dio, vol. 8, p. 82) 80,000 perished.

Νέρων Ὀρέστης Ἀλκμέων μητροκτόνος.

Νεόψηφον·[1] Νέρων ἰδίαν μητέρα ἀπέκτεινε.

Quis negat Aeneae magna de stirpe Neronem?
　　Sustulit hic matrem, sustulit ille patrem.

Dum tendit citharam noster, dum cornua Parthus,
　　Noster erit Paean, ille Hecatebeletes.

Roma domus fiet; Veios migrate, Quirites,
　　Si non et Veios occupat ista domus.

Sed neque auctores requisiit et quosdam per indicem delatos ad senatum adfici graviore poena prohibuit.

3　Transeuntem eum Isidorus Cynicus in publico clara voce corripuerat, quod Naupli mala bene cantitaret, sua bona male disponeret; et Datus Atellanarum histrio in cantico quodam

　　　　ὑγίαινε πάτερ, ὑγίαινε μῆτερ

ita demonstraverat, ut bibentem natantemque faceret, exitum scilicet Claudi Agrippinaeque significans, et in novissima clausula

　　Orcus vobis ducit pedes

senatum gestu notarat.[2] Histrionem et philosophum

---

[1] νεόψηφον, Ω; see Bücheler, Rh. Mus. 61, 308 f.; νεόνυμφον, ς.　　[2] notarat, Oudendorp; notaret, ς.

---

[a] The numerical value of the Greek letters in Nero's name (1005) is the same as that of the rest of the sentence; hence Nero = the slayer of one's own mother.　　[b] The pun is on sustulit = "get rid of" and "lift up."　　[c] Two names for two aspects of Apollo.　　[d] A reference to his "Golden House"; see xxxi. 1–2.
[e] Referring to Nero's design mentioned in chap. xxxvii. 3.

"Nero, Orestes, Alcmeon their mothers slew."

"A calculation new. Nero his mother slew."[a]

"Who can deny the descent from Aeneas' great line
   of our Nero?
   One his mother took out, the other one took up
      his sire."[b]

"While our ruler his lyre doth twang and the
      Parthian his bowstring,
   Paean-singer our prince shall be, and Far-darter
      our foe."[c]

"Rome is becoming one house; off with you to Veii,
      Quirites!
   If that house does not soon seize upon Veii as
      well."[d]

He made no effort, however, to find the authors; in fact, when some of them were reported to the senate by an informer, he forbade their being very severely punished. As he was passing along a public street, the Cynic Isidorus loudly taunted him, "because he was a good singer of the ills of Nauplius, but made ill use of his own goods." Datus also, an actor of Atellan farces, in a song beginning:

Farewell to thee, father; farewell to thee, mother,

represented drinking and swimming in pantomime, referring of course to the death of Claudius and Agrippina; and in the final tag,

Orcus guides your steps,

he indicated the senate by a gesture.[e] Nero contented

Nero nihil amplius quam urbe Italiaque summovit, vel contemptu omnis infamiae vel ne fatendo dolorem irritaret ingenia.

XL. Talem principem paulo minus quattuordecim annos perpessus terrarum orbis tandem destituit, initium facientibus Gallis duce Iulio Vindice, qui tum eam provinciam pro praetore optinebat.

2   Praedictum a mathematicis Neroni olim erat fore ut quandoque destitueretur; unde illa vox eius celeberrima: τὸ τέχνιον ἡμᾶς διατρέφει,[1] quo maiore scilicet venia meditaretur citharoedicam artem, principi sibi gratam, privato necessariam. Spoponderant tamen quidam destituto Orientis dominationem, nonnulli nominatim regnum Hierosolymorum, plures omnis pristinae fortunae restitutionem. Cui spei pronior, Britannia Armeniaque amissa ac rursus utraque recepta, defunctum se fatalibus malis

3 existimabat. Ut vero consulto Delphis Apolline septuagensimum ac tertium annum cavendum sibi audivit, quasi eo demum obiturus, ac nihil coniectans de aetate Galbae, tanta fiducia non modo senectam sed etiam perpetuam singularemque concepit felicitatem, ut amissis naufragio pretiosissimis rebus non dubitaverit inter suos dicere pisces eas sibi relaturos.

4   Neapoli de motu Galliarum cognovit die ipso quo

----

[1] διατρεσφει, MLS; *the rest of the mss. have* διατρεφει; διαθρέψει, *Turnebus from Dio*, 63. 27.

[a] If the text is right, the remark must be of a general nature ("us" = mankind). Dio, 63. 27, who reads διαθρέψει, says that Nero, when planning to kill the senators, burn Rome, and sail to Alexandria, said: "Even though we be driven from our empire,

himself with banishing the actor and the philosopher from the city and from Italy, either because he was impervious to all insults, or to avoid sharpening men's wits by showing his vexation.

XL. After the world had put up with such a ruler for nearly fourteen years, it at last cast him off, and the Gauls took the first step under the lead of Julius Vindex, who at that time governed their province as propraetor.

Astrologers had predicted to Nero that he would one day be repudiated, which was the occasion of that well known saying of his: "A humble art affords us daily bread,"[a] doubtless uttered to justify him in practising the art of lyre-playing, as an amusement while emperor, but a necessity for a private citizen. Some of them, however, had promised him the rule of the East, when he was cast off, a few expressly naming the sovereignty of Jerusalem, and several the restitution of all his former fortunes. Inclining rather to this last hope, after losing Armenia and Britain and recovering both, he began to think that he had suffered the misfortunes which fate had in store. And after consulting the oracle at Delphi and being told that he must look out for the seventy-third year, assuming that he would die only at that period, and taking no account of Galba's years, he felt so confident not only of old age, but also of unbroken and unusual good fortune, that when he had lost some articles of great value by shipwreck, he did not hesitate to say among his intimate friends that the fish would bring them back to him.

He was at Naples when he learned of the uprising of the Gallic provinces, on the anniversary of his mother's

yet this little artistic gift of ours shall support us there"; *i.e.* at Alexandria.

matrem occiderat, adeoque lente ac secure tulit ut gaudentis etiam suspicionem praeberet tamquam occasione nata spoliandarum iure belli opulentissimarum provinciarum; statimque in gymnasium progressus certantis athletas effusissimo studio spectavit. Cenae quoque tempore interpellatus tumultuosioribus litteris hactenus excanduit, ut malum iis qui descissent minaretur. Denique per octo continuos dies non rescribere cuiquam, non mandare quid aut praecipere conatus rem silentio obliteravit.

XLI. Edictis tandem Vindicis contumeliosis et frequentibus permotus senatum epistula in ultionem sui reique publicae adhortatus est, excusato languore faucium, propter quem non adesset. Nihil autem aeque doluit, quam ut malum se citharoedum increpitum ac pro Nerone Ahenobarbum appellatum; et nomen quidem gentile, quod sibi per contumeliam exprobraretur, resumpturum se professus est deposito adoptivo, cetera convicia, ut falsa, non alio argumento refellebat, quam quod etiam inscitia sibi tanto opere elaboratae[1] perfectaeque a se artis obiceretur, singulos subinde rogitans, nossentne quemquam praestantiorem. Sed urgentibus aliis super alios nuntiis Romam praetrepidus rediit; leviterque modo in itinere frivolo auspicio mente recreata, cum adnotasset insculptum monumento militem Gallum ab equite R. oppressum trahi crinibus, ad eam speciem exsiluit gaudio caelumque adoravit. Ac ne tunc

___

[1] elaboratae, *Bernegger*; laboratae, *mss.*

___

[a] Cf. chap. vii. 1.

murder, and received the news with such calmness and indifference that he incurred the suspicion of actually rejoicing in it, because it gave him an excuse for pillaging those wealthy provinces according to the laws of war. And he at once proceeded to the gymnasium, where he watched the contests of the athletes with rapt interest. At dinner too when interrupted by a more disturbing letter, he fired up only so far as to threaten vengeance on the rebels. In short for eight whole days making no attempt to write a reply to anyone, none to give any commission or command, he blotted out the affair with silence.

XLI. At last he was driven by numerous insulting edicts of Vindex, to urge the senate in a letter to avenge him and the state, alleging a throat trouble as his excuse for not appearing in person. Yet there was nothing which he so much resented as the taunt that he was a wretched lyre-player and that he was addressed as Ahenobarbus instead of Nero.[a] With regard to his family name, which was cast in his teeth as an insult, he declared that he would resume it and give up that of his adoption. He used no other arguments to show the falsity of the rest of the reproaches than that he was actually taunted with being unskilled in an art to which he had devoted so much attention and in which he had so perfected himself, and he asked various individuals from time to time whether they knew of any artist who was his superior. Finally, beset by message after message, he returned to Rome in a panic; but on the way, when but slightly encouraged by an insignificant omen, for he noticed a monument on which was sculptured the overthrow of a Gallic soldier by a Roman horseman, who was dragging him along by the hair, he leaped for joy at the sight and lifted up his hands

quidem aut senatu aut populo coram appellato quosdam e primoribus viris domum evocavit transactaque raptim consultatione reliquam diei partem per organa hydraulica[1] novi et ignoti generis circumduxit, ostendensque singula, de ratione ac difficultate cuiusque disserens, iam se etiam prolaturum omnia in theatrum affirmavit, si per Vindicem liceat.

XLII. Postquam deinde etiam Galbam et Hispanias descivisse cognovit, conlapsus animoque male facto diu sine voce et prope intermortuus[2] iacuit, utque resipiit, veste discissa, capite converberato, actum de se pronuntiavit consolantique nutriculae et aliis quoque iam principibus similia accidisse memoranti, se vero praeter ceteros inaudita et incognita pati respondit, qui summum imperium vivus amitteret. Nec eo setius quicquam ex consuetudine luxus atque desidiae omisit vel inminuit; quin immo, cum prosperi quiddam ex provinciis nuntiatum esset, super abundantissimam cenam iocularia in defectionis duces carmina lasciveque modulata, quae vulgo notuerunt, etiam gesticulatus est; ac spectaculis theatri clam inlatus cuidam scaenico placenti nuntium misit abuti eum occupationibus suis.

XLIII. Initio statim tumultus multa et inmania, verum non abhorrentia a natura sua creditur destinasse; successores percussoresque summittere exercitus et provincias

2

---

[1] ydraulica, *mss.* [2] intermortuus] intermortuos, *M.*

---

[a] This and the following sentences show Nero's utter failure to realize the real gravity of the situation and his fluctuation between panic fear and fatuous confidence.

[b] Implying that Nero would have been the centre of attraction, if he were not otherwise engaged.

to heaven.[a] Not even on his arrival did he personally address the senate or people, but called some of the leading men to his house and after a hasty consultation spent the rest of the day in exhibiting some water-organs of a new and hitherto unknown form, explaining their several features and lecturing on the theory and complexity of each of them; and he even declared that he would presently produce them all in the theatre "with the kind permission of Vindex."

XLII. Thereafter, having learned that Galba also and the Spanish provinces had revolted, he fainted and lay for a long time insensible, without a word and all but dead. When he came to himself, he rent his robe and beat his brow, declaring that it was all over with him; and when his old nurse tried to comfort him by reminding him that similar evils had befallen other princes before him, he declared that unlike all others he was suffering the unheard of and unparalleled fate of losing the supreme power while he still lived. Nevertheless he did not abandon or amend his slothful and luxurious habits; on the contrary, whenever any good news came from the provinces, he not only gave lavish feasts, but even ridiculed the leaders of the revolt in verses set to licentious music, which have since become public, and accompanied them with gestures; then secretly entering the audience room of the theatre, he sent word to an actor who was making a hit that he was taking advantage of the emperor's busy days.[b]

XLIII. At the very beginning of the revolt it is believed that he formed many plans of monstrous wickedness, but in no way inconsistent with his character: to depose and assassinate the commanders of the armies and

regentibus, quasi conspiratis idemque et unum sentien-
tibus; quidquid ubique exsulum, quidquid in urbe hominum Gallicanorum esset contrucidare, illos ne desciscen-
tibus adgregarentur, hos ut conscios popularium suorum
atque fautores; Gallias exercitibus diripiendas permittere;
senatum universum veneno per convivia necare; urbem
incendere feris in populum immissis, quo difficilius
2 defenderentur. Sed absterritus non tam paenitentia
quam perficiendi desperatione credensque expeditionem
necessariam, consules ante tempus privavit honore atque
in utriusque locum solus iniit consulatum, quasi fatale
esset non posse Gallias debellari nisi a[1] consule. Ac sus-
ceptis fascibus cum post epulas triclinio digrederetur,
innixus umeris familiarium affirmavit, simul ac primum
provinciam attigisset, inermem se in conspectum exercituum proditurum nec quicquam aliud quam fleturum,
revocatisque ad paenitentiam defectoribus insequenti die
laetum inter laetos cantaturum epinicia, quae iam nunc
sibi componi oporteret.

XLIV. In praeparanda expeditione primam curam
habuit deligendi vehicula portandis scaenicis organis con-
cubinasque, quas secum educeret, tondendi ad virilem
modum et securibus peltisque Amazonicis instruendi.
Mox tribus urbanas ad sacramentum citavit ac nullo ido-
neo respondente certum dominis servorum numerum
indixit; nec nisi ex tota cuiusque familia probatissimos, ne

---

[1] a] a se, ς.

---

[a] Since Nero commanded the army, the consul in question
must be himself; hence the *se* of ς is unnecessary.

the governors of the provinces, on the ground that they were all united in a conspiracy against him; to massacre all the exiles everywhere and all men of Gallic birth in the city: the former, to prevent them from joining the rebels; the latter, as sharing and abetting the designs of their countrymen; to turn over the Gallic provinces to his armies to ravage; to poison the entire senate at banquets; to set fire to the city, first letting the wild beasts loose, that it might be harder for the people to protect themselves. But he was deterred from these designs, not so much by any compunction, as because he despaired of being able to carry them out, and feeling obliged to take the field, he deposed the consuls before the end of their term and assumed the office alone in place of both of them, alleging that it was fated that the Gallic provinces could not be subdued except by a consul.[a] Having assumed the fasces, he declared as he was leaving the diningroom after a banquet, leaning on the shoulders of his comrades, that immediately on setting foot in the province he would go before the soldiers unarmed and do nothing but weep; and having thus led the rebels to change their purpose, he would next day rejoice among his rejoicing subjects and sing paeans of victory, which he ought at that very moment to be composing.

XLIV. In preparing for his campaign his first care was to select wagons to carry his theatrical instruments, to have the hair of his concubines, whom he planned to take with him, trimmed man-fashion, and to equip them with Amazonian axes and shields. Next he summoned the city tribes to enlist, and when no eligible person responded, he levied on their masters a stated number of slaves, accepting only the choicest from each household and not

161

dispensatoribus quidem aut amanuensibus exceptis,

2 recepit. Partem etiam census omnes ordines conferre iussit et insuper inquilinos privatarum aedium atque insularum pensionem annuam repraesentare fisco; exegitque ingenti fastidio et acerbitate nummum asperum, argentum pustulatum, aurum ad obrussam, ut plerique omnem collationem palam recusarent, consensu flagitantes a delatoribus potius revocanda praemia quaecumque cepissent.

XLV. Ex annonae quoque caritate lucranti[1] adcrevit invidia; nam et forte accidit, ut in publica fame Alexandrina navis nuntiaretur pulverem luctatoribus aulicis advexisse.

2 Quare omnium in se odio incitato nihil contumeliarum defuit quin subiret. Statuae eius a vertice cirrus appositus est cum inscriptione Graeca; nunc demum agona esse, et traderet tandem. Alterius collo ἀσκὸς praeligatus[2] simulque titulus: "Ego egi quod potui.[3] Sed tu cullum[4] meruisti." Ascriptum et columnis, etiam Gallos eum cantando excitasse. Iam noctibus iurgia cum servis plerique simulantes crebro vindicem poscebant.

---

[1] lucranti, *Oudendorp*; lucrantia, Ω; lucrantium, ⸂.

[2] ἀσκὸς praeligatus, *Howard* (*Harv. Stud.* vii. 208); ascopa deligata, *mss.*   [3] ego egi quod potui, *Howard*; ego quid potui, Ω.   [4] cullum, *Howard*; culleum, Ω.

---

[a] Instead of to their landlords. These people had no rating on the census list and their contribution took this form.   [b] That is, tested by fire; see Pliny, *N.H.* 33. 59.   [c] By using, for his own purposes, ships which would otherwise have been loaded with grain; but the text and the meaning are uncertain.

even exempting paymasters and secretaries. He also required all classes to contribute a part of their incomes, and all tenants of private houses and apartments to pay a year's rent at once to the privy purse.[a] With great fastidiousness and rigour he demanded newly minted coin, refined silver, and pure gold,[b] so that many openly refused to make any contribution at all, unanimously demanding that he should rather compel the informers to give up whatever rewards had been paid them.

XLV. The bitter feeling against him was increased because he also turned the high cost of grain to his profit;[c] for indeed, it so fell out that while the people were suffering from hunger it was reported that a ship had arrived from Alexandria, bringing sand for the court wrestlers.

When he had thus aroused the hatred of all, there was no form of insult to which he was not subjected. A curl[d] was placed on the head of his statue with the inscription in Greek: "Now there is a real contest[e] and you must at last surrender." To the neck of another statue a sack was tied and with it the words: "I have done what I could, but you have earned the sack."[f] People wrote on the columns that he had stirred up even the Gauls[g] by his singing. When night came on, many men pretended to be wrangling with their slaves and kept calling out for a defender.[h]

[d] Doubtless an allusion to the long hair which he wore during his Greek trip; see chap. li.   [e] In contrast with those of the stage.   [f] The one in which parricides were put; see *Aug.* xxxiii. 1. But the text and the meaning are uncertain. Cf. Juv. 8. 213.   [g] There is obviously a pun on *Galli*, "Gauls," and *galli*, "cocks," and on *cantare* in the sense of "sing" and of "crow."

[h] Punning of course on Vindex, the leader of the revolt.

XLVI. Terrebatur ad hoc evidentibus portentis somniorum et auspiciorum et ominum, cum veteribus tum novis. Numquam antea somniare solitus occisa demum matre vidit per quietem navem sibi regenti extortum gubernaculum trahique se ab Octavia uxore in artissimas tenebras et modo pinnatarum formicarum multitudine oppleri, modo a simulacris gentium ad Pompei theatrum dedicatarum circumiri arcerique progressu; asturconem, quo maxime laetabatur, posteriore corporis parte in simiae speciem transfiguratum ac tantum capite integro 2 hinnitus edere canoros. De Mausoleo, sponte foribus patefactis, exaudita vox est nomine eum cientis. Kal. Ian. exornati Lares in ipso sacrificii apparatu conciderunt; auspicanti Sporus anulum muneri optulit, cuius gemmae scalptura[1] erat Proserpinae raptus; votorum nuncupatione, magna iam ordinum frequentia, vix repertae Capi- 3 tolii claves. Cum ex oratione eius, qua in Vindicem perorabat, recitaretur in senatu daturos poenas sceleratos ac brevi dignum exitum facturos, conclamatum est ab universis: "Tu facies, Auguste." Observatum etiam fuerat novissimam fabulam cantasse eum publice Oedipodem exsulem atque in hoc desisse[2] versu:

$$\theta\alpha\nu\epsilon\hat{\iota}\nu\ \mu'\ \check{\alpha}\nu\omega\gamma\epsilon^3\ \sigma\acute{\upsilon}\gamma\gamma\alpha\mu\circ\varsigma,\ \mu\acute{\eta}\tau\eta\rho,\ \pi\alpha\tau\acute{\eta}\rho.$$

[1] scalptura] sculptura, Ω.
[2] desisse, ς; dedisse, MX (dixisse, P); finem dedisse, G; decidisse, Υ.
[3] μ' ἄνωγε] μενωγε, Ω.

---

[a] On the first of January, for the prosperity of the emperor and the State.

[b] Of course used in a double sense.

XLVI. In addition he was frightened by manifest portents from dreams, auspices and omens, both old and new. Although he had never before been in the habit of dreaming, after he had killed his mother it seemed to him that he was steering a ship in his sleep and that the helm was wrenched from his hands; that he was dragged by his wife Octavia into thickest darkness, and that he was now covered with a swarm of winged ants, and now was surrounded by the statues of the nations which had been dedicated in Pompey's theatre and stopped in his tracks. A Spanish steed of which he was very fond was changed into the form of an ape in the hinder parts of its body, and its head, which alone remained unaltered, gave forth tuneful neighs. The doors of the Mausoleum flew open of their own accord, and a voice was heard from within summoning him by name. After the Lares had been adorned on the Kalends of January, they fell to the ground in the midst of the preparations for the sacrifice. As he was taking the auspices, Sporus made him a present of a ring with a stone on which was engraved the rape of Proserpina. When the vows were to be taken[a] and a great throng of all classes had assembled, the keys of the Capitol could not be found for a long time. When a speech of his in which he assailed Vindex was being read in the senate, at the words "the wretches will suffer punishment and will shortly meet the end which they deserve," all who were present cried out with one voice: "You will do it, Augustus."[b] It also had not failed of notice that the last piece which he sang in public was "Oedipus in Exile," and that he ended with the line:

Wife, father, mother drive me to my death.

XLVII. Nuntiata interim etiam ceterorum exercituum defectione litteras prandenti sibi redditas concerpsit, mensam subvertit, duos scyphos gratissimi usus, quos Homerios a caelatura carminum Homeri vocabat, solo inlisit ac sumpto a Lucusta veneno et in auream pyxidem condito transiit in hortos Servilianos, ubi praemissis libertorum fidissimis Ostiam ad classem praeparandam tribunos centurionesque praetorii de fugae societate

2 temptavit. Sed partim tergiversantibus, partim aperte detrectantibus, uno vero etiam proclamante:

"Usque adeone mori miserum est?"

varie agitavit, Parthosne an Galbam supplex peteret, an atratus prodiret in publicum proque rostris quanta maxima posset miseratione veniam praeteritorum precaretur, ac ni flexisset animos, vel Aegypti praefecturam concedi sibi oraret. Inventus est postea in scrinio eius hac de re sermo formatus; sed deterritum putant, ne prius quam in Forum perveniret discerperetur.

3 Sic cogitatione in posterum diem dilata ad mediam fere noctem excitatus, ut comperit stationem militum recessisse, prosiliuit e lecto misitque circum amicos, et quia nihil a quoquam renuntiabatur, ipse cum paucis hospitia singulorum adiit. Verum clausis omnium foribus, respondente nullo, in cubiculum rediit, unde iam et

---

[a] Pliny, *N.H.* 37. 29, tells us that the cups were of crystal.
[b] Virg. *Aen.* 12. 646.
[c] In the Palace.

XLVII. When meanwhile word came that the other armies had revolted, he tore to pieces the dispatches which were handed to him as he was dining, tipped over the table, and dashed to the ground two favourite drinking cups, which he called "Homeric," because they were carved with scenes from Homer's poems.[a] Then taking some poison from Lucusta and putting it into a golden box, he crossed over into the Servilian gardens, where he tried to induce the tribunes and centurions of the Guard to accompany him in his flight, first sending his most trustworthy freedmen to Ostia, to get a fleet ready. But when some gave evasive answers and some openly refused, one even cried:

"Is it so dreadful a thing then to die?"[b]

Whereupon he turned over various plans in his mind, whether to go as a suppliant to the Parthians or Galba, or to appear to the people on the rostra, dressed in black, and beg as pathetically as he could for pardon for his past offences; and if he could not soften their hearts, to entreat them at least to allow him the prefecture of Egypt. Afterwards a speech composed for this purpose was found in his writing desk; but it is thought that he did not dare to deliver it for fear of being torn to pieces before he could reach the Forum.

Having therefore put off further consideration to the following day, he awoke about midnight and finding that the guard of soldiers had left, he sprang from his bed and sent for all his friends. Since no reply came back from anyone, he went himself to their rooms[c] with a few followers. But finding that all the doors were closed and that no one replied to him, he returned to his own cham-

custodes diffugerant, direptis etiam stragulis, amota et pyxide veneni; ac statim Spiculum murmillonem vel quemlibet alium percussorem, cuius manu periret, requisiit et nemine reperto: "Ergo ego," inquit, "nec amicum habeo nec inimicum?" procurritque, quasi praecipitaturus se in Tiberim.

XLVIII. Sed revocato rursus impetu aliquid secretioris latebrae ad colligendum animum desideravit, et offerente Phaonte liberto suburbanum suum inter Salariam et Nomentanam viam circa quartum miliarium, ut erat nudo pede atque tunicatus, paenulam obsoleti coloris superinduit adopertoque capite et ante faciem optento sudario equum inscendit, quattuor solis comitan-

2 tibus, inter quos et Sporus erat. Statimque tremore terrae et fulgure adverso pavefatus audiit e proximis castris clamorem militum et sibi adversa et Galbae prospera ominantium, etiam ex obviis viatoribus quendam dicentem: "Hi Neronem persequuntur," alium sciscitantem: "Ecquid[1] in urbe novi de Nerone?" Equo autem ex odore abiecti in via cadaveris consternato, detecta facie agnitus

3 est a quodam missicio praetoriano et salutatus. Ut ad deverticulum ventum est, dimissis equis inter fruticeta ac vepres per harundineti semitam aegre nec nisi strata sub pedibus veste ad aversum[2] villae parietem evasit. Ibi hortante eodem Phaonte, ut interim in specum egestae

[1] ecquid, *second Roman edition*; etquid, Ω.
[2] aversum, *J. F. Gronov*; adversum, Ω.

---

[a] See chap. xxx. 2.
[b] The word *percussor* implies experience in dealing death. Nero wished to be killed swiftly and painlessly.

ber, from which now the very caretakers had fled, taking with them even the bed-clothing and the box of poison. Then he at once called for the gladiator Spiculus[a] or any other adept[b] at whose hand he might find death, and when no one appeared, he cried "Have I then neither friend nor foe?" and ran out as if to throw himself into the Tiber.

XLVIII. Changing his purpose again, he sought for some retired place, where he could hide and collect his thoughts; and when his freedman Phaon offered his villa in the suburbs between the Via Nomentana and the Via Salaria near the fourth milestone, just as he was, bare-footed and in his tunic, he put on a faded cloak, covered his head, and holding a handkerchief before his face, mounted a horse with only four attendants, one of whom was Sporus. At once he was startled by a shock of earth-quake and a flash of lightning full in his face, and he heard the shouts of the soldiers from the camp hard by, as they prophesied destruction for him and success for Galba. He also heard one of the wayfarers whom he met say: "These men are after Nero," and another ask: "Is there anything new in the city about Nero?" Then his horse took fright at the smell of a corpse which had been thrown out into the road, his face was exposed, and a retired soldier of the Guard recognised him and saluted him. When they came to a by-path leading to the villa, they turned the horses loose and he made his way amid bushes and brambles and along a path through a thicket of reeds to the back wall of the house, with great difficulty and only when a robe was thrown down for him to walk on. Here the aforesaid Phaon urged him to hide for a time in a pit, from which sand had been dug, but he

harenae concederet, negavit se vivum sub terram iturum, ac parumper commoratus, dum clandestinus ad villam introitus pararetur, aquam ex subiecta lacuna poturus manu hausit et: "Haec est," inquit, "Neronis decocta."

4 Dein divolsa sentibus paenula traiectos surculos rasit, atque ita quadripes per angustias effossae cavernae receptus in proximam cellam decubuit super lectum modica culcita, vetere pallio strato, instructum; fameque et iterum siti interpellante panem quidem sordidum oblatum aspernatus est, aquae autem tepidae aliquantum bibit.

XLIX. Tunc uno quoque hinc inde instante ut quam primum se impendentibus contumeliis eriperet, scrobem coram fieri imperavit dimensus ad corporis sui modulum, componique simul, si qua invenirentur, frusta marmoris et aquam simul ac ligna conferri curando mox cadaveri, flens ad singula atque identidem dictitans: "Qualis artifex pereo!"

2 Inter moras perlatos a cursore Phaonti codicillos praeripuit legitque se hostem a senatu iudicatum et quaeri, ut puniatur more maiorum, interrogavitque quale id genus esset poenae; et cum comperisset nudi hominis cervicem inseri furcae, corpus virgis ad necem caedi, conterritus duos pugiones, quos secum extulerat, arripuit temptataque utriusque acie rursus condidit, causatus

---

ᵃ Referring to a drink of his own contrivance, distilled water cooled in snow; cf. Pliny, *N.H.* 31. 40.

ᵇ *Cella* implies a small room, for the use of slaves.

ᶜ The water was for washing the corpse and the fire for burning it.   ᵈ Cf. *Claud.* xxxiv. 1.

ᵉ Two pieces of wood, fastened together in the form of a ∨.

declared that he would not go under ground while still alive, and after waiting for a while until a secret entrance into the villa could be made, he scooped up in his hand some water to drink from a pool close by, saying: "This is Nero's distilled water."[a] Then, as his cloak had been torn by the thorns, he pulled out the twigs which had pierced it, and crawling on all fours through a narrow passage that had been dug, he entered the villa and lay down in the first room[b] he came to, on a couch with a common mattress, over which an old cloak had been thrown. Though suffering from hunger and renewed thirst, he refused some coarse bread which was offered him, but drank a little lukewarm water.

XLIX. At last, while his companions one and all urged him to save himself as soon as possible from the indignities that threatened him, he bade them dig a grave in his presence, proportioned to the size of his own person, collect any bits of marble that could be found, and at the same time bring water and wood for presently disposing of his body.[c] As each of these things was done, he wept and said again and again: "What an artist the world is losing!"

While he hesitated, a letter was brought to Phaon by one of his couriers. Nero snatching it from his hand read that he had been pronounced a public enemy by the senate, and that they were seeking him to punish him in the ancient fashion;[d] and he asked what manner of punishment that was. When he learned that the criminal was stripped, fastened by the neck in a fork[e] and then beaten to death with rods, in mortal terror he seized two daggers which he had brought with him, and then, after trying the point of each, put them up again, pleading that the fated

3   nondum adesse fatalem horam. Ac modo Sporum horta-
batur ut lamentari ac plangere inciperet, modo orabat ut
se aliquis ad mortem capessendam exemplo iuvaret; interdum segnitiem suam his verbis increpabat: "Vivo defor-
miter, turpiter—οὐ πρέπει Νέρωνι, οὐ πρέπει—νήφειν
δεῖ ἐν τοῖς τοιούτοις—ἄγε ἔγειρε σεαυτόν." Iamque
equites appropinquabant, quibus praeceptum erat ut
vivum eum adtraherent. Quod ut sensit, trepidanter
effatus:

ἵππων μ' ὠκυπόδων ἀμφὶ κτύπος οὔατα βάλλει,

ferrum iugulo adegit iuvante Epaphrodito a libellis.
4   Semianimisque adhuc irrumpenti centurioni et paenula
ad vulnus adposita in auxilium se venisse simulanti non
aliud respondit quam: "Sero," et: "Haec est fides." Atque
in ea voce defecit, exstantibus rigentibusque oculis usque
ad horrorem formidinemque visentium. Nihil prius aut
magis a comitibus exegerat quam ne potestas cuiquam
capitis sui fieret, sed ut quoquo modo totus cremaretur.
Permisit hoc Icelus,[1] Galbae libertus, non multo ante vinculis exsolutus, in quae primo tumultu coniectus fuerat.

   L. Funeratus est impensa ducentorum milium, stragulis albis auro intextis, quibus usus Kal. Ian. fuerat.
Reliquias Egloge[2] et Alexandria nutrices cum Acte con-
cubina gentili Domitiorum monimento condiderunt,
quod prospicitur e campo Martio impositum colli[3] Hortu-

---

[1] Icelus, *Politianus*; hiceius, Ω.
[2] Egloge] Ecloge, *Basle ed. of* 1533.
[3] colli, *Stephanus*; colle, ς; collo, Ω.

---

[a] *Iliad.* 10. 535.   [b] See *Domit.* xiv. 4.
[c] See *Galba*, xiv. 2.   [d] The modern Pincio.

hour had not yet come. Now he would beg Sporus to begin to lament and wail, and now entreat someone to help him take his life by setting him the example; anon he reproached himself for his cowardice in such words as these: "To live is a scandal and shame—this does not become Nero, does not become him—one should be resolute at such times—come, rouse thyself!" And now the horsemen were at hand who had orders to take him off alive. When he heard them, he quavered:

"Hark, now strikes on my ear the trampling of swift-footed coursers!"[a]

and drove a dagger into his throat, aided by Epaphroditus, his private secretary.[b] He was all but dead when a centurion rushed in, and as he placed a cloak to the wound, pretending that he had come to aid him, Nero merely gasped: "Too late!" and "This is fidelity!" With these words he was gone, with eyes so set and starting from their sockets that all who saw him shuddered with horror. First and beyond all else he had forced from his companions a promise to let no one have his head, but to contrive in some way that he be buried unmutilated. And this was granted by Icelus, Galba's freedman,[c] who had shortly before been released from the bondage to which he was consigned at the beginning of the revolt.

L. He was buried at a cost of two hundred thousand sesterces and laid out in white robes embroidered with gold, which he had worn on the Kalends of January. His ashes were deposited by his nurses, Egloge and Alexandria, accompanied by his mistress Acte, in the family tomb of the Domitii on the summit of the Hill of Gardens,[d] which is visible from the Campus Martius. In

lorum. In eo monimento solium porphyretici marmoris, superstante Lunensi ara, circumsaeptum est lapide Thasio.

LI. Statura fuit prope iusta, corpore maculoso et fetido, subflavo capillo, vultu pulchro magis quam venusto, oculis caesis et hebetioribus, cervice obesa, ventre proiecto, gracillimis cruribus, valitudine prospera; nam qui luxuriae immoderatissimae esset, ter omnino per quattuordecim annos languit, atque ita ut neque vino neque consuetudine reliqua abstineret; circa cultum habitumque adeo pudendus, ut comam semper in gradus formatam peregrinatione Achaica etiam pone verticem summiserit ac plerumque synthesinam indutus ligato circum collum sudario prodierit in publicum sine cinctu et discalciatus.

LII. Liberalis disciplinas omnis fere puer attigit. Sed a philosophia eum mater avertit monens imperaturo contrariam esse; a cognitione veterum oratorum Seneca praeceptor, quo diutius in admiratione sui detineret. Itaque ad poeticam pronus carmina libenter ac sine labore composuit nec, ut quidam putant, aliena pro suis edidit. Venere in manus meas pugillares libellique cum quibusdam notissimis versibus ipsius chirographo scriptis, ut facile appareret non tralatos aut dictante aliquo exceptos, sed plane quasi a cogitante atque generante exaratos; ita multa et deleta et inducta et superscripta inerant.

---

[a] The *synthesina* (sc. *vestis*), or *synthesis*, was a loose robe of bright-coloured silk, worn at dinner, during the Saturnalia, and by women at other times. Nero's is described by Dio, 63. 13, as "a short, flowered tunic with a muslin collar."

[b] Probably meaning "in slippers."

that monument his sarcophagus of porphyry, with an altar of Luna marble standing above it, is enclosed by a balustrade of Thasian stone.

LI. He was about the average height, his body marked with spots and malodorous, his hair light blond, his features regular rather than attractive, his eyes blue and somewhat weak, his neck over thick, his belly prominent, and his legs very slender. His health was good, for though indulging in every kind of riotous excess, he was ill but three times in all during the fourteen years of his reign, and even then not enough to give up wine or any of his usual habits. He was utterly shameless in the care of his person and in his dress, always having his hair arranged in tiers of curls, and during the trip to Greece also letting it grow long and hang down behind; and he often appeared in public in a dining-robe,[a] with a handkerchief bound about his neck, ungirt and unshod.[b]

LII. When a boy he took up almost all the liberal arts; but his mother turned him from philosophy, warning him that it was a drawback to one who was going to rule, while Seneca kept him from reading the early orators, to make his admiration for his teacher endure the longer. Turning therefore to poetry, he wrote verses with eagerness and without labour, and did not, as some think, publish the work of others as his own. I have had in my possession note-books and papers with some well-known verses of his, written with his own hand and in such wise that it was perfectly evident that they were not copied or taken down from dictation, but worked out exactly as one writes when thinking and creating; so many instances were there of words erased or struck through and written above the

Habuit et pingendi fingendique[1] non mediocre studium.

LIII. Maxime[2] autem popularitate efferebatur, omnium aemulus, qui quoquo modo animum vulgi moverent. Exiit opinio post scaenicas coronas proximo lustro descensurum eum ad Olympia[3] inter athletas; nam et luctabatur assidue nec aliter certamina gymnica tota Graecia spectaverat quam brabeutarum more in stadio humi assidens ac, si qua paria longius recessissent, in medium manibus suis protrahens. Destinaverat etiam, quia Apollinem cantu, Solem aurigando aequiperare existimaretur, imitari et Herculis facta; praeparatumque leonem aiunt, quem vel clava vel brachiorum nexibus in amphitheatri harena spectante populo nudus elideret.

LIV. Sub exitu quidem vitae palam voverat, si sibi incolumis status permansisset, proditurum se partae victoriae ludis etiam hydraulam et choraulam et utricularium ac novissimo die histrionem saltaturumque Vergili Turnum. Et sunt qui tradant Paridem histrionem occisum ab eo quasi gravem adversarium.

LV. Erat illi aeternitatis perpetuaeque famae cupido, sed inconsulta. Ideoque multis rebus ac locis vetere appellatione detracta novam indixit ex suo nomine, mensem quoque Aprilem Neroneum appellavit; destinaverat et Romam Neropolim nuncupare.

[1] Ω *had* maxime *after* fingendique, *a misplaced emendation of the following* maxima.
[2] maxime, ς; maxima, Ω.
[3] Olympia, ς; Olympiam, Ω.

---

[a] See note on *Aug.* xcvii. 1. Here *lustrum* is applied to the five-year period of the Olympic games.

lines. He likewise had no slight interest in painting and sculpture.

LIII. But above all he was carried away by a craze for popularity and he was jealous of all who in any way stirred the feeling of the mob. It was the general belief that after his victories on the stage he would at the next lustrum[a] have competed with the athletes at Olympia; for he practised wrestling constantly, and all over Greece he had always viewed the gymnastic contests after the fashion of the judges, sitting on the ground in the stadium; and if any pairs of contestants withdrew too far from their positions, he would force them forward with his own hand. Since he was acclaimed as the equal of Apollo in music and of the Sun in driving a chariot, he had planned to emulate the exploits of Hercules as well; and they say that a lion had been specially trained for him to kill naked in the arena of the amphitheatre before all the people, with a club or by the clasp of his arms.

LIV. Towards the end of his life, in fact, he had publicly vowed that if he retained his power, he would at the games in celebration of his victory give a performance on the water-organ, the flute, and the bagpipes, and that on the last day he would appear as an actor and dance "Virgil's Turnus." Some even assert that he put the actor Paris to death as a dangerous rival.

LV. He had a longing for immortality and undying fame, though it was ill-regulated. With this in view he took their former appellations from many things and numerous places and gave them new ones from his own name. He also called the month of April Neroneus and was minded to name Rome Neropolis.

LVI. Religionum usque quaque contemptor, praeter unius Deae Syriae,ᵃ hanc mox ita sprevit ut urina contaminaret, alia superstitione captus, in qua sola pertinacissime haesit, siquidem imagunculam puellarem, cum quasi remedium insidiarum a plebeio quodam et ignoto muneri accepisset, detecta confestim coniuratione pro summo numine trinisque in die sacrificiis colere perseveravit volebatque credi monitione eius futura praenoscere. Ante paucos quam periret menses attendit et extispicio nec umquam litavit.

LVII. Obiit tricensimo et secundo aetatis anno, die quo quondam Octaviam interemerat, tantumque gaudium publice praebuit, ut plebs pilleata tota urbe discurreret. Et tamen non defuerunt qui per longum tempus vernis aestivisque floribus tumulum eius ornarent ac modo imagines praetextatas in rostris proferrent, modo edicta quasi viventis et brevi magno inimicorum malo reversuri. Quin etiam Vologaesus Parthorum rex missis ad senatum legatis de instauranda societate hoc etiam magno opere oravit, ut Neronis memoria coleretur. Denique cum post viginti annos adulescente me exstitisset condicionis incertae qui se Neronem esse iactaret, tam favorabile nomen eius apud Parthos fuit, ut vehementer adiutus et vix redditus sit.ᵈ

ᵃ Atargatis, the principal deity of Northern Syria, identified with Magna Mater and Caelestis; often mentioned in inscriptions and called by Apul. *Metam.* 8. 25, *omnipotens et omniparens.*

ᵇ In A.D. 68.

ᶜ See note on *Tib.* iv. 2.

ᵈ In 88, Terentius Maximus by name; another pseudo-Nero had appeared in 70; see Tac. *Hist.* 2. 8.

LVI. He utterly despised all cults, with the sole exception of that of the Syrian Goddess,[a] and even acquired such a contempt for her that he made water on her image, after he was enamoured of another superstition, which was the only one to which he constantly clung. For he had received as a gift from some unknown man of the commons, as a protection against plots, a little image of a girl; and since a conspiracy at once came to light, he continued to venerate it as a powerful divinity and to offer three sacrifices to it every day, encouraging the belief that through its communication he had knowledge of the future. A few months before his death he did attend an inspection of victims, but could not get a favourable omen.

LVII. He met his death[b] in the thirty-second year of his age, on the anniversary of the murder of Octavia, and such was the public rejoicing that the people put on liberty-caps[c] and ran about all over the city. Yet there were some who for a long time decorated his tomb with spring and summer flowers, and now produced his statues on the rostra in the fringed toga, and now his edicts, as if he were still alive and would shortly return and deal destruction to his enemies. Nay more, Vologaesus, king of the Parthians, when he sent envoys to the senate to renew his alliance, earnestly begged this too, that honour be paid to the memory of Nero. In fact, twenty years later, when I was a young man, a person of obscure origin appeared, who gave out that he was Nero,[d] and the name was still in such favour with the Parthians that they supported him vigorously and surrendered him with great reluctance.

LIBER VII

GALBA · OTHO · VITELLIUS

GALBA

I. Progenies Caesarum in Nerone defecit: quod futurum compluribus quidem signis, sed vel evidentissimis duobus apparuit. Liviae olim post Augusti statim nuptias Veientanum suum revisenti praetervolans aquila gallinam albam ramulum lauri rostro tenentem, ita ut rapuerat, demisit in gremium; cumque nutriri alitem, pangi ramulum placuisset, tanta pullorum suboles provenit, ut hodieque ea villa "ad Gallinas" vocetur, tale vero lauretum, ut triumphaturi Caesares inde laureas decerperent; fuitque mos triumphantibus, alias confestim eodem loco pangere; et observatum est sub cuiusque obitum arborem ab ipso institutam elanguisse. Ergo novissimo Neronis anno et silva omnis exaruit radicitus, et quidquid ibi gallinarum erat interiit. Ac subinde tacta de caelo Caesarum

---

[a] Nero was the last who bore the name because of connection with the family of Augustus; after him it became a designation of rank.

[b] In 38 B.C.   [c] "The Hen Roost."

[d] Those which they carried in their triumph, according to Pliny, *N.H.* 15. 136 f.

BOOK VII

GALBA · OTHO · VITELLIUS

GALBA

I. The race of the Caesars ended with Nero.[a] That this would be so was shown by many portents and especially by two very significant ones. Years before, as Livia was returning to her estate near Veii, immediately after her marriage with Augustus,[b] an eagle which flew by dropped into her lap a white hen, holding in its beak a sprig of laurel, just as the eagle had carried it off. Livia resolved to rear the fowl and plant the sprig, whereupon such a great brood of chickens was hatched that to this day the villa is called *Ad Gallinas*,[c] and such a grove of laurel sprang up that the Caesars gathered their laurels from it when they were going to celebrate triumphs. Moreover it was the habit of those who triumphed to plant other branches[d] at once in that same place, and it was observed that just before the death of each of them the tree which he had planted withered. Now in Nero's last year the whole grove died from the root up, as well as all the hens. Furthermore, when shortly afterwards the temple of the Caesars[e] was struck by lightning, the heads

[e] Uncertain; but see Pliny *NH* 12. 94.

aede capita omnibus simul statuis deciderunt, Augusti etiam sceptrum e manibus excussum est.

II. Neroni Galba successit nullo gradu contingens Caesarum domum, sed haud dubie nobilissimus magnaque et vetere prosapia, ut qui statuarum titulis pronepotem se Quinti Catuli Capitolini semper ascripserit, imperator vero etiam stemma in atrio proposuerit, quo paternam originem ad Iovem, maternam ad Pasiphaam Minonis uxorem referret.

III. Imagines et elogia universi generis exsequi longum est, familiae breviter attingam. Qui primus Sulpiciorum cognomen Galbae tulit cur aut unde traxerit, ambigitur. Quidam putant, quod oppidum Hispaniae frustra diu oppugnatum inlitis demum galbano facibus succenderit; alii, quod in diuturna valitudine galbeo, id est remediis lana involutis, assidue uteretur; nonnulli, quod praepinguis fuerit visus, quem galbam Galli vocent; vel contra, quod tam exilis, quam sunt animalia quae in aesculis nascuntur appellanturque galbae.

2   Familiam illustravit Servius Galba consularis, temporum suorum vel[1] eloquentissimus, quem tradunt Hispaniam ex praetura optinentem, triginta Lusitanorum milibus perfidia trucidatis, Viriathini belli causam exstitisse. Eius nepos ob repulsam consulatus infensus Iulio Caesari, cuius legatus in Gallia fuerat, conspiravit cum

---

[1] vel, *Bentley*; et, *mss. except* II[1], *which omits the word.*

[a] In A.D. 68.

[b] No existing inscription confirms this statement.

[c] That is, of those of the Sulpicii who bore the surname Galba.   [d] The gum of a Syrian plant; see Pliny, *N.H.* 12. 126.

[e] In 145 B.C.   [f] In 150–136 B.C.

fell from all the statues at the same time, and his sceptre, too, was dashed from the hand of Augustus.

II. Nero was succeeded by Galba,[a] who was related in no degree to the house of the Caesars, although unquestionably of noble origin and of an old and powerful family; for he always added to the inscriptions on his statues that he was the great-grandson of Quintus Catulus Capitolinus,[b] and when he became emperor he even displayed a family tree in his hall in which he carried back his ancestry on his father's side to Jupiter and on his mother's to Pasiphae, the wife of Minos.

III. It would be a long story to give in detail his illustrious ancestors and the honorary inscriptions of the entire race, but I shall give a brief account of his immediate family.[c] It is uncertain why the first of the Sulpicii who bore the surname Galba assumed the name, and whence it was derived. Some think that it was because after having for a long time unsuccessfully besieged a town in Spain, he at last set fire to it by torches smeared with *galbanum*;[d] others because during a long illness he made constant use of *galbeum*, that is to say of remedies wrapped in wool; still others, because he was a very fat man, such as the Gauls term *galba*, or because he was, on the contrary, as slender as the insects called *galbae*, which breed in oak trees.

The family acquired distinction from Servius Galba, who became consul[e] and was decidedly the most eloquent speaker of his time. This man, they say, was the cause of the war with Viriathus,[f] because while governing Spain as propraetor, he treacherously massacred thirty thousand of the Lusitanians. His grandson had been one of Caesar's lieutenants in Gaul, but angered because

Cassio et Bruto, propter quod Pedia lege damnatus est.
3 Ab hoc sunt imperatoris Galbae avus ac pater: avus clarior
studiis quam dignitate—non enim egressus praeturae
gradum—multiplicem nec incuriosam historiam edidit;
pater consulatu functus, quanquam brevi corpore atque
etiam gibber modicaeque in dicendo facultatis, causas
4 industrie actitavit. Uxores habuit Mummiam Achaicam,
neptem Catuli proneptemque L. Mummi, qui Corinthum
excidit; item Liviam Ocellinam ditem admodum et pul-
chram, a qua tamen nobilitatis causa appetitus ultro existimatur et aliquanto enixius, postquam subinde instanti
vitium corporis secreto posita veste detexit, ne quasi
ignaram fallere videretur. Ex Achaica liberos Gaium et
Servium[1] procreavit, quorum maior Gaius attritis facul-
tatibus urbe cessit prohibitusque a Tiberio sortiri anno
suo proconsulatum voluntaria morte obiit.

IV. Ser. Galba imperator M. Valerio Messala Cn.[2]
Lentulo coss. natus est VIIII. Kal. Ian. in villa colli super-
posita prope Tarracinam[3] sinistrorsus Fundos petentibus,
adoptatusque a noverca sua Livia nomen et Ocellare cognomen assumpsit mutato praenomine; nam Lucium mox
pro Servio[4] usque ad tempus imperii usurpavit. Constat

---

[1] Servium, *Glareanus*; Sergium, Ω.
[2] Cn., *mss.*; *it should be* L.
[3] Terracinam, Ω.   [4] Sergio, Ω.

---

[a] See *Nero*, iii. 1.   [b] In A.D. 22.
[c] That is, after his consulship. Tiberius doubtless suspected
him of a desire to enrich himself at the expense of the provincials; cf. *Tib*. xxxii. 2, at the end.
[d] On December 24, 3 B.C.

his commander caused his defeat for the consulship, he joined the conspiracy with Brutus and Cassius, and was consequently condemned to death by the Pedian law.[a] From him were descended the grandfather and the father of the emperor Galba. The former, who was more eminent for his learning than for his rank—for he did not advance beyond the grade of praetor—published a voluminous and painstaking history. The father attained the consulship,[b] and although he was short of stature and even hunchbacked, besides being only an indifferent speaker, was an industrious pleader at the bar. He married Mummia Achaica, the granddaughter of Catulus and great-granddaughter of Lucius Mummius who destroyed Corinth; and later Livia Ocellina, a very rich and beautiful woman, who however is thought to have sought marriage with him because of his high rank, and the more eagerly when, in response to her frequent advances, he took off his robe in private and showed her his deformity, so as not to seem to deceive her by concealing it. By Achaica he had two sons, Gaius and Servius. Gaius, who was the elder, left Rome after squandering the greater part of his estate, and committed suicide because Tiberius would not allow him to take part in the allotment of the provinces in his year.[c]

IV. The emperor Servius Galba was born[d] in the consulship of Marcus Valerius Messala and Gnaeus Lentulus, on the ninth day before the Kalends of January, in a country house situated on a hill near Tarracina, on the left as you go towards Fundi. Adopted by his stepmother Livia, he took her name and the surname Ocella, and also changed his forename; for he used Lucius, instead of Servius, from that time until he became emperor. It is

Augustum puero adhuc, salutanti se inter aequales, apprehensa buccula dixisse: καὶ σὺ τέκνον τῆς ἀρχῆς ἡμῶν παρατρώξῃ.[1] Sed et Tiberius, cum comperisset imperaturum eum verum in senecta: "Vivat sane," ait,

2 "quando id ad nos nihil pertinet." Avo quoque eius fulgur procuranti, cum exta de manibus aquila rapuisset et in frugiferam quercum contulisset, responsum est summum sed serum imperium portendi familiae; et ille irridens; "Sane," inquit, "cum mula pepererit." Nihil aeque postea Galbam temptantem res novas confirmavit quam mulae partus, ceterisque ut obscaenum ostentum abhorrentibus, solus pro laetissimo accepit memor sacrificii dictique avi.

3 Sumpta virili toga somniavit Fortunam dicentem, stare se ante fores defessam et nisi ocius reciperetur, cuicumque obvio praedae futuram. Utque evigilavit, aperto atrio simulacrum aeneum deae cubitali maius iuxta limen invenit idque gremio suo Tusculum, ubi aestivare consueverat, avexit et in parte aedium consecratum menstruis deinceps supplicationibus et pervigilio anniversario coluit.

4 Quanquam autem nondum aetate constanti veterem civitatis exoletumque morem ac tantum in domo sua haerentem obstinatissime retinuit, ut liberti servique bis

---

[1] παρατρώξῃ, *Turnebus*; παρατρωζῃ, Ω.

a The usual procedure, to avert the evil omen.

b Proverbial for "never," like the Greek Kalends (*Aug.* lxxxvii. 1).

well known that when he was still a boy and called to pay his respects to Augustus with others of his age, the emperor pinched his cheek and said in Greek: "Thou too, child, wilt have a nibble at this power of mine." Tiberius too, when he heard that Galba was destined to be emperor, but in his old age, said: "Well, let him live then, since that does not concern me." Again, when Galba's grandfather was busy with a sacrifice for a stroke of lightning,[a] and an eagle snatched the intestines from his hand and carried them to an oak full of acorns, the prediction was made that the highest dignity would come to the family, but late; whereupon he said with a laugh: "Very likely, when a mule has a foal.[b]" Afterwards when Galba was beginning his revolt, nothing gave him so much encouragement as the foaling of a mule, and while the rest were horrified and looked on it as an unfavourable omen, he alone regarded it as most propitious, remembering the sacrifice and his grandfather's saying.

When he assumed the gown of manhood, he dreamt that Fortune said that she was tired of standing before his door, and that unless she were quickly admitted, she would fall a prey to the first comer. When he awoke, opening the door of the hall, he found close by the threshold a bronze statue of Fortune more than a cubit high. This he carried in his arms to Tusculum, where he usually spent the summer, and consecrated it in a room of his house; and from that time on he honoured it with monthly sacrifices and a yearly vigil.

Even before he reached middle life, he persisted in keeping up an old and forgotten custom of his country, which survived only in his own household, of having his

187

die frequentes adessent ac mane salvere, vesperi valere sibi singuli dicerent.

V. Inter liberales disciplinas attendit et iuri. Dedit et matrimonio operam; verum amissa uxore Lepida duobusque ex ea filiis remansit in caelibatu neque sollicitari ulla condicione amplius potuit, ne Agrippinae quidem quae[1] viduata morte Domiti maritum quoque adhuc necdum caelibem Galbam adeo omnibus sollicitaverat modis, ut in conventu matronarum correpta iurgio atque etiam manu pulsata sit a matre Lepidae.

2 Observavit ante omnis Liviam Augustam, cuius et vivae gratia plurimum valuit et mortuae testamento paene ditatus est; sestertium namque quingenties praecipuum inter legatorios habuit, sed quia notata, non perscripta erat summa, herede Tiberio legatum ad quingenta revocante, ne haec quidem accepit.

VI. Honoribus ante legitimum tempus initis praetor commissione ludorum Floralium novum spectaculi genus elephantos funambulos edidit; exim provinciae Aquitaniae anno fere praefuit; mox consulatum per sex menses ordinarium gessit, evenitque ut in eo ipse L.[2] Domitio patri Neronis, ipsi Salvius Otho pater Othonis succederet, velut praesagium insequentis casus, quo medius inter utriusque filios exstitit imperator.

2 A Gaio Caesare legatus Germaniae superioris in

---

[1] quae, *added by G. Becker*; II *and* Q *have it after* Domiti.
[2] L. *mss.* (Lucio, *G*); Cn., *Torrentius.*

---

[a] To marry and rear a family was regarded as one of the duties of a good citizen.   [b] Cf. *Nero*, xi. 2.   [c] That is, entering office on January 1, and with his colleague, L. Cornelius Sulla, giving his name to the year.   [d] In A.D. 33.   [e] Either Suetonius is in error or the manuscripts; the name should be Gnaeus.

freedmen and slaves appear before him twice a day in a body, greeting him in the morning and bidding him farewell at evening, one by one.

V. Among other liberal studies he applied himself to the law. He also assumed a husband's duties,[a] but after losing his wife Lepida and two sons whom he had by her, he remained a widower. And he could not be tempted afterwards by any match, not even with Agrippina, who no sooner lost Domitius by death than she set her cap for Galba so obviously, even before the death of his wife, that Lepida's mother scolded her roundly before a company of matrons and went so far as to slap her.

He showed marked respect to Livia Augusta, to whose favour he owed great influence during her lifetime and by whose last will he almost became a rich man; for he had the largest bequest among her legatees, one of fifty million sesterces. But because the sum was designated in figures and not written out in words, Tiberius, who was her heir, reduced the bequest to five hundred thousand, and Galba never received even that amount.

VI. He began his career of office before the legal age, and in celebrating the games of the Floralia in his praetorship he gave a new kind of exhibition, namely of elephants walking the rope.[b] Then he governed the province of Aquitania for nearly a year and soon afterwards held a regular consulship[c] for six months;[d] and it chanced that in this office he succeeded Lucius[e] Domitius, the father of Nero, and was succeeded by Salvius Otho, the father of the emperor Otho, a kind of omen of what happened later, when he became emperor between the reigns of the sons of these two men.

Appointed governor of Upper Germany by Gaius Cae-

locum Gaetulici[1] substitutus, postridie quam ad legiones venit, sollemni forte spectaculo plaudentes inhibuit data tessera, ut manus paenula[2] continerent; statimque per castra iactatum est:

> Disce miles militare; Galba est, non Gaetulicus.

3 Pari severitate interdixit commeatus peti. Veteranum ac tironem militem opere assiduo corroboravit matureque barbaris, qui iam in Galliam usque proruperant, coercitis, praesenti quoque Gaio talem et se et exercitum approbavit, ut inter innumeras contractasque ex omnibus provinciis copias neque testimonium neque praemia ampliora ulli perciperent; ipse maxime insignis, quod campestrem decursionem scuto moderatus, etiam ad essedum imperatoris per viginti passuum milia cucurrit.

VII. Caede Gai nuntiata multis ad occasionem stimulantibus quietem praetulit. Per hoc gratissimus Claudio receptusque in cohortem amicorum tantae dignationis est habitus, ut cum subita ei valitudo nec adeo gravis incidisset, dilatus sit expeditionis Britannicae dies. Africam pro consule biennio optinuit extra sortem electus ad ordinandam provinciam et intestina dissensione et barbarorum tumultu inquietam; ordinavitque magna severitatis ac 2 iustitiae cura etiam in parvulis rebus. Militi, qui per expe-

---

[1] legatus Germaniae superioris in locum Gaetu-, *supplied by Ihm.* [2] manus paenula, *Salmasius*; manus paenulas, *MXT* (paenulis, *OST*); manu paenulas, *G.*

---

[a] See *Calig.* xliv.
[b] Cf. *Calig.* xxvi. 2.
[c] Except in special cases, the governors were appointed by lot from among those who were eligible.

sar in place of Gaetulicus, the day after he appeared
before the legions he put a stop to their applause at a festival which chanced to fall at that time, by issuing a written order to keep their hands under their cloaks; and
immediately this verse was bandied about the camp:

> Soldiers, learn to play the soldier; it's Galba, not
> Gaetulicus.

With equal strictness he put a stop to the requests for
furloughs. He got both the veterans and the new recruits
into condition by plenty of hard work, speedily checked
the barbarians, who had already made inroads even into
Gaul, and when Gaius arrived,[a] Galba and his army made
such a good impression that out of the great body of
troops assembled from all the provinces none received
greater commendation or richer rewards. Galba particularly distinguished himself, while directing the military
manoeuvres shield in hand, by actually running for
twenty miles close beside the emperor's chariot.[b]

VII. When the murder of Gaius was announced,
although many urged Galba to take advantage of the
opportunity, he preferred quiet. Hence he was in high
favour with Claudius, became one of his staff of intimate
friends, and was treated with such consideration that the
departure of the expedition to Britain was put off because
Galba was taken with a sudden illness, of no great severity. He governed Africa for two years with the rank of
proconsul, being specially chosen[c] to restore order in the
province, which was disturbed both by internal strife and
by a revolt of the barbarians. And he was successful,
owing to his insistence on strict discipline and his
observance of justice even in trifling matters. When pro-

ditionem artissima annona residuum cibariorum tritici modium centum denariis vendidisse arguebatur, vetuit, simul atque indigere cibo coepisset, a quoquam opem ferri; et is fame extabuit. At in iure dicendo cum de proprietate iumenti quaereretur, levibus utrimque argumentis et testibus ideoque difficili coniectura veritatis, ita decrevit ut ad lacum, ubi adaquari solebat, duceretur capite involuto atque ibidem revelato eius esset, ad quem sponte se a potu recepisset.

VIII. Ob res et tunc in Africa et olim in Germania gestas ornamenta triumphalia accepit et sacerdotium triplex, inter quindecimviros sodalesque Titios item Augustales cooptatus; atque ex eo tempore prope ad medium Neronis principatum in secessu plurimum vixit, ne ad gestandum quidem umquam iter ingressus quam ut secum vehiculo proximo decies sestertium in auro efferret, donec in oppido Fundis moranti Hispania Tarraconensis 2 oblata est. Acciditque, ut cum provinciam ingressus sacrificaret, intra aedem publicam puero e ministris acerram tenenti capillus repente toto capite canesceret, nec defuerunt qui interpretarentur significari rerum mutationem successurumque iuveni senem, hoc est ipsum Neroni. Non multo post in Cantabriae lacum fulmen decidit repertaeque sunt duodecim secures, haud ambiguum summae imperii signum.

ᵃ The *modius* was 8.75 litres.   ᵇ See note on *Jul.* lxxix. 3.

ᶜ The *sodales Titii* were an ancient priesthood of uncertain origin. The tradition arose that they were established to keep up the ancient Sabine worship, and named from Titus Tatius.

ᵈ See note on *Claud.* vi. 2.   ᵉ So as to be able to leave the country on short notice.   ᶠ In A.D. 60.

visions were very scarce during a foray and a soldier was accused of having sold for a hundred denarii a peck[a] of wheat which was left from his rations, Galba gave orders that when the man began to lack food, he should receive aid from no one; and he starved to death. On another occasion when he was holding court and the question of the ownership of a beast of burden was laid before him, as the evidence on both sides was slight and the witnesses unreliable, so that it was difficult to get at the truth, he ruled that the beast should be led with its head muffled up to the pool where it was usually watered, that it should then be unmuffled, and should belong to the man to whom it returned of its own accord after drinking.

VIII. His services in Africa at that time, and previously in Germany, were recognised by the triumphal regalia and three priesthoods, for he was chosen a member of the Fifteen,[b] of the brotherhood of Titius,[c] and of the priests of Augustus.[d] After that he lived for the most part in retirement until about the middle of Nero's reign, never going out even for recreation without taking a million sesterces in gold with him in a second carriage;[e] until at last, while he was staying in the town of Fundi,[f] Hispania Tarraconensis was offered him. And it fell out that as he was offering sacrifice in a public temple after his arrival in the province, the hair of a young attendant who was carrying an incense-box suddenly turned white all over his head, and there were some who did not hesitate to interpret this as a sign of a change of rulers and of the succession of an old man to a young one; that is to say, of Galba to Nero. Not long after this lightning struck a lake of Cantabria and twelve axes were found there, an unmistakable token of supreme power.

IX. Per octo annos varie et inaequabiliter provinciam rexit, primo acer et vehemens et in coercendis quidem delictis vel immodicus. Nam et nummulario non ex fide versanti pecunias manus amputavit mensaeque eius adfixit, et tutorem, quod pupillum, cui substitutus heres erat, veneno necasset, cruce adfecit; implorantique leges et civem Romanum se testificanti, quasi solacio et honore aliquo poenam levaturus, mutari multoque praeter ceteras altiorem et dealbatam statui crucem iussit. Paulatim in desidiam segnitiamque conversus est, ne quid materiae praeberet Neroni et, ut dicere solebat, quod nemo rationem otii sui reddere cogeretur.

2   Carthagine nova conventum agens tumultuari Gallias comperit legato Aquitaniae auxilia implorante; supervenerunt et Vindicis litterae hortantis, ut humano generi assertorem ducemque se accommodaret. Nec diu cunctatus condicionem partim metu partim spe recepit; nam et mandata Neronis de nece sua ad procuratores clam missa deprenderat et confirmabatur cum secundissimis auspiciis et ominibus virginis honestae vaticinatione, tanto magis quod eadem illa carmina sacerdos Iovis Cluniae ex penetrali somnio monitus eruerat ante ducentos annos similiter a fatidica puella pronuntiata. Quorum carminum sententia erat oriturum quandoque ex Hispania principem dominumque rerum.

---

[a] See note on *Claud.* xxiv. 1.

[b] Such predictions, like the responses of oracles, were in verse.

IX. For eight years he governed the province in a variable and inconsistent manner. At first he was vigorous and energetic and even over severe in punishing offences; for he cut off the hands of a money-lender who carried on his business dishonestly and nailed them to his counter; crucified a man for poisoning his ward, whose property he was to inherit in case of his death; and when the man invoked the law and declared that he was a Roman citizen, Galba, pretending to lighten his punishment by some consolation and honour, ordered that a cross much higher than the rest and painted white be set up, and the man transferred to it. But he gradually changed to sloth and inaction, not to give Nero any cause for jealousy, and as he used to say himself, because no one could be forced to render an account for doing nothing.

As he was holding the assizes at New Carthage, he learned of the rebellion of the Gallic provinces through an urgent appeal for help from the governor of Aquitania; then came letters from Vindex, calling upon him to make himself the liberator and leader of mankind. So without much hesitation he accepted the proposal, led by fear as well as by hope. For he had intercepted despatches ordering his own death, which had been secretly sent by Nero to his agents.[a] He was encouraged too, in addition to most favourable auspices and omens, by the prediction of a young girl of high birth, and the more so because the priest of Jupiter at Clunia, directed by a dream, had found in the inner shrine of his temple the very same prediction, likewise spoken by an inspired girl two hundred years before. And the purport of the verses[b] was that one day there would come forth from Spain the ruler and lord of the world.

X. Igitur cum quasi manumissioni vacaturus conscendisset tribunal, propositis ante se damnatorum occisorumque a Nerone quam plurimis imaginibus et astante nobili puero, quem exsulantem e proxima Baliari insula ob id ipsum acciverat, deploravit temporum statum consalutatusque imperator legatum se senatus ac populi

2 R. professus est. Dein iustitio indicto, e plebe quidem provinciae legiones et auxilia conscripsit super exercitum veterem legionis unius duarumque alarum et cohortium trium; at e primoribus prudentia atque aetate praestantibus vel[1] instar senatus, ad quos de maiore re quotiens

3 opus esset referretur, instituit. Delegit et equestris ordinis iuvenes, qui manente anulorum aureorum usu evocati appellarentur excubiasque circa cubiculum suum vice militum agerent. Etiam per provincias edicta dimisit, auctor in[2] singulis universisque conspirandi simul et ut qua posset quisque opera communem causam iuvarent.

4 Per idem fere tempus in munitione oppidi, quod sedem bello delegerat, repertus est anulus opere antiquo, scalptura gemmae Victoriam cum tropaeo exprimente; ac subinde Alexandrina navis Dertosam appulit armis onusta, sine gubernatore, sine nauta aut vectore ullo, ut nemini dubium esset iustum piumque et faventibus diis

---

[1] vel] velut, T.

[2] ΠQ *and the editions omit* in.

---

[a] Instead of the emperor, as heretofore.

[b] *Evocati* were soldiers who, after serving their time, were invited to continue their service. It is here an honorary title.

[c] See note on *Jul.* xxxiii.

X. Accordingly, pretending that he was going to attend to the manumitting of slaves, he mounted the tribunal, on the front of which he had set up as many images as he could find of those who had been condemned and put to death by Nero; and having by his side a boy of noble family, whom he had summoned for that very purpose from his place of exile hard by in the Balearic Isles, he deplored the state of the times; being thereupon hailed as emperor, he declared that he was their governor, representing the senate and people of Rome.[a] Then proclaiming a holiday, he enrolled from the people of the province legions and auxiliaries in addition to his former force of one legion, two divisions of cavalry, and three cohorts. But from the oldest and most experienced of the nobles he chose a kind of senate, to whom he might refer matters of special importance whenever it was necessary. He also chose young men of the order of knights, who were to have the title of volunteers[b] and keep guard before his bedchamber in place of the regular soldiers, without losing their right to wear the gold ring.[c] He also sent proclamations broadcast throughout the province, urging all men individually and collectively to join the revolution and aid the common cause in every possible way.

At about this same time, during the fortification of a town which he had chosen as the seat of war, a ring of ancient workmanship was found, containing a precious stone engraved with a Victory and a trophy. Immediately afterwards a ship from Alexandria loaded with arms arrived at Dertosa without a pilot, without a single sailor or passenger, removing all doubt in anyone's mind that the war was just and holy and undertaken with the

bellum suscipi: cum repente ex inopinato prope cuncta
5 turbata sunt. Alarum altera castris appropinquantem
paenitentia mutati sacramenti destituere conata est
aegreque retenta in officio, et servi, quos a liberto Neronis ad fraudem praeparatos muneri acceperat, per angi-
portum in balneas transeuntem paene interemerunt, nisi
cohortantibus in vicem ne occasionem omitterent, inter-
rogatisque de qua occasione loquerentur, expressa cru-
ciatu confessio esset.

XI. Accessit ad tanta discrimina mors Vindicis, qua
maxime consternatus destitutoque similis non multum
afuit quin vitae renuntiaret. Sed supervenientibus ab
urbe nuntiis ut occisum Neronem cunctosque in verba
sua iurasse cognovit, deposita legati suscepit Caesaris
appellationem iterque ingressus est paludatus ac depen-
dente a cervicibus pugione ante pectus; nec prius usum
togae reciperavit quam oppressis qui novas res molieban-
tur, praefecto praetori Nymphidio Sabino Romae, in Germania Fonteio Capitone, in Africa Clodio Macro legatis.

XII. Praecesserat de eo fama saevitiae simul atque
avaritiae, quod civitates Hispaniarum Galliarumque,
quae cunctantius sibi accesserant, gravioribus tributis,
quasdam etiam murorum destructione punisset et praepositos procuratoresque supplicio capitis adfecisset cum

---

^a See chap. x. 2.
^b See note on chap. i.
^c See note on *Claud.* xxiv. 1.

198

approval of the gods. Then suddenly and unexpectedly the whole plan was almost brought to naught. One of the two divisions of cavalry,[a] repenting of its change of allegiance, attempted to desert Galba as he was approaching his camp and was with difficulty prevented. Some slaves too, whom one of Nero's freedmen had given Galba with treachery in view, all but slew him as he was going to the bath through a narrow passage-way. In fact they would have succeeded, had they not urged one another not to miss the opportunity and so been questioned as to what the opportunity was to which they referred; for when they were put to the torture, a confession was wrung from them.

XI. To these great perils was added the death of Vindex, by which he was especially panic-stricken and came near taking his own life, in the belief that all was lost. But when some messengers came from the city, reporting that Nero was dead and that all the people had sworn allegiance to him, he laid aside the title of governor and assumed that of Caesar.[b] He then began his march to Rome in a general's cloak with a dagger hanging from his neck in front of his breast; and he did not resume the toga until he had overthrown those who were plotting against him, Nymphidius Sabinus, prefect of the praetorian guard at Rome, in Germany and Africa the governors Fonteius Capito and Clodius Macer.

XII. His double reputation for cruelty and avarice had gone before him; men said that he had punished the cities of the Spanish and Gallic provinces which had hesitated about taking sides with him by heavier taxes and some even by the razing of their walls, putting to death the governors and imperial deputies[c] along with their wives and

coniugibus ac liberis; quodque oblatam a Tarraconensi-
bus e vetere templo Iovis coronam auream librarum quin-
decim conflasset ac tres uncias, quae ponderi deerant,
2 iussisset exigi. Ea fama et confirmata et aucta est, ut primum urbem introiit. Nam cum classiarios, quos Nero ex
remigibus iustos milites fecerat, redire ad pristinum statum cogeret, recusantis atque insuper aquilam et signa
pertinacius flagitantis non modo inmisso equite disiecit,
sed decimavit etiam. Item Germanorum cohortem a
Caesaribus olim ad custodiam corporis institutam multisque experimentis fidelissimam dissolvit ac sine commodo
ullo remisit in patriam, quasi Cn. Dolabellae, iuxta cuius
3 hortos tendebat, proniorem. Illa quoque verene an falso
per ludibrium iactabantur, adposita lautiore cena inge-
muisse eum, et ordinario quidem dispensatori breviarium
rationum offerenti paropsidem[1] leguminis pro sedulitate
ac diligentia porrexisse, Cano autem choraulae mire
placenti denarios quinque donasse prolatos manu sua e
peculiaribus loculis suis.

XIII. Quare adventus eius non perinde gratus fuit,
idque proximo spectaculo apparuit, siquidem Atellanis
notissimum canticum exorsis:[2]

---

[1] paropsidem] parobsidem, *M*; parabsidem, *G*; *the other mss.
have* parapsidem.   [2] exorsis, ς; exorsus, Ω.

---

[a] Cf. *Aug.* xxiv. 2; *Calig.* xlviii. 1.

[b] See *Aug.* xlix. 1; *Calig.* lviii. 3.

[c] Doubtless many of them were false or exaggerated. Galba's
frugality was naturally regarded as stinginess by a people accus-
tomed to a prince like Nero; see *Nero*, xxxi. 1.

[d] Plutarch, *Galba* xvi, gives the story quite a different aspect,
saying that the gift was of gold pieces, and that Galba said that it
came from his own pocket, and not from the public funds.

children. Further, that he had melted down a golden crown of fifteen pounds weight, which the people of Tarraco had taken from their ancient temple of Jupiter and presented to him, with orders that the three ounces which were found lacking be exacted from them. This reputation was confirmed and even augmented immediately on his arrival in the city. For having compelled some marines whom Nero had made regular soldiers to return to their former position as rowers, upon their refusing and obstinately demanding an eagle and standards, he not only dispersed them by a cavalry charge, but even decimated[a] them. He also disbanded a cohort of Germans, whom the previous Caesars had made their body-guard[b] and had found absolutely faithful in many emergencies, and sent them back to their native country without any rewards, alleging that they were more favourably inclined towards Gnaeus Dolabella, near whose gardens they had their camp. The following tales too were told in mockery of him, whether truly or falsely:[c] that when an unusually elegant dinner was set before him, he groaned aloud; that when his duly appointed steward presented his expense account, he handed him a dish of beans in return for his industry and carefulness; and that when the flute player Canus greatly pleased him, he presented him with five denarii, which he took from his own purse with his own hand.[d]

XIII. Accordingly his coming was not so welcome as it might have been, and this was apparent at the first performance in the theatre; for when the actors of an Atellan farce began the familiar lines:

201

Venit Onesimus[1] a villa

cuncti simul spectatores consentiente voce reliquam partem rettulerunt ac saepius versu repetito egerunt.

XIV. Maiore adeo et favore et auctoritate adeptus est quam gessit imperium, quanquam multa documenta egregii principis daret; sed nequaquam tam grata erant, quam invisa quae secus fierent.

2 Regebatur trium arbitrio, quos una et intra Palatium habitantis nec umquam non adhaerentis paedagogos vulgo vocabant. Ii erant T. Vinius legatus eius in Hispania, cupiditatis immensae; Cornelius Laco ex assessore praefectus praetorii, arrogantia socordiaque intolerabilis; libertus Icelus, paulo ante anulis aureis et Marciani cognomine ornatus ac iam summae equestris gradus candidatus. His diverso vitiorum genere grassantibus adeo se abutendum permisit et tradidit, ut vix sibi ipse constaret, modo acerbior parciorque, modo remissior ac neglegentior quam conveniret principi electo atque illud aetatis.

3 Quosdam claros ex utroque ordine viros suspicione minima inauditos condemnavit. Civitates R. raro dedit, iura trium liberorum vix uni atque alteri ac ne iis quidem nisi ad certum praefinitumque tempus. Iudicibus sextam decuriam adici precantibus non modo negavit, sed et con-

---

[1] venit Onesimus, δ; venitione simus, Ω; venit Dorsennus, *Lachmann.*

---

[a] The text is uncertain, but obviously the song ridiculed a stingy old countryman.   [b] Cf. the inimitable sentence of Tac. (*Hist.* 1. 49) *maior privatus visus, dum privatus, et omnium consensu capax imperii, nisi imperasset.*   [c] See note on *Jul.* xxxiii.   [d] Prefect of the praetorian guard.   [e] See note on *Claud.* xv. 1.

Here comes Onesimus from his farm[a]

all the spectators at once finished the song in chorus and repeated it several times with appropriate gestures, beginning with that verse.

XIV. Thus his popularity and prestige were greater when he won, than while he ruled the empire,[b] though he gave many proofs of being an excellent prince; but he was by no means so much loved for those qualities as he was hated for his acts of the opposite character.

He was wholly under the control of three men, who were commonly known as his tutors because they lived with him in the palace and never left his side. They were Titus Vinius, one of his generals in Spain, a man of unbounded covetousness; Cornelius Laco, advanced from the position of judge's assistant to that of prefect of the Guard and intolerably haughty and indolent; and his own freedman Icelus, who had only just before received the honour of the gold ring[c] and the surname of Marcianus, yet already aspired to the highest office open to the equestrian order.[d] To these brigands, each with his different vice, he so entrusted and handed himself over as their tool, that his conduct was far from consistent; for now he was more exacting and niggardly, and now more extravagant and reckless than became a prince chosen by the people and of his time of life.

He condemned to death divers distinguished men of both orders on trivial suspicions without a trial. He rarely granted Roman citizenship, and the privileges of three-fold paternity[e] to hardly one or two, and even to those only for a fixed and limited time. When the jurors petitioned that a sixth division be added to their number, he

cessum a Claudio beneficium, ne hieme initioque anni ad iudicandum evocarentur, eripuit.

XV. Existimabatur etiam senatoria et equestria officia bienni spatio determinaturus nec daturus nisi invitis ac recusantibus. Liberalitates Neronis non plus decimis concessis per quinquaginta equites R. ea condicione revocandas curavit exigendasque, ut et si quid scaenici ac xystici donatum olim vendidissent, auferretur emptoribus, quando illi pretio absumpto solvere nequirent. At contra nihil non per comites atque libertos pretio addici aut donari gratia passus est, vectigalia, immunitates, poenas innocentium, impunitates noxiorum. Quin etiam populo R. deposcente supplicium Haloti et Tigillini solos ex omnibus Neronis emissariis vel maleficentissimos incolumes praestitit atque insuper Halotum procuratione amplissima ornavit, pro Tigillino etiam saevitiae populum edicto increpuit.

XVI. Per haec prope universis ordinibus offensis vel praecipua flagrabat invidia apud milites. Nam cum in verba eius absentis iurantibus donativum grandius solito praepositi pronuntiassent, neque ratam rem habuit et subinde iactavit legere se militem, non emere consuesse; atque eo quidem nomine omnis, qui ubique erant, exacerbavit. Ceterum praetorianos etiam metu et indignitate

---

[a] See *Claud.* xxiii. 1, and the note.   [b] These offices were numerous and varied. Since his apparent purpose was to check ambition and avarice, the senatorial offices referred to were probably military commands and governorships, and the equestrian, procuratorships; see note on *Claud.* xxiv. 1.

[c] According to Plutarch (*Galba*, 2) it was Nymphidius Sabinus, prefect of the praetorian guard, who made this promise. *Praepositi* would include those who followed his example.

not only refused, but even deprived them of the privilege granted by Claudius,[a] of not being summoned for court duty in winter and at the beginning of the year.

XV. It was thought too that he intended to limit the offices open to senators and knights to a period of two years, and to give them only to such as did not wish them and declined them.[b] He had all the grants of Nero revoked, allowing only a tenth part to be retained; and he exacted repayment with the help of fifty Roman knights, stipulating that even if the actors and athletes had sold anything that had formerly been given them, it should be taken away from the purchasers, in case the recipient had spent the money and could not repay it. On the other hand, there was nothing that he did not allow his friends and freedmen to sell at a price or bestow as a favour, taxes and freedom from taxation, the punishment of the guiltless and impunity for the guilty. Nay more, when the Roman people called for the punishment of Halotus and Tigellinus, the most utterly abandoned of all Nero's creatures, not content with saving their lives, he honoured Halotus with a very important stewardship and in the case of Tigellinus even issued an edict rebuking the people for their cruelty.

XVI. Having thus incurred the hatred of almost all men of every class, he was especially detested by the soldiers; for although their officers[c] had promised them a larger gift than common when they swore allegiance to Galba in his absence, so far from keeping the promise, he declared more than once that it was his habit to levy troops, not buy them; and on this account he embittered the soldiers all over the empire. The praetorians he filled

commovit, removens subinde plerosque ut suspectos et
2 Nymphidi socios. Sed maxime fremebat superioris Germaniae exercitus fraudari se praemiis navatae adversus
Gallos et Vindicem operae. Ergo primi obsequium
rumpere ausi Kal. Ian. adigi sacramento nisi in nomen
senatus recusarunt statimque legationem ad praetorianos
cum mandatis destinaverunt: displicere imperatorem in
Hispania factum; eligerent ipsi quem cuncti exercitus
comprobarent.

XVII. Quod ut nuntiatum est, despectui esse non tam
senectam suam quam orbitatem ratus, Pisonem Frugi
Licinianum nobilem egregiumque iuvenem ac sibi olim
probatissimum testamentoque semper in bona et nomen
adscitum repente e media salutantium turba adprehendit
filiumque appellans perduxit in castra ac pro contione
adoptavit, ne tunc quidem donativi ulla mentione facta.
Quo faciliorem occasionem M. Salvio Othoni praebuit
perficiendi conata intra sextum adoptionis diem.

XVIII. Magna et assidua monstra iam inde a principio
exitum ei, qualis evenit, portenderant. Cum per omne
iter dextra sinistraque oppidatim victimae caederentur,
taurus securis ictu consternatus rupto vinculo essedum
eius invasit elatisque pedibus totum cruore perfudit; ac
descendentem speculator impulsu turbae lancea prope

---

a See chap. xi.
b As he was on his way to Rome.

besides with both fear and indignation by discharging many of them from time to time as under suspicion of being partisans of Nymphidius.[a] But loudest of all was the grumbling of the army in Upper Germany, because it was defrauded of the reward for its services against the Gauls and Vindex. Hence they were the first to venture on mutiny, refusing on the Kalends of January to swear allegiance to anyone save the senate, and at once resolving to send a deputation to the praetorians with the following message: that the emperor created in Spain did not suit them and the Guard must choose one who would be acceptable to all the armies.

XVII. When this was reported to Galba, thinking that it was not so much his age as his lack of children that was criticised, he picked out Piso Frugi Licinianus from the midst of the throng at one of his morning receptions, a young man of noble birth and high character, who had long been one of his special favourites and always named in his will as heir to his property and his name. Calling him son, he led him to the praetorian camp and adopted him before the assembled soldiers. But even then he made no mention of largess, thus making it easier for Marcus Salvius Otho to accomplish his purpose within six days after the adoption.

XVIII. Many prodigies in rapid succession from the very beginning of his reign had foretold Galba's end exactly as it happened. When victims were being slain to right and left all along his route in every town,[b] an ox, maddened by the stroke of an axe, broke its bonds and charged the emperor's chariot, and as it raised its feet, deluged him with blood. And as Galba dismounted, one of his guards, pushed forward by the crowd, almost

vulneravit. Urbem quoque et deinde Palatium ingressum excepit terrae tremor et assimilis quidam mugitui sonus. 2 Secuta sunt aliquanto manifestiora. Monile margaritis gemmisque consertum ad ornandam Fortunam suam Tusculanam ex omni gaza secreverat; id repente quasi augustiore dignius loco Capitolinae Veneri dedicavit, ac proxima nocte somniavit speciem Fortunae querentis fraudatam se dono destinato, minantisque erepturam et ipsam quae dedisset. Cumque exterritus luce prima ad expiandum somnium, praemissis qui rem divinam apparerent, Tusculum excucurrisset, nihil invenit praeter tepidam in ara favillam atratumque iuxta senem in catino 3 vitreo tus[1] tenentem et in calice fictili merum. Observatum etiam est Kal. Ian. sacrificanti coronam de capite excidisse, auspicanti pullos avolasse; adoptionis die neque milites adlocuturo castrensem sellam de more positam pro tribunali oblitis ministris et in senatu curulem perverse collocatam.

XIX. Prius vero quam occideretur sacrificantem mane haruspex identidem monuit, caveret periculum, non longe percussores abesse.

Haud multo post cognoscit teneri castra ab Othone, ac plerisque ut eodem quam primum pergeret suadenti-

---

[1] tus] thus, *mss.*

---

[a] See chap. iv. 3.
[b] The fire should have been blazing brightly and a youth clad in white should have carried the incense in a proper box (*acerra*, see chap. viii. 2), and the wine in a more costly and appropriate vessel.
[c] Of Piso.
[d] Of the praetorian guard.

wounded him with his lance. Again, as he entered the
city, and later the Palace, he was met by a shock of earth-
quake and a sound like the lowing of kine. There followed even clearer signs. He had set apart from all the
treasure a necklace fashioned of pearls and precious
stones, for the adornment of his image of Fortune at
Tusculum.[a] This on a sudden impulse he consecrated to
the Capitoline Venus, thinking it worthy of a more august
position. The next night Fortune appeared to him in his
dreams, complaining of being robbed of the gift intended
for her and threatening in her turn to take away what she
had bestowed. When Galba hastened in terror to Tusculum at daybreak, to offer expiatory sacrifices because of
the dream, and sent on men to make preparations for the
ceremony, he found on the altar nothing but warm ashes
and beside it an old man dressed in black, holding the
incense in a glass dish and the wine in an earthen cup.[b] It
was also remarked that as he was sacrificing on the
Kalends of January, the garland fell from his head, and
that as he took the auspices, the sacred chickens flew
away. As he was on the point of addressing the soldiers on
the day of the adoption,[c] his camp chair, through the for-
getfulness of his attendants, was not placed on the tribunal, as is customary, and in the senate his curule chair
was set wrong side foremost.

XIX. As he was offering sacrifice on the morning
before he was killed, a soothsayer warned him again and
again to look out for danger, since assassins were not far
off.

Not long after this he learned that Otho held possession of the Camp,[d] and when several advised him to proceed thither as soon as possible—for they said that he

bus—posse enim auctoritate et praesentia praevalere—
nihil amplius quam continere se statuit et legionariorum
firmare praesidiis, qui multifariam diverseque tendebant.
Loricam tamen induit linteam, quanquam haud dissimu-
2 lans parum adversus tot mucrones profuturam. Sed
extractus rumoribus falsis, quos conspirati, ut eum in
publicum elicerent, de industria dissiparant, paucis
temere affirmantibus transactum negotium, oppressos,
qui tumultuarentur, advenire frequentis ceteros gratula-
bundos et in omne obsequium paratos, iis ut occurreret
prodiit tanta fiducia, ut militi cuidam occisum a se Othonem glorianti: "Quo auctore?" responderit, atque in
Forum usque processit. Ibi equites, quibus mandata
caedes erat, cum per publicum dimota paganorum turba
equos adegissent, viso procul eo parumper restiterunt;
dein rursum incitati desertum a suis contrucidarunt.

XX. Sunt qui tradant, ad primum tumultum proclamasse eum: "Quid agitis commilitones? Ego vester sum
et vos mei,"[a] donativum etiam pollicitum. Plures autem
prodiderunt optulisse ultro iugulum et ut hoc agerent ac
ferirent, quando ita videretur, hortatum. Illud mirum
admodum fuerit, neque praesentium quemquam opem
imperatori ferre conatum et omnes qui arcesserentur[1]
sprevisse nuntium excepta Germanicianorum[2] vexilla-
tione. Ii ob recens meritum, quod se aegros et invalidos

---

[1] arcesserentur] arcessirentur, *MGT*.
[2] Germanicianorum, *Turnebus*; Germaniciorum, Ω.

---

[a] Which he had hitherto refused; see chap. xvi.1.
[b] See note on *Calig.* lviii. 2.

could win the day by his presence and prestige—he decided to do no more than hold his present position and strengthen it by getting together a guard of the legionaries, who were encamped in many different quarters of the city. He did however put on a linen cuirass, though he openly declared that it would afford little protection against so many swords. But he was lured out by false reports, circulated by the conspirators to induce him to appear in public; for when a few rashly assured him that the trouble was over, that the rebels had been overthrown, and that the rest were coming in a body to offer their congratulations, ready to submit to all his orders, he went out to meet them with so much confidence that, when one of the soldiers boasted that he had slain Otho, he asked him, "On whose authority?" and then he went on as far as the Forum. There the horsemen who had been bidden to slay him, spurring their horses through the streets and dispersing the crowd of civilians, caught sight of him from a distance and halted for a moment. Then they rushed upon him again and butchered him, abandoned by his followers.

XX. Some say that at the beginning of the disturbance he cried out, "What mean you, fellow soldiers? I am yours and you are mine," and that he even promised them largess.[a] But the more general account is that he offered them his neck without resistance, urging them to do their duty[b] and strike, since it was their will. It might seem very surprising that none of those present tried to lend aid to their emperor, and that all who were sent for treated the summons with contempt except a company of German troops. These, because of his recent kindness in showing them great indulgence when they were weak-

magno opere[1] fovisset, in auxilium advolaverunt, sed serius itinere devio per ignorantiam locorum retardati.

2   Iugulatus est ad lacum Curti ac relictus ita uti erat, donec gregarius miles a frumentatione rediens abiecto onere caput ei amputavit; et quoniam capillo arripere non poterat, in gremium abdidit, mox inserto per os pollice ad Othonem detulit. Ille lixis calonibusque donavit, qui hasta suffixum non sine ludibrio circum castra portarunt adclamantes identidem: "Galba Cupido, fruaris aetate tua," maxime irritati ad talem iocorum petulantiam, quod ante paucos dies exierat in vulgus, laudanti cuidam formam suam ut adhuc floridam et vegetam respondisse eum:

ἔτι μοι μένος ἔμπεδόν ἐστιν.

Ab iis Patrobii[2] Neroniani libertus centum aureis redemptum eo loco, ubi iussu Galbae animadversum in patronum suum fuerat, abiecit. Sero tandem dispensator Argivus et hoc et ceterum truncum in privatis eius hortis Aurelia via sepulturae dedit.

XXI. Statura fuit iusta, capite praecalvo, oculis caeruleis, adunco naso, manibus pedibusque articulari morbo distortissimis, ut neque calceum perpeti nec[3] libellos evolvere aut tenere omnino valeret. Excreverat etiam in dexteriore latere eius caro praependebatque adeo ut aegre fascia substringeretur.

XXII. Cibi plurimi traditur, quem tempore hiberno

---

[1] magno opere] magnopere, *mss.*
[2] Patrobii, ς (*Sabellicus*); Patrobil, Ω.
[3] nec] ne, *M*; neque, *Gδ*; *the other mss. have* nec.

[a] In the Forum; see *Aug.* lvii. 1, and Index.

ened by illness, flew to his help, but through their unfamiliarity with the city took a roundabout way and arrived too late.

He was killed beside the Lake of Curtius[a] and was left lying just as he was, until a common soldier, returning from a distribution of grain, threw down his load and cut off the head. Then, since there was no hair by which to grasp it, he put it under his robe, but later thrust his thumb into the mouth and so carried it to Otho. He handed it over to his servants and camp-followers, who set it on a lance and paraded it about the camp with jeers, crying out from time to time, "Galba, Cupid, exult in thy vigour!" The special reason for this saucy jest was that the report had gone abroad a few days before that, when someone had congratulated him on still looking young and vigorous, he replied:

"As yet my strength is unimpaired."[b]

From these it was bought by a freedman of Patrobius Neronianus for a hundred pieces of gold and thrown aside in the place where his patron had been executed by Galba's order. At last, however, his steward Argivus consigned it to the tomb with the rest of the body in Galba's private gardens on the Aurelian Road.

XXI. He was of average height, very bald, with blue eyes and a hooked nose. His hands and feet were so distorted by gout that he could not endure a shoe for long, unroll a book, or even hold one. The flesh on his right side too had grown out and hung down to such an extent that it could with difficulty be held in place by a bandage.

XXII. It is said that he was a heavy eater and in winter

[b] *Iliad*, 5. 254; *Odyss.* 21. 426.

etiam ante lucem capere consuerat, inter cenam vero usque eo abundantis,[1] ut congestas super manus reliquias circumferri iuberet spargique ad pedes stantibus. Libidinis in mares pronior[2] et eos non nisi praeduros exoletosque; ferebant in Hispania Icelum e veteribus concubinis de Neronis exitu nuntiantem non modo artissimis osculis palam exceptum ab eo, sed ut sine mora velleretur oratum atque seductum.

XXIII. Periit tertio et septuagesimo aetatis anno, imperii mense septimo. Senatus, ut primum licitum est, statuam ei decreverat rostratae columnae superstantem in parte Fori, qua trucidatus est; sed decretum Vespasianus abolevit, percussores sibi ex Hispania in Iudaeam submisisse opinatus.

OTHO

I. Maiores Othonis orti sunt oppido Ferentio, familia vetere et honorata atque ex principibus Etruriae. Avus M. Salvius[3] Otho, patre equite R., matre humili incertum an ingenua, per gratiam Liviae Augustae, in cuius domo creverat, senator est factus nec praeturae gradum excessit.

---

[1] abundantis, *Graevius*; abundanti, Ω; abundantem, *Milan ed. of* 1475; abundanter, *Gruter.*
[2] pronior, *mss.*; pronioris, *Stephanus.*
[3] Salvius, *Stephanus*; Silvius, Ω.

---

[a] The meaning of this passage is uncertain; interpretations differ. The meaning of *super manus* is particularly dark; the most plausible suggestion is that it is equivalent to *ante se*. The idea seems to be that Galba's leavings were so large that they fed his entire staff.

time was in the habit of taking food even before daylight, while at dinner he helped himself so lavishly that he would have the leavings which remained in a heap before him passed along and distributed among the attendants who waited on him.[a] He was more inclined to desire for males, and in gratifying it preferred full-grown, strong men. They say that when Icelus, one of his old-time favourites, brought him news in Spain of Nero's death, he not only received him openly with the fondest kisses, but begged him to prepare himself without delay and took him on one side.

XXIII. He met his end[b] in the seventy-third year of his age and the seventh month of his reign. The senate, as soon as it was allowed to do so, voted him a statue standing upon a column adorned with the beaks of ships, in the part of the Forum where he was slain; but Vespasian annulled this decree, believing that Galba had sent assassins from Spain to Judaea, to take his life.

OTHO

I. The ancestors of Otho came from an old and illustrious family in the town of Ferentium and were descended from the princes of Etruria.[c] His grandfather Marcus Salvius Otho, whose father was a Roman knight but whose mother was of lowly origin and perhaps not even free-born, became a senator through the influence of Livia Augusta, in whose house he was reared, but did not advance beyond the grade of praetor.

[b] In A.D. 69.
[c] Like Maecenas, Otho was *Tyrrhena regum progenies*; Hor. *Odes*, 3. 29. 1.

2   Pater L. Otho, materno genere praeclaro multarumque et magnarum propinquitatium, tam carus tamque non absimilis facie Tiberio principi fuit, ut plerique procreatum ex eo crederent. Urbanos honores, proconsulatum Africae et extraordinaria imperia severissime administravit. Ausus etiam est in Illyrico milites quosdam, quod motu Camilli ex paenitentia praepositos suos quasi defectionis adversus Claudium auctores occiderant, capite punire et quidem ante principia se coram, quamvis ob id ipsum promotos in ampliorem

3   gradum a Claudio sciret. Quo facto sicut gloriam auxit, ita gratiam minuit; quam tamen mature reciperavit detecta equitis R. fraude, quem prodentibus servis necem Claudio parare compererat. Namque et senatus honore rarissimo, statua in Palatio posita, prosecutus est eum et Claudius adlectum inter patricios conlaudans amplissimis verbis hoc quoque adiecit: "Vir, quo meliores liberos habere ne opto quidem." Ex Albia Terentia splendida femina duos filios tulit, L. Titianum et minorem M. cognominem sibi; tulit et filiam, quam vixdum nubilem Druso Germanici filio despondit.

II. Otho imperator IIII. Kal. Mai. natus est Camillo Arruntio Domitio Ahenobarbo coss. A prima adulescentia

---

[a] See *Claud.* xiii and xxxv. 2.

[b] Suetonius does not mention this among the conspiracies against Claudius; see *Claud.* xiii.

[c] April 28, A.D. 32.

His father Lucius Otho was of a distinguished family on his mother's side, with many powerful connections, and was so beloved by Tiberius and so like him in appearance that he was believed by many to be the emperor's son. In the regular offices at Rome, the proconsulate of Africa, and several special military commands he conducted himself with extreme severity. In Illyricum he even had the courage to punish some soldiers with death, because in the rebellion of Camillus,[a] repenting of their defection, they had killed their officers on the ground that they were the ringleaders in the revolt against Claudius; and they were executed in his presence before his headquarters, although he knew that they had been promoted to higher positions by Claudius because of that very act. By this deed, while he increased his reputation, he lost favour at court; but he speedily regained it by detecting the treachery of a Roman knight, whose slaves betrayed their master's design of killing the emperor.[b] For in consequence of this, the senate conferred a very unusual honour on him by setting up his statue in the Palace; and Claudius also enrolled him among the patricians, and after praising him in the highest terms, added these words: "a man of greater loyalty than I can even pray for in my own children." By Albia Terentia, a woman of an illustrious line, he had two sons, Lucius Titianus and a younger called Marcus, who had the same surname as himself; also a daughter, whom he betrothed to Drusus, son of Germanicus, almost before she was of marriageable age.

II. The emperor Otho was born on the fourth day before the Kalends of May in the consulate of Camillus Arruntius and Domitius Ahenobarbus.[c] From earliest

217

prodigus ac procax, adeo ut saepe flagris obiurgaretur a patre, ferebatur et vagari noctibus solitus atque invalidum quemque obviorum vel potulentum corripere ac distento

2 sago impositum in sublime iactare. Post patris deinde mortem libertinam aulicam gratiosam, quo efficacius coleret, etiam diligere simulavit quamvis anum ac paene decrepitam; per hanc insinuatus Neroni facile summum inter amicos locum tenuit congruentia morum, ut vero quidam tradunt, et consuetudine mutui stupri. Ac tantum potentia valuit, ut damnatum repetundis consularem virum, ingens praemium pactus, prius quam plane restitutionem ei impetrasset, non dubitaret in senatum ad agendas gratias introducere.

III. Omnium autem consiliorum secretorumque particeps die, quem necandae matri Nero destinarat, ad avertendas suspiciones cenam utrique exquisitissimae comitatis dedit; item Poppaeam Sabinam tunc adhuc amicam eius, abductam marito demandatamque interim sibi, nuptiarum specie recepit nec corrupisse contentus adeo dilexit, ut ne rivalem quidem Neronem aequo tulerit

2 animo. Creditur certe non modo missos ad arcessendam non recepisse, sed ipsum etiam exclusisse quondam pro foribus astantem miscentemque frustra minas et preces ac depositum reposcentem. Quare diducto matrimonio

---

[a] Instead of the modern blanket a *sagum*, or military cloak, was used, whence the operation was called *sagatio*.

[b] The penalty for extortion was expulsion from the senate; see *Jul.* xliii. 1.   [c] See note on *Nero*, xxxiv. 2.

[d] According to Tac. *Ann.* 13. 45, the marriage was a real one, as is also implied below at note *e*.

[e] See note *d* above.

youth he was so extravagant and wild that his father often
flogged him; and they say that he used to rove about at
night and lay hands on anyone whom he met who was feeble or drunk and toss him in a blanket.[a] After his father's
death he pretended love for an influential freedwoman of
the court, although she was an old woman and almost
decrepit, that he might more effectually win her favour.
Having through her wormed his way into Nero's good
graces, he easily held the first place among the emperor's
friends because of the similarity of their characters; but
according to some, also exchanged sexual gratification. At
any rate his influence was such that when he had bar-
gained for a huge sum of money to procure the pardon of
an ex-consul who had been condemned for extortion, he
had no hesitation in bringing him into the senate to give
thanks, before he had fully secured his restoration.[b]

III. He was privy to all the emperor's plans and
secrets, and on the day which Nero had chosen for the
murder of his mother he gave both of them a most elabo-
rate banquet,[c] in order to avert suspicion. Also when
Poppaea Sabina, who up to that time had been Nero's
mistress, was separated from her husband and turned
over for the time being to Otho, he pretended marriage
with her;[d] but not content with seducing her he became
so devoted that he could not endure the thought of having
Nero even as a rival. At all events it is believed that he
not only would not admit those whom Nero sent to fetch
her, but that on one occasion he even shut out the
emperor himself, who stood before his door, vainly mingling threats and entreaties and demanding the return of
his trust. Therefore Nero annulled the marriage[e] and

sepositus est per causam legationis in Lusitaniam. Et[1] satis visum, ne poena acrior mimum omnem divulgaret, qui tamen sic quoque hoc districho enotuit:

Cur Otho mentito sit, quaeritis, exsul honore?
Uxoris moechus coeperat esse suae.

Provinciam administavit quaestorius per decem annos, moderatione atque abstinentia singulari.

IV. Ut tandem occasio ultionis data est, conatibus Galbae primus accessit; eodemque momento et ipse spem imperii cepit magnam quidem et ex condicione temporum, sed aliquanto maiorem ex affirmatione Seleuci mathematici. Qui cum eum olim superstitem Neroni fore spopondisset, tunc ultro inopinatus advenerat imperaturum quoque brevi repromittens.

2 Nullo igitur officii aut ambitionis in quemquam genere omisso, quotiens cena principem acciperet, aureos excubanti cohorti viritim dividebat, nec minus alium alia via militum demerebatur; cuidam etiam de parte finium cum vicino litiganti adhibitus arbiter totum agrum redemit emancipavitque, ut iam vix ullus esset, qui non et sentiret et praedicaret solum successione imperii dignum.

V. Speraverat autem fore ut adoptaretur a Galba,

---

[1] et, Ω; id, *Casaubon*.

---

[a] Tacitus and Plutarch give Ptolemaeus as the name of the astrologer.

under colour of an appointment as governor banished Otho to Lusitania, contenting himself with this through fear that by inflicting a severe punishment he would make the whole farce public; but even as it was, it was published abroad in this couplet:

Why you ask, is Otho in exile under false pretense?
He had been the adulterer of his own wife.

With the rank of quaestor Otho governed the province for ten years with remarkable moderation and integrity.

IV. When at last an opportunity for revenge was given him, Otho was the first to espouse Galba's cause, at the same time conceiving on his own account high hopes of imperial power, because of the state of the times, but still more because of a declaration of the astrologer Seleucus.[a] For he had not only promised Otho some time before that he would survive Nero, but had at this time unexpectedly appeared unsought and made the further promise that he would soon become emperor as well.

Accordingly Otho let slip no opportunity for flattery or attention to anyone. Whenever he entertained the prince at dinner, he gave a gold piece to each man of the cohort on guard, and put all the soldiers under obligation in one form or another. Chosen arbiter by a man who was at law with his neighbour about a part of his estate, he bought the whole property and presented it to him. As a result there was hardly anyone who did not both think and openly declare that he alone was worthy to succeed to the empire.

V. Now he had hoped to be adopted by Galba, and

idque in dies exspectabat. Sed postquam Pisone praelato
spe decidit, ad vim conversus est instigante super animi
dolorem etiam magnitudine aeris alieni. Neque enim dissimulabat, nisi principem se stare non posse, nihilque
referre ab hoste in acie an in Foro sub creditoribus
caderet.

2 Ante paucos dies servo Caesaris pro impetrata dispen-
satione decies sestertium expresserat; hoc subsi-
dium tanti coepti fuit. Ac primo quinque speculatoribus
commissa res est, deinde decem aliis, quos singuli binos
produxerant; omnibus dena sestertia repraesentata et
quinquagena promissa. Per hos sollicitati reliqui, nec
adeo multi, haud dubia fiducia in ipso negotio pluris adfu-
turos.

VI. Tulerat animus post adoptionem statim castra
occupare cenantemque in Palatio Galbam adgredi, sed
obstitit respectus cohortis, quae tunc excubabat, ne one-
raretur invidia, quod eiusdem statione et Gaius fuerat
occisus et desertus Nero. Medium quoque tempus religio et Seleucus exemit.

2 Ergo destinata die praemonitis consciis, ut se in Foro
sub aede Saturni ad miliarium aureum opperirentur,
mane Galbam salutavit, utque consueverat osculo excep-
tus, etiam sacrificanti interfuit audivitque praedicta

---

[a] Between the adoption and the death of Galba, a space of
five days.

[b] A pillar covered with gilded bronze, erected by Augustus, in
20 B.C., on which were engraved the names of the principal cities
of the empire and their distance from Rome. The Roman roads
were supposed to converge at that point, but the distances on
them were reckoned from the gates.

looked forward to it from day to day. But when Piso was preferred and he at last lost that hope, he resorted to force, spurred on not merely by feelings of resentment, but also by the greatness of his debts. For he flatly declared that he could not keep on his feet unless he became emperor, and that it made no difference whether he fell at the hands of the enemy in battle or at those of his creditors in the Forum.

He had extorted a million sesterces from one of the emperor's slaves a few days before for getting him a stewardship. This was the entire capital for his great undertaking. At first the enterprise was entrusted to five of his body-guard, then to ten others, two being chosen by each of the first five; to all of them ten thousand sesterces were paid at once and they were promised fifty thousand more. Through these others were won over, but not so very many, since he had full confidence that more would join him when the business was afoot.

VI. He had been inclined to seize the Camp immediately after the adoption, and set upon Galba as he was dining in the Palace, but had been prevented by consideration for the cohort which was on guard at the time, and a reluctance to increase its ill repute; for it was while that same cohort was at its post that both Gaius had been slain and Nero had been forsaken. The intervening time[a] was lost owing to bad omens and the warnings of Seleucus.

Accordingly, when the day was set, after admonishing his confederates to await him in the Forum at the golden mile-post[b] hard by the temple of Saturn, he called upon Galba in the morning and was welcomed as usual with a kiss. He also attended the emperor as he was offering sacrifice, and heard the predictions of the soothsayer.

haruspicis. Deinde liberto adesse architectos nuntiante,
quod signum convenerat, quasi venalem domum inspec-
turus abscessit proripuitque se postica parte Palati ad
constitutum. Alii febrem simulasse aiunt eamque excusa-
3 tionem proximis mandasse, si quaereretur. Tunc abditus
propere muliebri sella in castra contendit ac deficientibus
lecticariis[1] cum descendisset cursumque cepisset, laxato
calceo restitit, donec omissa mora succollatus et a prae-
sente comitatu imperator consalutatus inter faustas adcla-
mationes strictosque gladios ad principia devenit, obvio
quoque non aliter ac si conscius et particeps foret adhae-
rente. Ibi missis qui Galbam et Pisonem trucidarent, ad
conciliandos pollicitationibus militum animos nihil magis
pro contione testatus est, quam id demum se habiturum,
quod sibi illi reliquissent.

VII. Dein vergente iam die ingressus senatum posi-
taque brevi ratione[2] quasi raptus de publico et suscipere
imperium vi coactus gesturusque communi omnium arbitrio, Palatium petit. Ac super ceteras gratulantium adu-
lantiumque blanditias ab infima plebe appellatus Nero
nullum indicium recusantis dedit, immo, ut quidam tradiderunt, etiam diplomatibus primisque epistulis suis ad
quosdam provinciarum praesides Neronis cognomen
adiecit. Certe et imagines statuasque eius reponi passus
est et procuratores atque libertos ad eadem officia revo-

---

[1] lecticariis, *X*; lecticaris, *Roth*; lecticaribus, *MGϒ*.
[2] ratione, *Erasmus*; oratione, *mss.*

Then a freedman announced that the architects had
come, which was the signal agreed on, and going off as if
to inspect a house which was for sale, he rushed from the
Palace by a back door and hastened to the appointed
place. Others say that he feigned an attack of fever and
asked those who stood near him to give that excuse, in
case he should be missed. Then hurriedly entering a
closed sedan, such as women use, he hurried to the camp,
but got out when the bearers' strength flagged, and
started to run. His shoe came untied and he stopped,
whereupon without delay he was at once taken up on the
shoulders of his companions and hailed as emperor. In
this way he arrived at headquarters, amid acclamations
and drawn swords, while everyone whom he met fell in,
just as though he were an accomplice and a participator in
the plot. He then sent emissaries to kill Galba and Piso,
and made no further promises in the assembly to win the
loyalty of the soldiers than to declare that he would have
that—and only that—which they should leave to him.

VII. Next, as the day was drawing to its close, he
entered the senate and after giving a brief account of
himself, alleging that he had been carried off in the
streets and forced to undertake the rule, which he would
exercise in accordance with the general will, he went to
the Palace. When in the midst of the other adulations
of those who congratulated and flattered him, he was hailed
by the common herd as Nero, he made no sign of dissent;
on the contrary, according to some writers, he even made
use of that surname in his commissions and his first letters
to some of the governors of the provinces. Certain it is
that he suffered Nero's busts and statues to be set up
again, and reinstated his procurators and freedmen in

cavit, nec quicquam prius pro potestate subscripsit quam quingenties sesterium ad peragendam Auream Domum.

2 Dicitur ea nocte per quietem pavefactus gemitus maximos edidisse repertusque a concursantibus humi ante lectum iacens per omnia piaculorum genera Manes Galbae, a quo deturbari expellique se viderat, propitiare temptasse; postridie quoque in augurando tempestate orta graviter prolapsum identidem obmurmurasse:

τί γάρ μοι καὶ μακροῖς αὐλοῖς;[1]

VIII. Sub idem vero tempus Germaniciani exercitus in Vitelli verba iurarant. Quod ut comperit, auctor senatui fuit mittendae legationis, quae doceret electum iam principem, quietem concordiamque[2] suaderet; et tamen per internuntios ac litteras consortem imperii generumque se Vitellio optulit. Verum haud dubio bello iamque ducibus et copiis, quas Vitellius praemiserat, appropinquantibus animum fidemque erga se praetorianorum paene internecione amplissimi ordinis expertus est.

2 Placuerat[3] per classiarios arma transferri remittique navibus; ea cum in castris sub noctem promerentur, insidias quidam suspicati tumultum excitaverunt; ac repente omnes nullo certo duce in Palatium cucurrerunt caedem senatus flagitantes, repulsisque tribunorum qui inhibere

---

[1] αὐλοῖς, ς; *M and the greater number of the other mss. have* δουλοις.   [2] concordiamque, *GT*δ; et concordiam, Υ; *the other mss. have only* concordiam.
[3] placuerat, ς (*Torrentius*); et placuerat, Ω; ei pl., *Bücheler.*

---

[a] Proverbial of undertaking something beyond one's powers; cf. Cic. *ad Att.* ii. 16.
[b] To Ostia.   [c] Of the armoury.

their former posts, while the first grant that he signed as emperor was one of fifty million sesterces for finishing the Golden House.

It is said that he had a fearful dream that night, uttered loud groans, and was found by those who ran to his aid lying on the ground beside his couch; that he tried by every kind of expiatory rite to propitiate the shade of Galba, by whom he dreamt that he was ousted and thrown out; and that next day, as he was taking the auspices, a great storm arose and he had a bad fall, whereat he muttered from time to time:

"With long flutes what concern have I?"[a]

VIII. Now at about this same time the armies in Germany swore allegiance to Vitellius. When Otho learned of this, he persuaded the senate to send a deputation, to say that an emperor had already been chosen and to counsel peace and harmony; but in spite of this he offered Vitellius by messengers and letters a share in the imperial dignity and proposed to become his son-in-law. But when it became clear that war was inevitable, and the generals and troops which Vitellius had sent in advance were already drawing near, he was given a proof of the affection and loyalty of the praetorians towards himself which almost resulted in the destruction of the senate. It had been resolved that some arms should be removed and carried back[b] on shipboard by the marines; but as these were being taken out[c] in the Camp towards nightfall, some suspected treachery and started a riot; then on a sudden all the soldiers hastened to the Palace without any particular leader, demanding the death of the senators. After putting to flight some of the tribunes who attempted to

temptabant, nonnullis et occisis, sic ut erant cruenti, ubinam imperator esset requirentes perruperunt in triclinium usque nec nisi viso destiterunt.

3   Expeditionem autem inpigre atque etiam praepropere incohavit, nulla ne religionum quidem cura, sed et motis necdum conditis ancilibus, quod antiquitus infaustum habetur, et die, quo cultores deum Matris lamentari et plangere incipiunt, praeterea adversissimis auspiciis. Nam et victima Diti patri caesa litavit, cum tali sacrificio contraria exta potiora sint, et primo egressu inundationibus Tiberis retardatus ad vicensimum etiam lapidem ruina aedificiorum praeclusam viam offendit.

IX. Simili temeritate, quamvis dubium nemini esset quin trahi bellum oporteret, quando et fame et angustiis locorum urgeretur hostis, quam primum tamen decertare statuit, sive impatiens longioris sollicitudinis speransque ante Vitelli adventum profligari plurimum posse, sive impar militum ardori pugnam deposcentium. Nec ulli pugnae affuit substititque Brixelli.

2   Et tribus quidem, verum mediocribus proeliis apud

ᵃ This difficult passage is obscure because of its brevity and perhaps through corruption of the text. The same story is told by Tacitus (*Hist.* 1. 80) and Plutarch (*Otho*, 3), but the three accounts seem to vary. According to Suetonius the arms were sent from the praetorian camp to Ostia, to fit out the (eighteenth) cohort, and the riot started in the praetorian camp; the account of Tacitus seems to imply that it was the soldiers from Ostia (joined by the praetorians) that burst into Otho's dining room: *insidentes equis* urbem ac Palatium *petunt.* The arms in question would seem to be a part of those belonging to the cohort; hence *remitti.* See however Hofstee, *ad loc.*

stop them, and killing others, just as they were, all blood-stained, they burst right into the dining-room, demanding to know where the emperor was; and they could not be quieted until they had seen him.[a]

He began his expedition with energy and in fact too hastily, without any regard even for the omens, and in spite of the fact that the sacred shields had been taken out,[b] but not yet put back, which for ages has been considered unlucky; on the very day, too, when the worshippers of the Mother of the Gods[c] begin their wailing and lamentation, and also with most unfavourable auspices. For having offered up a victim to father Dis, he had good omens, whereas in such a sacrifice adverse indications are more favourable; and when he first left the city, he was delayed by floods of the Tiber, while at the twentieth milestone he found the road blocked by fallen buildings.

IX. With like rashness, although no one doubted that the proper course was to protract the war, since the enemy were hard pressed by hunger and by the narrowness of their quarters, he decided to fight a decisive battle as soon as possible, either because he could not endure the continued worry and hoped that the war could be ended before the arrival of Vitellius, or from inability to resist the impetuosity of his soldiers, who clamoured for the fight. He himself did not take part in any of the battles, but remained behind at Brixellum.

He was victorious in three contests, but they were of

[b] From the temple of Mars, to be carried through the streets in the sacred procession. To begin any enterprise during that time was considered unlucky, and weddings were avoided; see Ovid, *Fasti*, iii. 393.

[c] Cybele, whose festival was from March 24 to 30.

Alpes circaque Placentiam et ad Castoris, quod loco nomen est, vicit; novissimo maximoque apud Betriacum[1] fraude superatus est, cum spe conloquii facta, quasi ad condicionem pacis militibus eductis, ex inproviso atque in ipsa consalutatione[2] dimicandum fuisset. Ac statim moriendi impetum cepit, ut multi nec frustra opinantur, magis pudore, ne tanto rerum hominumque periculo dominationem sibi asserere perseveraret, quam desperatione ulla aut diffidentia copiarum; quippe residuis integrisque etiam nunc quas secum ad secundos casus detinuerat, et supervenientibus aliis e Dalmatia Pannoniaque et Moesia, ne victis quidem adeo afflictis ut non in ultionem ignominiae quidvis discriminis ultro et vel solae subirent.

X. Interfuit huic bello pater meus Suetonius Laetus, tertiae decimae legionis tribunus angusticlavius. Is mox referre crebro solebat Othonem etiam privatum usque adeo detestatum civilia arma, ut memorante quodam inter epulas de Cassi Brutique exitu cohorruerit; nec concursurum cum Galba fuisse, nisi confideret sine bello rem transigi posse; tunc ad despiciendam vitam exemplo manipularis militis concitatum, qui cum cladem exercitus nuntiaret nec cuiquam fidem faceret ac nunc mendaci nunc timoris, quasi fugisset, ex acie argueretur, gladio ante pedes eius incubuerit. Hoc viso proclamasse eum

3

---

[1] Betriacum] Bretiacum, Ω.

[2] consalutatione, Π[1]Q (*cf. Tac. Hist.* 2. 42); *the other mss. have* consultatione.

---

[a] Tacitus, *Hist.* 2. 24, says *locus Castorum* (= *Castoris et Pollucis*) *vocatur*, and that it was twelve miles from Cremona. There was probably a temple there to the Twin Brethren.

little moment: in the Alps, near Placentia, and "at Castor's,"[a] as the place is called. In the final and decisive struggle at Betriacum he was defeated, but through treachery. For hope of a conference was offered, and when his soldiers were led out in the belief that they were to discuss terms of peace, a battle was forced upon them unexpectedly, just as they were exchanging greetings with the foe. After the defeat, Otho at once resolved to take his own life, rather from a feeling of shame, as many have thought with good reason, and an unwillingness to persist in a struggle for imperial power at the expense of such danger to life and property, than from any despair of success or distrust of his troops; for even then he had a fresh and strong force which he had held in reserve for a second attempt, while others were on their way from Dalmatia, Pannonia, and Moesia. Even the defeated troops were not so crushed as not to undergo any danger, and even without support undertake to avenge their disgrace.

X. My father Suetonius Laetus took part in that war, as a tribune of the equestrian order in the Thirteenth legion. He used often to declare afterwards that Otho, even when he was a private citizen, so loathed civil strife that at the mere mention of the fate of Brutus and Cassius at a banquet he shuddered; that he would not have engaged with Galba, if he had not felt confident that the affair could be settled peacefully; further, that he was led to hold his life cheap at that time by the example of a common soldier. This man on bringing news of the defeat of the army was believed by no one, but was charged by the soldiers now with falsehood and now with cowardice, and accused of running away; whereupon he fell on his sword at the emperor's feet. My father used to say that at this sight

231

aiebat, non amplius se in periculum talis tamque bene meritos coniecturum.

2 Fratrem igitur fratrisque filium et singulos amicorum cohortatus, ut sibi quisque pro facultate consuleret, ab amplexu et osculo suo dimisit omnis, secretoque capto binos codicillos exaravit, ad sororem consolatorios et ad Messalinam Neronis, quam matrimonio destinarat, commendans reliquias suas et memoriam. Quicquid deinde epistularum erat, ne cui periculo aut noxae apud victorem forent, concremavit. Divisit et pecunias domesticis ex copia praesenti.

XI. Atque ita paratus intentusque iam morti, tumultu inter moras exorto ut eos, qui discedere et abire coeptabant, corripi quasi desertores detinerique sensit: "Adiciamus," inquit, "vitae et hanc noctem," his ipsis totidemque verbis, vetuitque vim cuiquam fieri; et in serum usque patente cubiculo, si quis adire vellet, potestatem sui prae-

2 buit. Post hoc sedata siti gelidae aquae potione arripuit duos pugiones et explorata utriusque acie, cum alterum pulvino subdidisset, foribus adopertis artissimo somno quievit. Et circa lucem demum expergefactus uno se traiecit ictu infra laevam papillam irrumpentibusque ad primum gemitum modo celans modo detegens plagam exanimatus est et celeriter, nam ita praeceperat, funeratus, tricensimo et octavo aetatis anno et nonagensimo et quinto imperii die.

Otho cried out that he would no longer endanger the lives of such brave men, who had deserved so well.

Having therefore advised his brother, his nephew, and his friends one by one to look out each for his own safety as best they could, he embraced and kissed them all and sent them off. Then going to a retired place he wrote two notes, one of consolation to his sister, and one to Nero's widow Messalina, whom he had intended to marry, commending to her his corpse and his memory. Then he burned all his letters, to prevent them from bringing danger or harm to anyone at the hands of the victor. He also distributed what money he had with him among his servants.

XI. When he had thus made his preparations and was now resolved upon death, learning from a disturbance which meantime arose that those who were beginning to depart and leave the camp were being seized and detained as deserters, he said "Let us add this one more night to our life" (these were his very words), and he forbade the offering of violence to anyone. Leaving the door of his bedroom open until a late hour, he gave the privilege of speaking with him to all who wished to come in. After that, quenching his thirst with a draught of cold water, he caught up two daggers, and having tried the point of both of them, put one under his pillow. Then closing the doors, he slept very soundly. When he at last woke up at about daylight, he stabbed himself with a single stroke under the left breast; and now concealing the wound, and now showing it to those who rushed in at his first groan, he breathed his last and was hastily buried (for such were his orders) in the thirty-eighth year of his age and on the ninety-fifth day of his reign.

XII. Tanto Othonis animo nequaquam corpus aut habitus competit. Fuisse enim et modicae staturae et male pedatus scambusque[1] traditur, munditiarum vero paene muliebrium, vulso corpore, galericulo capiti propter raritatem capillorum adaptato et adnexo, ut nemo dinosceret; quin et faciem cotidie rasitare ac pane madido linere consuetum, idque instituisse a prima lanugine, ne barbatus umquam esset; sacra etiam Isidis saepe in lintea

2 religiosaque veste propalam celebrasse. Per quae factum putem, ut mors eius minime congruens vitae maiore miraculo fuerit. Multi praesentium militum cum plurimo fletu manus ac pedes iacentis exosculati, fortissimum virum, unicum imperatorem praedicantes, ibidem statim nec procul a rogo vim suae vitae attulerunt; multi et absentium accepto nuntio prae dolore armis inter se ad internecionem concurrerunt. Denique magna pars hominum incolumem gravissime detestata mortuum laudibus tulit, ut vulgo iactatum sit etiam, Galbam ab eo non tam dominandi quam rei p. ac libertatis restituendae causa interemptum.

VITELLIUS

I. Vitelliorum originem alii aliam et quidem diversissimam tradunt, partim veterem et nobilem, partim vero novam et obscuram atque etiam sordidam; quod ego per

---

[1] scambusque, *Turnebus*; cambusque, Ω; *cf. Bonnet, A.L.L.* 13, 579.

XII. Neither Otho's person nor his bearing suggested such great courage. He is said to have been of moderate height, splay-footed and bandy-legged, but almost feminine in his care of his person. He had the hair of his body plucked out, and because of the thinness of his locks wore a wig so carefully fashioned and fitted to his head that no one suspected it. Moreover, they say that he used to shave every day and smear his face with moist bread, beginning the practice with the appearance of the first down, so as never to have a beard; also that he used to celebrate the rites of Isis publicly in the linen garment prescribed by the cult. I am inclined to think that it was because of these habits that a death so little in harmony with his life excited the greater marvel. Many of the soldiers who were present kissed his hands and feet as he lay dead, weeping bitterly and calling him the bravest of men and an incomparable emperor, and then at once slew themselves beside his bier. Many of those who were absent, too, on receiving the news attacked and killed one another from sheer grief. In short the greater part of those who hated him most bitterly while he lived lauded him to the skies when he was dead; and it was even commonly declared that he had put an end to Galba, not so much for the sake of ruling, as of restoring the republic and liberty.

VITELLIUS

I. Of the origin of the Vitellii different and widely varying accounts are given, some saying that the family was ancient and noble, others that it was new and obscure, if not of mean extraction. I should believe that

adulatores obtrectatoresque imperatoris Vitelli evenisse
opinarer, nisi aliquanto prius de familiae condicione
2   variatum esset. Exstat Q. Elogi[1] ad Quintum Vitellium
Divi Augusti quaestorem libellus, quo continetur, Vitel-
lios Fauno Aboriginum rege et Vitellia, quae multis locis
pro numine coleretur, ortos toto Latio imperasse; horum
residuam stirpem ex Sabinis transisse Romam atque inter
3   patricios adlectam; indicia stirpis mansisse diu viam Vitel-
liam ab Ianiculo ad mare usque, item coloniam eiusdem
nominis, quam gentili copia adversus Aequiculos tutan-
dam olim depoposcissent; tempore deinde Samnitici belli
praesidio in Apuliam misso quosdam ex Vitellis subsedisse Nuceriae eorumque progeniem longo post intervallo repetisse urbem atque ordinem senatorium.

II. Contra plures auctorem generis libertinum prodiderunt, Cassius Severus nec minus alii eundem et
sutorem veteramentarium, cuius filius sectionibus et cog-
nituris uberius compendium nanctus, ex muliere vulgari,
Antiochi cuiusdam furnariam exercentis filia, equitem R.
genuerit. Sed quod discrepat, sit in medio.

2   Ceterum P. Vitellius domo Nuceria, sive ille stirpis
antiquae sive pudendis parentibus atque avis, eques certe
R. et rerum Augusti procurator, quattuor filios amplissi-

---

[1] exstatq(ue) elogi, Ω (elogii, XΥ; elogium, G).

these came respectively from the flatterers and detractors of the emperor, were it not for a difference of opinion about the standing of the family at a considerably earlier date. We have a book of Quintus Elogius addressed to Quintus Vitellius, quaestor of the Deified Augustus, in which it is written that the Vitellii were sprung from Faunus, king of the Aborigines, and Vitellia, who was worshipped as a goddess in many places; and that they ruled in all Latium. That the surviving members of the family moved from the Sabine district to Rome and were enrolled among the patricians. That traces of this stock endured long afterwards in the Vitellian Road, running from the Janiculum all the way to the sea, as well as in a colony of the same name, which in ancient days the family had asked the privilege of defending against the Aequicoli with troops raised from their own line. That when afterwards a force was sent into Apulia at the time of the Samnite war, some of the Vitellii settled at Nuceria, and that after a long time their descendants returned to the city and resumed their place in the senatorial order.

II. On the other hand several have written that the founder of the family was a freedman, while Cassius Severus and others as well say further that he was a cobbler, and that his son, after making a considerable fortune from the sale of confiscated estates and the profession of informer, fathered a child by a common woman, the daughter of one Antiochus who kept a bakery, and this son became a Roman knight. But this difference of opinion may be left unsettled.

In any event Publius Vitellius of Nuceria, whether of ancient stock or of parents and forefathers in whom he could take no pride, unquestionably a Roman knight and a steward of Augustus' property, left four sons of high

mae dignitatis cognomines ac tantum praenominibus distinctos reliquit Aulum, Quintum, Publium, Lucium. Aulus in consulatu obiit, quem cum Domitio Neronis Caesaris patre inierat, praelautus[1] alioqui famosusque cenarum magnificentia. Quintus caruit ordine, cum auctore Tiberio secerni minus idoneos senatores removerique placuisset. Publius, Germanici comes, Cn.

3 Pisonem inimicum et interfectorem eius accusavit condemnavitque, ac post praeturae honorem inter Seiani conscios arreptus et in custodiam fratri datus scalpro librario venas sibi incidit, nec tam mortis paenitentia quam suorum obtestatione obligari curarique se passus in

4 eadem custodia morbo periit. Lucius ex consulatu Syriae praepositus, Artabanum Parthorum regem summis artibus non modo ad conloquium suum, sed etiam ad veneranda legionum signa pellexit. Mox cum Claudio principe duos insuper ordinarios consulatus censuramque gessit. Curam quoque imperii sustinuit absente eo expeditione Britannica; vir innocens et industrius, sed amore libertinae perinfamis, cuius etiam salivis melle commixtis, ne clam quidem aut raro sed cotidie ac palam, arterias et

5 fauces pro remedio fovebat. Idem miri in adulando ingenii primus C. Caesarem adorare ut deum instituit,

---

[1] praelautus, *Basle ed. of* 1533; praelatus, Ω.

---

[a] In A.D. 32.

[b] See Tac. *Ann.* 2. 48.

[c] In A.D. 20.   [d] In A.D. 35.

[e] In A.D. 34.

[f] See *Calig.* xiv. 3.

[g] In A.D. 43 and 47.

[h] In A.D. 47.

[i] In A.D. 43.

rank with the same name and differing only in their fore-names: Aulus, Quintus, Publius and Lucius. Aulus, who was given to luxury and especially notorious for the magnificence of his feasts, died a consul,[a] appointed to the office with Domitius, father of the emperor Nero. Quintus lost his rank at the time when it was resolved, at the suggestion of Tiberius, to depose and get rid of undesirable senators.[b] Publius, a member of Germanicus' staff, arraigned Gnaeus Piso,[c] the enemy and murderer of his commander, and secured his condemnation. Arrested among the accomplices of Sejanus, after holding the praetorship, and handed over to his own brother to be kept in confinement,[d] he opened his veins with a penknife, but allowed himself to be bandaged and restored, not so much from unwillingness to die, as because of the entreaties of his friends; and he met a natural death while still in confinement. Lucius attained the consulate[e] and then was made governor of Syria, where with supreme diplomacy he not only induced Artabanus, king of the Parthians, to hold a conference with him,[f] but even to do obeisance to the standards of the legion. Later he held, with the emperor Claudius, two more regular consulships[g] and the censorship.[h] He also bore the charge of the empire while Claudius was away on his expedition to Britain.[i] He was an honest and active man, but of very ill repute because of his passion for a freed-woman, which went so far that he used her spittle mixed with honey to rub on his throat and jaws as a medicine, not secretly nor seldom, but openly and every day. He had also a wonderful gift for flattery and was the first to begin to worship Gaius Caesar as a god; for on his return

cum reversus ex Syria non aliter adire ausus esset quam
capite velato circumvertensque se, deinde procumbens.
Claudium uxoribus libertisque addictum ne qua non arte
demereretur, proximo munere a Messalina petit ut sibi
pedes praeberet excalciandos[1]; detractumque socculum
dextrum inter togam tunicasque gestavit assidue, nonnumquam osculabundus. Narcissi quoque et Pallantis
imagines aureas inter Lares coluit. Huius et illa vox est:
"Saepe facias," cum saeculares ludos edenti Claudio gratularetur.

III. Decessit paralysi altero die quam correptus est,
duobus filiis superstitibus, quos ex Sestilia[2] probatissima
nec ignobili femina editos consules vidit, et quidem
eodem ambos totoque anno, cum maiori minor in sex
menses successisset. Defunctum senatus publico funere
honoravit, item statua pro rostris cum hac inscriptione:
PIETATIS IMMOBILIS ERGA PRINCIPEM.

2   A. Vitellius L. filius imperator natus est VIII. Kal. Oct.,
vel ut quidam VII. Id. Sept., Druso Caesare Norbano
Flacco coss. Genituram eius praedictam a mathematicis
ita parentes exhorruerunt, ut pater magno opere semper
contenderit, ne qua ei provincia vivo se committeretur,
mater et missum ad legiones et appellatum imperatorem
pro afflicto statim lamentata sit. Pueritiam primamque
adulescentiam Capreis egit inter Tiberiana scorta, et

---

[1] excalciandos] exculciandos, *MGII*[1]*R*; exosculandos, *Q*.
[2] Sestilia, *the mss. except POST, which have* Sextilia.

[a] See *Claud.* xxix. 1.
[b] See *Claud.* xxi. 2.
[c] Sept. 24, A.D. 15.   [d] Sept. 7.

from Syria he did not presume to approach the emperor except with veiled head, turning himself about and then prostrating himself. To neglect no means of gaining the favour of Claudius, who was a slave to his wives and freedmen,[a] he begged of Messalina as the highest possible favour that she would allow him to take off her shoes; and when he had taken off her right slipper, he constantly carried it about between his toga and his tunic, and sometimes kissed it. Narcissus also and Pallas he honoured by cherishing their images among his household gods. It was he who made the famous remark, "May you often do it," when he was congratulating Claudius at the celebration of the Secular games.[b]

III. He died of a paralytic stroke on the second day after he was seized, leaving two sons, begotten of Sestilia, a most worthy woman and of no mean family, and having lived to see them consuls both in the same year, and for the whole year, since the younger succeeded the elder for six months. On his decease the senate honoured him with a public funeral and with a statue on the rostra with this inscription: "Of unwavering loyalty to his emperor."

The emperor Aulus Vitellius, son of Lucius, was born on the eighth day before the Kalends of October[c] or, according to some, on the seventh day before the Ides of September,[d] in the consulship of Drusus Caesar and Norbanus Flaccus. His parents were so aghast at his horoscope as announced by the astrologers that his father tried his utmost, while he lived, to prevent the assignment of any province to his son; and when he was sent to the legions and hailed as emperor, his mother immediately mourned over him as lost. He spent his boyhood and early youth at Capreae among Tiberius' lewd entourage

ipse perpetuo Spintriae[1] cognomine notatus existima-
tusque corporis gratia initium et causa incrementorum
patri fuisse.

IV. Sequenti quoque aetate omnibus probris contami-
natus, praecipuum in aula locum tenuit, Gaio per aurigandi, Claudio per aleae studium familiaris, sed aliquanto
Neroni acceptior, cum propter eadem haec, tum peculiari
merito, quod praesidens certamini Neroneo cupientem
inter citharoedos contendere nec quamvis flagitantibus
cunctis promittere audentem ideoque egressum theatro
revocaverat, quasi perseverantis populi legatione suscepta, exorandumque praebuerat.

V. Trium itaque principum indulgentia non solum
honoribus verum et sacerdotiis amplissimis auctus, proconsulatum Africae post haec curamque operum publicorum administravit et voluntate dispari et existimatione.
In provincia singularem innocentiam praestitit biennio
continuato, cum succedenti fratri legatus substitisset; at
in urbano officio dona atque ornamenta templorum subripuisse et commutasse quaedam ferebatur proque auro
et argento stagnum[2] et aurichalcum supposuisse.

VI. Uxorem habuit Petroniam consularis viri filiam et
ex ea filium Petronianum captum altero oculo. Hunc
heredem a matre sub condicione institutum, si de potestate patris exiisset, manu emisit brevique, ut creditum est,

---

[1] Spintriae] spintheriae, *mss.*
[2] stagnum, *the mss. except G* (stamnum) $\Pi^1\varsigma$ (stannum).

---

[a] See *Tib.* xliii. 1.
[b] See *Nero*, xii. 3 and xxi.
[c] In A.D. 60.

being branded for all time with the nickname Spintria[a] and suspected of having been the cause of his father's first advancement at the expense of his own chastity.

IV. Stained by every sort of baseness as he advanced in years, he held a prominent place at court, winning the intimacy of Gaius by his devotion to driving and of Claudius by his passion for dice. But he was still dearer to Nero, not only because of these same qualities, but because of a special service besides; for when he was presiding at the contests of the Neronia[b] and Nero wished to compete among the lyre-players, but did not venture to do so although there was a general demand for him and accordingly left the theatre, Vitellius called him back alleging that he came as an envoy from the insistent people, and thus gave Nero a chance to yield to their entreaties.

V. Having in this way through the favour of three emperors been honoured not only with political positions but with distinguished priesthoods as well, he afterwards governed Africa[c] as proconsul and served as curator of public works, but with varying purpose and reputation. In his province he showed exceptional integrity for two successive years, for he served as deputy to his brother, who succeeded him; but in his city offices he was said to have stolen some of the offerings and ornaments from the temples and changed others, substituting tin and brass for gold and silver.

VI. He had as wife Petronia, daughter of an ex-consul, and by her a son Petronianus, who was blind in one eye. Since this son was named as his mother's heir on condition of being freed from his father's authority, he manumitted him, but shortly afterwards killed him, according

interemit, insimulatum insuper parricidii et quasi paratum ad scelus venenum ex conscientia hausisset. Duxit mox Galeriam Fundanam praetorio patre ac de hac quoque liberos utriusque sexus tulit, sed marem titubantia oris prope mutum et elinguem.

VII. A Galba in inferiorem Germaniam contra opinionem missus est. Adiutum putant T. Vini[1] suffragio, tunc potentissimi et cui iam pridem per communem factionis Venetae favorem conciliatus esset; nisi quod Galba prae se tulit nullos minus metuendos quam qui de solo victu cogitarent, ac posse provincialibus copiis profundam gulam eius expleri, ut cuivis evidens sit contemptu

2   magis quam gratia electum. Satis constat exituro viaticum defuisse, tanta egestate rei familiaris, ut uxore et liberis, quos Romae relinquebat, meritorio cenaculo abditis domum in reliquam partem anni ablocaret utque ex aure matris detractum unionem pigneraverit ad itineris impensas. Creditorum quidem praestolantium ac detinentium turbam et in iis Sinuessanos Formianosque, quorum publica vectigalia interverterat, non nisi terrore calumniae amovit, cum libertino cuidam acerbius debitum reposcenti iniuriarum formulam, quasi calce ab eo percussus, intendisset nec aliter quam extortis quinquaginta sestertiis remisisset.

---

[1] Vini, *Torrentius*; Iuni, Ω.

---

[a] A faction in the Circus; see note on *Calig.* lv. 2.

to the general belief, charging him besides with attempted parricide, and alleging that his guilty conscience had led him to drink the poison which he had mixed for his intended crime. Soon afterwards he married Galeria Fundana, daughter of an ex-praetor, and from her too he had a son and a daughter, but the former stammered so badly that he was all but dumb and tongue-tied.

VII. Galba surprised everyone by sending him to Lower Germany. Some think that it was due to Titus Vinius, who had great influence at the time, and whose friendship Vitellius had long since won through their common support of the Blues.[a] But since Galba openly declared that no men were less to be feared than those who thought of nothing but eating, and that Vitellius' bottomless gullet might be filled from the resources of the province, it is clear to anyone that he was chosen rather through contempt than favour. It is notorious that when he was about to start, he lacked means for his travelling expenses, and that his need of funds was such that, after consigning his wife and children, whom he left in Rome, to a hired garret, he let his house for the rest of the year; and that he took a valuable pearl from his mother's ear and pawned it, to defray the expenses of his journey. He had to resort to false accusation to get rid of the throng of creditors that lay in wait for him and tried to detain him, including the people of Sinuessa and of Formiae, whose public revenues he had embezzled; for he brought an action for damages against a freedman who was somewhat persistent in demanding what was due to him, alleging that he had been kicked by him, and would not let him off until he had squeezed him to the tune of fifty thousand sesterces.

3   Advenientem male animatus erga principem exercitus
pronusque ad res novas libens ac supinis manibus excepit
velut dono deum oblatum, ter consulis filium, aetate inte-
gra, facili ac prodigo animo. Quam veterem de se persua-
sionem Vitellius recentibus etiam experimentis auxerat,
tota via caligatorum quoque militum obvios exosculans
perque stabula ac deversoria mulionibus ac viatoribus
praeter modum comis, ut mane singulos iamne iantassent
sciscitaretur seque fecisse ructu quoque ostenderet.

VIII. Castra vero ingressus nihil cuiquam poscenti
negavit atque etiam ultro ignominiosis notas, reis sordes,
damnatis supplicia dempsit. Quare vixdum mense transacto, neque diei neque temporis ratione habita, ac iam
vespere, subito a militibus e cubiculo raptus, ita ut erat in
veste domestica, imperator est consalutatus circumlatus-
que per celeberrimos vicos, strictum Divi Iuli gladium
tenens detractum delubro Martis atque in prima gratula-
2   tione porrectum sibi a quodam. Nec ante in praetorium
rediit quam flagrante triclinio ex conceptu camini, cum
quidem consternatis et quasi omine adverso anxiis
omnibus: "Bono," inquit, "animo estote! nobis adluxit,"
nullo sermone alio apud milites usus. Consentiente
deinde etiam superioris provinciae exercitu, qui prior a
Galba ad senatum defecerat, cognomen Germanici dela-

    ᵃ *Supinis manibus*, "with hands uplifted," to the gods in grati-
tude.

    ᵇ See *Aug.* xxxii. 2.

    ᶜ Cf. *Aug.* lxxiii and the note. See also Seneca, *De Tranq. An.*
1. 5, *placet . . . non ex arcula prolata vestis . . . sed domestica et
vilis, nec servata nec sumenda sollicite.*

On his arrival the army, which was disaffected towards the emperor and inclined to mutiny, received him gladly with open arms,[a] as if he had come to them as a gift from the gods, since he was the son of the man who had thrice been consul, in the prime of life, and of an easy-going and lavish disposition. This earlier good opinion Vitellius had also strengthened by recent acts, for throughout the march he kissed even the common soldiers whom he met, and at the posthouses and inns he was unusually affable to the mule drivers and travellers, asking each of them in the morning whether they had breakfasted and even showing by belching that he had done so.

VIII. As soon as he entered the camp, he granted every request that anyone made and even of his own accord freed those in disgrace from their penalties, defendants of suits from their mourning,[b] and the convicted from punishment. Therefore hardly a month had passed, when the soldiers, regardless of the hour, for it was already evening, hastily took him from his bedroom, just as he was, in his common houseclothes,[c] and hailed him as emperor. Then he was carried about the most populous villages, holding a drawn sword of the Deified Julius, which someone had taken from a shrine of Mars and handed him during the first congratulations. He did not return to headquarters until the dining-room caught fire from the stove and was ablaze; and then, when all were shocked and troubled at what seemed a bad omen, he said: "Be of good cheer; to us light is given"; and this was his only address to the soldiers. When he presently received the support of the army of the upper province too, which had previously transferred its allegiance from Galba to the senate, he eagerly accepted the surname of

tum ab universis cupide recepit, Augusti distulit, Caesaris in perpetuum recusavit.

IX. Ac subinde caede Galbae adnuntiata, compositis Germanicis rebus, partitus est copias, quas adversus Othonem praemitteret quasque ipse perduceret. Praemisso agmine laetum evenit auspicium, siquidem a parte dextra repente aquila advolavit lustratisque[1] signis ingressos viam sensim antecessit. At contra ipso movente statuae equestres, cum plurifariam ei ponerentur, fractis repente cruribus pariter corruerunt, et laurea, quam religiosissime circumdederat, in profluentem excidit; mox Viennae pro tribunali iura reddenti gallinaceus supra umerum ac deinde in capite astitit. Quibus ostentis par respondit exitus; nam confirmatum per legatos suos imperium per se retinere non potuit.

X. De Betriacensi victoria et Othonis exitu, cum adhuc in Gallia esset, audiit nihilque cunctatus, quicquid praetorianarum cohortium fuit, ut pessimi exempli, uno exauctoravit edicto iussas tribunis tradere arma. Centum autem atque viginti, quorum libellos Othoni datos invenerat exposcentium praemium ob editam in caede Galbae operam, conquiri et supplicio adfici imperavit, egregie prorsus atque magnifice et ut summi principis spem ostenderet, nisi cetera magis ex natura et priore vita sua

---

[1] lustratisque, ς (*second Roman edition*); lustravitque, Ω.

---

[a] Vienne, on the Rhone.
[b] See chap. xviii below.
[c] In deserting Galba for Otho.

Germanicus, which was unanimously offered him, put off accepting the title of Augustus, and forever refused that of Caesar.

IX. Then hearing of the murder of Galba, he settled affairs in Germany and made two divisions of his forces, one to send on against Otho, and the other to lead in person. The former was greeted with a lucky omen at the start, for an eagle suddenly flew towards them from the right and after hovering about the standards, slowly preceded their line of march. But, on the contary, when he himself began his advance, the equestrian statues which were being set up everywhere in his honour on a sudden all collapsed with broken legs, and the laurel crown which he had put on with due ceremony fell into a running stream. Later, as he was sitting in judgment on the tribunal at Vienna,[a] a cock perched on his shoulder and then on his head.[b] And the outcome corresponded with these omens; for he was not by his own efforts able to retain the power which his lieutenants secured for him.

X. He heard of the victory at Betriacum and of the death of Otho when he was still in Gaul, and without delay by a single edict he disbanded all the praetorian cohorts, as having set a pernicious example,[c] and bade them hand over their arms to their tribunes. Furthermore, he gave orders that one hundred and twenty of them should be hunted up and punished, having found petitions which they had written to Otho, asking for a reward for services rendered in connection with Galba's murder. These acts were altogether admirable and noble, and such as to give hope that he would be a great prince, had it not been that the rest of his conduct was more in harmony with his natural disposition and his former

249

2   quam ex imperii maiestate gessisset. Namque itinere
incohato per medias civitates ritu triumphantium vectus
est perque flumina delicatissimis navigiis et variarum
coronarum genere redimitis, inter profusissimos obsonio-
rum apparatus, nulla familiae aut militis disciplina, rapinas ac petulantiam omnium in iocum vertens, qui non
contenti epulo ubique publice praebito, quoscumque
libuisset in libertatem asserebant, verbera et plagas,
saepe vulnera, nonnumquam necem repraesentantes

3   adversantibus. Utque campos, in quibus pugnatum est,
adit, abhorrentis quosdam cadaverum tabem detestabili
voce confirmare ausus est, optime olere occisum hostem
et melius civem. Nec eo setius ad leniendam gravitatem
odoris plurimum meri propalam hausit passimque divisit.
Pari vanitate atque insolentia lapidem memoriae Othonis
inscriptum intuens dignum eo Mausoleo ait, pugionem-
que, quo is se occiderat, in Agrippinensem coloniam misit
Marti dedicandum. In Appennini quidem iugis etiam
pervigilium egit.

    XI. Urbem denique ad classicum introiit paludatus
ferroque succinctus, inter signa atque vexilla, sagulatis
comitibus ac detectis commilitonum armis.

2   Magis deinde ac magis omni divino humanoque iure
neglecto Alliensi die pontificatum maximum cepit, comitia in decem annos ordinavit seque perpetuum consulem.

---

    [a] Modern Cologne.

    [b] See note on *Calig*. liv. 2. The connection suggests an orgy
in celebration of his victory.

    [c] A day of special ill omen because of the defeat by the Gauls
in 390 B.C.

habits of life than with imperial dignity. For when he had begun his march, he rode through the middle of the cities like a triumphing general, and on the rivers he sailed in most exquisite craft wreathed with various kinds of garlands, amid lavish banqueting with no discipline among his household or the soldiers, making a jest of the pillage and wantonness of all his followers. For not content with the banquets which were furnished them everywhere at public expense, they set free whatever slaves they pleased, promptly paying those who remonstrated with blows and stripes, often with wounds, and sometimes with death. When he came to the plains where the battle was fought and some shuddered with horror at the mouldering corpses, he had the audacity to encourage them by the abominable remark that the odour of a dead enemy was sweet and that of a fellow-citizen sweeter still. But nevertheless, the better to bear the awful stench, he openly drained a great draught of unmixed wine and distributed some among the troops. With equal bad taste and arrogance, gazing upon the stone inscribed to the memory of Otho, he declared that he deserved such a Mausoleum, and sent the dagger with which his rival had killed himself to the Colony of Agrippina,[a] to be dedicated to Mars. He also held an all night festival[b] on the heights of the Apennines.

XI. Finally he entered the city to the sound of the trumpet, wearing a general's mantle and a sword at his side, amid standards and banners, with his staff in military cloaks and his troops with drawn swords.

Then showing greater and greater disregard for the laws of gods and men, he assumed the office of high priest on the day of Allia,[c] held elections for ten years to come,

Et ne cui dubium foret, quod exemplar regendae rei p. eligeret, medio Martio campo adhibita publicorum sacerdotum frequentia inferias Neroni dedit ac sollemni convivio citharoedum placentem palam admonuit, ut aliquid et de dominico diceret, incohantique Neroniana cantica primus exsultans etiam plausit.

XII. Talibus principiis magnam imperii partem non nisi consilio et arbitrio vilissimi cuiusque histrionum et aurigarum administravit et maxime Asiatici liberti. Hunc adulescentulum mutua libidine constupratum, mox taedio profugum cum Puteolis poscam vendentem reprehendisset, coniecit in compedes statimque solvit[1] et rursus in deliciis habuit; iterum deinde ob nimiam contumaciam et furacitatem gravatus circumforano[2] lanistae vendidit dilatumque ad finem muneris repente subripuit et provincia demum accepta manumisit ac primo imperii die aureis donavit anulis super cenam, cum mane rogantibus pro eo cunctis detestatus esset severissime talem equestris ordinis maculam.

XIII. Sed vel praecipue luxuriae saevitiaeque deditus epulas trifariam semper, interdum quadrifariam dispertiebat, in iantacula et prandia et cenas comissationesque,

---

[1] solvit, *Basle edition of* 1533; coluit, Ω.
[2] circumforano] circumforaneo, ϛ.

---

[a] *Dominicus* (*liber*) was the name applied to a collection of Nero's compositions.

[b] A drink made of sour wine or vinegar mixed with water.

[c] The *iantaculum* (also *ient-* and *ieient-*) was ordinarily a very light breakfast; Vitellius made a banquet of it.

and made himself consul for life. And to leave no doubt in anyone's mind what model he chose for the government of the State, he made funerary offerings to Nero in the middle of the Campus Martius, attended by a great throng of the official priests; and when at the accompanying banquet a flute-player was received with applause, he openly urged him "to render something from the Master's Book[a] as well"; and when he began the songs of Nero, Vitellius was the first to applaud him and even leaped to his feet.

XII. Beginning in this way, he regulated the greater part of his rule wholly according to the advice and whims of the commonest of actors and chariot-drivers, and in particular of his freedman Asiaticus. In his youth this fellow had been sexually violated by Vitellius to their mutual pleasure, but later grew weary of him and ran away. When Vitellius came upon him selling *posca*[b] at Puteoli, he put him in irons, but at once freed him again and made him one of his favourites. His vexation was renewed by the man's excessive insolence and thievishness, and he sold him to an itinerant keeper of gladiators. When, however, he was once reserved for the end of a gladiatorial show, Vitellius suddenly spirited him away, and finally on getting his province set him free. On the first day of his reign he presented him with the golden ring at a banquet, although in the morning, when there was a general demand that Asiaticus be given that honour, he had deprecated in the strongest terms such a blot on the equestrian order.

XIII. But his besetting sins were luxury and cruelty. He divided his feasts into three, sometimes into four a day, breakfast,[c] luncheon, dinner, and a drinking bout; and he was readily able to do justice to all of them

facile omnibus sufficiens vomitandi consuetudine. Indicebat autem aliud alii eadem die, nec cuiquam minus singuli apparatus quadringenis milibus nummum con-
2 stiterunt. Famosissima super ceteras fuit cena data ei adventicia a fratre, in qua duo milia lectissimorum piscium, septem avium apposita traduntur. Hanc quoque exsuperavit ipse dedicatione patinae, quam ob immensam magnitudinem clipeum Minervae πολιούχου[1] dictitabat. In hac scarorum iocinera, phasianarum[2] et pavonum cerebella, linguas phoenicopterum, murenarum lactes a Parthia usque fretoque Hispanico per nauarchos ac
3 triremes petitarum commiscuit. Ut autem homo non profundae modo sed intempestivae quoque ac sordidae gulae, ne in sacrificio quidem umquam aut itinere ullo temperavit, quin inter altaria ibidem statim viscus et farris frusta[3] paene rapta e foco manderet circaque viarum popinas fumantia obsonia vel pridiana atque semesa.

XIV. Pronus vero ad cuiuscumque et quacumque de causa necem atque supplicium nobiles viros, condiscipulos et aequales suos, omnibus blanditiis tantum non ad societatem imperii adlicefactos vario genere fraudis occidit, etiam unum veneno manu sua porrecto in aquae
2 frigidae potione, quam is adfectus febre poposcerat. Tum faeneratorum et stipulatorum publicanorumque, qui

---

[1] πολιούχου, *Stephanus*; τονδυχον, Ω.
[2] phasianarum] fasianarum, Ω.
[3] farris frusta *and* farra, ⸸; farris, Ω.

---

[a] Probably referring to the colossal statue of Athena Promachos on the Acropolis at Athens. Pliny, *N.H.* 35. 163 ff., says that the platter cost a million sesterces, and that to make it a special furnace was built in the open fields.   [b] That is, from the eastern to the western limits of the Roman world.

through his habit of vomiting. Moreover, he had himself invited to each of these meals by different men on the same day, and the materials for any one of them never cost less than four hundred thousand sesterces. Most notorious of all was the dinner given by his brother to celebrate the emperor's arrival in Rome, at which two thousand of the choicest fishes and seven thousand birds are said to have been served. He himself eclipsed even this at the dedication of a platter, which on account of its enormous size he called the "Shield of Minerva, Defender of the City."[a] In this he mingled the livers of pike, the brains of pheasants and peacocks, the tongues of flamingoes and the milk of lampreys, brought by his captains and triremes from the whole empire, from Parthia to the Spanish strait.[b] Being besides a man of an appetite that was not only boundless, but also regardless of time or decency, he could never refrain, even when he was sacrificing or making a journey, from snatching bits of meat and cakes amid the altars, almost from the very fire, and devouring them on the spot; and in the cookshops along the road, food smoking hot or even those left over from the day before and partly consumed.

XIV. He delighted in inflicting death and torture on anyone whatsoever and for any cause whatever, putting to death several men of rank, fellow students and comrades of his, whom he had solicited to come to court by every kind of deception, all but offering them a share in the rule. This he did in various treacherous ways, even giving poison to one of them with his own hand in a glass of cold water, for which the man had called when ill of a fever. Besides he spared hardly one of the money-lenders, contractors, and tax-gatherers who had ever demanded of

umquam se aut Romae debitum aut in via portorium flagitassent, vix ulli pepercit; ex quibus quendam in ipsa salutatione supplicio traditum statimque revocatum, cunctis clementiam laudantibus, coram interfici iussit, velle se dicens pascere oculos; alterius poenae duos filios

3 adiecit deprecari pro patre conatos. Sed et equitem R. proclamantem, cum raperetur ad poenam: "Heres meus es," exhibere testamenti tabulas coegit, utque legit coheredem sibi libertum eius ascriptum, iugulari cum liberto imperavit. Quosdam et de plebe ob id ipsum, quod Venetae factioni clare male dixerant, interemit con-

4 temptu sui et nova spe id ausos opinatus.[1] Nullis tamen infensior quam vernaculis et mathematicis, ut quisque deferretur, inauditum capite puniebat exacerbatus, quod post edictum suum, quo iubebat intra Kal. Oct. urbe Italiaque mathematici excederent, statim libellus propositus est, et Chaldaeos dicere, bonum factum, ne Vitellius Germanicus intra eundem Kalendarum diem usquam esset.

5 Suspectus et in morte matris fuit, quasi aegrae praeberi cibum prohibuisset, vaticinante Chatta[2] muliere, cui velut oraculo adquiescebat, ita demum firmiter ac diutissime imperaturum, si superstes parenti exstitisset. Alii

---

[1] opinatus] obstinatus, *M*Υ; obstinatosque, *G*.
[2] Chatta] Chattha, *MG*; catha, Υ; cata, *X*.

---

[a] See *Calig.* iv. 2 and note.   [b] *Vernaculus* and *verna* are used by Martial 10. 3. 1 and 1. 41. 2 in the sense of "buffoons," a meaning derived from the proverbial insolence of the *vernae*, or home-born slaves. The connection of the word here with *mathematicis*, and the fact that only the astrologers are mentioned in what follows, would seem to imply that the lampoons of these jesters contained predictions about Vitellius.   [c] That is, the astrologers, for whom *Chaldaei* became a general term.

him the payment of a debt at Rome or of a toll on a journey. When one of these had been handed over for execution just as he was paying his morning call and at once recalled, as all were praising the emperor's mercy, Vitellius gave orders to have him killed in his presence, saying that he wished to feast his eyes. In another case he had two sons who attempted to intercede for their father put to death with him. A Roman knight also, who cried as he was being taken off to execution, "You are my heir," he compelled to show his will; and reading that one of the man's freedmen was put down as joint-heir with himself, he ordered the death of both the knight and the freedman. He even killed some of the common people, merely because they had openly spoken ill of the Blue faction,[a] thinking that they had ventured to do this from contempt of himself and the anticipation of a change of rulers. But he was especially hostile to writers of lampoons[b] and to astrologers, and whenever any one of them was accused, he put him to death without trial, particularly incensed because after a proclamation of his in which he ordered the astrologers to leave the city and Italy before the Kalends of October, a placard was at once posted, reading: "By proclamation of the Chaldeans,[c] God bless the State![d] Before the same day and date let Vitellius Germanicus have ceased to live." Moreover, when his mother died, he was suspected of having forbidden her being given food when she was ill, because a woman of the Chatti, in whom he believed as he would in an oracle, prophesied that he would rule securely and for a long time, but only if he should survive his parent. Others say

[d] See note on *Jul.* lxxx. 2.

tradunt ipsam taedio praesentium et imminentium metu
venenum a filio impetrasse, haud sane difficulter.

XV. Octavo imperii mense desciverunt ab eo exercitus
Moesiarum atque Pannoniae, item ex transmarinis
Iudaicus et Syriaticus, ac pars in absentis pars in praesen-
tis Vespasiani verba iurarunt. Ad retinendum ergo ceterorum hominum studium ac favorem nihil non publice
privatimque nullo adhibito modo largitus est. Dilectum
quoque ea condicione in urbe egit, ut voluntariis non
modo missionem post victoriam, sed etiam veteranorum
2 iustaeque militiae commoda polliceretur. Urgenti deinde
terra marique hosti hinc fratrem cum classe ac tironibus
et gladiatorum manu opposuit, hinc Betriacenses copias
et duces; atque ubique aut superatus aut proditus salutem
sibi et milies sestertium a Flavio Sabino Vespasiani fratre
pepigit; statimque pro gradibus Palati apud frequentes
milites cedere se imperio quod invitus recepisset professus, cunctis reclamantibus[1] rem distulit ac nocte inter-
posita primo diluculo sordidatus descendit ad rostra multisque cum lacrimis eadem illa, verum e libello testatus
3 est. Rursus interpellante milite ac populo et ne deficeret
hortante omnemque operam suam certatim pollicente,
animum resumpsit Sabinumque et reliquos Flavianos

---

[1] reclamantibus, S⊊; declamantibus, Ω.

that through weariness of present evils and fear of those which threatened, she asked poison of her son, and obtained it with no great difficulty.

XV. In the eighth month of his reign the armies of the Moesian provinces and Pannonia revolted from him, and also in the provinces beyond the seas those of Judaea and Syria, the former swearing allegiance to Vespasian in his absence and the latter in his presence. Therefore, to retain the devotion and favour of the rest of the people, there was nothing that he did not lavish publicly and privately, without any limit whatever. He also held a levy in the city, promising those who volunteered not only their discharge upon his victory but also the rewards and privileges given to veterans after their regular term of service. Later, when his enemies were pressing him hard by land and sea, he opposed to them in one quarter his brother with a fleet manned by raw recruits and a band of gladiators, and in another the forces and leaders who had fought at Betriacum. And after he was everywhere either worsted or betrayed, he made a bargain with Flavius Sabinus, the brother of Vespasian, that he should have his own life and a hundred million sesterces. Thereupon he immediately declared from the steps of the Palace before his assembled soldiers that he withdrew from the rule which had been given him against his will; but when all cried out against this, he postponed the matter, and after a night had passed, went at daybreak to the rostra in mourning garb and with many tears made the same declaration, but from a written document. When the people and soldiers again interrupted him and besought him not to lose heart, vying with one another in promising him all their efforts in his behalf, he again took courage and by a sudden onslaught drove Sabinus and the rest of the

nihil iam metuentis vi subita in Capitolium compulit succensoque templo Iovis Optimi Maximi oppressit, cum et proelium et incendium e Tiberiana prospiceret domo inter epulas. Non multo post paenitens facti et in alios culpam conferens vocata contione iuravit coegitque iurare et ceteros nihil sibi antiquius quiete publica fore.

4 Tunc solutum a latere pugionem consuli primum, deinde illo recusante magistratibus ac mox senatoribus singulis porrigens, nullo recipiente, quasi in aede Concordiae positurus abscessit. Sed quibusdam adclamantibus ipsum esse Concordiam, rediit nec solum retinere se ferrum affirmavit, verum etiam Concordiae recipere cognomen.

XVI. Suasitque senatui, ut legatos cum virginibus Vestalibus mitterent pacem aut certe tempus ad consultandum petituros.

Postridie responsa opperienti nuntiatum est per exploratorem hostes appropinquare. Continuo igitur abstrusus gestatoria sella duobus solis comitibus, pistore et coco, Aventinum et paternam domum clam petit, ut inde in Campaniam fugeret; mox levi rumore et incerto, tamquam pax impetrata esset, referri se in Palatium passus est. Ubi cum deserta omnia repperisset, dilabentibus et qui simul erant, zona se aureorum plena circumdedit confugitque in cellulam ianitoris, religato pro foribus cane lectoque et culcita obiectis.

---

[a] As a sign that he was willing to renounce the power of life and death over the people; Tac. *Hist.* 3. 68.

Flavians, who no longer feared an attack, into the Capitol. Then he set fire to the temple of Jupiter Optimus Maximus and destroyed them, viewing the battle and the fire from the house of Tiberius, where he was feasting. Not long afterwards, repenting of his action and throwing the blame upon others, he called an assembly and took oath, compelling the rest to do the same, that there was nothing for which he would strive more earnestly than for the public peace. Then he took a dagger from his side and offered it first to the consul, and when he refused it, to the magistrates, and then to the senators, one by one.[a] When no one would take it, he went off as if he would place it in the temple of Concord; but when some cried out that he himself was Concord, he returned and declared that he would not only retain the steel but would also adopt the surname Concordia.

XVI. He also persuaded the senate to send envoys with the Vestal virgins, to sue for peace or at least to gain time for conference.

The following day, as he was waiting for a reply, word was brought by a scout that the enemy were drawing near. Then he was at once hurried into a sedan chair with only two companions, a baker and a cook, and secretly went to his father's house on the Aventine, intending to flee from there to Campania. Presently, on a slight and dubious rumour that peace had been granted, he allowed himself to be taken back to the Palace. Finding everything abandoned there, and that even those who were with him were making off, he put on a girdle filled with gold pieces and took refuge in a lodge of the door-keeper, tying a dog before the door and putting a couch and a mattress against it.

XVII. Irruperant iam agminis antecessores ac nemine obvio rimabantur, ut fit, singula. Ab his extractus e latebra, sciscitantes, quis esset—nam ignorabatur—et ubi esse Vitellium sciret, mendacio elusit; deinde agnitus rogare non destitit, quasi quaedam de salute Vespasiani dicturus, ut custodiretur interim vel in carcere, donec religatis post terga manibus, iniecto cervicibus laqueo, veste discissa seminudus in Forum tractus est inter magna rerum verborumque ludibria per totum viae Sacrae spatium, reducto coma capite, ceu noxii solent, atque etiam mento mucrone gladii subrecto, ut visendam praeberet faciem neve summitteret; quibusdam stercore et caeno incessentibus, aliis incendiarium et patinarium vociferantibus, parte vulgi etiam corporis vitia exprobrante; erat enim in eo enormis proceritas, facies rubida plerumque ex vinulentia, venter obesus, alterum femur subdebile impulsu olim quadrigae, cum auriganti Gaio ministratorem exhiberet. Tandem apud Gemonias minutissimis ictibus excarnificatus atque confectus est et inde unco tractus in Tiberim.

XVIII. Periit cum fratre et filio anno vitae septimo quinquagesimo; nec fefellit coniectura eorum qui augurio, quod factum ei Viennae ostendimus, non aliud portendi praedixerant quam venturum in alicuius Gallicani hominis potestatem, siquidem ab Antonio Primo adversarum partium duce oppressus est, cui Tolosae nato cognomen in pueritia Becco fuerat: id valet gallinacei rostrum.

---

[a] Chap. ix, above.

[b] *Gallus* means "a cock," as well as "a Gaul."

XVII. The foremost of the army had now forced their way in, and since no one opposed them, were ransacking everything in the usual way. They dragged Vitellius from his hiding-place and when they asked him his name (for they did not know him) and if he knew where Vitellius was, he attempted to escape them by a lie. Being soon recognised, he did not cease to beg that he be confined for a time, even in the prison, alleging that he had something to say of importance to the safety of Vespasian. But they bound his arms behind his back, put a noose about his neck, and dragged him with rent garments and half-naked to the Forum. All along the Sacred Way he was greeted with mockery and abuse, his head held back by the hair, as is common with criminals, and even the point of a sword placed under his chin, so that he could not look down but must let his face be seen. Some pelted him with dung and filth, others called him incendiary and glutton, and some of the mob even taunted him with his bodily defects. He was in fact abnormally tall, with a face usually flushed from hard drinking, a huge belly, and one thigh crippled from being struck once upon a time by a four-horse chariot, when he was in attendance on Gaius as he was driving. At last on the Stairs of Wailing he was tortured by many small stabbings and then despatched and dragged off with a hook to the Tiber.

XVIII. He met his death, along with his brother and his son, in the fifty-seventh year of his age, fulfilling the prediction of those who had declared from an omen which befell him at Vienna, as we have stated,[a] that he was destined to fall into the power of some man of Gaul. For he was slain by Antonius Primus, a leader of the opposing faction, who was born at Tolosa and in his youth bore the surname Becco, which means a rooster's beak.[b]

LIBER VIII

DIVUS VESPASIANUS
DIVUS TITUS · DOMITIANUS

Divus Vespasianus

I. Rebellione trium principum et caede incertum diu
et quasi vagum imperium suscepit firmavitque tandem
gens Flavia, obscura illa quidem ac sine ullis maiorum
imaginibus, sed tamen rei p. nequaquam paenitenda,
constet licet Domitianum cupiditatis ac saevitiae merito
poenas luisse.

2   T. Flavius Petro, municeps Reatinus, bello civili Pom-
peianarum partium centurio an evocatus, profugit ex
Pharsalica acie domumque se contulit, ubi deinde venia
et missione impetrata coactiones argentarias factitavit.
Huius filius, cognomine Sabinus, expers militiae—etsi
quidam eum primipilarem, nonnulli, cum adhuc ordines
duceret, sacramento solutum per causam valitudinis
tradunt—publicum quadragesimae in Asia egit; mane-
bantque imagines a civitatibus ei positae sub hoc titulo:

---

[a] See note on *Galba*, x. 3.
[b] A duty (*portorium*) of two and a half percent on imports
and exports; cf. *Jul.* xliii. 1.

BOOK VIII

THE DEIFIED VESPASIAN
THE DEIFIED TITUS · DOMITIAN

THE DEIFIED VESPASIAN

I. The empire, which had long been unsettled and, as it were, drifting, through the usurpation and violent death of three emperors, was at last taken in hand and given stability by the Flavian family. This house was, it is true, obscure and without family portraits, yet it was one of which our country had no reason whatever to be ashamed, even though it is the general opinion that the penalty which Domitian paid for his avarice and cruelty was fully merited.

Titus Flavius Petro, a burgher of Reate and during the civil war a centurion or a volunteer veteran[a] on Pompey's side, fled from the field of Pharsalus and went home, where, after at last obtaining pardon and an honourable discharge, he carried on the business of a collector of moneys. His son, surnamed Sabinus, although some say that he was an ex-centurion of the first grade, others that while still in command of a cohort he was retired because of ill-health, took no part in military life, but farmed the public tax of a fortieth[b] in Asia. And there existed for some time statues erected in his honour by the cities of

265

LIVES OF THE CAESARS, VIII

3 ΚΑΛΩΣ ΤΕΛΩΝΗΣΑΝΤΙ. Postea faenus apud Helvetios exercuit ibique diem obiit superstitibus uxore Vespasia Polla et duobus ex ea liberis, quorum maior Sabinus ad praefecturam urbis, minor Vespasianus ad principatum usque processit. Polla Nursiae honesto genere orta patrem habuit Vespasium Pollionem, ter tribunum militum praefectumque castrorum, fratrem senatorem praetoriae dignitatis. Locus etiam ad sextum miliarium a Nursia Spoletium euntibus in monte summo appellatur Vespasiae, ubi Vespasiorum complura monumenta exstant, magnum indicium splendoris familiae et vetustatis.

4 Non negaverim iactatum a quibusdam Petronis patrem e regione Transpadana fuisse mancipem operarum, quae ex Umbria in Sabinos ad culturam agrorum quotannis commeare soleant; subsedisse autem in oppido Reatino uxore ibidem ducta. Ipse ne vestigium quidem de hoc, quamvis satis curiose inquirerem, inveni.

II. Vespasianus natus est in Sabinis[1] ultra Reate vico modico, cui nomen est Falacrinae,[2] XV. Kal. Decb. vesperi, Q.[3] Sulpicio Camerino C. Poppaeo Sabino coss., quinquennio ante quam Augustus excederet; educatus sub paterna avia Tertulla in praediis Cosanis. Quare princeps quoque et locum incunabulorum assidue frequentavit, manente villa qualis fuerat olim, ne quid scilicet

---

[1] Sabinis, ς; Samnis, Ω.   [2] Falacrinae] Phalacrinae (-ne), Ω.   [3] vesperiq(ue), Ω; *corrected in* ς.

---

[a] A position held by tried and skilful officers, especially centurions of the first grade (*primipili*; *C.I.L.* iii. 6809, etc.). Cf. Vegetius, *Epit. Rei Milit.* 2. 10, *is post longam probatamque militiam peritissimus omnium legebatur, ut recte doceret alios quod ipse cum laude fecisset.*   [b] Nov. 17, A.D. 9.

Asia, inscribed "To an honest tax-gatherer." Later he carried on a banking business in the Helvetian country and there he died, survived by his wife, Vespasia Polla, and by two of her children, of whom the elder, Sabinus, rose to the rank of prefect of Rome, and the younger, Vespasian, even to that of emperor. Polla, who was born of an honourable family at Nursia, had for father Vespasius Pollio, thrice tribune of the soldiers and prefect of the camp,[a] while her brother became a senator with the rank of praetor. There is moreover on the top of a mountain, near the sixth milestone on the road from Nursia to Spoletium, a place called Vespasiae, where many monuments of the Vespasii are to be seen, affording strong proof of the renown and antiquity of the house. I ought to add that some have bandied about the report that Petro's father came from the region beyond the Po and was a contractor for the day-labourers who come regularly every year from Umbria to the Sabine district, to till the fields; but that he settled in the town of Reate and there married. Personally I have found no evidence whatever of this, in spite of rather careful investigation.

II. Vespasian was born in the Sabine country, in a small village beyond Reate, called Falacrina, on the evening of the fifteenth day before the Kalends of December,[b] in the consulate of Quintus Sulpicius Camerinus and Gaius Poppaeus Sabinus, five years before the death of Augustus. He was brought up under the care of his paternal grandmother Tertulla on her estates at Cosa. Therefore even after he became emperor he used constantly to visit the home of his infancy, where the manor house was kept in its original condition, since he did not

oculorum consuetudini deperiret; et aviae memoriam tanto opere dilexit, ut sollemnibus ac festis diebus pocillo quoque eius argenteo potare perseveraverit.

2   Sumpta virili toga latum clavum, quanquam fratre adepto, diu aversatus est, nec ut tandem appeteret compelli nisi a matre potuit. Ea demum extudit magis convicio quam precibus vel auctoritate, dum eum identidem per contumeliam anteambulonem fratris appellat.

3   Tribunatu[1] militum in Thracia meruit; quaestor Cretam et Cyrenas provinciam sorte cepit; aedilitatis ac mox praeturae candidatus, illam[2] non sine repulsa sextoque vix adeptus est loco, hanc[3] prima statim petitione et in primis. Praetor infensum[4] senatui Gaium ne quo non genere demereretur, ludos extraordinarios pro victoria eius Germanica depoposcit poenaeque coniuratorum addendum censuit, ut insepulti proicerentur. Egit et gratias ei apud amplissimum ordinem, quod se honore cenae dignatus esset.

    III. Inter haec Flaviam Domitillam duxit uxorem, Statili Capellae equitis R. Sabratensis ex Africa delicatam olim Latinaeque condicionis, sed mox ingenuam et civem Rom. reciperatorio iudicio pronuntiatam, patre asserente Flavio Liberale Ferenti genito nec quicquam amplius

---

[1] tribunatu, *Lipsius;* tribunatum *mss.;* tribunus *Torrentius.*
[2] illam, *Torrentius;* etiam, Ω.
[3] hanc, *Bentley, Duker;* ac, Ω.
[4] infensum, *Lipsius;* infensus (-os), *mss.*

---

[a] The *anteambulo* was the client who walked before his patron on the street and compelled people to make way for him; cf. Mart. 2. 18. 5, *tumidique anteambulo regis,* where *regis* means "patron," as in Hor. *Epist.* 1. 17. 43 and elsewhere.
    [b] In A.D. 38.   [c] In A.D. 39.   [d] See *Calig.* xlviii and xlix.

wish to miss anything which he was wont to see there; and he was so devoted to his grandmother's memory that on religious and festival days he always drank from a little silver cup that had belonged to her.

After assuming the garb of manhood he for a long time made no attempt to win the broad stripe of senator, though his brother had gained it, and only his mother could finally induce him to sue for it. She at length drove him to it, but rather by sarcasm than by entreaties or parental authority, since she constantly taunted him with being his brother's footman.[a]

He served in Thrace as tribune of the soldiers; as quaestor was assigned by lot to the province of Crete and Cyrene; became a candidate for the aedileship and then for the praetorship, attaining[b] the former only after one defeat and then barely landing in the sixth place, but the latter[c] on his first canvass and among the foremost. In his praetorship, to lose no opportunity of winning the favour of Gaius, who was at odds with the senate,[d] he asked for special games because of the emperor's victory in Germany and recommended as an additional punishment of the conspirators[e] that they be cast out unburied. He also thanked the emperor before that illustrious body[f] because he had deigned to honour him with an invitation to dinner.

III. Meanwhile he took to wife Flavia Domitilla, formerly the mistress of Statilius Capella, a Roman knight of Sabrata in Africa, a woman originally only of Latin rank,[g] but afterwards declared a freeborn citizen of Rome in a suit before arbiters, brought by her father Flavius Libe-

[e] Lepidus and Gaetulicus; see *Claud.* ix. 1.
[f] The senate.   [g] See note on *Aug.* xlvii.

quam quaestorio scriba. Ex hac liberos tulit Titum et Domitianum et Domitillam. Uxori ac filiae superstes fuit atque utramque adhuc privatus amisit. Post uxoris excessum Caenidem, Antoniae libertam et a manu, dilectam quondam sibi revocavit in contubernium habuitque etiam imperator paene iustae uxoris loco.

IV. Claudio principe Narcissi gratia legatus legionis in Germaniam missus est; inde in Britanniam translatus tricies cum hoste conflixit. Duas validissimas gentes superque viginti oppida et insulam Vectem Britanniae proximam in dicionem redegit partim Auli Plauti legati consularis partim Claudi ipsius ductu. Quare triumphalia ornamenta et in brevi spatio duplex sacerdotium accepit, praeterea consulatum, quem gessit per duos novissimos anni menses. Medium tempus ad proconsulatum usque in otio secessuque egit, Agrippinam timens potentem adhuc apud filium et defuncti quoque Narcissi amici perosam.

III. Exim[1] sortitus Africam integerrime nec sine magna dignatione administravit, nisi quod Hadrumeti seditione quadam rapa in eum iacta sunt. Rediit certe nihilo opulentior, ut qui prope labefactata iam fide omnia praedia fratri obligaret necessarioque ad mangonicos quaestus sustinendae dignitatis causa descenderit; propter quod

---

[1] exim, *M*; *the other mss. have* exin.

---

[a] See *Claud.* xvii.   [b] The Isle of Wight.
[c] In A.D. 51.   [d] In A.D. 63.   [e] *Mango* (cf. Gk. μάγγανον, "charm") was the term applied to a dealer in slaves, cattle, or wares, to which he tried to give an appearance of greater value than they actually possessed. The nickname applied to Vespasian implies that his trade was in mules.

ralis, a native of Ferentum and merely a quaestor's clerk. By her he had three children, Titus, Domitian, and Domitilla. He outlived his wife and daughter; in fact lost them both before he became emperor. After the death of his wife he resumed his relations with Caenis, freedwoman and amanuensis of Antonia, and formerly his mistress; and even after he became emperor he treated her almost as a lawful wife.

IV. In the reign of Claudius he was sent in command of a legion to Germany, through the influence of Narcissus; from there he was transferred to Britain,[a] where he fought thirty battles with the enemy. He reduced to subjection two powerful nations, more than twenty towns, and the island of Vectis,[b] near Britain, partly under the leadership of Aulus Plautius, the consular governor, and partly under that of Claudius himself. For this he received the triumphal regalia, and shortly after two priesthoods, besides the consulship,[c] which he held for the last two months of the year. The rest of the time up to his proconsulate he spent in rest and retirement, through fear of Agrippina, who still had a strong influence over her son and hated any friend of Narcissus, even after the latter's death.

The chance of the lot then gave him Africa,[d] which he governed with great justice and high honour, save that in a riot at Hadrumetum he was pelted with turnips. Certain it is that he came back none the richer, for his credit was so nearly gone that he mortgaged all his estates to his brother, and had to resort to trading in mules[e] to keep up his position; whence he was commonly known as "the

271

vulgo mulio vocabatur. Convictus quoque dicitur ducenta sestertia expressisse iuveni, cui[1] latum clavum adversus patris voluntatem impetrarat, eoque nomine graviter increpitus.

4 Peregrinatione Achaica inter comites Neronis cum cantante eo aut discederet saepius aut praesens obdormisceret, gravissimam contraxit offensam, prohibitusque non contubernio modo sed etiam publica salutatione secessit in parvam ac deviam civitatem, quoad latenti etiamque extrema metuenti provincia cum exercitu oblata est.

5 Percrebruerat Oriente toto vetus et constans opinio esse in fatis ut eo tempore Iudaea profecti rerum potirentur. Id de imperatore Romano, quantum postea eventu paruit, praedictum Iudaei ad se trahentes rebellarunt caesoque praeposito legatum insuper Syriae consularem suppetias ferentem rapta aquila fugaverunt. Ad hunc motum comprimendum cum exercitu ampliore et non instrenuo duce, cui tamen tuto tanta res committeretur, opus esset, ipse potissimum delectus est ut et industriae expertae nec metuendus ullo modo ob humilitatem

6 generis ac nominis. Additis igitur ad copias duabus legionibus, octo alis, cohortibus decem, atque inter legatos maiore filio assumpto, ut primum provinciam attigit, proximas quoque convertit in se, correcta statim

---

[1] cui, ᔓ (*Sabellicus*); qui, Ω.

---

[a] See *Nero*, xxii ff.
[b] Probably of auxiliaries.

Muleteer." He is also said to have been found guilty of squeezing two hundred thousand sesterces out of a young man for whom he obtained the broad stripe against his father's wish, and to have been severely rebuked in consequence.

On the tour through Greece, among the companions of Nero,[a] he bitterly offended the emperor by either going out often while Nero was singing, or falling asleep, if he remained. Being in consequence banished, not only from intimacy with the emperor but even from his public receptions, he withdrew to a little out-of-the-way town, until a province and an army were offered him while he was in hiding and in fear of his life.

There had spread over all the Orient an old and established belief, that it was fated at that time for men coming from Judaea to rule the world. This prediction, referring to the emperor of Rome, as afterwards appeared from the event, the people of Judaea took to themselves; accordingly they revolted and after killing their governor, they routed the consular ruler of Syria as well, when he came to the rescue, and took one of his eagles. Since to put down this rebellion required a considerable army with a leader of no little enterprise, yet one to whom so great power could be entrusted without risk, Vespasian was chosen for the task, both as a man of tried energy and as one in no wise to be feared because of the obscurity of his family and name. Therefore there were added to the forces in Judaea two legions with eight divisions of cavalry and ten cohorts.[b] He took his elder son as one of his lieutenants, and as soon as he reached his province he attracted the attention of the neighbouring provinces also; for he at once reformed the discipline of the army

273

castrorum disciplina, unoque et altero proelio tam constanter inito, ut in oppugnatione castelli lapidis ictum genu scutoque sagittas aliquot exceperit.

V. Post Neronem Galbamque Othone ac Vitellio de principatu certantibus in spem imperii venit iam pridem sibi per haec ostenta conceptam.

2   In suburbano Flaviorum quercus antiqua, quae erat Marti sacra, per tres Vespasiae partus singulos repente ramos a frutice dedit, haud dubia signa futuri cuiusque fati: primum exilem et cito arefactum, ideoque puella nata non perannavit, secundum praevalidum ac prolixum et qui magnam felicitatem portenderet, tertium vero instar arboris. Quare patrem Sabinum ferunt, haruspicio insuper confirmatum, renuntiasse matri, nepotem ei Caesarem genitum; nec illam quicquam aliud quam cachinnasse, mirantem quod adhuc se mentis compote deliraret iam filius suus.

3   Mox, cum aedilem eum C. Caesar, succensens curam verrendis viis non adhibitam, luto iussisset oppleri congesto per milites in praetextae sinum, non defuerunt qui interpretarentur, quandoque proculcatam desertamque rem p. civili aliqua perturbatione in tutelam eius ac velut in gremium deventuram.

4   Prandente eo quondam canis extrarius e trivio manum humanam intulit mensaeque subiecit. Cenante rursus

---

[a] The hand was typical of power, and *manus* is often used in the sense of *potestas*.

and fought one or two battles with such daring that in the storming of a fortress he was wounded in the knee with a stone and received several arrows in his shield.

V. While Otho and Vitellius were fighting for the throne after the death of Nero and Galba, he began to cherish the hope of imperial dignity, which he had long since conceived because of the following portents.

On the suburban estate of the Flavii an old oak tree, which was sacred to Mars, on each of the three occasions when Vespasia was delivered suddenly put forth a branch from its trunk, obvious indications of the destiny of each child. The first was slender and quickly withered, and so too the girl that was born died within the year; the second was very strong and long and portended great success, but the third was the image of a tree. Therefore their father Sabinus, so they say, being further encouraged by an inspection of sacrificial victims, announced to his mother that a grandson had been born to her who would be a Caesar. But she only laughed, marvelling that her son should already be in his dotage, while she was still of strong mind.

Later, when Vespasian was aedile, Gaius Caesar, incensed at his neglect of his duty of cleaning the streets, ordered that he be covered with mud, which the soldiers accordingly heaped into the bosom of his purple-bordered toga; this some interpreted as an omen that one day in some civil commotion his country, trampled under foot and forsaken, would come under his protection and as it were into his embrace.

Once when he was taking breakfast, a stray dog brought in a human hand from the cross-roads and dropped it under the table.[a] Again, when he was dining,

275

bos arator decusso iugo triclinium irrupit ac fugatis ministris quasi repente defessus procidit ad ipsos accumbentis pedes cervicemque summisit. Arbor quoque cupressus in agro avito sine ulla vi tempestatis evulsa radicitus atque prostrata insequenti die viridior ac firmior resurrexit.

5 At in Achaia somniavit initium sibi suisque felicitatis futurum, simul ac dens Neroni exemptus esset; evenitque ut sequenti die progressus in atrium medicus dentem ei ostenderet tantumque quod exemptum.

6 Apud Iudaeam Carmeli dei oraculum consulentem ita confirmavere sortes, ut quidquid cogitaret volveretque animo quamlibet magnum, id esse proventurum pollicerentur; et unus ex nobilibus captivis Iosephus, cum coiceretur in vincula, constantissime asseveravit fore ut

7 ab eodem brevi solveretur, verum iam imperatore. Nuntiabantur et ex urbe praesagia: Neronem diebus ultimis monitum per quietem, ut tensam Iovis Optimi Maximi e sacrario in domum Vespasiani et inde in Circum deduceret; ac non multo post comitia secundi consulatus ineunte Galba statuam Divi Iuli ad Orientem sponte conversam, acieque Betriacensi, prius quam committeretur, duas aquilas in conspectu omnium conflixisse victaque altera supervenisse tertiam ab solis exortu ac victricem abegisse.

VI. Nec tamen quicquam ante temptavit, promptis-

---

[a] Of Nero's lodging.

an ox that was ploughing shook off its yoke, burst into the dining-room, and after scattering the servants, fell at the very feet of Vespasian as he reclined at table, and bowed its neck as if suddenly tired out. A cypress tree, also, on his grandfather's farm was torn up by the roots, without the agency of any violent storm, and thrown down, and on the following day rose again greener and stronger than before.

He dreamed in Greece that the beginning of good fortune for himself and his family would come as soon as Nero had a tooth extracted; and on the next day it came to pass that a physician walked into the hall[a] and showed him a tooth which he had just then taken out.

When he consulted the oracle of the god of Carmel in Judaea, the lots were highly encouraging, promising that whatever he planned or wished, however great it might be, would come to pass; and one of his high-born prisoners, Josephus by name, as he was being put in chains, declared most confidently that he would soon be released by the same man, who would then, however, be emperor. Omens were also reported from Rome: Nero in his latter days was admonished in a dream to take the sacred chariot of Jupiter Optimus Maximus from its shrine to the house of Vespasian and from there to the Circus. Not long after this, too, when Galba was on his way to the elections which gave him his second consulship, a statue of the Deified Julius of its own accord turned towards the East; and on the field of Betriacum, before the battle began, two eagles fought in the sight of all, and when one was vanquished, a third came from the direction of the rising sun and drove off the victor.

VI. Yet he made no move, although his followers were

simis atque etiam instantibus suis, quam sollicitatus
quorundam et ignotorum et absentium fortuito favore.
2 Moesiaci exercitus bina e tribus legionibus milia missa
auxilio Othoni, postquam ingressis iter nuntiatum est
victum eum ac vim vitae suae attulisse, nihilo setius
Aquileiam usque perseveraverunt, quasi rumori minus
crederent. Ibi per occasionem ac licentiam omni ra-
pinarum genere grassati, cum timerent ne sibi reversis
reddenda ratio ac subeunda poena esset, consilium
inierunt eligendi creandique imperatoris; neque enim
deteriores esse aut Hispaniensi exercitu qui Galbam, aut
praetoriano qui Othonem, aut Germaniciano qui Vitel-
3 lium fecissent. Propositis itaque nominibus legatorum
consularium, quot ubique tunc erant, cum ceteros alium
alia de causa improbarent et quidam e legione tertia,
quae sub exitu Neronis translata ex Syria in Moesiam
fuerat, Vespasianum laudibus ferrent, assensere cuncti
nomenque eius vexillis omnibus sine mora inscripserunt.
Et tunc quidem compressa res est revocatis ad officium
numeris parumper. Ceterum divulgato facto Tiberius
Alexander praefectus Aegypti primus in verba Vespasiani
legiones adegit Kal. Iul., qui principatus dies in posterum
observatus est; Iudaicus deinde exercitus V. Idus Iul.
apud ipsum iuravit.
4 Plurimum coeptis contulerunt iactatum exemplar

ª July 11; according to Tac. *Hist.* 2. 79, it was the fifth day
before the Nones, July 3.

quite ready and even urgent, until he was roused to it by the accidental support of men unknown to him and at a distance. Two thousand soldiers of the three legions that made up the army in Moesia had been sent to help Otho. When word came to them after they had begun their march that he had been defeated and had taken his own life, they none the less kept on as far as Aquileia, because they did not believe the report. There, taking advantage of the lawless state of the times, they indulged in every kind of pillage; then, fearing that if they went back, they would have to give an account and suffer punishment, they took it into their heads to select and appoint an emperor, saying that they were just as good as the Spanish army which had appointed Galba, or the praetorian guard which had elected Otho, or the German army which had chosen Vitellius. Accordingly the names of all the consular governors who were serving anywhere were taken up, and since objection was made to the rest for one reason or another, while some members of the third legion, which had been transferred from Syria to Moesia just before the death of Nero, highly commended Vespasian, they unanimously agreed on him and forthwith inscribed his name on all their banners. At the time, however, the movement was checked and the soldiers recalled to their allegiance for a while. But when their action became known, Tiberius Alexander, prefect of Egypt, was the first to compel his legions to take the oath for Vespasian on the Kalends of July, the day which was afterwards celebrated as that of his accession; then the army in Judaea swore allegiance to him personally on the fifth day before the Ides of July.[a]

The enterprise was greatly forwarded by the circula-

epistulae verae sive falsae defuncti Othonis ad Vespasianum extrema obtestatione ultionem mandantis et ut rei p. subveniret optantis, simul rumor dissipatus destinasse victorem Vitellium permutare hiberna legionum et Germanicas transferre in Orientem ad securiorem mollioremque militiam, praeterea ex praesidibus provinciarum Licinius Mucianus et e regibus Vologaesus Parthus; ille deposita simultate, quam in id tempus ex aemulatione non obscure gerebat, Syriacum promisit exercitum, hic quadraginta milia sagittariorum.

VII. Suscepto igitur civili bello ac ducibus copiisque in Italiam praemissis interim Alexandriam transiit, ut claustra Aegypti optineret. Hic cum de firmitate imperii capturus auspicium aedem Serapidis summotis omnibus solus intrasset ac propitiato multum deo tandem se convertisset, verbenas coronasque et panificia, ut illic assolet, Basilides libertus obtulisse ei visus est; quem neque admissum a quoquam et iam pridem propter nervorum valitudinem vix ingredi longeque abesse constabat. Ac statim advenere litterae fusas apud Cremonam Vitelli copias, ipsum in urbe interemptum nuntiantes.

2 Auctoritas et quasi maiestas quaedam ut scilicet inopinato et adhuc novo principi deerat; haec quoque accessit. E plebe quidam luminibus orbatus, item alius debili crure sedentem pro tribunali pariter adierunt

---

[a] Governor of the neighbouring province of Syria.

[b] The strategic importance of Egypt is shown by Tac. *Ann.* 2. 59; cf. *Jul.* xxxv. 1 (at the end); *Aug.* xviii. 2.

[c] The freedman's name, connected with Greek Βασιλεύς, "king," was an additional omen.

tion of a copy of a letter of the late emperor Otho to Vespasian, whether genuine or forged, urging him with the utmost earnestness to vengeance and expressing the hope that he would come to the aid of his country; further, by a rumour which spread abroad that Vitellius had planned, after his victory, to change the winter quarters of the legions and to transfer those in Germany to the Orient, to a safer and milder service; and finally, among the governors of provinces, by the support of Licinius Mucianus,[a] and among the kings, by that of Vologaesus, the Parthian. The former, laying aside the hostility with which up to that time jealousy had obviously inspired him, promised the Syrian army; and the latter forty thousand bowmen.

VII. Therefore beginning a civil war and sending ahead generals with troops to Italy, he crossed meanwhile to Alexandria, to take possession of the key to Egypt.[b] There he dismissed all his attendants and entered the temple of Serapis alone, to consult the auspices as to the duration of his power. And when after many propitiatory offerings to the god he at length turned about, it seemed to him that his freedman Basilides[c] offered him sacred boughs, garlands and loaves, as is the custom there; and yet he knew well that no one had let him in, and that for some time he had been hardly able to walk by reason of rheumatism, and was besides far away. And immediately letters came with the news that Vitellius had been routed at Cremona and the emperor himself slain at Rome.

Vespasian as yet lacked prestige and a certain divinity, so to speak, since he was an unexpected and still new-made emperor; but these also were given him. A man of the people who was blind, and another who was lame, came to him together as he sat on the tribunal, begging

orantes opem valitudini demonstratam a Serapide per quietem: restituturum oculos, si inspuisset; confirmaturum crus, si dignaretur calce contingere. Cum vix fides esset ullo modo rem successuram ideoque ne experiri quidem auderet, extremo hortantibus amicis palam pro contione utrumque temptavit; nec eventus defuit. Per idem tempus Tegeae in Arcadia instinctu vaticinantium effossa sunt sacrato loco vasa operis antiqui atque in iis assimilis Vespasiano imago.

VIII. Talis tantaque cum fama in urbem reversus acto de Iudaeis triumpho consulatus octo veteri addidit; suscepit et censuram ac per totum imperii tempus nihil habuit antiquius quam prope afflictam nutantemque rem p. stabilire primo, deinde et ornare.

Milites pars victoriae fiducia, pars ignominiae dolore ad omnem licentiam audaciamque processerant; sed et provinciae civitatesque liberae, nec non et regna quaedam tumultuosius inter se agebant. Quare Vitellianorum quidem et exauctoravit plurimos et coercuit, participibus autem victoriae adeo nihil extra ordinem indulsit, ut etiam legitima praemia sero persolverit. Ac ne quam occasionem corrigendi disciplinam praetermitteret, adulescentulum fragrantem unguento, cum sibi pro impetrata praefectura gratias ageret, nutu aspernatus, voce etiam gravissima increpuit: "Maluissem alium

---

[a] In A.D. 70, 71, 72, 74, 75, 76, 77, 79.

for the help for their disorders which Serapis had promised in a dream; for the god declared that Vespasian would restore the eyes, if he would spit upon them, and give strength to the leg, if he would deign to touch it with his heel. Though he had hardly any faith that this could possibly succeed, and therefore shrank even from making the attempt, he was at last prevailed upon by his friends and tried both things in public before a large crowd; and with success. At this same time, by the direction of certain soothsayers, some vases of antique workmanship were dug up in a consecrated spot at Tegea in Arcadia and on them was an image very like Vespasian.

VIII. Returning to Rome under such auspices and attended by so great renown, after celebrating a triumph over the Jews, he added eight consulships[a] to his former one; he also assumed the censorship and during the whole period of his rule he considered nothing more essential than first to strengthen the State, which was tottering and almost overthrown, and then to embellish it as well.

The soldiery, some emboldened by their victory and some resenting their humiliating defeat, had abandoned themselves to every form of licence and recklessness; the provinces, too, and the free cities, as well as some of the kingdoms, were in a state of internal dissension. Therefore he discharged many of the soldiers of Vitellius and punished many; but so far from showing any special indulgence to those who had shared in his victory, he was even tardy in paying them their lawful rewards. To let slip no opportunity of improving military discipline, when a young man reeking with perfumes came to thank him for a commission which had been given him, Vespasian drew back his head in disgust, adding the stern reprimand: "I

oboluisses," litterasque revocavit. Classiarios vero, qui ab Ostia et Puteolis Romam pedibus per vices commeant, petentes constitui aliquid sibi calciarii nomine, quasi parum esset sine responso abegisse, iussit posthac excalciatos cursitare; et ex eo ita cursitant.

4   Achaiam, Lyciam, Rhodum, Byzantium, Samum libertate adempta, item Trachiam[1] Ciliciam et Commagenen dicionis regiae usque ad id tempus, in provinciarum formam redegit. Cappadociae propter adsiduos barbarorum incursus legiones addidit consularemque rectorem imposuit pro eq. R.

5   Deformis urbs veteribus incendiis ac ruinis erat; vacuas areas occupare et aedificare, si possessores cessarent, cuicumque permisit. Ipse restitutionem Capitolii adgressus ruderibus purgandis manus primus admovit ac suo collo quaedam extulit; aerearumque tabularum tria milia, quae simul conflagraverant, restituenda suscepit undique investigatis exemplaribus: instrumentum imperii pulcherrimum ac vetustissimum, quo continebantur paene ab exordio urbis senatus consulta, plebi scita de societate et foedere ac privilegio cuicumque concessis.

    IX. Fecit et nova opera templum Pacis Foro proximum Divique Claudi in Caelio monte coeptum quidem ab Agrippina, sed a Nerone prope funditus destructum;

---

[1] Trachiam, *Bentley* (II); Thraciam, Ω.

---

[a] They were stationed at Ostia and Puteoli as a fire brigade (see *Claud.* xxv. 2), and the various divisions were on duty now in one town, now in the other, and again in Rome.

[b] Literally, "on his own neck"; in a basket.

would rather you had smelt of garlic"; and he revoked the appointment. When the marines who march on foot by turns from Ostia and Puteoli to Rome[a] asked that an allowance be made them under the head of shoe money, not content with sending them away without a reply, he ordered that in future they should make the run barefooted; and they have done so ever since.

He made provinces of Achaia, Lycia, Rhodes, Byzantium and Samos, taking away their freedom, and likewise of Trachian Cilicia and Commagene, which up to that time had been ruled by kings. He sent additional legions to Cappadocia because of the constant inroads of the barbarians, and gave it a consular governor in place of a Roman knight.

As the city was unsightly from former fires and fallen buildings, he allowed anyone to take possession of vacant sites and build upon them, in case the owners failed to do so. He began the restoration of the Capitol in person, was the first to lend a hand in clearing away the debris, and carried some of it off on his own head.[b] He undertook to restore the three thousand bronze tablets which were destroyed with the temple, making a thorough search for copies: priceless and very ancient records of the empire, containing the decrees of the senate and the acts of the commons almost from the foundation of the city, regarding alliances, treaties, and special privileges granted to individuals.

IX. He also undertook new works, the temple of Peace hard by the Forum and one to the Deified Claudius on the Caelian mount, which was begun by Agrippina, but almost utterly destroyed by Nero; also an amphi-

item amphitheatrum urbe media, ut destinasse compererat Augustum.[a]

2　　Amplissimos ordines et exhaustos caede varia et contaminatos veteri neglegentia purgavit supplevitque recenso senatu et equite, summotis indignissimis et honestissimo quoque Italicorum ac provincialium allecto. Atque uti notum esset, utrumque ordinem non tam libertate inter se quam dignitate differre, de iurgio quodam senatoris equitisque R. ita pronuntiavit, non oportere maledici senatoribus, remaledici civile fasque esse.[b]

X. Litium series ubique maiorem in modum excreverant, manentibus antiquis intercapedine iuris dictionis, accedentibus novis ex condicione tumultuque temporum;[c] sorte elegit per quos rapta bello restituerentur quique iudicia centumviralia, quibus peragendis vix suffectura litigatorum videbatur aetas, extra ordinem diiudicarent redigerentque ad brevissimum numerum.

XI. Libido atque luxuria coercente nullo invaluerat; auctor senatui fuit decernendi, ut quae se alieno servo iunxisset, ancilla haberetur; neve filiorum familiarum[e] faeneratoribus exigendi crediti ius umquam esset, hoc est ne post patrum quidem mortem.

XII. Ceteris in rebus statim ab initio principatus

---

[a] The Colosseum, known as the Flavian amphitheatre until the Middle Ages.

[b] That is, a citizen could return the abuse of another citizen, regardless of their respective ranks.

[c] During the civil wars.　　[d] See note on *Aug.* xxxvi.

[e] In the legal sense; *filii familiarum* were sons who were still under the control of their fathers, regardless of their age; cf. *Tib.* xv. 2.

theatre[a] in the heart of the city, a plan which he learned that Augustus had cherished.

He reformed the two great orders, reduced by a series of murders and sullied by long standing neglect, and added to their numbers, holding a review of the senate and the knights, expelling those who least deserved the honour and enrolling the most distinguished of the Italians and provincials. Furthermore, to let it be known that the two orders differed from each other not so much in their privileges as in their rank, in the case of an altercation between a senator and a Roman knight, he rendered this decision: "Unseemly language should not be used towards senators, but to return their insults in kind is proper and lawful."[b]

X. Lawsuit upon lawsuit had accumulated in all the courts to an excessive degree, since those of long standing were left unsettled through the interruption of court business[c] and new ones had arisen through the disorder of the times. He therefore chose commissioners by lot to restore what had been seized in time of war, and to make special decisions in the court of the Hundred,[d] reducing the cases to the smallest possible number, since it was clear that the lifetime of the litigants would not suffice for the regular proceedings.

XI. Licentiousness and extravagance had flourished without restraint; hence he induced the senate to vote that any woman who formed a connection with the slave of another person should herself be treated as a bond-woman; also that those who lend money to minors[e] should never have a legal right to enforce payment, that is to say, not even after the death of the fathers.

XII. In other matters he was unassuming and lenient

287

usque ad exitum civilis et clemens, mediocritatem pristinam neque dissimulavit umquam ac frequenter etiam prae se tulit. Quin et conantis quosdam originem Flavii generis ad conditores Reatinos comitemque Herculis, cuius monimentum exstat Salaria via, referre irrisit ultro. Adeoque nihil ornamentorum extrinsecus cupide appetivit, ut triumphi die fatigatus tarditate et taedio pompae non reticuerit, merito se plecti, qui triumphum, quasi aut debitum maioribus suis aut speratum umquam sibi, tam inepte senex concupisset. Ac ne tribuniciam quidem potestatem statim nec[1] patris patriae appellationem nisi sero recepit. Nam consuetudinem scrutandi salutantes manente adhuc bello civili omiserat.

XIII. Amicorum libertatem, causidicorum figuras ac philosophorum contumaciam lenissime tulit. Licinium Mucianum notae impudicitiae, sed meritorum fiducia minus sui reverentem, numquam nisi clam et hactenus retaxare sustinuit, ut apud communem aliquem amicum querens adderet clausulam:[2] "Ego tamen vir sum." Salvium Liberalem in defensione divitis rei ausum dicere: "Quid ad Caesarem, si Hipparchus sestertium milies habet?" et ipse laudavit. Demetrium Cynicum in itinere obvium sibi post damnationem ac neque assurgere neque salutare se dignantem, oblatrantem etiam nescio quid, satis habuit canem appellare.

[1] statim nec, *supplied by Bücheler*; aut, *Roth*; statim, *O. Hirschfeld*.   [2] clausulam, *Duker*; clausulae, Ω.

[a] His tribunician power was reckoned from July 1, 69, the day when he was proclaimed emperor by the army. The meaning of the sentence is not clear.   [b] See *Claud.* xxxv.

[c] See chap. vi. 4. He boasted that the rule had been at his disposal and that he had given it to Vespasian; see Tac. *Hist.* 4. 4.

from the very beginning of his reign until its end, never tryng to conceal his former lowly condition, but often even parading it. Indeed, when certain men tried to trace the origin of the Flavian family to the founders of Reate and a companion of Hercules whose tomb still stands on the Via Salaria, he laughed at them for their pains. So far was he from a desire for pomp and show that on the day of his triumph, exhausted by the slow and tiresome procession, he did not hesitate to say: "It serves me right for being such a fool as to want a triumph in my old age, as if it were due to my ancestors or had even been among my own ambitions." He did not even assume the tribunician power at once nor the title of Father of his Country until late.[a] As for the custom of searching those who came to pay their morning calls,[b] he gave that up before the civil war was over.

XIII. He bore the frank language of his friends, the quips of pleaders, and the impudence of the philosophers with the greatest patience. Though Licinius Mucianus,[c] a man of notorious homosexual practices, presumed upon the services he had rendered him to treat Vespasian with scant respect, he never had the heart to criticise him except privately and then only to the extent of adding to a complaint made to a common friend, the significant words: "I at least am a man."[d] When Salvius Liberalis ventured to say while defending a rich client, "What is it to Caesar if Hipparchus has a hundred millions," he personally commended him. When the Cynic Demetrius met him abroad after being condemned to banishment, and without deigning to rise in his presence or to salute him, even snarled out some insult, he merely called him "cur."

[d] Thus casting aspersions on Mucianus' masculinity.

XIV. Offensarum inimicitiarumque minime memor exsecutorve Vitelli hostis sui filiam splendidissime maritavit, dotavit etiam et instruxit. Trepidum eum interdicta aula sub Nerone quaerentemque, quidnam ageret aut quo abiret, quidam ex officio admissionis simul expellens abire Morboviam[a] iusserat. In hunc postea deprecantem non ultra verba excanduit, et quidem totidem fere atque eadem. Nam ut suspicione aliqua vel metu ad perniciem cuiusquam compelleretur tantum afuit, ut monentibus amicis cavendum esse Mettium Pompusianum, quod volgo crederetur genesim habere imperatoriam, insuper consulem fecerit, spondens quandoque beneficii memorem futurum.

XV. Non temere quis punitus insons reperietur[1] nisi absente eo et ignaro aut certe invito atque decepto. Helvidio Prisco, qui et reversum se ex Syria solus privato nomine Vespasianum salutaverat et in praetura omnibus edictis sine honore ac mentione ulla transmiserat,[b] non ante succensuit quam altercationibus insolentissimis paene in ordinem redactus.[c] Hunc quoque, quamvis relegatum primo, deinde et interfici iussum, magni aestimavit servare quoquo modo, missis qui percussores revocarent; et servasset, nisi iam perisse falso renuntiatum esset.

---

[1] reperietur, ς (*Scriverius, Salmasius*); reperiretur, Ω.

---

[a] A made-up name from *morbus,* "illness"; the expression is equivalent to "go to the devil."

[b] That is, in their superscriptions; see note on *Tib.* xxxii. 2.

[c] *Cogere (redigere) in ordinem* is used of one who resists or does not show proper respect to a magistrate; that is, attempts to reduce him to the level of an ordinary citizen. It seems to have

XIV. He was not inclined to remember or to avenge affronts or enmities, but made a brilliant match for the daughter of his enemy Vitellius, and even provided her with a dowry and household furnishings. When he was in terror at being forbidden Nero's court, and asked what on earth he was to do or where he was to go, one of the ushers put him out and told him to "go to Morbovia[a]"; but when the man later begged for forgiveness, Vespasian confined his resentment to words, and those of about the same number and purport. Indeed, so far was he from being led by any suspicion or fear to cause anyone's death that when his friends warned him that he must keep an eye on Mettius Pompusianus, since it was commonly believed that he had an imperial horoscope, he even made him consul, guaranteeing that he would one day be mindful of the favour.

XV. It cannot readily be shown that any innocent person was punished save in Vespasian's absence and without his knowledge, or at any rate against his will and by misleading him. Although Helvidius Priscus was the only one who greeted him on his return from Syria by his private name of "Vespasian," and moreover in his praetorship left the emperor unhonoured and unmentioned in all his edicts,[b] he did not show anger until by the extravagance of his railing Helvidius had all but degraded him.[c] But even in his case, though he did banish him and later order his death, he was most anxious for any means of saving him, and sent messengers to recall those who were to slay him; and he would have saved him, but for a false report that Helvidius had already been done to death.

been originally a military expression. Cf. *Claud.* xxxviii. 1; Pliny, *Epist.* 1. 23. 1; Livy, 3. 51. 13.

Ceterum neque caede cuiusquam umquam laetatus[1] iustis suppliciis inlacrimavit etiam et ingemuit.

XVI. Sola est, in qua merito culpetur, pecuniae cupiditas. Non enim contentus omissa sub Galba vectigalia revocasse, nova et gravia addidisse, auxisse tributa provinciis, nonnullis et duplicasse, negotiationes quoque vel privato pudendas propalam exercuit, coemendo
2 quaedam tantum ut pluris postea distraheret. Ne candidatis quidem honores reisve tam innoxiis quam nocentibus absolutiones venditare cunctatus est. Creditur etiam procuratorum rapacissimum quemque ad ampliora officia ex industria solitus promovere, quo locupletiores mox condemnaret; quibus quidem volgo pro spongiis dicebatur uti, quod quasi et siccos madefaceret et exprimeret umentis.
3 Quidam natura cupidissimum tradunt, idque exprobratum ei a sene bubulco, qui negata sibi gratuita libertate,[2] quam imperium adeptum[3] suppliciter orabat, proclamaverit, vulpem pilum mutare, non mores. Sunt contra qui opinentur ad manubias et rapinas necessitate compulsum summa aerarii fiscique inopia, de qua testificatus sit initio statim principatus, professus quadringenties milies opus esse, ut res p. stare posset. Quod et veri similius videtur, quando et male partis optime usus est.

[1] laetatus, ⌐; *omitted by the earlier mss.*
[2] negata ... gratuita libertate, Π[1]QST; *the other mss. have* negatam ... gratuitam libertatem.
[3] adeptum, S[2]T⌐; ademptum, Ω.

Certainly he never took pleasure in the death of anyone, but even wept and sighed over those who suffered merited punishment.

XVI. The only thing for which he can fairly be censured was his love of money. For not content with reviving the taxes which had been repealed under Galba, he added new and heavy burdens, increasing the amount of tribute paid by the provinces, in some cases actually doubling it, and quite openly carrying on traffic which would be shameful even for a man in private life; for he would buy up certain commodities merely in order to distribute them at a profit. He made no bones of selling offices to candidates and acquittals to men under prosecution, whether innocent or guilty. He is even believed to have had the habit of designedly advancing the most rapacious of his procurators to higher posts, that they might be the richer when he later condemned them; in fact, it was common talk that he used these men as sponges, because he, so to speak, soaked them when they were dry and squeezed them when they were wet.

Some say that he was naturally covetous and was taunted with it by an old herdsman of his who, on being forced to pay for the freedom for which he earnestly begged Vespasian when he became emperor, cried: "The fox changes his fur, but not his nature." Others on the contrary believe that he was driven by necessity to raise money by spoliation and robbery because of the desperate state of the treasury and the privy purse; to which he bore witness at the very beginning of his reign by declaring that forty thousand millions were needed to set the State upright. This latter view seems the more probable, since he made the best use of his gains, ill-gotten though they were.

XVII. In omne hominum genus liberalissimus explevit censum senatorium, consulares inopes quingenis sestertiis annuis sustentavit, plurimas per totum orbem civitates terrae motu aut incendio afflictas restituit in melius, ingenia et artes vel maxime fovit.

XVIII. Primus e fisco Latinis Graecisque rhetoribus annua centena constituit; praestantis poetas, nec non et artifices, Coae Veneris,[1] item Colossi refectorem insigni congiario magnaque mercede donavit; mechanico quoque grandis columnas exigua impensa perducturum in Capitolium pollicenti praemium pro commento non mediocre optulit, operam remisit praefatus sineret se plebiculam pascere.

XIX. Ludis, per quos scaena Marcelliani theatri restituta dedicabatur, vetera quoque acroamata revocaverat. Apellae[2] tragoedo quadringenta, Terpno Diodoroque citharoedis ducena, nonnullis centena, quibus minimum, quadragena sestertia super plurimas coronas aureas dedit. Sed et convivabatur assidue ac saepius recta et dapsile, ut macellarios adiuvaret. Dabat sicut Saturnalibus viris apophoreta, ita per Kal. Mart. feminis.

Et tamen ne sic quidem pristina cupiditatis infamia caruit. Alexandrini Cybiosacten[3] eum vocare persevera-

2

---

[1] Coae Veneris, *Graevius*; coevenerit, *MGϒ*; coemerit, *LPS*[1]; coemit, *S*[2]*T*. [2] Apellae, *Bücheler*; Apellari, *mss.* (apelli, *ρϛ*). [3] Cybiosacten, *Torrentius from Strabo*, 17. 796; cybiotanten, Ω.

---

[a] This had been increased to 1,200,000 sesterces by Augustus. [b] See note on *Aug.* xli. 2. [c] Doubtless referring to the statue of Venus consecrated by Vespasian in his temple of Peace, the sculptor of which, according to Pliny, was unknown. The Venus of Cos was the work of Praxiteles.

XVII. He was most generous to all classes, making up the requisite estate[a] for senators, giving needy ex-consuls an annual stipend of five hundred thousand sesterces, restoring to a better condition many cities throughout the empire which had suffered from earthquakes or fires, and in particular encouraging men of talent and the arts.

XVIII. He was the first to establish a regular salary of a hundred thousand sesterces for Latin and Greek teachers of rhetoric, paid from the privy purse. He also presented eminent poets with princely largess[b] and great rewards, and artists, too, such as the restorer of the Venus of Cos[c] and of the Colossus.[d] To a mechanical engineer, who promised to transport some heavy columns to the Capitol at small expense, he gave no mean reward for his invention, but refused to make use of it, saying: "You must let me feed my poor commons."

XIX. At the plays with which he dedicated the new stage of the theatre of Marcellus he revived the old musical entertainments. To Apelles, the tragic actor, he gave four hundred thousand sesterces; to Terpnus and Diodorus, the lyre-players, two hundred thousand each; to several a hundred thousand; while those who received least were paid forty thousand, and numerous golden crowns were awarded besides. He gave constant dinner-parties, too, usually formally[e] and sumptuously, to help the marketmen. He gave gifts[f] to women on the Kalends of March,[g] as he did to the men on the Saturnalia.

Yet even so he could not be rid of his former ill-repute for covetousness. The Alexandrians persisted in calling

[d] The colossal statue of Nero; see *Nero*, xxxi. 1.

[e] See *Aug*. lxxiv and the note.   [f] See note on *Calig*. lv. 2.

[g] The Matronalia or feast of married women; see Hor. *Odes*, 3. 8, 1.

verunt, cognomine unius e regibus suis turpissimarum sordium. Sed et in funere Favor archimimus personam eius ferens imitansque, ut est mos, facta ac dicta vivi, interrogatis palam procuratoribus, quanti funus et pompa constaret, ut audit sestertium centiens, exclamavit, centum sibi sestertia darent ac se vel in Tiberim proicerent.

XX. Statura fuit quadrata, compactis firmisque membris, vultu veluti nitentis; de quo quidam urbanorum non infacete, siquidem petenti, ut et in se aliquid diceret: "Dicam," inquit, "cum ventrem exonerare desieris." Valitudine prosperrima usus est, quamvis ad tuendam eam nihil amplius quam fauces ceteraque membra sibimet ad numerum in sphaeristerio defricaret inediamque unius diei per singulos menses interponeret.

XXI. Ordinem vitae hunc fere tenuit. In principatu maturius semper ac de nocte vigilabat; dein perlectis epistulis officiorumque omnium breviariis, amicos admittebat, ac dum salutabatur, et calciabat ipse se et amiciebat; postque decisa quaecumque obvenissent negotia gestationi et inde quieti vacabat, accubante aliqua pallacarum, quas in locum defunctae Caenidis[1] plurimas constituerat; a secreto in balineum tricliniumque transibat. Nec ullo tempore facilior aut indulgentior traditur, eaque momenta domestici ad aliquid petendum magno opere captabant.

---

[1] Caenidis, *Q*; Cenidis, ΠS[2]; *the other mss. have* G(a)enidis.

---

[a] A transliterated Greek word, κυβιοσάκτης, meaning "dealer in square pieces (κύβοι) of salt fish."

[b] According to Celsus, 2. 1, *quadratum* is applied to a well-proportioned body, neither slender nor fat.

him Cybiosactes,[a] the surname of one of their kings who was scandalously stingy. Even at his funeral, Favor, a leading actor of mimes, who wore his mask and, according to the usual custom, imitated the actions and words of the deceased during his lifetime, having asked the procurators in a loud voice how much his funeral procession would cost, and hearing the reply "Ten million sesterces," cried out: "Give me a hundred thousand and fling me even into the Tiber."

XX. He was well built,[b] with strong, sturdy limbs, and the expression of one who was straining at stool. Apropos of which a witty fellow, when Vespasian asked him to make a joke on him also, replied rather cleverly: "I will, when you have finished relieving your bowels." He enjoyed excellent health, though he did nothing to keep it up except to rub his throat and the other parts of his body a certain number of times in the ball court, and to fast one day in every month.

XXI. This was in general his manner of life. While emperor, he always rose very early, in fact before daylight; then after reading his letters and the reports of all the officials, he admitted his friends, and while he was receiving their greetings, he put on his own shoes and dressed himself. After despatching any business that came up, he took time for a drive and then for a nap, lying with one of his concubines, of whom he had taken several after the death of Caenis. After his siesta he went to the bath and the dining-room; and it is said that at no time was he more good-natured or indulgent, so that the members of his household eagerly watched for these opportunities of making requests.

XXII. Et super cenam autem et semper alias comissimus multa ioco transigebat; erat enim dicacitatis plurimae, etsi scurrilis et sordidae, ut ne praetextatis quidem verbis abstineret. Et tamen nonnulla eius facetissima exstant, in quibus et haec. Mestrium Florum consularem, admonitus ab eo "plaustra" potius quam "plostra" dicenda, postero die "Flaurum" salutavit. Expugnatus autem a quadam, quasi amore suo deperiret, cum perductae pro concubitu sestertia quadringenta donasset, admonente dispensatore, quem ad modum summam rationibus vellet inferri: "Vespasiano," inquit, "adamato."

XXIII. Utebatur et versibus Graecis tempestive satis, et de quodam procerae staturae improbiusque nato:

μακρὰ βιβάς, κραδάων δολιχόσκιον ἔγχος,

et de Cerylo liberto, qui dives admodum ob subterfugiendum quandoque ius fisci ingenuum se et Lachetem mutato nomine coeperat ferre:

ὦ Λάχης, Λάχης,
ἐπὰν ἀποθάνῃς,[1] αὖθις ἐξ ἀρχῆς[2] ἔσει
σὺ[3] Κηρύλος.[4]

[1] ἀποθάνῃς] αποθανες, Ω.
[2] ἀρχῆς, Casaubon; αιχαρχης, M; αυχαρης, G; the rest of the mss. for the most part have αυχαρχης.
[3] ἔσει σύ, Bücheler; ειρσυ, Ω.
[4] Γηρυλος, Ω.

---

[a] Cf. Macrobius, Saturn. 2. 1. 9, impudica et praetextata verba; Gell. N.A. 9. 10. 4, non praetextatis sed puris honestisque verbis. Various explanations of the term are given. It perhaps means words such as boys use; but see Festus, s.v. praetextum sermonem.

XXII. Not only at dinner but on all other occasions he was most affable, and he turned off many matters with a jest; for he was very ready with sharp sayings, albeit of a low and buffoonish kind, so that he did not even refrain from obscene expressions.[a] Yet many of his remarks are still remembered which are full of fine wit, and among them the following. When an ex-consul called Mestrius Florus called his attention to the fact that the proper pronunciation was *plaustra*[b] rather than *plostra*, he greeted him next day as "Flaurus." When he was importuned by a woman who said that she was dying with love for him, he took her to his bed and gave her four hundred sesterces for her favours. Being asked by his steward how he would have the sum entered in his accounts, he replied: "To a passion for Vespasian."

XXIII. He also quoted Greek verses with great timeliness, saying of a man of tall stature and monstrous genitals:

"Striding along and waving a lance that casts a long
  shadow,"[c]

and of the freedman Cerylus, who was very rich and who, to cheat the privy purse of its dues at his death, had begun to give himself out as freeborn, changing his name to Laches:

"O Laches, Laches,
When you are dead, you'll change your name at once
To Cerylus again."[d]

[b] *Plaustra* was the urban form of the word for "wagons," but there was also a plebeian form *plostra*; see Hor. *Serm.* 1. 6. 42 and cf. *Claudius, Clodius.* The original form was *plostra.*
[c] *Iliad* 7. 213. [d] Menander, Fr. 223. 2, Koch.

Maxime tamen dicacitatem adfectabat in deformibus lucris, ut invidiam aliqua cavillatione dilueret transferretque ad sales.

2 Quendam e caris ministris dispensationem cuidam quasi fratri petentem cum distulisset, ipsum candidatum ad se vocavit; exactaque pecunia, quantam is cum suffragatore suo pepigerat, sine mora ordinavit; interpellanti mox ministro: "Alium tibi," ait, "quaere fratrem; hic, quem tuum putas, meus est." Mulionem in itinere quodam suspicatus ad calciandas mulas desiluisse,[1] ut adeunti litigatori spatium moramque praeberet, interrogavit

3 quanti calciasset, et pactus est[2] lucri partem. Reprehendenti filio Tito, quod etiam urinae vectigal commentus esset, pecuniam ex prima pensione admovit ad nares, sciscitans num odore offenderetur; et illo negante: "Atqui,"[3] inquit, "e lotio est." Nuntiantis legatos decretam ei publice non mediocris summae statuam colosseam, iussit vel continuo ponere,[4] cavam manum

4 ostentans et paratam basim dicens. Ac ne in metu quidem ac periculo mortis extremo abstinuit iocis. Nam cum inter cetera prodigia Mausoleum derepente patuisset et stella crinita in caelo apparuisset, alterum ad Iuniam Calvinam e gente Augusti pertinere dicebat, alterum ad Parthorum regem qui capillatus esset; prima quoque morbi accessione: "Vae," inquit, "puto deus fio."

---

[1] desiluisse, *M; the other mss. have* desilisse.

[2] et pactus est, *J. Gronov.;* pactusque est, *L³ᴤ; the other mss. have* pactus.   [3] atqui] atquin, *M.*

[4] ponere, *Bentley; the mss. have* poneret *or* ponerent.

---

[a] Of Augustus; see *Aug.* c. 4.   [b] The connection between the *stella crinita* and the long hair of the Parthian king is obvious; it does not seem accidental that Calvina is conected with *calvus,*

But he particularly resorted to witticisms about his unseemly means of gain, seeking to diminish their odium by some jocose saying and to turn them into a jest.

Having put off one of his favourite attendants, who asked for a stewardship for a pretended brother, he summoned the candidate himself, and after compelling him to pay him as much money as he had agreed to give his advocate, appointed him to the position without a delay. On his attendant's taking up the matter again, he said: "Find yourself another brother; the man that you thought was yours is mine." On a journey, suspecting that his muleteer had got down to shoe the mules merely to make delay and give time for a man with a lawsuit to approach the emperor, he asked how much he was paid for shoeing the mules and insisted on a share of the money. When Titus found fault with him for contriving a tax upon public latrines, he held a piece of money from the first payment to his son's nose, asking whether its odour was offensive to him. When Titus said "No," he replied, "Yet it comes from urine." On the report of a deputation that a colossal statue of great cost had been voted him at public expense, he demanded to have it set up at once, and holding out his open hand, said that the base was ready. He did not cease his jokes even when in apprehension of death and in extreme danger; for when among other portents the Mausoleum[a] opened on a sudden and a comet appeared in the heavens, he declared that the former applied to Junia Calvina of the family of Augustus, and the latter to the king of the Parthians, who wore his hair long;[b] and as death drew near, he said: "Woe's me. Methinks I'm turning into a god."

"bald," though this word-play seems to have been overlooked.

XXIV. Consulatu suo nono temptatus in Campania motiunculis levibus protinusque urbe repetita, Cutilias[1] ac Reatina rura, ubi aestivare quotannis solebat, petit. Hic cum super urgentem valitudinem creberrimo frigidae aquae usu etiam intestina vitiasset nec eo minus muneribus imperatoriis ex consuetudine fungeretur, ut etiam legationes audiret cubans, alvo repente usque ad defectionem soluta, imperatorem ait stantem mori oportere; dumque consurgit ac nititur, inter manus sublevantium extinctus est VIIII. Kal. Iul. annum agens aetatis sexagensimum ac nonum superque mensem ac diem septimum.

XXV. Convenit inter omnis, tam certum eum de sua suorumque genitura semper fuisse, ut post assiduas in se coniurationes ausus sit adfirmare senatui aut filios sibi successuros aut neminem. Dicitur etiam vidisse quondam per quietem stateram media parte vestibuli Palatinae domus positam examine aequo, cum in altera lance Claudius et Nero starent, in altera ipse ac filii. Nec res fefellit, quando totidem annis parique temporis spatio utrique imperaverunt.

Divus Titus

I. Titus, cognomine paterno, amor ac deliciae generis humani—tantum illi ad promerendam omnium voluntatem vel ingenii vel artis vel fortunae superfuit, et, quod difficillimum est, in imperio, quando privatus atque etiam

---

[1] Cutilias, ⊊ (*Beroaldus*); Cutillas, Ω.

[a] In A.D. 79.   [b] June 23, A.D. 79.   [c] Claudius and Nero reigned thirteen and fourteen years respectively; Vespasian, ten; Titus, two; and Domitian, fifteen.

XXIV. In his ninth consulship[a] he had a slight illness in Campania, and returning at once to the city, he left for Cutiliae and the country about Reate, where he spent the summer every year. There, in addition to an increase in his illness, having contracted a bowel complaint by too free use of the cold waters, he nevertheless continued to perform his duties as emperor, even receiving embassies *attention* as he lay in bed. Taken on a sudden with such an attack of *to death* diarrhoea that he all but swooned, he said: "An emperor ought to die standing," and while he was struggling to get on his feet, he died in the arms of those who tried to help him, on the ninth day before the Kalends of July,[b] at the age of sixty-nine years, one month and seven days.

XXV. All agree that he had so much faith in his own horoscope and those of his family that even after constant conspiracies were made against him he had the assurance to say to the senate that either his sons would succeed him or he would have no successor. It is also said that he once dreamed that he saw a balance with its beam on a level placed in the middle of the vestibule of the Palace, in one pan of which stood Claudius and Nero and in the other himself and his sons. And the dream came true, since both houses reigned for the same space of time and the same term of years.[c]

THE DEIFIED TITUS

I. Titus, of the same surname as his father, was the delight and darling of the human race; such surpassing ability had he, by nature, art, or good fortune, to win the affections of all men, and that, too, which is no easy task, while he was emperor; for as a private citizen, and even

sub patre principe ne odio quidem, nedum vituperatione publica caruit—natus est III. Kal. Ian. insigni anno Gaiana nece, prope Septizonium sordidis aedibus, cubiculo vero perparvo et obscuro, nam manet adhuc et ostenditur.

II. Educatus in aula cum Britannico simul ac paribus disciplinis et apud eosdem magistros institutus. Quo quidem tempore aiunt metoposcopum a Narcisso Claudi liberto adhibitum, ut Britannicum inspiceret, constantissime affirmasse illum quidem nullo modo, ceterum Titum, qui tunc prope astabat, utique imperaturum. Erant autem adeo familiares, ut de potione, qua Britannicus hausta periit, Titus quoque iuxta cubans gustasse credatur gravique morbo adflictatus diu. Quorum omnium mox memor statuam ei auream in Palatio posuit et alteram ex ebore equestrem, quae circensi pompa hodieque praefertur, dedicavit prosecutusque est.

III. In puero statim corporis animique dotes exsplenduerunt, magisque ac magis deinceps per aetatis gradus: forma egregia et cui non minus auctoritatis inesset quam gratiae, praecipuum robur, quanquam neque procera statura et ventre paulo proiectiore; memoria[1] singularis, docilitas ad omnis fere tum belli tum pacis artes. Armorum et equitandi peritissimus, Latine Graeceque vel in orando vel in fingendis poematibus promptus et facilis ad extemporalitatem usque; sed ne musicae quidem rudis, ut qui cantaret et psalleret iucunde scienterque. E pluribus

2

---

[1] memoria, Π[1]Q; *the other mss. have* memoriae.

---

[a] Dec. 30, A.D. 41.   [b] Some building of seven stories; the famous Septizonium on the Palatine was the work of Septimius Severus.   [c] Cf. *Nero*, xxxiii. 2 and 3.

during his father's rule, he did not escape hatred, much less public criticism. He was born on the third day before the Kalends of January,[a] in the year memorable for the death of Gaius, in a mean house near the Septizonium[b] and in a very small dark room besides; for it still remains and is on exhibition.

II. He was brought up at court in company with Britannicus and taught the same subjects by the same masters. At that time, so they say, a physiognomist was brought in by Narcissus, the freedman of Claudius, to examine Britannicus and declared most positively that he would never become emperor; but that Titus, who was standing near by at the time, would surely rule. The boys were so intimate, too, that it is believed that when Britannicus drained the fatal draught,[c] Titus, who was reclining at his side, also tasted of the potion and for a long time suffered from an obstinate disorder. Titus did not forget all this, but later set up a golden statue of his friend in the Palace, and dedicated another equestrian statue of ivory, which is to this day carried in the procession in the Circus, and he attended it on its first appearance.

III. Even in boyhood his bodily and mental gifts were conspicuous and they became more and more so as he advanced in years. He had a handsome person, in which there was no less dignity than grace, and was uncommonly strong, although he was not tall of stature and had a rather protruding belly. His memory was extraordinary and he had an aptitude for almost all the arts, both of war and of peace. Skilful in arms and horsemanship, he made speeches and wrote verses in Latin and Greek with ease and readiness, and even off-hand. He was besides not unacquainted with music, but sang and played the harp

305

comperi, notis quoque excipere velocissime solitum, cum amanuensibus suis per ludum iocumque certantem, imitarique chirographa quaecumque vidisset, ac saepe profiteri maximum falsarium esse potuisse.

IV. Tribunus militum et in Germania et in Britannia meruit summa industriae nec minore modestiae fama,[1] sicut apparet statuarum et imaginum eius multitudine ac titulis per utramque provinciam.

2   Post stipendia Foro operam dedit honestam magis quam assiduam, eodemque tempore Arrecinam[2] Tertullam, patre eq. R. sed praefecto quondam praetorianarum cohortium, duxit uxorem et in defunctae locum Marciam Furnillam splendidi generis; cum qua sublata filia divortium fecit.

3   Ex quaesturae deinde honore legioni praepositus Taricheaes[3] et Gamalam urbes Iudaeae validissimas in potestatem redegit, equo quadam acie sub feminibus amisso alteroque inscenso, cuius rector circa se dimicans occubuerat.

V. Galba mox tenente rem p. missus ad gratulandum, quaqua iret convertit homines, quasi adoptionis gratia arcesseretur. Sed ubi turbari rursus cuncta sensit, redit ex itinere, aditoque Paphiae Veneris oraculo, dum de navigatione consulit, etiam de imperii spe confirmatus est.

2   Cuius brevi compos et ad perdomandam Iudaeam relic-

---

[1] summa industriae ... modestiae fama, ς; summae industriae ... modestia et fama, Ω.

[2] Arrecinam, *Roth*; adrecidiam, Ω.

[3] Taricheas, *Ursinus* (Tarichias, *Bentley*); Thracias, Ω.

---

[a] See *Galba* xiv. 2, and note *d*.   [b] In A.D. 67.

[c] By the accession of his father Vespasian.

agreeably and skilfully. I have heard from many sources that he used also to write shorthand with great speed and would amuse himself by playful contests with his secretaries; also that he could imitate any handwriting that he had ever seen and often declared that he might have been the prince of forgers.

IV. He served as military tribune both in Germany and in Britain, winning a high reputation for energy and no less for integrity, as is evident from the great number of his statues and busts in both those provinces and from the inscriptions they bear.

After his military service he pleaded in the Forum, rather for glory than as a profession, and at the same time took to wife Arrecina Tertulla, whose father, though only a Roman knight, had once been prefect of the praetorian cohorts;[a] on her death he replaced her by Marcia Furnilla, a lady of a very distinguished family, but divorced her after he had acknowledged a daughter which she bore him.

Then, after holding the office of quaestor,[b] as commander of a legion he subjugated the two strong cities of Tarichaeae and Gamala in Judaea, having his horse killed under him in one battle and mounting another, whose rider had fallen fighting by his side.

V. Presently he was sent to congratulate Galba on becoming ruler of the state, and attracted attention wherever he went, through the belief that he had been sent for to be adopted. But observing that everything was once more in a state of turmoil, he turned back, and visiting the oracle of the Paphian Venus, to consult it about his voyage, he was also encouraged to hope for imperial power. Soon realising his hope[c] and left behind to complete the

307

tus, novissima Hierosolymorum oppugnatione duodecim propugnatores totidem sagittarum confecit ictibus, cepitque ea[1] natali filiae suae tanto militum gaudio ac favore, ut in gratulatione imperatorem eum consalutaverint et subinde decedentem provincia detinuerint, suppliciter nec non et minaciter efflagitantes, aut

3 remaneret aut secum omnis pariter abduceret. Unde nata suspicio est, quasi desciscere a patre Orientisque sibi regnum vindicare temptasset; quam suspicionem auxit, postquam Alexandriam petens in consecrando apud Memphim bove Apide diadema gestavit, de more quidem rituque priscae religionis; sed non deerant qui sequius interpretarentur. Quare festinans in Italiam, cum Regium, dein Puteolos oneraria nave appulisset, Romam inde contendit expeditissimus inopinantique patri, velut arguens rumorum de se temeritatem: "Veni," inquit, "pater, veni."

VI. Neque ex eo destitit participem atque etiam tutorem imperii agere. Triumphavit cum patre censuramque gessit una, eidem collega et in tribunicia potestate et in septem consulatibus fuit; receptaque ad se prope omnium officiorum cura, cum patris nomine et epistulas ipse dictaret et edicta conscriberet orationesque in senatu recitaret etiam quaestoris vice, praefecturam quoque praetori suscepit numquam ad id tempus nisi ab eq. R. administratam, egitque aliquanto incivilius et

---

[1] ea, *M; the other mss. have* eam.

---

[a] See *Aug.* xiii. 2.   [b] In A.D. 73.

[c] In A.D. 70, 72, 74, 75, 76, 77, 79.

[d] See *Nero* xv. 2, and note *b*.

conquest of Judaea, in the final attack on Jerusalem he slew twelve of the defenders with as many arrows; and he took the city on his daughter's birthday, so delighting the soldiers and winning their devotion that they hailed him as Imperator[a] and detained him from time to time, when he would leave the province, urging him with prayers and even with threats either to stay or to take them all with him. This aroused the suspicion that he had tried to revolt from his father and make himself king of the East; and he strengthened this suspicion on his way to Alexandria by wearing a diadem at the consecration of the bull Apis in Memphis, an act quite in accord with the usual ceremonial of that ancient religion, but unfavourably interpreted by some. Because of this he hastened to Italy, and putting in at Regium and then at Puteoli in a transport ship, he went with all speed from there to Rome, where as if to show that the reports about him were groundless, he surprised his father with the greeting, "I am here, father; I am here."

VI. From that time on he never ceased to act as the emperor's partner and even as his protector. He took part in his father's triumph[b] and was censor with him. He was also his colleague in the tribunicial power and in seven consulships.[c] He took upon himself the discharge of almost all duties, personally dictated letters and wrote edicts in his father's name, and even read his speeches in the senate in lieu of a quaestor.[d] He also assumed the command of the praetorian guard, which before that time had never been held except by a Roman knight, and in this office conducted himself in a somewhat arrogant and tyrannical fashion. For whenever he himself regarded

violentius, siquidem suspectissimum quemque sibi summissis qui per theatra et castra quasi consensu ad poenam
2 deposcerent, haud cunctanter oppressit. In his Aulum
Caecinam consularem vocatum ad cenam ac vixdum triclinio egressum confodi iussit, sane urgente discrimine,
cum etiam chirographum eius praeparatae apud milites
contionis deprehendisset. Quibus rebus sicut in
posterum securitati satis cavit, ita ad praesens plurimum
contraxit invidiae, ut non temere quis tam adverso
rumore magisque invitis omnibus transierit ad principatum.

VII. Praeter saevitiam suspecta in eo etiam luxuria
erat, quod ad mediam noctem comissationes cum profu-
sissimo quoque familiarium extenderet; nec minus libido
propter exoletorum et spadonum greges propterque
insignem reginae Berenices amorem, cui etiam nuptias
pollicitus ferebatur; suspecta rapacitas, quod constabat in
cognitionibus[1] patris nundinari praemiarique solitum;
denique propalam alium Neronem et opinabantur et
praedicabant. At illi ea fama pro bono cessit conversaque
est in maximas laudes neque vitio ullo reperto et contra
virtutibus summis.

2 Convivia instituit iucunda magis quam profusa. Amicos elegit, quibus etiam post eum principes ut et sibi et
rei p. necessariis adquieverunt praecipueque sunt usi.
Berenicen statim ab urbe dimisit invitus invitam. Quosdam e gratissimis delicatorum quanquam tam artifices

---

[1] cognitionibus, *Torrentius*; contionibus, Ω.

anyone with suspicion, he would secretly send some of the Guard to the various theatres and camps, to demand their punishment as if by consent of all who were present; and then he would put them out of the way without delay. Among these was Aulus Caecina, an ex-consul, whom he invited to dinner and then ordered to be stabbed almost before he left the dining-room; but in this case he was led by a pressing danger, having got possession of an autograph copy of an harangue which Caecina had prepared to deliver to the soldiers. Although by such conduct he provided for his safety in the future, he incurred such odium at the time that hardly anyone ever came to the throne with so evil a reputation or so much against the desires of all.

VII. Besides cruelty, he was also suspected of riotous living, since he protracted his revels until the middle of the night with the most prodigal of his friends; likewise of unchastity because of his troops of male prostitutes and eunuchs, and his notorious passion for queen Berenice, to whom it was even said that he promised marriage. He was suspected of greed as well; for it was well known that in cases which came before his father he put a price on his influence and accepted bribes. In short, people not only thought, but openly declared, that he would be a second Nero. But this reputation turned out to his advantage and gave place to the highest praise, when no fault was discovered in him, but on the contrary the highest virtues.

His banquets were pleasant rather than extravagant. He chose as his friends men whom succeeding emperors also retained as indispensable alike to themselves and to the State, and of whose services they made special use. Berenice he sent from Rome at once, against her will and against his own. Some of his most beloved paramours,

saltationis, ut mox scaenam tenuerint, non modo fovere prolixius, sed spectare omnino in publico coetu supersedit.

3   Nulli civium quicquam ademit; abstinuit alieno, ut si quis umquam; ac ne concessas quidem ac solitas conlationes recepit. Et tamen nemine ante se munificentia minor, amphitheatro dedicato thermisque iuxta celeriter[1] exstructis munus edidit apparatissimum largissimumque; dedit et navale proelium in veteri naumachia, ibidem et gladiatores atque uno die quinque milia omne genus ferarum.

VIII. Natura autem benevolentissimus, cum ex instituto Tiberi omnes dehinc Caesares beneficia a superioribus concessa principibus aliter rata[2] non haberent, quam si eadem iisdem et ipsi dedissent, primus praeterita omnia uno confirmavit edicto nec a se peti passus est. In ceteris vero desideriis hominum obstinatissime tenuit, ne quem sine spe dimitteret; quin et admonentibus domesticis, quasi plura polliceretur quam praestare posset, non oportere ait quemquam a sermone principis tristem discedere; atque etiam recordatus quondam super cenam, quod nihil cuiquam toto die praestitisset, memorabilem illam meritoque laudatam vocem edidit: "Amici, diem perdidi."

2   Populum in primis universum tanta per omnis occasiones comitate tractavit, ut proposito gladiatorio

---

[1] celeriter, *Calderinus, in note on Mart. Spect.* 2. 7; celebriter, Ω.   [2] rata, *inserted by Egnatius.*

---

[a] In A.D. 80.
[b] See note on *Vesp.* ix. 1.
[c] See *Aug.* xliii. 1.

although they were such skilful dancers that they later became stage favourites, he not only ceased to cherish any longer, but even to witness their public performances.

He took away nothing from any citizen. He respected others' property, if anyone ever did; in fact, he would not accept even proper and customary presents. And yet he was second to none of his predecessors in munificence. At the dedication[a] of the amphitheatre[b] and of the baths which were hastily built near it he gave a most magnificent and costly gladiatorial show. He presented a sham sea-fight too in the old naumachia,[c] and in the same place a combat of gladiators,[d] exhibiting five thousand wild beasts of every kind in a single day.

VIII. He was most kindly by nature, and whereas, in accordance with a custom established by Tiberius, all the Caesars who followed him refused to regard favours granted by previous emperors as valid, unless they had themselves conferred the same ones on the same individuals, Titus was the first to ratify them all in a single edict, without allowing himself to be asked. Moreover, in the case of other requests made of him, it was his fixed rule not to let anyone go away without hope. Even when his household officials warned him that he was promising more than he could perform, he said that it was not right for anyone to go away sorrowful from an interview with his emperor. On another occasion, remembering at dinner that he had done nothing for anybody all that day, he gave utterance to that memorable and praiseworthy remark: "Friends, I have lost a day."

The whole body of the people in particular he treated with such indulgence on all occasions that once at a

[d] When the water had been let out; cf. *Nero*, xxvii. 2.

munere, non ad suum, sed ad spectantium arbitrium editurum se professus sit; et plane ita fecit. Nam neque negavit quicquam petentibus et ut quae vellent peterent ultro adhortatus est. Quin et studium armaturae Thraecum prae se ferens saepe cum populo et voce et gestu ut fautor cavillatus est, verum maiestate salva nec minus aequitate. Ne quid popularitatis praetermitteret, nonnumquam in thermis suis admissa plebe lavit.

3   Quaedam sub eo fortuita ac tristia acciderunt, ut conflagratio Vesuvii[1] montis in Campania, et incendium Romae per triduum totidemque noctes, item pestilentia quanta non temere alias. In iis tot adversis ac talibus non modo principis sollicitudinem sed et parentis affectum unicum praestitit, nunc consolando per edicta, nunc 4 opitulando quatenus suppeteret facultas. Curatores restituendae Campaniae e consularium numero sorte duxit; bona oppressorum in Vesuvio,[2] quorum heredes non exstabant, restitutioni afflictarum civitatium attribuit. Urbis incendio nihil publice nisi periisse testatus,[3] cuncta praetoriorum suorum ornamenta operibus ac templis destinavit praeposuitque compluris ex equestri ordine, quo quaeque maturius peragerentur. Medendae valitudini leniendisque morbis nullam divinam humanamque

---

[1] Vesuvii] ve*bii, *M*; vesubii, *G*.

[2] Vesuvio, *M*; vesubio, *G*.

[3] nichil nisi sibi perisse testatus publice, Υ; nichil nisi sibi publice perisse testatus, *OT*; nihil publice perisse testatus, *Roth, following a ms. of Torrentius.*

---

[a] By humorously pretending to wrangle with those who favoured other gladiators than the Thracians; see Index, s.v. *gladiator.*   [b] In A.D. 79.   [c] In A.D. 80.

gladiatorial show he declared that he would give it, "not after his own inclinations, but those of the spectators"; and what is more, he kept his word. For he refused nothing which anyone asked, and even urged them to ask for what they wished. Furthermore, he openly displayed his partiality for Thracian gladiators and bantered the people about it by words and gestures,[a] always however preserving his dignity, as well as observing justice. Not to omit any act of condescension, he sometimes bathed in the baths which he had built, in company with the common people.

There were some dreadful disasters during his reign, such as the eruption of Mount Vesuvius in Campania,[b] a fire at Rome[c] which continued three days and as many nights, and a plague the like of which had hardly ever been known before. In these many great calamities he showed not merely the concern of an emperor, but even a father's surpassing love, now offering consolation in edicts, and now lending aid so far as his means allowed. He chose commissioners by lot from among the ex-consuls for the relief of Campania; and the property of those who lost their lives by Vesuvius and had no heirs left alive he applied to the rebuilding of the buried cities. During the fire in Rome he made no remark except "I am ruined,"[d] and he set aside all the ornaments of his villas for the public buildings and temples, and put several men of the equestrian order in charge of the work, that everything might be done with the greater dispatch. For curing the plague and diminishing the force of the epidemic there was no aid, human or divine, which he did not

[d] Implying that it was his personal loss, which he would make good.

315

opem non adhibuit inquisito omni sacrificiorum remedio-
rumque genere.

5   Inter adversa temporum et delatores mandatoresque[1]
erant ex licentia veteri. Hos assidue in Foro flagellis ac
fustibus caesos ac novissime traductos per amphitheatri
harenam partim subici ac venire imperavit, partim in
asperrimas insularum avehi. Utque etiam similia quandoque ausuros perpetuo coerceret, vetuit inter cetera de
eadem re pluribus legibus agi quaerive de cuiusquam
defunctorum statu ultra certos annos.

IX. Pontificatum maximum ideo se professus accipere
ut puras servaret manus, fidem praestitit, nec auctor
posthac cuiusquam necis nec conscius, quamvis interdum
ulciscendi causa non deesset, sed periturum se potius
quam perditurum adiurans. Duos patricii generis convictos in adfectatione imperii nihil amplius quam ut desiste-
rent monuit, docens principatum fato dari, si quid[2]
2   praeterea desiderarent promittens se tributurum. Et
confestim quidem ad alterius matrem quae procul aberat
cursores suos misit, qui anxiae salvum filium nuntiarent,
ceterum ipsos non solum familiari cenae adhibuit, sed et
insequenti die gladiatorum spectaculo circa se ex industria conlocatis oblata sibi ferramenta pugnantium in-

---

[1] mandatoresque, *X*; amendatoresque, *M*; amandatoresque,
*G*δ.   [2] quid, *GN*δ; *the other mss. have* quod.

---

[a] To propitiate the gods, who were supposed to inflict such
evils upon mankind by way of punishment.

[b] The office was seldom taken so seriously. Julius Caesar, for
instance, held it during his campaigns in Gaul.

[c] The weapons of gladiators were regularly examined by the
editor, or giver of the games, to see if they were sharp enough; cf.
Dio, 68. 3, who tells a similar story of the emperor Nerva.

employ, searching for every kind of sacrifice[a] and all kinds of medicines.

Among the evils of the times were the informers and their instigators, who had enjoyed a long standing license. After these had been soundly beaten in the Forum with scourges and cudgels, and finally led in procession across the arena of the amphitheatre, he had some of them put up and sold, and other deported to the wildest of the islands. To further discourage for all time any who might think of venturing on similar practices, among other precautions he made it unlawful for anyone to be tried under several laws for the same offence, or for any inquiry to be made as to the legal status of any deceased person after a stated number of years.

IX. Having declared that he would accept the office of pontifex maximus[b] for the purpose of keeping his hands unstained, he was true to his promise; for after that he neither caused nor connived at the death of any man, although he sometimes had no lack of reasons for taking vengeance; but he swore that he would rather be killed than kill. When two men of patrician family were found guilty of aspiring to the throne, he satisfied himself with warning them to abandon their attempt, saying that imperial power was the gift of fate, and promising that if there was anything else they desired, he himself would bestow it. Then he sent his couriers with all speed to the mother of one of them, for she was some distance off, to relieve her anxiety by reporting that her son was safe; and he not only invited the men themselves to dinner among his friends, but on the following day at a gladiatorial show he purposely placed them near him, and when the swords of the contestants were offered him,[c] handed them over for

spicienda porrexit. Dicitur etiam cognita utriusque genitura imminere ambobus periculum adfirmasse, verum
quandoque et ab alio, sicut evenit.

3 Fratrem insidiari sibi non desinentem, sed paene
ex professo sollicitantem exercitus, meditantem fugam,
neque occidere neque seponere ac ne in minore quidem
honore habere sustinuit, sed, ut a primo imperii die, consortem successoremque testari perseveravit, nonnumquam secreto precibus et lacrimis orans, ut tandem
mutuo erga se animo vellet esse.

X. Inter haec morte praeventus est maiore hominum
damno quam suo. Spectaculis absolutis, in quorum fine
populo coram ubertim fleverat, Sabinos petit aliquanto
tristior, quod sacrificanti hostia aufugerat quodque tempestate serena tonuerat. Deinde ad primam statim man-
sionem febrim nanctus, cum inde lectica transferretur,
suspexisse dicitur dimotis pallulis caelum, multumque
conquestus eripi sibi vitam immerenti; neque enim
exstare ullum suum factum paenitendum excepto dum
2 taxat uno. Id quale fuerit, neque ipse tunc prodidit
neque cuiquam facile succurrat. Quidam opinantur consuetudinem recordatum, quam cum fratris uxore
habuerit; sed nullam habuisse persancte Domitia iurabat,
haud negatura, si qua omnino fuisset, immo etiam glo-
riatura, quod illi promptissimum erat in omnibus probris.

---

[a] Possibly Domitian's charge was true; cf. *Dom.* ii. 3 and
note *d*.

their inspection. It is even said that inquiring into the horoscope of each of them, he declared that danger threatened them both, but at some future time and from another, as turned out to be the case.

Although his brother never ceased plotting against him, but almost openly stirred up the armies to revolt and meditated flight to them, he had not the heart to put him to death or banish him from the court, or even to hold him in less honour than before. On the contrary, as he had done from the very first day of his rule, he continued to declare that he was his partner and successor, and sometimes he privately begged him with tears and prayers to be willing at least to return his affection.

X. In the meantime he was cut off by death, to the loss of mankind rather than to his own. After finishing the public games, at the close of which he wept bitterly in the presence of the people, he went to the Sabine territory, somewhat cast down because a victim had escaped as he was sacrificing and because it had thundered from a clear sky. Then at the very first stopping place he was seized with a fever, and as he was being carried on from there in a litter, it is said that he pushed back the curtains, looked up to heaven, and lamented bitterly that his life was being taken from him contrary to his deserts; for he said that there was no act of his life of which he had cause to repent, save one only. What this was he did not himself disclose at the time, nor could anyone easily divine.[a] Some think that he recalled the intimacy which he had with his brother's wife; but Domitia swore most solemnly that this did not exist, although she would not have denied it if it had been in the least true, but on the contrary would have boasted of it, as she was most ready to do of all her scandalous actions.

XI. Excessit in eadem qua pater villa Id. Sept. post biennium ac menses duos diesque XX quam successerat patri, altero et quadragesimo aetatis anno. Quod ut palam factum est, non secus atque in domestico luctu maerentibus publice cunctis, senatus prius quam edicto convocaretur ad curiam concurrit, obseratisque adhuc foribus, deinde apertis, tantas mortuo gratias egit laudesque congessit, quantas ne vivo quidem umquam atque praesenti.

DOMITIANUS

I. Domitianus natus est VIIII. Kal. Novemb. patre consule designato inituroque mense insequenti honorem, regione urbis sexta ad Malum Punicum, domo quam postea in templum gentis Flaviae convertit. Pubertatis ac primae adulescentiae tempus tanta inopia tantaque infamia gessisse fertur, ut nullum argenteum vas in usu haberet. Satisque constat Clodium Pollionem praetorium virum, in quem est poema Neronis quod inscribitur "Luscio," chirographum eius conservasse et nonnumquam protulisse noctem sibi pollicentis; nec defuerunt qui affirmarent, corruptum Domitianum et a Nerva successore
2   mox suo. Bello Vitelliano confugit in Capitolium cum

ᵃ The old homestead at Cutilae, near Reate; see *Vesp.* xxiv. That this continued to be a *villa rustica* is implied in *Vesp.* ii. 1.   ᵇ Sept. 13, A.D. 81.   ᶜ Oct. 24, A.D. 51.   ᵈ Various quarters and streets of the city were designated in this way; cf. *ad Capita Bubula, Aug.* v; *ad Pirum*, Mart. 1. 117. 6. *Ad Malum Punicum* was a street on the Quirinal hill, probably corresponding with the modern Via delle Quattro Fontane.

XI. He died in the same farmhouse[a] as his father, on the Ides of September,[b] two years, two months and twenty days after succeeding Vespasian, in the forty-second year of his age. When his death was made known, the whole populace mourned as they would for a loss in their own families, the senate hastened to the House before it was summoned by proclamation, and with the doors still shut, and then with them open, rendered such thanks to him and heaped such praise on him after death as they had never done even when he was alive and present.

DOMITIAN

I. Domitian was born[c] on the ninth day before the Kalends of November of the year when his father was consul elect and was about to enter on the office in the following month, in a street of the sixth region called "the Pomegranate,"[d] in a house which he afterwards converted into a temple of the Flavian family. He is said to have passed the period of his boyhood and his early youth in great poverty and infamy. For he did not possess a single piece of plate and it is a well known fact that Clodius Pollio, a man of praetorian rank, against whom Nero's poem entitled "The One-eyed Man" is directed, preserved a letter in Domitian's handwriting and sometimes exhibited it, in which the future emperor promised him an assignation; and there have not been wanting those who declared that Domitian was also debauched by Nerva, who succeeded him. In the war with Vitellius he took refuge in the Capitol with his paternal uncle Sabinus and a part

patruo Sabino ac parte praesentium copiarum, sed irrumpentibus adversariis et ardente templo apud aedituum clam pernoctavit, ac mane Isiaci celatus habitu interque sacrificulos variae[1] superstitionis cum se trans Tiberim ad condiscipuli sui matrem comite uno contulisset, ita latuit, ut scrutantibus qui vestigia subsecuti erant, deprehendi non potuerit. Post victoriam demum progressus et Caesar consalutatus honorem praeturae urbanae consulari potestate suscepit titulo tenus, nam[2] iuris dictionem ad collegam proximum transtulit, ceterum omnem vim dominationis tam licenter exercuit, ut iam tum qualis futurus esset ostenderet. Ne[3] exsequar singula, contractatis multorum uxoribus Domitiam Longinam Aelio Lamiae nuptam etiam in matrimonium abduxit, atque uno die super XX officia urbana aut peregrina distribuit, mirari se Vespasiano dictitante, quod successorem non et sibi mitteret.

II. Expeditionem quoque in Galliam Germaniasque neque necessariam et dissuadentibus paternis amicis incohavit, tantum ut fratri se et opibus et dignatione adaequaret. Ob haec correptus, quo magis et aetatis et condicionis admoneretur, habitabat cum patre una sellamque eius ac fratris, quotiens prodirent, lectica sequebatur ac triumphum utriusque Iudaicum equo albo

---

[1] variae, Ω; vanae, ⊊ *and the editors.*
[2] nam, *J. Gronov.*; quam, Ω; quia, ⊊.
[3] ne, ΠQ; *the other mss. have* nec.

---

[a] Cf. *Otho*, xii. 1, at the end.   [b] See note on *Galba*, i.
[c] As son of the emperor.   [d] That is, in the provinces.
[e] He was but eighteen years old at the time.

of the forces under him. When the enemy forced an entrance and the temple was fired, he hid during the night with the guardian of the shrine, and in the morning, disguised in the garb of a follower of Isis[a] and mingling with the priests of that fickle superstition, he went across the Tiber with a single companion to the mother of one of his school-fellows. There he was so effectually concealed that, though he was closely followed, he could not be found, in spite of a thorough search. It was only after the victory that he ventured forth and after being hailed as Caesar,[b] he assumed the office of city praetor with consular powers, but only in name, turning over all the judicial business to his next colleague. But he exercised all the tyranny of his high position[c] so lawlessly, that it was even then apparent what sort of a man he was going to be. Not to mention all details, after making free with the wives of many men, he went so far as to marry Domitia Longina, who was the wife of Aelius Lamia, and in a single day he assigned more than twenty positions in the city and abroad,[d] which led Vespasian to say more than once that he was surprised that he did not appoint the emperor's successor with the rest.

II. He began an expedition against Gaul and the Germanies, which was uncalled for and from which his father's friends dissuaded him, merely that he might make himself equal to his brother in power and rank. For this he was reprimanded, and to give him a better realisation of his youth[e] and position, he had to live with his father, and when they appeared in public he followed the emperor's chair and that of his brother in a litter, while he also attended their triumph over Judaea riding on a white

comitatus est. Quin et e sex[1] consulatibus non nisi unum ordinarium gessit eumque cedente ac suffragante fratre.

2 Simulavit et ipse mire modestiam in primisque poeticae studium, tam insuetum antea sibi quam postea spretum et abiectum, recitavitque etiam publice. Nec tamen eo setius, cum Vologaesus Parthorum rex auxilia adversus Alanos ducemque alterum ex Vespasiani liberis depoposcisset, omni ope contendit ut ipse potissimum mitteretur; et quia discussa res est, alios Orientis reges ut idem postularent donis ac pollicitationibus sollicitare temptavit.

3 Patre defuncto diu cunctatus an duplum donativum militi offerret, numquam iactare dubitavit relictum se participem imperii, sed fraudem testamento adhibitam; neque cessavit ex eo insidias struere fratri clam palamque,[2] quoad correptum gravi valitudine, prius quam plane efflaret animam, pro mortuo deseri iussit; defunctumque nullo praeterquam consecrationis honore dignatus, saepe etiam carpsit obliquis orationibus et edictis.

III. Inter initia principatus cotidie secretum sibi horarum sumere solebat nec quicquam amplius quam muscas captare ac stilo praeacuto configere, ut cuidam interroganti, essetne quis intus cum Caesare, non absurde responsum sit a Vibio Crispo, ne muscam quidem.

[1] quin et e sex, *Ihm* (quin ex, *Bentley*); qui sex *or* quis ex, *MGRLP*δ; *the rest of the mss. have* in sex.

[2] palamque, *T*ς; et palam, *L*; *the other mss. have* palam.

---

[a] The usual procedure for a youthful prince; cf. *Tib.* vi. 4.

[b] See note *c* on *Galba*, vi. 1. The reference is to his consulships before he became emperor; see chap. xiii. 3.

[c] That is, twice as large as his brother's.

[d] Titus had the ability to do this; cf. *Tit.* iii. 2, at the end.

horse.[a] Moreover, of his six consulships only one was a regular one,[b] and he obtained that only because his brother gave place to him and recommended his appointment.

He himself too made a remarkable pretence of modesty and especially of an interest in poetry, an art which had previously been as unfamiliar to him as it was later despised and rejected, and he even gave readings in public. Yet in spite of all this, when Vologaesus, king of the Parthians, had asked for auxiliaries against the Alani and for one of Vespasian's sons as their leader, Domitian used every effort to have himself sent rather than Titus; and because the affair came to nothing, he tried by gifts and promises to induce other eastern kings to make the same request.

On the death of his father he hesitated for some time whether to offer a double largess[c] to the soldiers, and he never had any compunction about saying that he had been left a partner in the imperial power, but that the will had been tampered with.[d] And from that time on he never ceased to plot against his brother secretly and openly, until Titus was seized with a dangerous illness, when Domitian ordered that he be left for dead, before he had actually drawn his last breath. And after his death he bestowed no honour upon him, save that of deification, and he often assailed his memory in ambiguous phrases, both in his speeches and in his edicts.

III. At the beginning of his reign he used to spend hours in seclusion every day, doing nothing but catch flies and stab them with a keenly-sharpened stylus. Consequently when someone once asked whether anyone was in there with Caesar, Vibius Crispus made the witty reply:

Deinde uxorem Domitiam, ex qua in secundo suo consulatu filium tulerat alteroque anno quam imperium adeptus est amisit,[1] consalutavit Augustam; eandem Paridis histrionis amore deperditam repudiavit intraque breve tempus inpatiens discidii quasi efflagitante populo reduxit.

2   Circa administrationem autem imperii aliquamdiu se varium praestitit, mixtura quoque[2] aequabili vitiorum atque virtutum, donec virtutes quoque in vitia deflexit; quantum coniectare licet, super ingenii naturam inopia rapax, metu saevus.

IV. Spectacula assidue magnifica et sumptuosa edidit non in amphitheatro modo, verum et in Circo, ubi praeter sollemnes bigarum quadrigarumque cursus proelium etiam duplex, equestre ac pedestre, commisit; at in amphitheatro navale quoque. Nam venationes gladiatoresque et noctibus ad lychnuchos, nec virorum modo pugnas, sed et feminarum. Praeterea quaestoriis muneribus, quae olim omissa revocaverat, ita semper interfuit, ut populo potestatem faceret bina paria e suo ludo postu-

2 landi eaque novissima aulico apparatu induceret. Ac per omne gladiatorum spectaculum ante pedes ei stabat puerulus coccinatus parvo portentosoque capite, cum quo plurimum fabulabatur, nonnumquam serio. Auditus est certe, dum ex eo quaerit, ecquid[3] sciret, cur sibi visum esset ordinatione proxima Aegypto praeficere Mettium

---

[1] quam . . . amisit, *supplied by Ihm.*
[2] mixturaque, *Lipsius*; mixtura prope, *Bentley.*
[3] ecquid, *second Roman edition*; et quid, Ω (et qui, X).

---

[a] See chaps. ix and xi. 1.
[b] See note on *Vesp.* ix. 1.

"Not even a fly." Then he saluted his wife Domitia as Augusta. He had had a son by her in his second consulship, whom he lost the second year after he became emperor; he divorced her because of her love for the actor Paris, but could not bear the separation and soon took her back, alleging that the people demanded it.

In his administration of the government he for some time showed himself inconsistent, with about an equal number of virtues and vices, but finally he turned the virtues also into vices; for so far as one may guess, it was contrary to his natural disposition[a] that he was made rapacious through need and cruel through fear.

IV. He constantly gave grand and costly entertainments, both in the amphitheatre[b] and in the Circus, where in addition to the usual races between two-horse and four-horse chariots, he also exhibited two battles, one between forces of infantry and the other by horsemen; and he even gave a naval battle in the amphitheatre. Besides he gave hunts of wild beasts, gladiatorial shows at night by the light of torches, and not only combats between men but between women as well. He was always present too at the games given by the quaestors, which he revived after they had been abandoned for some time, and invariably granted the people the privilege of calling for two pairs of gladiators from his own school, and brought them in last in all the splendour of the court. During the whole of every gladiatorial show there always stood at his feet a small boy clad in scarlet, with an abnormally small head, with whom he used to talk a great deal, and sometimes seriously. At any rate, he was overheard to ask him if he knew why he had decided at the last appointment day to make Mettius Rufus prefect of

Rufum. Edidit navalis pugnas paene iustarum classium, effosso et circumstructo iuxta Tiberim lacu, atque inter maximos imbres perspectavit.

3   Fecit et ludos saeculares, computata ratione temporum ad annum non quo Claudius proxime, sed quo olim Augustus ediderat; in iis circensium die, quo facilius centum missus peragerentur, singulos e septenis spatiis ad quina corripuit.

4   Instituit et quinquennale certamen Capitolino Iovi triplex, musicum equestre gymnicum, et aliquanto plurium quam nunc est coronatorum. Certabant enim et prosa oratione Graece Latineque ac praeter citharoedos chorocitharistae quoque et psilocitharistae, in stadio vero cursu etiam virgines.[1] Certamini praesedit crepidatus purpureaque amictus toga Graecanica, capite gestans coronam auream cum effigie Iovis ac Iunonis Minervaeque, adsidentibus Diali sacerdote et collegio Flavialium pari habitu, nisi quod illorum coronis inerat et ipsius imago. Celebrabat et in Albano quotannis Quinquatria Minervae, cui collegium instituerat, ex quo sorte ducti magisterio fungerentur ederentque eximias venationes et scaenicos ludos superque oratorum ac poetarum certamina.

5   Congiarium populo nummorum trecenorum ter dedit atque inter spectacula muneris largissimum epulum

---

[1] virgines, *Lipsius*; virginis, Ω.

---

[a] See note on *Claud.* xxi. 2.

[b] See note on *Claud.* xxi. 3.

[c] As well as in poetry.   [d] Established for the worship of the deified Flavian emperors, after the manner of the Augustales; see note on *Claud.* vi. 2.   [e] See *Aug.* lxxi. 3.

Egypt. He often gave sea-fights almost with regular fleets, having dug a pool near the Tiber and surrounded it with seats; and he continued to witness the contests amid heavy rains.

He also celebrated Secular games,[a] reckoning the time, not according to the year when Claudius had last given them, but by the previous calculation of Augustus. In the course of these, to make it possible to finish a hundred races on the day of the contests in the Circus, he diminished the number of laps from seven to five.[b]

He also established a quinquennial contest in honour of Jupiter Capitolinus of a threefold character, comprising music, riding, and gymnastics, and with considerably more prizes than are awarded nowadays. For there were competitions in prose declamation[c] both in Greek and in Latin; and in addition to those of the lyre-players, between choruses of such players and in the lyre alone, without singing; while in the stadium there were races even between maidens. He presided at the competitions in half-boots, clad in a purple toga in the Greek fashion, and wearing upon his head a golden crown with figures of Jupiter, Juno, and Minerva, while by his side sat the priest of Jupiter and the college of the Flaviales,[d] similarly dressed, except that their crowns bore his image as well. He celebrated the Quinquatria[e] too every year in honour of Minerva at his Alban villa, and established for her a college of priests, from which men were chosen by lot to act as officers and give splendid shows of wild beasts and stage plays, besides holding contests in oratory and poetry.

He made a present to the people of three hundred sesterces each on three occasions, and in the course of one of

Septimontiali sacro, cum[1] quidem senatui equitique panariis, plebei sportellis cum obsonio distributis initium vescendi primus fecit; dieque proximo omne genus rerum missilia sparsit, et quia pars maior intra popularia deciderat, quinquagenas tesseras in singulos cuneos equestris ac senatorii ordinis pronuntiavit.

V. Plurima et amplissima opera incendio absumpta restituit, in quis et Capitolium, quod rursus arserat; sed omnia sub titulo tantum suo ac sine ulla pristini auctoris memoria. Novam autem excitavit aedem in Capitolio Custodi Iovi et forum quod nunc Nervae vocatur, item Flaviae templum gentis et stadium et odium et naumachiam, e cuius postea lapide Maximus Circus deustis utrimque lateribus exstructus est.

VI. Expeditiones partim sponte suscepit, partim necessario: sponte in Chattos, necessario unam in Sarmatas legione cum legato simul caesa; in Dacos duas, primam Oppio Sabino consulari oppresso, secundam Cornelio Fusco praefecto cohortium praetorianarum, cui belli summam commiserat. De Chattis Dacisque post varia

---

[1] sacro cum, *J. Gronov*; sacro (quidem), ⊊ (*Torrentius*); sacrorum, Ω.

---

[a] While the spectators remained in their seats; cf. Dio, 67. 4.

[b] Represented in many cases by *tesserae*, or tickets; see note on *Aug.* xli. 2.

[c] In 80; it had previously been destroyed by fire in 69; see *Vit.* xv. 3.

[d] Who finished and dedicated it; it was also called the *Forum Transitorium* because it connected the Forum of Augustus with the Forum Pacis, as well as the Subura with the Forum Romanum. It occupied a part of the Argiletum.

his shows in celebration of the feast of the Seven Hills gave a plentiful banquet,[a] distributing large baskets of victuals to the senate and knights, and smaller ones to the commons; and he himself was the first to begin to eat. On the following day he scattered gifts of all sorts of things[b] to be scrambled for, and since the greater part of these fell where the people sat, he had five hundred tickets thrown into each section occupied by the senatorial and equestrian orders.

V. He restored many splendid buildings which had been destroyed by fire, among them the Capitolium, which had again been burned,[c] but in all cases with the inscription of his own name only, and with no mention of the original builder. Furthermore, he built a new temple on the Capitoline hill in honour of Jupiter Custos and the forum which now bears the name of Nerva;[d] likewise a temple to the Flavian family, a stadium, an Odeum,[e] and a pool for sea-fights.[f] From the stone used in this last the Circus Maximus was afterwards rebuilt, when both sides of it had been destroyed by fire.

VI. His campaigns he undertook partly without provocation and partly of necessity. That against the Chatti was uncalled for, while the one against the Sarmatians was justified by the destruction of a legion with its commander. He made two against the Dacians, the first when Oppius Sabinus an ex-consul was defeated, and the second on the overthrow of Cornelius Fuscus, prefect of the praetorian guard, to whom he had entrusted the conduct of the war. After several battles of varying success he celebrated a double triumph over the Chatti and the

[e] Or Music Hall.   [f] See chap. iv. 2.

proelia duplicem triumphum egit, de Sarmatis lauream modo Capitolino Iovi rettulit.

2   Bellum civile motum a L. Antonio, superioris Germaniae praeside, confecit absens felicitate mira, cum ipsa dimicationis hora resolutus repente Rhenus transituras ad Antonium copias barbarorum inhibuisset. De qua victoria praesagiis prius quam nuntiis comperit, siquidem ipso quo dimicatum erat die statuam eius Romae insignis aquila circumplexa pinnis clangores laetissimos edidit; pauloque post occisum Antonium adeo vulgatum est, ut caput quoque adportatum eius vidisse se plerique contenderent.

VII. Multa etiam in communi rerum usu novavit: sportulas publicas sustulit revocata rectarum cenarum consuetudine; duas circensibus gregum[1] factiones aurati purpureique panni ad quattuor pristinas addidit; interdixit histrionibus scaenam, intra domum quidem exercendi artem iure concesso; castrari mares vetuit; spadonum, qui residui apud mangones erant, pretia moderatus est. Ad summam quondam ubertatem vini, frumenti vero inopiam existimans nimio vinearum studio neglegi arva, edixit, ne quis in Italia novellaret utque in provinciis vineta succiderentur, relicta ubi plurimum dimidia parte; nec exsequi rem perseveravit. Quaedam

---

[1] gregum, *Beroaldus*; grecum, Ω.

---

[a] Tac. *Agr.* 39 says that his unjustified triumph over the Germans (and the Dacians) was a laughing-stock.

[b] See *Nero*, xvi. 2.

[c] See *Aug.* lxxiv.

[d] See *Calig.* lv. 2.

[e] See chap. xiv. 2.

Dacians.[a] His victories over the Sarmatians he commemorated merely by the offering of a laurel crown to Jupiter of the Capitol.

A civil war which was set on foot by Lucius Antonius, governor of Upper Germany, was put down in the emperor's absence by a remarkable stroke of good fortune; for at the very hour of the battle the Rhine suddenly thawed and prevented his barbarian allies from crossing over to Antonius. Domitian learned of this victory through omens before he actually had news of it, for on the very day when the decisive battle was fought a magnificent eagle enfolded his statue at Rome with its wings, uttering exultant shrieks; and soon afterwards the report of Antony's death became so widespread that several went so far as to assert positively that they had seen his head brought to Rome.

VII. He made many innovations also in common customs. He did away with the distribution of food to the people[b] and revived that of formal dinners.[c] He added two factions of drivers in the Circus, with gold and purple as their colours, to the four former ones.[d] He forbade the appearance of actors on the stage, but allowed the practice of their art in private houses. He prohibited the castration of males, and kept down the price of the eunuchs that remained in the hands of the slave dealers. Once upon the occasion of a plentiful wine crop, attended with a scarcity of grain, thinking that the fields were neglected through too much attention to the vineyards, he made an edict forbidding anyone to plant more vines in Italy and ordering that the vineyards in the provinces be cut down, or but half of them at most be left standing; but he did not persist in carrying out the measure.[e] He opened some of

333

ex maximis officiis inter libertinos equitesque R. commu-
3 nicavit. Geminari legionum castra prohibuit nec plus
quam mille nummos a quoquam ad signa deponi, quod
L. Antonius apud duarum legionum hiberna res novas
moliens fiduciam cepisse etiam ex depositorum summa
videbatur. Addidit et quartum stipendium militi aureos
ternos.

VIII. Ius diligenter et industrie dixit, plerumque et in
Foro pro tribunali extra ordinem; ambitiosas centumviro-
rum sententias rescidit; reciperatores, ne se perfusoriis
assertionibus accommodarent, identidem admonuit;
nummarios iudices cum suo quemque consilio notavit.
2 Auctor et tribunis plebis fuit aedilem sordidum repetun-
darum accusandi iudicesque in eum a senatu petendi.
Magistratibus quoque urbicis provinciarumque praesidibus coercendis tantum curae adhibuit, ut neque mo-
destiores umquam neque iustiores exstiterint; e quibus
plerosque post illum reos omnium criminum vidimus.
3 Suscepta correctione[1] morum licentiam theatralem
promiscue in equite spectandi inhibuit; scripta famosa

---

[1] correctione, $L\varsigma$; *the other mss. have* correptione.

---

[a] That is, those which had formerly been restricted to the
senatorial order.

[b] Where the soldiers deposited their surplus money with the
general for safe keeping, until the end of their term of service;
see Veget. 2. 20.

[c] That is, raised the amount from nine to twelve *aurei* (the
aureus contained 100 sesterces).

[d] That is, to gain favour with influential men or their advocates; cf. *Tib.* xxxiii.

the most important offices of the court[a] to freedmen and
Roman knights. He prohibited the uniting of two legions
in one camp and the deposit of more than a thousand sesterces by any one soldier at headquarters,[b] because it was
clear that Lucius Antonius had been especially led to
attempt a revolution by the amount of such deposits
in the combined winter quarters of two legions. He
increased the pay of the soldiers one fourth, by the addition of three gold pieces each year.[c]

VIII. He administered justice scrupulously and conscientiously, frequently holding special sittings on the tribunal in the Forum. He rescinded such decisions of the
Hundred Judges as were made from interested motives.[d]
He often warned the arbiters[e] not to grant claims for freedom made under false pretences. He degraded jurors
who accepted bribes, together with all their associates.[f]
He also induced the tribunes of the commons to prose-
cute a corrupt aedile for extortion, and to ask the senate
to appoint jurors in the case. He took such care to exercise restraint over the city officials and the governors of
the provinces that at no time were they more honest or
just, whereas after his time we have seen many of them
charged with all manner of offences. Having undertaken
the correction of public morals,[g] he put an end to the
licence at the theatres, where the general public occupied
the seats reserved for the knights; did away with the pre-
vailing publication of scurrilous lampoons, in which dis-

[e] Cf. *Nero*, xvii.
[f] That is, all who sat in judgment on the same case.
[g] As censor.

vulgoque edita, quibus primores viri ac feminae notabantur, abolevit non sine auctorum ignominia; quaestorium virum, quod gesticulandi saltandique studio teneretur, movit senatu; probrosis feminis lecticae usum ademit iusque capiendi legata hereditatesque; equitem R. ob reductam in matrimonium uxorem, cui dimissae adulterii crimen intenderat, erasit iudicum albo; quosdam ex utroque ordine lege Scantinia condemnavit; incesta Vestalium virginum, a patre quoque suo et fratre neglecta, varie ac severe coercuit, priora capitali suppli-

4 cio, posteriora more veteri. Nam cum Oculatis sororibus, item Varronillae liberum mortis permisisset arbitrium corruptoresque earum relegasset, mox Corneliam maximam virginem absolutam olim, dein longo intervallo repetitam atque convictam defodi imperavit stupratoresque virgis in Comitio ad necem caedi, excepto praetorio viro, cui, dubia etiam tum causa et incertis quaestionibus atque tormentis de semet professo, exsilium

5 indulsit. Ac ne qua religio deum impune contaminaretur, monimentum, quod libertus eius e lapidibus templo Capitolini Iovis destinatis filio exstruxerat, diruit per milites ossaque et reliquias quae inerant mari mersit.

IX. Inter initia usque adeo ab omni caede abhorrebat, ut absente adhuc patre recordatus Vergili versum:

---

[a] Which prescribed penalties for homosexual behavior.

tinguished men and women were attacked, and imposed ignominious penalties on their authors; expelled an ex-quaestor from the senate, because he was given to acting and dancing; deprived notorious women of the use of litters, as well as of the right to receive inheritances and legacies; struck the name of a Roman knight from the list of jurors, because he had taken back his wife after divorcing her and charging her with adultery; condemned several men of both orders, offenders against the Scantinian law;[a] and the unchaste behavior of Vestal virgins, condoned even by his father and his brother, he punished severely in divers ways, at first by capital punishment, and afterwards in the ancient fashion. For while he allowed the sisters Oculata and also Varronilla free choice of the manner of their death, and banished their paramours, he later ordered that Cornelia, a chief-vestal who had been acquitted once but after a long interval again arraigned and found guilty, he buried alive; and her lovers were beaten to death with rods in the Comitium, with the exception of an ex-praetor, whom he allowed to go into exile, because he admitted his guilt while the case was still unsettled and the examination and torture of the witnesses had led to no result. To protect the gods from being dishonoured with impunity by any sacrilege, he caused a tomb which one of his freedmen had built for his son from stones intended for the temple of Jupiter of the Capitol to be destroyed by the soldiers and the bones and ashes contained in it thrown into the sea.

IX. In the earlier part of his reign he so shrank from any form of bloodshed that, while his father was still absent from the city, he planned to issue an edict that no oxen should be offered up, recalling the line of Virgil,

Impia quam caesis gens est epulata iuvencis[a]

edicere destinarit, ne boves immolarentur. Cupiditatis
quoque atque avaritiae vix suspicionem ullam aut privatus
umquam aut princeps aliquamdiu dedit, immo e diverso
magna saepe non abstinentiae modo sed etiam liberali-
2 tatis experimenta. Omnis circa se largissime prosecutus
nihil prius aut acrius monuit quam ne quid sordide facerent. Relictas sibi hereditates ab iis, quibus liberi erant,
non recepit. Legatum etiam ex testamento Rusti[1] Caepi-
onis, qui caverat ut quotannis ingredientibus curiam senatoribus[b] certam summam viritim praestaret heres suus,
irritum fecit. Reos, qui ante quinquennium proximum
apud aerarium pependissent, universos discrimine libe-
ravit nec repeti nisi intra annum eaque condicione permisit, ut accusatori qui causam non teneret exsilium
3 poena esset. Scribas quaestorios negotiantis ex consuetudine sed contra Clodiam legem[c] venia in praeteritum donavit. Subsiciva, quae divisis per veteranos agris carptim
superfuerunt, veteribus possessoribus ut usu capta concessit. Fiscales calumnias magna calumniantium poena
repressit, ferebaturque vox eius: "Princeps qui delatores
non castigat, irritat."

X. Sed neque in clementiae neque in abstinentiae

---

[1] Rusti, ⊊ (*Torrentius, Burman*); rusci, Ω.

---

[a] *Georg.* 2. 537.　　[b] Probably referring to new senators,
entering the House for the first time.

[c] Nothing is known of this law. Livy, 21. 63. 3–4, mentions a
law of Q. Claudius, which forbade senators to engage in business,
and that law may have had a chapter referring to the *scribae
quaestorii* and other "civil servants"; or, as some suppose, Publius
Clodius may have passed such a law.

Before an impious race feasted upon slaughtered
  bullocks.[a]

He was equally free from any suspicion of love of gain
or of avarice, both in private life and for some time after
becoming emperor; on the contrary, he often gave strong
proofs not merely of integrity, but even of liberality. He
treated all his intimates most generously, and there was
nothing which he urged them more frequently, or with
greater insistence, than that they should be niggardly in
none of their acts. He would not accept inheritances left
him by those who had children. He even annulled a
legacy in the will of Rustus Caepio, who had provided
that his heir should yearly pay a specified sum to each of
the senators on his entrance into the House.[b] He can-
celled the suits against those who had been posted as
debtors to the public treasury for more than five years,
and would not allow a renewal except within a year and
on the condition that an accuser who did not win his suit
should be punished with exile. Scribes of the quaestors
who carried on business, which had become usual
although contrary to the Clodian law,[c] he pardoned for
past offences. Parcels of land which were left unoccupied
here and there after the assignment of lands to the veterans he granted to their former owners as by right of possession. He checked false accusations designed for the
profit of the privy purse[d] and inflicted severe penalties
on offenders; and a saying of his was current, that an
emperor who does not punish informers hounds them on.

X. But he did not continue this course of mercy or

[d] That is, charges which resulted in the confiscation of the
goods of the accused to the privy purse.

tenore permansit, et tamen aliquanto celerius ad saevitiam descivit quam ad cupiditatem. Discipulum Paridis pantomimi impuberem[1] adhuc et cum maxime aegrum, quod arte formaque non absimilis magistro videbatur, occidit; item Hermogenem Tarsensem propter quasdam in historia figuras, librariis etiam, qui eam descripserant, cruci fixis. Patrem familias, quod Thraecem murmilloni parem, munerario imparem dixerat, detractum spectaculis in harenam canibus obiecit cum hoc titulo: "Impie locutus parmularius."

2   Complures senatores, in iis aliquot consulares, interemit; ex quibus Civicam Cerealem in ipso Asiae proconsulatu, Salvidienum Orfitum, Acilium Glabrionem in[2] exsilio, quasi molitores rerum novarum, ceteros levissima quemque de causa. Aelium Lamiam ob suspiciosos quidem, verum et veteres et innoxios iocos, quod post abductam[3] uxorem laudanti vocem suam "Eutacto" dixerat quodque Tito hortanti se ad alterum matrimonium

3   responderat: μὴ καὶ σὺ γαμῆσαι θέλεις; Salvium Cocceianum, quod Othonis imperatoris patrui sui diem natalem celebraverat; Mettium Pompusianum,[4] quod habere imperatoriam genesim vulgo ferebatur et quod depictum orbem terrae in membrana[5] contionesque

---

[1] impuberem, *Basle ed. of* 1533; puberem, Ω.
[2] in, *added by Torrentius.*   [3] abductam, T⌐; adductam, Ω.
[4] Pompusianum, *Roth* (*cf. Vesp.* xiv); Pomposianum, Ω.
[5] membrana, *Scriverius*; membranis, ⌐; membranas, Ω.

---

[a] See chap. iii. 1.
[b] Implying unfairness on the part of Domitian, who favoured the Thracians; cf. Pliny, *Paneg.* xi and xxxiii.
[c] There is an added insult in *parmularius*, "one armed with

integrity, although he turned to cruelty somewhat more
speedily than to avarice. He put to death a pupil of the
pantomimic actor Paris, who was still a beardless boy and
ill at the time, because in his skill and his appearance
he seemed not unlike his master;[a] also Hermogenes of
Tarsus because of some allusions in his History, besides
crucifying even the slaves who had written it out. A
householder who said that a Thracian gladiator was a
match for the *murmillo*, but not for the giver of the
games,[b] he caused to be dragged from his seat and
thrown into the arena to dogs, with this placard: "A
favourer of the Thracians who spoke impiously."[c]

He put to death many senators, among them several
ex-consuls, including Civica Cerealis, at the very time
when he was proconsul in Asia, Salvidienus Orfitus, Acilius Glabrio while he was in exile—these on the ground of
plotting revolution, the rest on any charge, however trivial. He slew Aelius Lamia for joking remarks, which were
reflections on him, it is true, but made long before and
harmless. For when Domitian had taken away Lamia's
wife,[d] the latter replied to someone who praised his voice:
"I practise continence";[e] and when Titus urged him to
marry again, he replied: "Are you too looking for a wife?"
He put to death Salvius Cocceianus, because he had kept
the birthday of the emperor Otho, his paternal uncle;
Mettius Pompusianus, because it was commonly reported
that he had an imperial nativity and carried about a map
of the world on parchment and speeches of the

the buckler," "a Thracian," as applied to a Roman citizen (*pater
familias*).   [d] See chap. i. 3.

[e] Sexual abstinence was part of an artist's regimen; cf. *Nero*,
xx. 1.

341

regum ac ducum ex Tito Livio circumferret quodque
servis nomina Magonis et Hannibalis indidisset; Sallustium Lucullum Britanniae legatum, quod lanceas
novae formae appellari Luculleas passus esset; Iunium
Rusticum, quod Paeti Thraseae et Helvidi[1] Prisci laudes
edidisset appellassetque eos sanctissimos viros; cuius cri-
minis occasione philosophos omnis urbe Italiaque sum-

4   movit. Occidit et Helvidium filium, quasi scaenico exodio
sub persona Paridis et Oenones divortium suum cum
uxore taxasset; Flavium Sabinum alterum e patruelibus,
quod eum comitiorum consularium die destinatum per-
peram praeco non consulem ad populum, sed imperatorem pronuntiasset.

5   Verum aliquanto post civilis belli victoriam saevior,
plerosque partis adversae, dum etiam latentis conscios
investigat,[2] novo quaestionis genere distorsit immisso per
obscaena igne; nonnullis et manus amputavit. Satisque
constat duos solos e notioribus venia donatos, tribunum
laticlavium et centurionem qui se, quo facilius expertes
culpae ostenderent, impudicos probaverant et ob id
neque apud ducem neque apud milites ullius momenti
esse potuisse.

XI. Erat autem non solum magnae, sed etiam callidae
inopinataeque saevitiae. Actorem[3] summarum pridie
quam cruci figeret in cubiculum vocavit, assidere in toro
iuxta coegit, securum hilaremque dimisit, partibus etiam
de cena dignatus est. Arrecinum[4] Clementem consu-

---

[1] *Mace, Suétone, p.* 413, *would insert* Herennium Sene-
cionem quod *before* Helvidi.   [2] investigat, *Stephanus*; inves-
tigato, Ω; per conscios investigatos, *Casaubon*.

[3] actorem, ς (*Torrentius*); auctorem, Ω.

[4] Arrecinum, Π[1]QN; arretinum, Ω.

kings and generals from Titus Livius, besides giving two of his slaves the names of Mago and Hannibal; Sallustius Lucullus, governor of Britain, for allowing some lances of a new pattern to be called "Lucullean," after his own name; Junius Rusticus, because he had published eulogies of Paetus Thrasea and Helvidius Priscus and called them the most upright of men; and on the occasion of this charge he banished all the philosophers from the city and from Italy. He also executed the younger Helvidius, alleging that in a farce composed for the stage he had under the characters of Paris and Oenone censured Domitian's divorce from his wife; Flavius Sabinus too, one of his cousins, because on the day of the consular elections the crier had inadvertently announced him to the people as emperor elect, instead of consul.

After his victory in the civil war he became even more cruel, and to discover any conspirators who were in hiding, tortured many of the opposite party by a new form of inquisition, inserting fire in their privates; and he cut off the hands of some of them. It is certain that of the more conspicuous only two were pardoned, a tribune of senatorial rank and a centurion who, the more clearly to prove their freedom from guilt, showed that they were of shameless unchastity and could therefore have had no influence with the general or with the soldiers.

XI. His savage cruelty was not only excessive, but also cunning and sudden. He invited one of his stewards to his bed-chamber the day before crucifying him, made him sit beside him on his couch, and dismissed him in a secure and gay frame of mind, even deigning to send him a share of his dinner. When he was on the point of condemning the ex-consul Arrecinus Clemens, one of his

larem, unum e familiaribus et emissariis suis, capitis con-
demnaturus in eadem vel etiam maiore gratia habuit,
quoad novissime simul gestanti, conspecto delatore eius:
"Vis," inquit, "hunc nequissimum servum cras audia-
mus?"

2   Et quo contemptius abuteretur patientia hominum,
numquam tristiorem sententiam sine praefatione clementiae pronuntiavit, ut non aliud iam certius atrocis exitus
signum esset quam principii lenitas. Quosdam maiestatis
reos in curiam induxerat, et cum praedixisset experturum
se illa die quam carus senatui esset, facile perfecerat ut
3   etiam more maiorum puniendi condemnarentur; deinde
atrocitate poenae conterritus, ad leniendam invidiam
intercessit his verbis—neque enim ab re fuerit ipsa
cognoscere: "Permittite, patres conscripti, a pietate vestra
impetrari, quod scio me difficulter impetraturum, ut
damnatis liberum mortis arbitrium indulgeatis; nam et
parcetis oculis vestris et intellegent me omnes senatui
interfuisse."

XII. Exhaustus operum ac munerum inpensis stipen-
dioque, quod adiecerat, temptavit quidem ad relevandos
castrenses sumptus numerum militum deminuere; sed
cum et obnoxium se barbaris per hoc animadverteret
neque eo setius in explicandis oneribus haereret, nihil
pensi habuit quin praedaretur omni modo. Bona vivorum
ac mortuorum usquequaque quolibet et accusatore et
crimine corripiebantur. Satis erat obici qualecumque

---

a See *Nero*, xlix. 2.

344

intimates and tools, he treated him with as great favour as before, if not greater, and finally, as he was taking a drive with him, catching sight of his accuser he said: "Pray, shall we hear this base slave tomorrow?"

To abuse men's patience the more insolently, he never pronounced an unusually dreadful sentence without a preliminary declaration of clemency, so that there came to be no more certain indication of a cruel death than the leniency of his preamble. He had brought some men charged with treason into the senate, and when he had introduced the matter by saying that he would find out that day how dear he was to the members, he had no difficulty in causing them to be condemned to suffer the ancient method of punishment.[a] Then appalled at the cruelty of the penalty, he interposed a veto, to lessen the odium, in these words (for it will be of interest to know his exact language): "Allow me, Fathers of the senate, to prevail on you by your love for me to grant a favour which I know I shall obtain with difficulty, namely that you allow the condemned free choice of the manner of their death; for thus you will spare your own eyes and all men will know that I was present at the meeting of the senate."

XII. Reduced to financial straits by the cost of his buildings and shows, as well as by the additions which he had made to the pay of the soldiers, he tried to lighten the military expenses by diminishing the number of his troops; but perceiving that in this way he exposed himself to the attacks of the barbarians, and nevertheless had difficulty in easing his burdens, he had no hesitation in resorting to every sort of robbery. The property of the living and the dead was seized everywhere on any charge brought by any accuser. It was enough to allege any

2   factum dictumve[1] adversus maiestatem principis. Confiscabantur alienissimae hereditates vel uno exsistente, qui diceret audisse se ex defuncto, cum viveret, heredem sibi Caesarem esse. Praeter ceteros Iudaicus fiscus acerbissime actus est; ad quem deferebantur, qui vel inprofessi[2] Iudaicam viverent vitam vel dissimulata origine imposita genti tributa non pependissent. Interfuisse me adulescentulum memini, cum a procuratore frequentissimoque consilio inspiceretur nonagenarius senex, an circumsectus esset.

3   Ab iuventa minime civilis animi, confidens etiam et cum verbis tum rebus immodicus, Caenidi patris concubinae ex Histria reversae osculumque, ut assuerat, offerenti manum praebuit; generum fratris indigne ferens albatos et ipsum ministros habere, proclamavit:

οὐκ ἀγαθὸν πολυκοιρανίη.

XIII. Principatum vero adeptus neque in senatu iactare dubitavit et patri se et fratri imperium dedisse, illos sibi reddidisse, neque in reducenda post divortium uxore edicere revocatam[3] eam in pulvinar suum. Adclamari etiam in amphitheatro epuli die libenter audiit: "Domino et dominae feliciter!" Sed et Capitolino cer-

---

[1] dictumve, δϚ; dictumque, Ω.
[2] vel inprofessi, *J. F. Gronov*; velut inprofessi, *MGϒδ*; velut professi, *X.*   [3] revocatam, *Salmasius*; vocatam, Ω.

---

[a] A tax of two drachmas a head, imposed by Titus in return for free permission to practise their religion; see Josephus, *Bell. Jud.* 7. 6. 6.   [b] These may have been Christians, whom the Romans commonly confounded with the Jews.
[c] See *Vesp.* iii.   [d] *Iliad.* 2. 204.   [e] *Pulvinar* here means the couch for the images of the gods; cf. *Aug.* xlv. 1.

action or word derogatory to the majesty of the prince. ✓
Estates of those in no way connected with him were confiscated, if but one man came forward to declare that he
had heard from the deceased during his lifetime that Caesar was his heir. Besides other taxes, that on the Jews[a]
was levied with the utmost rigour, and those were prose-
cuted who without publicly acknowledging that faith yet
lived as Jews, as well as those who concealed their origin
and did not pay the tribute levied upon their people.[b] I
recall being present in my youth when the person of a
man ninety years old was examined before the procurator
and a very crowded court, to see whether he was circum-
cised.

From his youth he was far from being of an affable disposition, but was on the contrary presumptuous and
unbridled both in act and in word. When his father's con-
cubine Caenis[c] returned from Histria and offered to kiss
him as usual, he held out his hand to her. He was vexed
that his brother's son-in-law had attendants clad in white,
as well as he, and uttered the words:

"Not good is a number of rulers."[d]

XIII. When he became emperor, he did not hesitate
to boast in the senate that he had conferred their power
on both his father and his brother, and that they had but
returned him his own; nor on taking back his wife after
their divorce, that he had "recalled her to his divine
couch."[e] He delighted to hear the people in the amphitheatre shout on his feast day:[f] "Good Fortune attend our
Lord[g] and Mistress." Even more, in the Capitoline com-

[f] See chap. iv. 5.   [g] See note on *Aug*. liii. 1.

tamine cunctos ingenti consensu precantis, ut Palfurium
Suram restitueret pulsum olim senatu ac tunc de oratoribus coronatum, nullo responso dignatus tacere tan-
2 tum modo iussit voce praeconis. Pari arrogantia, cum
procuratorum suorum nomine formalem dictaret epistu-
lam, sic coepit: "Dominus et deus noster hoc fieri iubet."
Unde institutum posthac, ut ne scripto quidem ac sermone cuiusquam appellaretur aliter. Statuas sibi in Capitolio non nisi aureas et argenteas poni permisit ac pon-
deris certi. Ianos arcusque cum quadrigis et insignibus
triumphorum per regiones urbis tantos ac tot exstruxit,
3 ut cuidam Graece inscriptum sit: "Arci."[1] Consulatus
septemdecim cepit, quot[2] ante eum nemo; ex quibus
septem medios continuavit, omnes autem paene titulo
tenus gessit nec quemquam ultra Kal. Mai., plerosque ad
Idus usque Ianuarias. Post autem duos triumphos Germanici cognomine assumpto Septembrem mensem et
Octobrem ex appellationibus suis Germanicum Domi-
tianumque transnominavit, quod altero suscepisset
imperium, altero natus esset.

XIV. Per haec terribilis cunctis et invisus, tandem
oppressus est insidiis[3] amicorum libertorumque intimorum simul et uxoris. Annum diemque ultimum vitae iam
pridem suspectum habebat, horam etiam nec non et
genus mortis. Adulescentulo Chaldaei cuncta praedixe-

---

[1] arci, *MGδ* = ἀρκεῖ (*Turnebus*).   [2] quot, ς; quod, Ω.
[3] insidiis, *G*; conspiratione, *after* intimorum, Υ'ON.

---

[a] See chap. iv. 4.   [b] *Arci* is a transliteration of the Greek
word ἀρκεῖ with a pun on its resemblance in sound to *arcus*,
"arch."   [c] In A.D. 71, 73, 75, 76, 77, 79, 80, 82–88, 90, 92, 95.

petition,[a] when all the people begged him with great una-
nimity to restore Palfurius Sura, who had been banished
some time before from the senate, and on that occasion
received the prize for oratory, he deigned no reply, but
merely had a crier bid them be silent. With no less arrogance he began as follows in issuing a circular letter in the
name of his procurators, "Our Master and our God bids
that this be done." And so the custom arose henceforth of
addressing him in no other way even in writing or in conversation. He suffered no statues to be set up in his honour in the Capitol, except of gold and silver and of a fixed
weight. He erected so many and such huge vaulted pas-
sage-ways and arches in the various regions of the city,
adorned with chariots and triumphal emblems, that on
one of them someone wrote in Greek: "It is enough."[b]
He held the consulship seventeen times,[c] more often
than any of his predecessors. Of these the seven middle
ones were in successive years, but all of them he filled in
name only, continuing none beyond the first of May and
few after the Ides of January. Having assumed the surname Germanicus after his two triumphs, he renamed
the months of September and October from his own
names, calling them "Germanicus" and "Domitianus,"
because in the former he had come to the throne and in
the latter he was born.

XIV. In this way he became an object of terror and
hatred to all, but he was overthrown at last by a conspiracy of his friends and favourite freedmen, to which his
wife was also privy. He had long since had a premonition
of the last year and day of his life, and even of the very
hour and manner of his death. In his youth astrologers
had predicted all this to him, and his father once even

rant; pater quoque super cenam quondam fungis absti-
nentem palam irriserat ut ignarum sortis suae, quod non
2 ferrum potius timeret. Quare pavidus semper atque anxius minimis etiam suspicionibus praeter modum com-
movebatur. Ut edicti de excidendis vineis propositi gratiam faceret, non alia magis re compulsus creditur, quam
quod sparsi libelli cum his versibus erant:

$$\kappa\ddot{\alpha}\nu^1 \mu\epsilon \ \phi\acute{\alpha}\gamma\eta\varsigma \ \grave{\epsilon}\pi\grave{\iota} \ \acute{\rho}\acute{\iota}\zeta\alpha\nu, \ \ddot{o}\mu\omega\varsigma \ \ddot{\epsilon}\tau\iota \ \kappa\alpha\rho\pio\phio\rho\acute{\eta}\sigma\omega,$$
$$\ddot{o}\sigma\sigma o\nu \ \grave{\epsilon}\pi\iota\sigma\pi\epsilon\hat{\iota}\sigma\alpha\iota \ \sigma o\acute{\iota}, \ \tau\rho\acute{\alpha}\gamma\epsilon, \ \theta\upsilon o\mu\acute{\epsilon}\nu\omega.$$

3 Eadem formidine oblatum a senatu novum et excogita-
tum honorem, quamquam omnium talium appetentissimus, recusavit, quo decretum erat ut, quotiens gereret
consulatum, equites R. quibus sors obtigisset, trabeati et
cum hastis militaribus praecederent eum inter lictores
apparitoresque.

4 Tempore vero suspecti periculi appropinquante sol-
licitior in dies porticuum, in quibus spatiari consuerat,
parietes phengite lapide distinxit, e cuius splendore per
imagines quidquid a tergo fieret provideret. Nec nisi
secreto atque solus plerasque custodias, receptis quidem
in manum catenis, audiebat. Utque domesticis per-
suaderet, ne bono quidem exemplo audendam² esse

---

¹ κἄν, *Roth*; καὶ, Ω; *cf. C.I.L.* iv. 3407, 6.
² audendam, ρL³; audiendam, Ω.

ᵃ See chap. vii. 2.   ᵇ Cf. Ovid, *Fasti*, 1. 357.
ᶜ A toga ornamented with horizontal stripes of purple, worn
by the knights on public occasions, as well as by the early kings
and the consuls; Tac. *Ann.* 3. 2; Val. Max. 3. 2. 9.

ᵈ According to Pliny, *N.H.* 36. 163, a hard, white, translucent
stone discovered in Cappodocia in the reign of Nero. According

openly ridiculed him at dinner for refusing mushrooms,
saying that he showed himself unaware of his destiny in
not rather fearing the sword. Therefore he was at all
times timorous and worried, and was disquieted beyond
measure by even the slightest suspicions. It is thought
that nothing had more effect in inducing him to ignore his
proclamation about cutting down the vineyards[a] than the
circulation of notes containing the following lines:

> Gnaw at my root, if you will; even then shall I have
> juice in plenty
> To pour upon thee, O goat, when at the altar you
> stand.[b]

It was because of this same timorousness that although
he was most eager for all such honours, he refused a new
one which the senate had devised and offered to him, a
decree, namely, that whenever he held the consulship
Roman knights selected by lot should precede him among
his lictors and attendants, clad in the trabea[c] and bearing
lances.

As the time when he anticipated danger drew near,
becoming still more anxious every day, he lined the walls
of the colonnades in which he used to walk with phengite
stone,[d] to be able to see in its brilliant surface the reflection of all that went on behind his back. And he did not
give a hearing to any prisoners except in private and
alone, even holding their chains in his hands. Further, to
convince his household that one must not venture to kill a
patron even on good grounds, he condemned Epaphrodi-

to Tzetzes, *Lyc.* 98, φεγγίτης = σεληνίτης, "moon-stone."
Pliny also mentions similar mirrors of black obsidian; *N.H.*
36. 196.

patroni necem, Epaphroditum a libellis capitali poena condemnavit, quod post destitutionem Nero in adipiscenda morte manu eius adiutus existimabatur.

XV. Denique Flavium Clementem patruelem suum contemptissimae inertiae, cuius filios etiam tum parvulos successores palam destinaverat abolitoque[1] priore nomine alterum Vespasianum appellari, alterum Domitianum, repente ex tenuissima suspicione tantum non in ipso eius consulatu interemit. Quo maxime facto maturavit sibi exitium.

2 Continuis octo mensibus tot fulgura facta nuntiataque sunt, ut exclamaverit: "Feriat iam, quem volet." Tactum de caelo Capitolium templumque Flaviae gentis, item domus Palatina et cubiculum ipsius, atque etiam e basi statuae triumphalis titulus excussus vi procellae in monimentum proximum decidit. Arbor, quae privato adhuc Vespasiano eversa surrexerat, tunc rursus repente corruit. Praenestina Fortuna, toto imperii spatio annum novum commendanti laetam eandemque semper sortem dare assueta, extremo tristissimam reddidit[2] nec sine sanguinis mentione.

3 Minervam, quam superstitiose colebat, somniavit excedere sacrario negantemque[3] ultra se tueri eum posse, quod exarmata esset a Iove. Nulla tamen re perinde com-

---

[1] abolitoque, *N*; et abolito, *Υ*; abolito, *MGX* (*Bentley*).

[2] reddidit, *Υ'*; *the other mss. have* reddit.

[3] negantemque, *mss.*; negantem, *Stephanus*; negantem quoque, *Oudendorp*; *lacuna before* negantemque, *Roth*.

---

[a] Cf. *Nero*, xlvii. 3.   [b] See *Nero*, xlix. 4.   [c] It was evidently on a metal plate, attached to the marble base.

[d] See *Vesp.* v. 4.   [e] Fortuna Primigenia; cf. *Tib.* lxiii. 1.

tus, his confidential secretary, to death, because it was
believed that after Nero was abandoned[a] the freedman's
hand had aided him in taking his life.[b]

XV. Finally he put to death his own cousin Flavius
Clemens, suddenly and on a very slight suspicion, almost
before the end of his consulship; and yet Flavius was a
man of most contemptible laziness and Domitian had
besides openly named his sons, who were then very
young, as his successors, changing their former names
and calling the one Vespasian and the other Domitian.
And it was by this deed in particular that he hastened his
own destruction.

For eight successive months so many strokes of lightning occurred and were reported that at last he cried:
"Well, let him now strike whom he will." The temple of
Jupiter of the Capitol was struck and that of the Flavian
family, as well as the Palace and the emperor's own bedroom. The inscription too on the base of a triumphal
statue of his was torn off in a violent tempest and fell
upon a neighbouring tomb.[c] The tree which had been
overthrown when Vespasian was still a private citizen but
had sprung up anew[d] then on a sudden fell down again.
Fortune of Praeneste[e] had throughout his whole reign,
when he commended the new year to her protection,
given him a favourable omen and always in the same
words. Now at last she returned a most direful one, not
without the mention of bloodshed.

He dreamed that Minerva, whom he worshipped with
superstitious veneration, came forth from her shrine and
declared that she could no longer protect him, since she
had been disarmed by Jupiter. Yet there was nothing by

LIVES OF THE CAESARS, VIII

motus est quam responso casuque Ascletarionis[1] mathematici. Hunc delatum nec infitiantem iactasse se quae providisset ex arte, sciscitatus est, quis ipsum maneret exitus; et affirmantem fore ut brevi laceraretur a canibus, interfici quidem sine mora, sed ad coarguendam temeritatem artis sepeliri quoque accuratissime imperavit. Quod cum fieret, evenit ut repentina tempestate deiecto funere semiustum cadaver discerperent canes, idque ei cenanti a mimo Latino, qui praeteriens forte animadverterat, inter ceteras diei fabulas referretur.

XVI. Pridie quam periret, cum oblatos tubures servari iussisset in crastinum, adiecit: "Si modo uti licuerit," et conversus ad proximos affirmavit fore ut sequenti die luna se in aquario cruentaret factumque aliquod exsisteret, de quo loquerentur homines per terrarum orbem. At circa mediam noctem ita est exterritus, ut e strato prosiliret. Dehinc mane haruspicem ex Germania missum, qui consultus de fulgure mutationem rerum praedixerat, audiit condemnavitque. Ac dum exulceratam in fronte verrucam vehementius scalpit, profluente sanguine: "Utinam," inquit, "hactenus." Tunc horas requirenti pro quinta, quam metuebat, sexta ex industria nuntiata est. His velut transacto iam periculo laetum festinantemque ad corporis

---

[1] Asclationis, *F. Cumont, Cat. Codd. Astrol. Graec.* v. *p.* 205, *n.* 1.

---

[a] Including the burning of the body, to prevent the fulfilment of the prophecy.

which he was so much disturbed as a prediction of the astrologer Ascletarion and what befell him. When this man was accused before the emperor and did not deny that he had spoken of certain things which he had foreseen through his art, he was asked what his own end would be. When he replied that he would shortly be rent by dogs, Domitian ordered him killed at once; but to prove the fallibility of his art, he ordered besides that his funeral be attended to with the greatest care.[a] While this was being done, it chanced that the pyre was overset by a sudden storm and that the dogs mangled the corpse, which was only partly consumed; and that an actor of farces called Latinus, who happened to pass by and see the incident, told it to Domitian at the dinner table, with the rest of the day's gossip.

XVI. The day before he was killed he gave orders to have some apples which were offered him kept until the following day, and added: "If only I am spared to eat them"; then turning to his companions, he declared that on the following day the moon would be stained with blood in Aquarius, and that a deed would be done of which men would talk all over the world. At about midnight he was so terrified that he leaped from his bed. The next morning he conducted the trial of a soothsayer sent from Germany, who when consulted about the lightning strokes had foretold a change of rulers, and condemned him to death. While he was vigorously scratching a festered wart on his forehead, and had drawn blood, he said: "May this be all." Then he asked the time, and by prearrangement the sixth hour was announced to him, instead of the fifth, which he feared. Filled with joy at this, and believing all danger now past, he was hastening

355

curam Parthenius cubiculo praepositus convertit, nuntians esse qui magnum nescio quid afferret, nec differendum. Itaque summotis omnibus in cubiculum se recepit atque ibi occisus est.

XVII. De insidiarum caedisque genere haec fere divulgata sunt. Cunctantibus conspiratis, quando et quo modo, id est lavantemne an cenantem adgrederentur, Stephanus, Domitillae[a] procurator et tunc interceptarum pecuniarum reus, consilium operamque obtulit. Ac sinisteriore brachio velut aegro lanis fasciisque per aliquot dies ad avertendam suspicionem obvoluto, sub ipsam horam dolonem[1] interiecit; professusque conspirationis indicium et ob hoc admissus legenti traditum a se libellum et attonito suffodit inguina. Saucium ac repugnantem adorti Clodianus cornicularius et Maximus Partheni libertus et Satur decurio cubiculariorum et quidam e gladiatorio ludo vulneribus septem contrucidarunt. Puer, qui curae Larum cubiculi ex consuetudine assistens interfuit caedi, hoc amplius narrabat, iussum se a Domitiano ad primum statim vulnus pugionem pulvino subditum porrigere ac ministros vocare, neque ad caput quidquam excepto capulo et praeterea clausa omnia repperisse; atque illum interim arrepto deductoque ad terram Stephano conluctatum diu, dum modo ferrum extorquere, modo quanquam laniatis digitis oculos effodere conatur.

---

[1] dolonem, *Ferrarius*; dolum, Ω; dolo, δ.

---

[a] Niece of Domitian.
[b] See *Aug.* vii. 1.

to the bath, when his chamberlain Parthenius changed his purpose by announcing that someone had called about a matter of great moment and would not be put off. Then he dismissed all his attendants and went to his bedroom, where he was slain.

XVII. Concerning the nature of the plot and the manner of his death, this is about all that became known. As the conspirators were deliberating when and how to attack him, whether at the bath or at dinner, Stephanus, Domitilla's[a] steward, at the time under accusation for embezzlement, offered his aid and counsel. To avoid suspicion, he wrapped up his left arm in woollen bandages for some days, pretending that he had injured it, and concealed in them a dagger. Then pretending to betray a conspiracy and for that reason being given an audience, he stabbed the emperor in the groin as he was reading a paper which the assassin handed him, and stood in a state of amazement. As the wounded prince attempted to resist, he was slain with seven wounds by Clodianus, a subaltern, Maximus, a freedman of Parthenius, Satur, decurion of the chamberlains, and a gladiator from the imperial school. A boy who was engaged in his usual duty of attending to the Lares in the bedroom,[b] and so was a witness of the murder, gave this additional information. He was bidden by Domitian, immediately after he was dealt the first blow, to hand him the dagger hidden under his pillow and to call the servants; but he found nothing at the head of the bed save the hilt, and besides all the doors were closed. Meanwhile the emperor grappled with Stephanus and bore him to the ground, where they struggled for a long time, Domitian trying now to wrest the dagger from his assailant's hands and now to gouge out his eyes with his lacerated fingers.

3   Occisus est XIIII. Kal. Octb. anno aetatis quadragen-
simo quinto, imperii quinto decimo. Cadaver eius popu-
lari sandapila per vispillones[1] exportatum Phyllis[2] nutrix
in suburbano suo Latina via funeravit, sed reliquias
templo Flaviae gentis clam intulit cineribusque Iuliae Titi
filiae, quam et ipsam educarat, conmiscuit.

    XVIII. Statura fuit procera, vultu modesto ruborisque
pleno, grandibus oculis, verum acie hebetiore; praeterea
pulcher ac decens, maxime in iuventa, et quidem toto
corpore exceptis pedibus, quorum digitos restrictiores
habebat; postea calvitio quoque deformis et obesitate
ventris et crurum gracilitate, quae tamen ei valitudine
2 longa remacruerant. Commendari se verecundia oris
adeo sentiebat, ut apud senatum sic quondam iactaverit:
"Usque adhuc certe et animum meum probastis et vul-
tum." Calvitio ita offendebatur, ut in contumeliam suam
traheret, si cui alii ioco vel iurgio obiectaretur; quamvis
libello, quem de cura capillorum ad amicum edidit, haec
etiam, simul illum seque consolans, inseruerit:

    "οὐχ ὁράᾳς,[3] οἷος κἀγὼ καλός τε μέγας τε;

Eadem me tamen manent capillorum fata, et forti animo
fero comam in adulescentia senescentem. Scias nec
gratius quicquam decore nec brevius."

[1] vespillones, *Beroaldus*.
[2] Phyllis, ρ϶; Phyllix, Ω.   [3] ὁρᾷς, Ω.

---

[a] Sept. 18, A.D. 96.   [b] This in its connection suggests the
blush of modesty, but cf. Tac. *Agr.* 45, *ille vultus et rubor quo se
contra pudorem muniebat*; and in general, Sen. *Epist.* 11. 3.
Doubtless Domitian's ruddy complexion was a recommendation
in his youth.   [c] *Iliad*, 21. 108.

He was slain on the fourteenth day before the Kalends of October[a] in the forty-fifth year of his age and the fifteenth of his reign. His corpse was carried out on a common bier by those who bury the poor, and his nurse Phyllis cremated it at her suburban estate on the Via Latina; but his ashes she secretly carried to the temple of the Flavian family and mingled them with those of Julia, daughter of Titus, whom she had also reared.

XVIII. He was tall of stature, with a modest expression and a high colour.[b] His eyes were large, but his sight was somewhat dim. He was handsome and graceful too, especially when a young man, and indeed in his whole body with the exception of his feet, the toes of which were somewhat cramped. In later life he had the further disfigurement of baldness, a protruding belly, and spindling legs, though the latter had become thin from a long illness. He was so conscious that the modesty of his expression was in his favour, that he once made this boast in the senate: "So far, at any rate, you have approved my heart and my countenance." He was so sensitive about his baldness that he regarded it as a personal insult if anyone else was twitted with that defect in jest or in earnest; though in a book "On the Care of the Hair," which he published and dedicated to a friend, he wrote the following by way of consolation to the man and himself:

"Do you not see that I too am tall and comely to
    look on?[c]

And yet the same fate awaits my hair, and I bear with resignation the ageing of my locks in youth. Be assured that nothing is more pleasing than beauty, but nothing shorter-lived."

XIX. Laboris impatiens pedibus per urbem non temere ambulavit, in expeditione et agmine equo rarius, lectica assidue vectus est. Armorum nullo, sagittarum vel praecipuo studio tenebatur. Centenas varii generis feras saepe in Albano secessu conficientem spectavere plerique atque etiam ex industria ita quarundam capita figentem, ut duobus ictibus quasi cornua efficeret. Nonnumquam in pueri procul stantis praebentisque pro scopulo dispansam dexterae manus palmam sagittas tanta arte derexit,[1] ut omnes per intervalla digitorum innocue evaderent.

XX. Liberalia studia imperii initio neglexit, quanquam bibliothecas incendio absumptas impensissime reparare curasset, exemplaribus undique petitis missisque Alexandream qui describerent emendarentque. Numquam tamen aut historiae carminibusve noscendis operam ullam aut stilo vel necessario dedit. Praeter commentarios et acta Tiberi Caesaris nihil lectitabat; epistulas orationesque et edicta alieno[2] formabat ingenio. Sermonis tamen nec inelegantis, dictorum interdum etiam notabilium: "Vellem," inquit, "tam formosus esse, quam Maecius sibi videtur"; et cuiusdam caput varietate capilli subrutilum et incanum perfusam nivem mulso dixit.

[1] derexit, ς; derexerit, Q; *the other mss. have* direxit.
[2] alieno, ς; alfeno, MGT; *the greater number of the X class have* alieno alfeno.

---

[a] Cf. *Tit.* v. 2. The bow and arrow were not included by the Romans in the term *arma*.   [b] Cf. chap. ii. 2.

[c] The great library of Ptolemy Philadelphus at Alexandria was destroyed during Caesar's Alexandrine war. The Pergamene library was given by Antony to Cleopatra and transferred to Alexandria, where it was kept in the temple of Serapis. It was

XIX. He was incapable of exertion and seldom went about the city on foot, while on his campaigns and journeys he rarely rode on horseback, but was regularly carried in a litter. He took no interest in arms, but was particularly devoted to archery.[a] There are many who have more than once seen him slay a hundred wild beasts of different kinds on his Alban estate, and purposely kill some of them with two successive shots in such a way that the arrows gave the effect of horns. Sometimes he would have a slave stand at a distance and hold out the palm of his right hand for a mark, with the fingers spread; then he directed his arrows with such accuracy that they passed harmlessly between the fingers.

XX. At the beginning of his rule he neglected liberal studies,[b] although he provided for having the libraries, which were destroyed by fire,[c] renewed at very great expense, seeking everywhere for copies of the lost works, and sending scribes to Alexandria to transcribe and correct them. Yet he never took any pains to become acquainted with history or poetry, or even to acquiring an ordinarily good style. He read nothing except the memoirs and transactions of Tiberius Caesar; for his letters, speeches and proclamations he relied on others' talents. Yet his conversation was not inelegant, and some of his sayings were even noteworthy, "How I wish," said he "that I were as fine looking as Maecius thinks he is." He declared too that the head of a certain man, whose hair had changed colour in such a way that it was partly reddish and partly grey, was like "snow on which mead had been poured."

frequently damaged during civil disturbances. Burman thinks that the reference is to the latter; but the plural suggests both.

XXI. Condicionem principum miserrimam aiebat, quibus de coniuratione comperta non crederetur nisi occisis.

Quotiens otium esset, alea se oblectabat, etiam profestis diebus matutinisque horis, ac lavabat de die prandebatque ad satietatem, ut non temere super cenam praeter Matianum malum et modicam in ampulla potiunculam sumeret. Convivabatur frequenter ac large, sed paene raptim; certe non ultra solis occasum nec ut postea comissaretur. Nam ad horam somni nihil aliud quam solus secreto deambulabat.

XXII. Libidinis nimiae, assiduitatem concubitus velut exercitationis genus clinopalen[1] vocabat; eratque fama, quasi concubinas ipse develleret[2] nataretque inter vulgatissimas meretrices. Fratris filiam adhuc virginem oblatam in matrimonium sibi cum devinctus Domitiae nuptiis pertinacissime recusasset, non multo post alii conlocatam corrupit ultro et quidem vivo etiam tum Tito; mox patre ac viro orbatam ardentissime palamque dilexit, ut etiam causa mortis exstiterit coactae conceptum a se abigere.

XXIII. Occisum eum populus indifferenter, miles gravissime tulit statimque Divum appellare conatus est, paratus et ulcisci, nisi duces defuissent; quod quidem

---

[1] clinopalem, Ω.
[2] develleret, *G; the other mss. have* divelleret.

---

[a] Named after C. Matius, a friend of Augustus and a writer on cookery and gardening.
[b] Cf. *Juv.* ii. 32 f.

XXI. He used to say that the lot of princes was most unhappy, since when they discovered a conspiracy, no one believed them unless they had been killed.

Whenever he had leisure he amused himself with playing at dice, even on working days and in the morning hours. He went to the bath before the end of the forenoon and lunched to the point of satiety, so that at dinner he rarely took anything except a Matian apple[a] and a moderate amount of wine from a jug. He gave numerous and generous banquets, but usually ended them early; in no case did he protract them beyond sunset, or follow them by a drinking bout. In fact, he did nothing until the hour for retiring except walk alone in a retired place.

XXII. He was excessively lustful. His constant sexual intercourse he called bed-wrestling, as if it were a kind of exercise. It was reported that he depilated his concubines with his own hand and swam with common prostitutes. After persistently refusing his niece, who was offered him in marriage when she was still a maid, because he was entangled in an intrigue with Domitia, he seduced her shortly afterwards when she became the wife of another, and that too during the lifetime of Titus. Later, when she was bereft of father and husband, he loved her ardently and without disguise, and even became the cause of her death by compelling her to get rid of a child of his by abortion.[b]

XXIII. The people received the news of his death with indifference, but the soldiers were greatly grieved and at once attempted to call him the Deified Domitian, while they were prepared also to avenge him, had they not lacked leaders. This, however, they did accomplish a little

paulo post fecit expostulatis ad poenam pertinacissime caedis auctoribus. Contra senatus adeo laetatus est, ut repleta certatim curia non temperaret, quin mortuum contumeliosissimo atque acerbissimo adclamationum genere laceraret, scalas etiam inferri clipeosque et imagines eius coram detrahi et ibidem solo affligi iuberet, novissime eradendos ubique titulos abolendamque omnem memoriam decerneret.

2   Ante paucos quam occideretur menses cornix in Capitolio elocuta est: ἔσται πάντα καλῶς, nec defuit qui ostentum sic interpretaretur:

> Nuper Tarpeio quae sedit culmine cornix
> 'Est bene' non potuit dicere, dixit: 'Erit.'

Ipsum etiam Domitianum ferunt somniasse gibbam sibi pone cervicem auream enatam, pro certoque habuisse beatiorem post se laetioremque portendi rei publicae statum,[1] sicut sane brevi evenit abstinentia et moderatione insequentium principum.

---

[1] rerum statum publice, *M*; rei statum publicae, *G*; statum rei publicae, *X*.

later by most insistently demanding the execution of his murderers. The senators on the contrary were so over-joyed that they raced to fill the House, where they did not refrain from assailing the dead emperor with the most insulting and stinging kind of outcries. They even had ladders brought and his shields[a] and images torn down before their eyes and dashed upon the ground; finally they passed a decree that his inscriptions should every-where be erased, and all record of him obliterated.[b]

A few months before he was killed, a raven perched on the Capitolium and cried "All will be well," an omen which some interpreted as follows:

> Recently a crow which was sitting on a Tarpeian[c]
> rooftop
> Could not say 'It is well,' only declared 'It will
> be.'

Domitian himself, it is said, dreamed that a golden hump grew out on his back, and he regarded this as an infallible sign that the condition of the empire would be happier and more prosperous after his time; and this was shortly shown to be true through the uprightness and moderate rule of the succeeding emperors.

[a] Votive shields, adorned with the emperor's image; see *Calig.* xvi. 4.

[b] Cf. Plin. *Paneg.* lii.

[c] The Capitoline hill was sometimes called *mons Tarpeius*, from the Tarpeian Rock at its southwest corner. It was not, how-ever, the original name of the hill, as some Roman antiquarians supposed.

365

LIVES OF ILLUSTRIOUS MEN

PREFATORY NOTE

The manuscripts of the *Dialogus* and *Agricola* of Tacitus contain also a treatise "On Grammarians and Rhetoricians," attributed to Suetonius. This work was used by Gellius (*Noct. Att.* 15. 11) and by Jerome, but after the latter's day was lost for many centuries.

About the middle of the fifteenth century,[1] in the course of a journey through Germany and Denmark, Enoc of Ascoli[2] found the two works of Tacitus and the treatise on Grammarians and Rhetoricians, apparently at Hersfeld and in a single codex, and brought them to Italy. This codex is now lost,[3] but some eighteen copies of the *De Grammaticis et Rhetoribus* are in existence, all belonging to the fifteenth century, which show remarkable differences in reading, considering that they are derived from a single archetype, and are separated from it by so short a time. These manuscripts, not all of which have been collated, fall into two classes, distinguished from each other by the presence or absence of the index

[1] The date is variously given: 1455, Teuffel, *Gesch. d. röm. Lit.*[6]; 1457–8, Gudeman, *Grund. z. Gesch. d. kl. Phil.*; etc.

[2] Enoc's discovery of this manuscript has been doubted by some, but is now accepted by most scholars.

[3] Except for one *quaternio*, now at Esinus (Jesi).

of names at the beginning of the treatise. Roth in his edition of 1858 asserted the superiority of the former class, and Ihm is inclined to agree with him.[1] For a list of the better codices with their sigla see p. 375.

The work begins with an index, containing a list of the grammarians and rhetoricians who are to be discussed, which, as has been said, is omitted by some of the manuscripts. This is followed by an introduction on the origin and development of grammatical studies at Rome, and the connection of grammar with rhetoric, after which the individual representatives of the subject are treated. The part devoted to rhetoricians also begins with an introduction on the history of the study, but the work comes to an end after dealing with five of the fifteen persons named in the index.

It has been generally recognized that this treatise on "Grammarians and Rhetoricians" formed part of a larger work by Suetonius, entitled *De Viris Illustribus*, which treated of Romans who were eminent in the field of literature.[2] It seems to have consisted of five divisions, devoted respectively to Poets, Orators, Historians, Philosophers, and Grammarians and Rhetoricians under one head. The order of the various divisions, or books, cannot be determined.[3]

[1] *Rhein. Museum*, 61 (1906), p. 543.

[2] See Volume I, p. xi.

[3] Jerome used the *De Viris Illustribus* of Suetonius as his model in the composition of a work of the same title, devoted to the worthies of the Church, as well as in his translation and enlargement of the "Chronicle" of Eusebius. From the latter numerous fragments of the *De Viris Illustribus* of Suetonius have been recovered, and the general plan of his work made out.

To judge from the personages treated by Suetonius and those whom he omits, the *De Viris Illustribus* appears to have been written between 106 and 113. It was therefore his earliest work, and is in all probability the one to which Pliny refers in *Ep.* 5. 10. As was the case with the *Lives of the Caesars*, he apparently set as his limit the close of the reign of Domitian, so that Juvenal, Tacitus and the younger Pliny were not included.

While the greater part of the *De Viris Illustribus* has been lost, some passages of considerable length, in addition to the "Grammarians and Rhetoricians," have been recovered from various sources. These consist of Lives of various Roman writers, prefixed to their works by way of introduction. None of these has come down to us in its original form, and they differ greatly in the amount of abridgement or of interpolation to which they have been subjected. Those which may properly be included in an edition of Suetonius are the following.

From the book on Poets (*De Poetis*), to which an index of thirty-three names has been compiled from the references in Jerome, we have a Life of Terence, preserved in the Commentary of Aelius Donatus, of the fourth century, and ascribed by him to Suetonius. Similarly the Life of Virgil in Donatus' Commentary is by H. Naumann and other experts unhesitatingly identified as almost wholly Suetonius'. A Life of Horace, which is found in some of the manuscripts, is not directly attributed to Suetonius, but is believed to be his because of the occurrence in it of certain statements which are credited to Suetonius by the scholiasts.[1] A very fragmentary Life of Lucan is assigned

[1] See for example Porphyrio on *Epist.* 2. 1. 1.

to Suetonius also on internal evidence. With regard to the ultimate authorship of these four lives there is little, if any, difference of opinion. It is however, improbable that the Lives of Tibullus and Persius derive from Suetonius.

From the Orators (*De Oratoribus*), with an index of fifteen names, only the brief abstract of the Life of Passienus Crispus has come down to us, preserved in the scholia Pithoeana on Juvenal 4. 81, where Passienus is confused with Vibius Crispus. Although his source is not given by the scholiast, the Life is generally attributed to Suetonius. Since in the excerpts from the *De Oratoribus* made by Jerome we find no orator earlier than Cicero, it has been inferred that Suetonius began his biographies with Cicero and treated the earlier orators in a general introduction.

From the Historians, with an index of six names, we have only the Life of Pliny the Elder, which is attributed to Suetonius in the manuscripts which contain it. Here Suetonius seems to have begun with Sallust, discussing the earlier historians in his introduction.

From the *De Philosophis* we have only an index of three names, Marcus Terentius Varro, Publius Nigidius Figulus, and Lucius Annaeus Seneca, which have been recovered from Jerome.

As in the *Lives of the Caesars*, Suetonius' sources for the *Lives of Illustrious Men* were in the main literary, in particular Varro, the previous writers of books of the same title (Nepos, Santra and Hyginus), Asconius and Fenestella. In part through these writers, and perhaps in part directly, his work goes back to the Greek authors Antigonus of Carystos, Aristoxenes, Satyros, and Hermip-

pos. He also made some use of private letters, public documents, hearsay evidence and personal recollection.

Addendum (1997): All previous editions and discussion of the text of the *De Grammaticis et Rhetoribus* have now been superseded by the two volumes of Robert A. Kaster listed in the following bibliographical note.

BIBLIOGRAPHICAL NOTE

There are three editions of the *De Grammaticis et Rhetoribus* that rank as *principes* (c. 1472, 1474, and 1478). But of Suetonius' works other than *De Vita Caesarum* we only really begin with the editions of Roth and Reifferscheid, which complement each other in a curious way: Roth admitted only fragments specifically authenticated as Suetonian; Reifferscheid included anything which might conceivably have been derived from him, so that to Suetonius are imputed substantial portions of such sources as the grammarians, Censorinus, Servius, and Macrobius, not to mention Isidore, whose *Etymologiae* he thought derived from an encyclopaedic work of Suetonius called *Pratum* (cf. Gellius, *praef.* 8) or *Prata* (so Priscian).

Editions

C. L. Roth: *Suetonius*, Teubner, Leipzig 1858.

A. Reifferscheid: *C. Suetoni Tranquilli praeter Caesarum libros reliquiae*, Leipzig 1860.

R. P. Robinson, *C. Suetoni Tranquilli De grammaticis et rhetoribus*, Paris 1925.

372

BIBLIOGRAPHICAL NOTE

A. Rostagni, *Suetonio: De poetis e Biografi minori*, Turin 1944.

G. Brugnoli, *C. Suetoni Tranquilli De grammaticis et rhetoribus*, Teubner, Leipzig 1960.

Robert A. Kaster, *Suetonius De grammaticis et rhetoribus*, Oxford 1995.

Studies

R. P. Robinson, *De fragmenti Suetoniani de grammaticis et rhetoribus codicum, nexu et fide*, Urbana 1920.

E. Paratore, *Una Nuova Ricostruzione del 'De Poetis' di Suetonio*, Rome 1946.

M. Winterbottom, Suetonius, *De Grammaticis et Rhetoribus*, pp. 404–405; Tacitus, *Minor Works*, pp. 410–411 in *Texts and Transmission* (ed. L. D. Reynolds), Oxford 1983.

Robert A. Kaster, *Studies on the Text of Suetonius De grammaticis et rhetoribus*, Atlanta 1992.

General

W. Steidle, *Sueton und die antike Biographie*, Munich 1951[1], 1963[2].

Andrew Wallace-Hadrill, *Suetonius: The Scholar and His Caesars*, Duckworth, London 1983. The best study of the author.

Reference

D. Thomas Benediktson, 'A survey of Suetonian Scholarship, 1938–1987,' *Classical World* 86 (1993) 377–447.

DE GRAMMATICIS ET
RHETORIBUS

Several of the manuscripts have before or after the title the following table of contents (without the chapter numbers, which, however, are added for the reader's convenience):

[1] *del. Reifferscheid*
[2] *add. Reifferscheid*

19   Scribonius Aphrodisius
20   C. Iulius Hyginus
21   C. Melissus
22   M. Pomponius Marcellus
23   Q. Remmius Palaemon
24   Valerius Probus

25=I   ITEM RHETORES

26=II   Plotius Gallus
27=III   †L. Voltacilius Pilutus†
28=IV   M. Epidius
29=V   Sex. Clodius
30=VI   C. Albucius Silus
31   L. Cestius Pius
32   M. Porcius Latro
33   Q. Curtius Rufus
34   L. Valerius Primanus
35   Verg<inius>² Flavus
36   L. Statius Ursulus
37   P. Clodius Quirinalis
38   M. Antonius Liberalis
39   Sex. Iulius Gabinianus
40   M. Fabius Quintilianus
41   Iulius Tiro

The following sigla will be used to identify ms. readings:

G   Wolfenbüttel, Gudianus 93   O   Vatican, Ottob.
I   Vatican, lat.1518   lat.1455
L   Leiden, Periz.Q.21   V   Vatican, lat.1862
N   Naples, IV.C.21   W   Vienna, 711

DE GRAMMATICIS

I. Grammatica Romae ne in usu quidem olim, nedum in honore ullo erat, rudi scilicet ac bellicosa etiam tum civitate, necdum magnopere liberalibus disciplinis vacante. Initium quoque eius mediocre exstitit, siquidem antiquissimi doctorum, qui iidem[1] et poetae et semigraeci erant (Livium et Ennium dico, quos utraque lingua domi forisque docuisse adnotatum est), nihil amplius quam Graecos interpretabantur, aut si quid ipsi Latine composuissent praelegebant. Nam quod nonnulli tradunt duos libros "De Litteris Syllabisque," item "De Metris" ab eodem Ennio editos, iure arguit L. Cotta non poetae sed posterioris Ennii esse, cuius etiam "De Augurandi Disciplina" volumina ferantur.

II. Primus igitur, quantum opinamur, studium grammaticae in urbem intulit Crates Mallotes, Aristarchi aequalis, qui missus ad senatum ab Attalo rege inter secundum ac tertium Punicum bellum sub ipsam Ennii mortem, cum regione Palatii prolapsus in cloacae fora-

---

[1] qui iidem, *Stephanus*; qui idem, *Lachmann*; quidem, *VLOIG*; quidam, *N*.

---

[a] The *grammaticus* was a critic and teacher of literature, but "grammarian" has become conventional in this sense, as well as in its more restricted meaning.

ON GRAMMARIANS[a]

I. The study of Grammar was not even pursued at Rome in early days, still less held in any esteem; and naturally enough, since the state was then still uncultivated and given to war, and had as yet little leisure for liberal pursuits. The beginnings of the subject, too, were humble, for the earliest teachers, who were also both poets and Italian[b] Greeks (I refer to Livius and Ennius, who gave instruction in both tongues at home and abroad, as is well known), did no more than interpret the Greeks or give readings from whatever they themselves had composed in the Latin language. For while some tell us that this same Ennius published a book "On Letters and Syllables" and another "On Metres," Lucius Cotta is right in maintaining that these were not the work of the poet, but of a later Ennius, who is also the author of the volumes "On the Science of Augury."

II. In my opinion, then, the first to introduce the study of grammar into our city was Crates of Mallos, a contemporary of Aristarchus. He was sent to the senate by king Attalus between the second and third Punic wars, at about the time when Ennius died;[c] and having fallen into the opening of a sewer in the Palatine quarter and

---

[b] Livius Andronicus came from Tarentum, and Ennius was a native of Rudiae in Calabria.

[c] In 169 B.C.

377

men crus fregisset, per omne legationis simul et valitudinis tempus plurimas acroasis subinde fecit assidue-
que disseruit, ac nostris exemplo fuit ad imitandum.
Hactenus tamen imitati, ut carmina parum adhuc divol-
gata vel defunctorum amicorum vel si quorum aliorum
probassent, diligentius retractarent ac legendo commen-
tandoque etiam[1] ceteris nota facerent; ut C. Octavius
Lampadio Naevii "Punicum Bellum," quod uno volumine
et continenti scriptura expositum divisit in septem libros;
ut postea Q. Vargunteius Annales Ennii, quos certis
diebus in magna frequentia pronuntiabat; ut Laelius
Archelaus Vettiusque Philocomus Lucilii saturas familiaris sui, quas legisse se apud Archelaum Pompeius
Lenaeus, apud Philocomum Valerius Cato praedicant.

III. Instruxerunt auxeruntque ab omni parte grammaticam L. Aelius Lanuvinus generque Aelii Ser.
Clodius, uterque eques Ro. multique ac varii et in doctrina et in re p. usus. Aelius cognomine duplici fuit; nam
et Praeconinus,[2] quod pater eius praeconium fecerat,
vocabatur, et Stilo,[3] quod orationes nobilissimo cuique
scribere solebat; tantum optimatium fautor, ut Metellum[4]
Numidicum in exsilium comitatus sit. Servius, cum
librum soceri nondum editum fraude intercepisset, et ob
hoc repudiatus pudore ac taedio secessisset ab urbe, in

---

[1] etiam, *NGOIW*; et, *VL.*

[2] Praeconinus, *Beroaldus*; Praeconius *or* Preconius, *mss.*

[3] Stilo, *Stephanus*; istilo, *mss.*

[4] Metellum, *W (Roth)*; *the other mss. have* M. Metellum.

---

[a] *praeco.*   [b] From *stylus*, an instrument for writing; see
note on *Jul.* lxxxii. 2.

broken his leg, he held numerous and frequent conferences during the whole time both of his embassy and of his convalescence, at which he constantly gave instruction, and thus set an example for our countrymen to imitate. Their imitation, however, was confined to a careful criticism of poems which had as yet but little circulation, either those of deceased friends or others that met with their approval, and to making them known to the public by reading and commenting on them. For example, Gaius Octavius Lampadio thus treated the "Punic War" of Naevius, which was originally written in a single volume without a break, but was divided by Lampadio into seven books. At a later time Quintus Vargunteius took up the "Annals" of Ennius, which he expounded on set days to large audiences; and Laelius Archelaus and Vettius Philocomus the satires of their friend Lucilius, which Lenaeus Pompeius prides himself on having read with Archelaus, and Valerius Cato with Philocomus.

III. The foundations of the study were laid, and it was advanced in all directions, by Lucius Aelius of Lanuvium and his son-in-law Servius Clodius, both of whom were Roman knights and men of wide and varied experience in scholarship and statecraft. Aelius had two surnames, for he was called Praeconinus because his father had followed the occupation of a crier,[a] and Stilo[b] because he used to write speeches for all the great men of the day; and he was so devoted to the aristocratic party, that he accompanied Metellus Numidicus into exile. Servius stole one of his father-in-law's books before it was published, and being in consequence disowned, left the city through shame and remorse, and fell ill of the

podagrae morbum incidit; cuius impatiens veneno sibi
perunxit pedes et enecuit ita, ut parte ea corporis quasi
praemortua[1] viveret.

Posthac magis ac magis et gratia et cura artis increvit,
ut ne clarissimi quidem viri abstinuerint quo minus et ipsi
aliquid de ea scriberent, utque temporibus quibusdam
super viginti celebres scholae fuisse in urbe tradantur;
pretia vero grammaticorum tanta mercedesque tam magnae, ut constet Lutatium Daphnidem, quem Laevius
Melissus per cavillationem nominis Panos ἀγάπημα[2]
dicit, DCC. milibus nummum a Q. Catulo emptum ac
brevi manumissum, L. Appuleium ab Eficio Calvino
equite Romano praedivite quadringenis annuis conduc-
tum ut Oscae doceret.[3] Nam in provincias quoque grammatica penetraverat, ac nonnulli de notissimis doctoribus
peregre docuerunt, maxime in Gallia Togata; inter quos
Octavius Teucer et Sescenius[4] Iaccus et Oppius Chares;
hic quidem ad ultimam aetatem, et cum iam non ingressu
modo deficeretur sed et visu.

IV. Appellatio grammaticorum Graeca consuetudine
invaluit; sed initio litterati vocabantur. Cornelius quoque
Nepos libello quo distinguit litteratum ab erudito, litte-

---

[1] praemortua, *Stephanus*; praemortui *or* premortui, *mss.*

[2] ἀγάπημα, *Toup* (*Reifferscheid*); ἄγασμα, *Baum.-Crusius*
(*Roth*).   [3] ut Oscae doceret, *Robinson*: mutoscedo[do]ceret,
archetype.

[4] Pescennius, *Roth*; Sescennius *or* Fescennius, *mss.*

---

[a] The pun consists in likening him to the Sicilian Daphnis, the
"ideal shepherd," whom Pan taught to play the shepherd's pipe.
If we read ἄγασμα, the meaning is "the prodigy (or 'wonder-
child') of Pan." The early commentators saw a reference to Pan's

gout. Unable to endure the pain, he applied a poisonous drug to his feet, which finally killed him, after he had lived for a time with that part of his body as it were prematurely dead.

After this the science constantly grew in favour and popularity, so much so that even the most eminent men did not hesitate to make contributions to it, while at times there are said to have been more than twenty well-attended schools in the city. The grammarians too were so highly esteemed, and their compensation was so ample, that Lutatius Daphnis, whom Laevius Melissus, punning on his name, often called the "darling of Pan,"[a] is known to have been bought for seven hundred thousand sesterces and soon afterwards set free, while Lucius Appuleius was hired for four hundred sesterces a year by Eficius Calvinus, a wealthy Roman knight, to teach at Osca. In fact, Grammar even made its way into the provinces, and some of the most famous teachers gave instruction abroad, especially in Gallia Togata, including Octavius Teucer, Sescenius Iaccus and Oppius Chares; indeed the last named taught until the very end of his life, when he could no longer walk, or even see.

IV. The term *grammaticus* became prevalent through Greek influence, but at first such men were called *litterati*.[b] Cornelius Nepos, too, in a little book in which he explains the difference between *litteratus* and *eruditus*[c] says that the former is commonly applied to

---

love for the flocks and shepherds (cf. Virg. *Ecl.* 2. 33) and an implication that Lutatius was *rusticus* or *pecus*.   [b] "Men of letters," from *littera*, while *grammaticus* is from the corresponding Greek word γράμμα.   [c] "Man of learning, scholar."

ratos quidem vulgo appellari ait eos qui aliquid diligenter[1] et acute scienterque possint aut dicere aut scribere, ceterum proprie sic appellandos poetarum interpretes, qui a Graecis grammatici nominentur. Eosdem litteratores vocitatos Messala Corvinus in quadam epistula ostendit, non esse sibi dicens rem cum Furio Bibaculo, ne cum Ticida quidem aut litteratore Catone; significat enim haud dubie Valerium Catonem, poetam simul grammaticumque notissimum. Sunt qui litteratum a litteratore distinguant, ut Graeci grammaticum a grammatista, et illum quidem absolute, hunc mediocriter doctum existiment. Quorum opinionem Orbilius etiam exemplis confirmat; namque apud maiores ait, cum familia alicuius venalis produceretur, non temere quem litteratum in titulo, sed litteratorem inscribi solitum esse, quasi non perfectum litteris, sed imbutum.

Veteres grammatici et rhetoricam docebant, ac multorum de utraque arte commentarii feruntur. Secundum quam consuetudinem posteriores quoque existimo, quanquam iam discretis professionibus, nihilo minus vel retinuisse vel instituisse et ipsos quaedam genera meditationum[2] ad eloquentiam praeparandam, ut problemata, paraphrasis, allocutiones, ethologias[3] atque alia hoc genus; ne scilicet sicci omnino atque aridi pueri rhetoribus traderentur. Quae quidem omitti iam video, desidia quorundam et infantia; non enim fastidio putem.

---

[1] aliquid diligenter, *NGIOW*; diligenter aliquid, *VL*.

[2] meditationum, *OW, G in margin, N as correction (cf. Gell.* xx. 5. 2); *the other mss. have* institutionum.

[3] ethologias, *Beroaldus*; aethiologias, *mss.*

---

[a] *Sicci* and *aridi* both mean "dry, juiceless."

those who can speak or write on any subject accurately, cleverly and with authority; but that it should strictly be used of interpreters of the poets, whom the Greeks call *grammatici*. That these were also called *litteratores* is shown by Messala Corvinus in one of his letters, in which he says: "I am not concerned with Furius Bibaculus, nor with Ticidas either, or with the *litterator* Cato." For he unquestionably refers to Valerius Cato, who was famous both as a poet and as a grammarian. Some however make a distinction between *litteratus* and *litterator*, as the Greeks do between *grammaticus* and *grammatista*, using the former of a master of his subject, the latter of one moderately proficient. Orbilius too supports this view by examples, saying: "In the days of our forefathers, when anyone's slaves were offered for sale, it was not usual except in special cases to advertise any one of them as *litteratus* but rather as *litterator*, implying that he had a smattering of letters, but was not a finished scholar."

The grammarians of early days taught rhetoric as well, and we have treatises from many men on both subjects. It was this custom, I think, which led those of later times also, although the two professions had now become distinct, nevertheless either to retain or to introduce certain kinds of exercises suited to the training of orators, such as problems, paraphrases, addresses, character sketches and similar things; doubtless that they might not turn over their pupils to the rhetoricians wholly ignorant and unprepared.[a] But I observe that such instruction is now given up, because of the lack of application and the youth of some of the pupils; for I do not believe that it is because the subjects are underrated. I remember that at

383

Me quidem adulescentulo, repeto quendam Principem nomine alternis diebus declamare, alternis disputare, nonnullis vero mane[1] disserere, post meridiem remoto pulpito declamare solitum. Audiebam etiam, memoria patrum quosdam e grammatici statim ludo transisse in Forum atque in numerum praestantissimorum patronorum receptos.

Clari professores et de quibus prodi possit aliquid dum taxat a nobis, fere hi fuerunt.

V. Sevius Nicanor primus ad famam dignationemque docendo pervenit, fecitque praeter commentarios, quorum tamen pars maxima intercepta dicitur, saturam quoque, in qua libertinum se ac duplici cognomine esse per haec indicat:

Sevius Nicanor Marci libertus negabit;
Sevius Posthumius vero[2] idem ac Marcus docebit.

Sunt qui tradant, ob infamiam quandam eum in Sardiniam secessisse ibique diem obisse.

VI. Aurelius Opillus, Epicurei cuiusdam libertus, philosophiam primo, deinde rhetoricam, novissime grammaticam docuit. Dimissa autem schola, Rutilium Rufum damnatum in Asiam secutus, ibidem Smyrnae[3] simul consenuit, composuitque variae eruditionis aliquot

[1] vero mane] mane vero, *mss.*   [2] Posthumius vero, *E. H. Brewster*, in *Class. Phil.* x, pp. 84 ff.; post huius, *VL*; posthus, *O*; post hoc, *G*; post h', *I*.   [3] Zmyrnae, *V.*

---

[a] The text and the meaning are uncertain, but it is obvious from the preceding sentence that we must have two *cognomina*. The man's name appears to have been M. Sevius Postumius Nicanor. Thus he was Sevius Nicanor, Sevius Postumius, and

any rate when I was a young man, one of these teachers, Princeps by name, used to declaim and engage in discussion on alternate days; and that sometimes he would give instruction in the morning, and in the afternoon remove his desk and declaim. I used to hear, too, that within the memory of our forefathers some passed directly from the grammar school to the Forum and took their place among the most eminent advocates.

The following list includes about all the distinguished teachers of the subject, at least those of whose life I am able to give any account.

V. Sevius Nicanor was the first to attain to fame and recognition through his teaching, and besides his commentaries, the greater part of which, however, are said to be stolen, he wrote a satire, in which he shows by the following lines that he was a freedman and had two surnames:

> Sevius Nicanor, the freedman of Marcus, may deny
> this; but Saevius Postumius, who is the same man,
> and a Marcus as well, will prove it.[a]

Some write that because of some disgrace he retired to Sardinia and there died.

VI. Aurelius Opilius, freedman of an Epicurean, first taught philosophy, afterwards rhetoric, and finally grammar. But when Rutilius Rufus was banished, he gave up his school and followed him to Asia, where he lived with him in Smyrna to old age. He wrote several books on

Marcus. The meaning of the verbs and of the lines as a whole is obscured by the lack of a context. The textual variants show that the mss. had the spelling Posthumius.

volumina, ex quibus novem unius corporis, quia[1] scriptores ac poetas sub clientela Musarum iudicaret, non absurde et fecisse et inscripsisse[2] se ait ex numero divarum et appellatione. Huius cognomen in plerisque indicibus et titulis per unam L litteram[3] scriptum animadverto, verum ipse id per duas effert in parastichide libelli, qui inscribitur "Pinax."

VII. M. Antonius Gnipho, ingenuus in Gallia natus sed expositus, a nutritore suo manumissus institutusque (Alexandriae quidem, ut aliqui tradunt, in contubernio Dionysi Scytobrachionis; quod equidem non temere crediderim, cum temporum ratio vix congruat) fuisse dicitur ingenii magni, memoriae singularis, nec minus Graece quam Latine doctus; praeterea comi facilique natura, nec unquam de mercedibus pactus, eoque plura ex liberalitate discentium consecutus. Docuit primum in Divi Iulii domo pueri adhuc,[4] deinde in sua privata. Docuit autem et rhetoricam, ita ut quotidie praecepta eloquentiae traderet, declamaret vero nonnisi nundinis. Scholam eius claros quoque viros frequentasse aiunt, in iis M. Ciceronem, etiam cum praetura fungeretur. Scripsit multa, quamvis annum aetatis quinquagesimum non excesserit. Etsi Ateius Philologus duo tantum volumina "De Latino Sermone" reliquisse eum tradit; nam cetera scripta discipulorum eius esse, non ipsius; in quibus et suum alicubi reperiri nomen, ut hoc ∗ ∗ ∗

[1] quia, *Ernesti*; qui quia, *mss.*
[2] inscripsisse, *Wolf*; scripsisse, *mss.* (se scripsisse, *O*).
[3] L litteram, *J. F. Gronov*; litteram *or* literam, *mss.*
[4] adhuc, *omitted by L.*

---

[a] The Tablet. [b] See note on *Tib.* vii. 2.
[c] That is, the man who found and reared him.

various learned topics, nine of which, so he tells us, form-
ing a single work, he appropriately made to correspond
with the number of the Muses, and called them by their
names, because he considered writers and poets to be
under the protection of those divinities. I observe that his
surname is given in numerous catalogues and titles with a
single L, but he himself writes it with two in an acrostic in
a little book of his called "Pinax."[a]

VII. Marcus Antonius Gnipho was born in Gaul of
free parents, but was disowned.[b] He was set free by his
foster-father[c] and given an education, at Alexandria,
according to some, and in intimate association with
Dionysius Scytobrachion; but this I can hardly credit for
chronological reasons. It is said that he was a man of
great talent, of unexampled powers of memory, and well
read not only in Latin but in Greek as well; that his disposition, too, was kindly and good-natured, and that he
never made any stipulation about his fees, and therefore
received the more from the generosity of his pupils. He
first gave instruction in the house of the Deified Julius,
when the latter was still a boy, and then in his own home.
He taught rhetoric too, giving daily instruction in speaking, but declaiming only once a week.[d] They say also that
distinguished men attended his school, including Cicero
even while he was praetor. Although he did not live
beyond his fiftieth year, he wrote a great deal. Ateius
Philologus, however, declares that he left but two volumes, "On the Latin Language," maintaining that the
other works attributed to him were those of his pupils and
not his own. Yet his own name is sometimes found in
them, for example * * *

[d] Literally, "on market days"; see note on *Aug.* xcii. 2.

VIII. M. Pompilius Andronicus, natione Syrus, studio Epicureae sectae desidiosior in professione grammatica[1] habebatur minusque idoneus ad tuendam scholam. Itaque cum se in urbe non solum Antonio Gniphoni, sed ceteris etiam deterioribus postponi videret, Cumas transiit ibique in otio vixit et multa composuit; verum adeo inops atque egens, ut coactus sit praecipuum illud opusculum suum "Annalium Ennii Elenchorum" XVI milibus nummum cuidam vendere, quos libros Orbilius suppressos redemisse se dicit vulgandosque curasse nomine auctoris.

IX. L.[2] Orbilius Pupillus Beneventanus, morte parentum, una atque eadem die inimicorum dolo interemptorum, destitutus, primo apparituram magistratibus fecit; deinde in Macedonia corniculo, mox equo meruit; functusque militia, studia repetit, quae iam inde a puero non leviter attigerat; ac professus diu in patria, quinquagesimo demum anno Romam consule Cicerone transiit docuitque maiore fama quam emolumento. Namque iam persenex pauperem se et habitare sub tegulis quodam scripto fatetur. Librum etiam, cui est titulus Περὶ ἀλο-γίας,[3] edidit continentem querelas de iniuriis, quas professores neglegentia aut ambitione parentum acciperent. Fuit autem naturae acerbae, non modo in antisophistas, quos omni occasione[4] laceravit, sed etiam in discipulos,

---

[1] grammatica, *NOGIW*; grammaticae, *VL.*

[2] L., *added by Roth.*   [3] Περὶ ἀλογίας, *Turnebus*: perialogos, *mss.*   [4] omni in occasione, *mss. except W, in which* in *is stricken out*; *cf. Claud.* xlii. 1.

---

[a] *Elenchus* is a transliteration of the Greek ἔλεγχος, "refutation," "cross-examination." The work was apparently an attack on the *Annals*, like those on the writings of Virgil; cf. the *Life of Virgil*, 44 and 45.   [b] In 63 B.C.

VIII. Marcus Pompilius Andronicus, a native of Syria, because of his devotion to the Epicurean sect was considered somewhat indolent in his work as a grammarian and not qualified to conduct a school. Therefore, realizing that he was held in less esteem at Rome, not only than Antonius Gnipho, but than others of even less ability, he moved to Cumae, where he led a quiet life and wrote many books. But he was so poor and needy that he was forced to sell that admirable little work of his "Criticisms of the Annals of Ennius"[a] to someone or other for sixteen thousand sesterces. Orbilius tells us that he bought up these books after they had been suppressed, and caused them to be circulated under their author's name.

IX. Lucius Orbilius Pupillus of Beneventum, left alone in the world by the death of his parents, both of whom were slain on the selfsame day by treacherous enemies, at first earned a living as an attendant on the magistrates. He then served as a subaltern in Macedonia, and later in the cavalry. After completing his military service, he resumed his studies, to which he had given no little attention from boyhood; and after teaching for a long time in his native place, he at last went to Rome in his fiftieth year, when Cicero was consul,[b] where he gave instruction with greater renown than profit. For in one of his books, written when he was well on in years, he admits that he was poor and lived under the tiles.[c] He also wrote a book called "On Folly," full of complaints of the wrongs which teachers suffered from the indifference or selfishness of parents. Indeed he was sour-tempered, not only towards rival scholars,[d] whom he assailed at every opportunity, but also towards his pupils, as Horace implies

[c] That is, in a garret.   [d] Cf. *Tib.* xi. 3.

ut et Horatius significat "plagosum" eum appellans, et Domitius Marsus scribens:

Si quos Orbilius ferula scuticaque cecidit.

Ac ne principum quidem virorum insectatione abstinuit; siquidem ignotus adhuc cum iudicio frequenti testimonium diceret, interrogatus a Varrone diversae partis advocato, quidnam ageret et quo artificio uteretur, gibberosos se de sole in umbram transferre respondit; quod Murena gibber erat. Vixit prope ad centesimum aetatis annum, amissa iam pridem memoria, ut versus Bibaculi docet:

Orbilius ubinam est, litterarum oblivio?

Statua eius Beneventi ostenditur in Capitolio ad sinistrum latus marmorea habitu sedentis ac palliati, appositis duobus scriniis. Reliquit filium Orbilium,[1] et ipsum grammaticum professorem.

X. L.[2] Ateius Philologus libertinus Athenis est natus. Hunc Capito Ateius notus iuris consultus inter grammaticos rhetorem, inter rhetores grammaticum fuisse ait. De eodem Asinius Pollio in libro, quo Sallustii scripta reprehendit ut nimia priscorum verborum affectatione oblita, ita tradit: "In eam rem adiutorium ei fecit maxime quidam Ateius praetextatis nobis grammaticus Latinus,

---

[1] Orbilium, *bracketed for omission by Reiff.*
[2] L., *added by Roth.*

---

[a] *Epist.* 2. 1. 70.   [b] Varro Murena. Macrobius, *Saturn.* 2. 6, tells the same story of Galba, father of the emperor (cf. *Galba,* iii), but gives the reply of Orbilius as: *in sole gibbos soleo fricare,* "I rub humps in the sun." Neither remark seems to have any point except the allusion to Murena's deformity, unless Sueto-

when he calls him "the flogger,"[a] and Domitius Marsus in the line:

> Whomever Orbilius thrashed with rod or with
> whiplash of leather.

He did not even refrain from gibes at men of distinction; for when he was still obscure and was giving testimony in a crowded court-room, being asked by Varro, the advocate on the other side, what he did and what his profession was, he replied: "I remove hunchbacks from the sun into the shade." Now Murena[b] was hunchbacked. Orbilius lived to be nearly a hundred, having long since lost his memory, as is shown by the verse of Bibaculus:

> Where is Orbilius, pray, great learning's tomb?

His marble statue may be seen at Beneventum, on the left side of the capitol, representing him seated and clad in a Greek mantle, with two book-boxes by his side. He left a son Orbilius, who was also a teacher of grammar.

X. Lucius Ateius Philologus was a freedman, born at Athens. The well-known jurist Ateius Capito says that he was "a rhetorician among grammarians and a grammarian among rhetoricians." Asinius Pollio, too, in the book in which he criticizes the writings of Sallust as marred by an excessive effort for archaism, writes as follows: "He was especially abetted in this by a certain Ateius, when I was a boy a Latin grammarian and later a critic and teacher of

nius' version means "I put them into the background," or "consign them to obscurity." The commentators confine themselves to quoting Macrobius.

declamantium deinde auditor atque praeceptor, ad summam Philologus ab semet nominatus." Ipse ad Laelium Hermam scripsit, se in Graecis litteris magnum processum habere et in Latinis nonnullum, audisse Antonium Gniphonen eiusque †haere postea docuisse. Praecepisse autem multis et claris iuvenibus, in quis Appio quoque et Pulchro Claudiis fratribus, quorum etiam comes in provincia fuerit. Philologi appellationem assumpsisse videtur, quia sic ut Eratosthenes, qui primus hoc cognomen sibi vindicavit, multiplici variaque doctrina censebatur. Quod sane ex commentariis eius apparet, quanquam paucissimi exstent; de quorum tamen copia sic altera ad eundem Hermam epistula significat: "Hylen nostram aliis memento commendare, quam omnis generis coegimus, uti scis, octingentos in libros." Coluit postea familiarissime C. Sallustium et eo defuncto Asinium Pollionem, quos historiam componere aggressos, alterum breviario rerum omnium Romanarum, ex quibus quas vellet eligeret, instruxit, alterum praeceptis de ratione scribendi. Quo magis miror Asinium credidisse, antiqua eum verba et figuras solitum esse colligere Sallustio; cum sibi sciat nihil aliud suadere quam ut noto civilique et proprio sermone utatur, vitetque maxime obscuritatem Sallustii et audaciam in translationibus.

---

[a] The text is corrupt and no satisfactory emendation has as yet been proposed; see Ihm, *Rh. Mus.* 61, p. 551. Vahlen, *Index Lectionum*, Berlin, 1877, suggested *theoremata*, which would give the meaning "and afterwards taught his (Gnipho's) theories."   [b] A Greek word, equivalent to *Silva*, meaning literally "timber" for building, and used metaphorically of material in a rough form; here of material for oratory. *Silva* is also applied

declamation, in short a self-styled 'Philologus.'" Ateius himself wrote to Laelius Hermas that he had made great progress in Greek letters and some in Latin, had been a pupil of Antonius Gnipho * * *,[a] and afterwards a teacher; further, that he had given instruction to many eminent young men, including the brothers Appius and Claudius Pulcher, whom he had also accompanied to their province. He seems to have assumed the title Philologus, because like Eratosthenes, who was first to lay claim to that surname, he regarded himself as a man of wide and varied learning. And that he was such is evident from his commentaries, though very few of them survive; but he gives some idea of their number in a second letter to the aforesaid Hermas: "Remember to recommend my *Hyle*[b] to others; as you know, it consists of material of every kind, collected in eight hundred books." He was afterwards a close friend of Gaius Sallustius, and after Sallust's death, of Asinius Pollio; and when they set about writing history, he provided the one with an epitome of all Roman story, from which to select what he wished, and the other with rules on the art of composition. This makes me wonder all the more that Asinius believed that Ateius used to collect archaic words and expressions for Sallust; for he knows that the grammarian's strongest recommendation to him was to use familiar, unassuming, natural[c] language, especially avoiding Sallust's obscurity and his bold figures of speech.

technically to hasty and more or less extempore productions; cf. *Quint.* 10. 3. 17, *diversum est huic eorum vitium, qui primo decurrere per materiam stilo quam velocissimo volunt et sequentes calorem atque impetum ex tempore scribunt; hanc silvam vocant.*   [c] That is, his own, without borrowing or imitation.

XI. P.[1] Valerius Cato, ut nonnulli tradiderunt, Burseni cuiusdam libertus ex Gallia; ipse libello, cui est titulus "Indignatio," ingenuum se natum ait et pupillum relictum, eoque facilius licentia Sullani temporis exutum patrimonio. Docuit multos et nobiles, visusque est peridoneus praeceptor, maxime ad poeticam tendentibus, ut quidem apparere vel his versiculis potest:

Cato grammaticus, Latina Siren,
Qui solus legit ac facit poetas.

Is scripsit praeter grammaticos libellos etiam poemata, ex quibus praecipue probantur "Lydia" et "Diana." "Lydiae" Ticida meminit:

Lydia doctorum maxima cura liber;

"Dianae" Cinna:

Saecula permaneat nostri Dictynna Catonis.

Vixit ad extremam senectam, sed in summa pauperie[2] et paene inopia,[3] abditus modico gurgustio, postquam Tusculana villa creditoribus cesserat, ut auctor est Bibaculus:

Si quis forte mei domum Catonis,
Depictas minio assulas,[4] et illos
Custodis videt hortulos Priapi:
Miratur, quibus ille disciplinis

[1] P., *added by Roth.*
[2] pauperie] pauperiem, *mss.*
[3] inopia] inopiam, *mss.*
[4] assulas, *Beroaldus*; assylas, *G*; assyllas, *NOI*; asillas, *VL.*

XI. Publius Valerius Cato, according to some writers, was the freedman of a certain Bursenus from Gaul; but he himself, in a little work called "Indignation," declares that he was freeborn but was left an orphan; so that he was the more easily stripped of his patrimony in the lawless times of Sulla. He had many distinguished pupils and was regarded as a very competent teacher, especially of those who had a bent for poetry, as indeed is especially evident from these verses:

Cato, teacher of letters, Siren Latin-born,
He, and none other, poets reads and makes.

Besides books of a grammatical character, he wrote poems also, of which the most highly esteemed are the "Lydia" and the "Diana." Ticidas says of the former:

Lydia, a book most dear to cultured minds,

and Cinna of the latter:

For ages may our Cato's Dian[a] live.

He reached an advanced age, but in extreme poverty and almost in destitution, buried in a little hovel, after he had given up his villa at Tusculum to his creditors, as Bibaculus tells us:

If haply one has seen my Cato's house,
His shingles stained with red,
His garden over which Priapus watched:
One can but wonder by what training he

[a] Dictynna is a name of Diana as goddess of the chase, from δίκτυον, "hunting-net."

Tantam sit sapientiam[1] assecutus,
Quem tres cauliculi, selibra farris.
Racemi duo tegula sub una
Ad summam prope nutriant senectam.

Et rursus:

Catonis modo, Galle, Tusculanum
Tota creditor urbe venditabat.
Mirati sumus, unicum magistrum,
Summum grammaticum, optimum poetam
Omnes solvere posse quaestiones,
Unum difficile expedire nomen.
En cor Zenodoti, en iecur Cratetis.

XII. Cornelius Epicadus, L. Cornelii Sullae dictatoris libertus calatorque in sacerdotio augurali, filio quoque eius Fausto gratissimus fuit; quare nunquam non utriusque se libertum edidit. Librum autem, quem Sulla novissimum "De Rebus Suis" imperfectum reliquerat, ipse supplevit.

XIII. Staberius Eros, suomet aere[2] emptus de catasta et propter litterarum studium manumissus, docuit inter ceteros Brutum et Cassium. Sunt qui tradant tanta eum honestate praeditum, ut temporibus Sullanis proscriptorum liberos gratis et sine mercede ulla in disciplinam receperit.

---

[1] sit sapientiam, *L (Pontanus)*; sapientiam sit, *VNGOI*.
[2] suomet aere, *Roth*; nametra, *mss. The text is corrupt and the meaning most uncertain*; *see Ihm, Rh. Mus.* 61, *p.* 551.

---

[a] *Unum expedire nomen*, "make shift to find one name," as surety for his debts. [b] That is, "what a fate for a man with such a mind and heart." *Cor* here, as often, = "intelligence," and

To such a height of wisdom has attained
That three small cabbages, half a pound of meal,
And clusters twain of grapes beneath one roof
Suffice for him when well-nigh at life's end.

And again:

Gallus, but now our Cato's creditor
His Tusculanum offered through the town.
We wondered that the master without peer,
The great grammarian, chief among our poets,
Could solve all questions, solvent[a] could not be.
Lo! Crates' heart, mind of Zenodotus.[b]

XII. Cornelius Epicadus was a freedman of Lucius Cornelius Sulla, the dictator, and one of his servants[c] in the augural priesthood, besides being a great favourite of his son Faustus. Therefore he always declared that he was the freedman of both. He himself completed the last book of Sulla's "Autobiography," which the dictator left unwritten.

XIII. Staberius Eros was purchased with his own savings at a public sale[d] and formally manumitted because of his devotion to literature. He numbered among his pupils Brutus and Cassius. Some say that he was so noble-minded that in the times of Sulla he admitted the children of the proscribed to his school free of charge and without any fee.

iecur may have the same meaning, although it is commonly spoken of as the seat of the emotions, especially anger and the like.

[c] The *calatores*, literally "summoners," were attendants on the augurs and other religious officials.

[d] *Catasta* was the scaffolding or platform on which slaves were exposed to view at public sales.

XIV. Curtius Nicia haesit Cn. Pompeio et C. Memmio; sed cum codicillos Memmi ad Pompei uxorem de stupro pertulisset, proditus ab ea, Pompeium offendit, domoque ei interdictum est. Fuit et M. Ciceronis familiaris; in cuius epistula ad Dolabellam haec de eo legimus: "Nihil Romae geritur quod te putem scire curare, nisi forte scire vis, me inter Niciam nostrum et Vidium iudicem esse. Profert alter, opinor duobus versiculis, expensum Niciae;[1] alter Aristarchus hos obelizei: ego tanquam criticus antiquus[2] iudicaturus sum, utrum sint τοῦ ποιητοῦ an παρεμβεβλημένοι.[3]" Item ad Atticum: "De Nicia quod scribis, si ita me haberem ut eius humanitate frui possem, in primis vellem mecum illum habere; sed mihi solitudo et recessus provincia est. Praeterea nosti Niciae nostri imbecillitatem, mollitiam, consuetudinem victus. Cur ergo illi molestus esse velim, cum mihi ille iucundus esse[4] non possit? Voluntas tamen eius mihi grata est." Huius "De Lucilio" libros etiam Santra[5] comprobat.

XV. Lenaeus, Magni Pompei libertus et paene omnium expeditionum comes, defuncto eo filiisque eius schola se sustentavit; docuitque in Carinis ad Telluris, in qua regione Pompeiorum domus fuerat, ac tanto amore erga patroni memoriam exstitit, ut Sallustium historicum, quod eum oris probi, animo inverecundo scripsisset, acer-

---

[1] Niciae, *omitted by VLNGW; added from Cicero by OI.*

[2] antiquus] antiquos, *mss.*   [3] ποιητοῦ an παρεμβεβλημένοι, *omitted by the mss.; restored from Cicero by Aldus.*   [4] velim ... esse, *om. by mss.; restored from Cic. by Aldus.*   [5] Santra, *Statius*; satyra *or* satura, *mss.* (*W. has* santyra *corr. to* satyra).

---

[a] *Ad Fam.* 9. 10.   [b] The critical mark used to indicate spurious or interpolated lines; that is, Vidius denies the debt.

XIV. Curtius Nicias was an adherent of Gnaeus Pompeius and Gaius Memmius; but having brought a note from Memmius to Pompey's wife with an infamous proposal, he was betrayed by her, lost favour with Pompey, and was forbidden his house. He was an intimate friend of Marcus Cicero too, and in a letter of the orator's to Dolabella[a] we read these words about Nicias: "I think there is nothing going on in Rome which you are interested in knowing, unless perhaps you would like to know that I am acting as arbiter between our friend Nicias and Vidius. The one presents a note for payment, consisting of two lines, I believe. The other, like an Aristarchus, marks them with an obelus.[b] I, like a critic of old, am to decide whether they are the poet's, or a forgery." In another letter to Atticus:[c] "As to what you write of Nicias, if I were in a position to enjoy his learned society, I should particularly like to have him with me; but my province is solitude and retirement. Besides you know our friend Nicias' weakness, self-indulgence, and mode of life. Why then should I wish to bore him, when he can give me no pleasure? Nevertheless I appreciate his desire." Santra likewise commends his books "On Lucilius."

XV. Lenaeus, freedman of Pompey the Great and his companion in almost all his campaigns, on the death of his patron and his sons supported himself by a school, teaching in the Carinae,[d] near the temple of Tellus, the quarter of the city in which the house of the Pompeys was formerly situated. He was so devoted to his patron's memory that, because the historian Sallust wrote that Pompey had "an honest face but a shameless character," he tore Sallust to pieces in a biting satire, calling him "a

[c] *Ad Att.* 12. 26.   [d] See note on *Tib.* xv. 1.

bissima satura laceraverit, lastaurum et lurconem et ne-
bulonem popinonemque appellans, et vita scriptisque
monstrosum, praeterea priscorum Catonis verborum
ineruditissimum furem. Traditur autem puer adhuc
catenis[1] subreptis,[2] refugisse in patriam, perceptisque
liberalibus disciplinis, pretium suum domino[3] rettulisse,
verum ob ingenium atque doctrinam gratis manumissus.

XVI. Q. Caecilius Epirota, Tusculi natus, libertus
Attici[4] equitis Romani, ad quem sunt Ciceronis epistulae,
cum filiam patroni nuptam M. Agrippae doceret, suspectus in ea et ob hoc remotus, ad Cornelium Gallum se contulit vixitque una familiarissime, quod ipsi Gallo inter
gravissima crimina ab Augusto obicitur. Post deinde
damnationem mortemque Galli scholam aperuit, sed ita
ut paucis et tantum adulescentibus praeciperet, praetex-
tato nemini, nisi si cuius parenti hoc officium negare non
posset. Primus dicitur Latine ex tempore disputasse,
primusque Vergilium et alios poetas novos praelegere
coepisse, quod etiam Domitii Marsi versiculus indicat:

Epirota, tenellorum nutricula vatum.

XVII. M.[5] Verrius Flaccus libertinus docendi genere
maxime claruit. Namque ad exercitanda discentium ingenia aequales inter se committere solebat, proposita non
solum materia quam scriberent, sed et praemio quod victor auferret. Id erat liber aliquis antiquus pulcher aut

---

[1] catenis] Athenis, *Heinsius.*   [2] subreptus, *some mss.*
[3] domino, *NGOIW; the other mss. omit.*
[4] Attici, *Beroaldus;* Satti, *etc., mss.*
[5] M., *added by Roth.*

---

[a] Cf. *Aug.* lxvi. 1–2.   [b] In 25 B.C.

debauchee, a gourmandizer, a spendthrift, and a tippler, a man whose life and writings were monstrous, and who was besides an ignorant pilferer of the archaic language of Cato." It is further said that when Lenaeus was still a boy he escaped from his chains and fled back to his native land, and after acquiring a liberal education, offered the price of his liberty to his former master, but received his freedom as a gift because of his ability and learning.

XVI. Quintus Caecilius Epirota, born at Tusculum, was a freedman of Atticus, a Roman knight, the correspondent of Cicero. While he was teaching his patron's daughter, who was the wife of Marcus Agrippa, he was suspected of improper conduct towards her and dismissed; whereupon he attached himself to Cornelius Gallus and lived with him on most intimate terms, a fact which Augustus made one of his heaviest charges against Gallus himself.[a] After the conviction and death of Gallus[b] he opened a school, but took few pupils and only grown up young men, admitting none under age, except those to whose fathers he was unable to refuse that favour. He is said to have been the first to hold extempore discussions in Latin, and the first to begin the practice of reading Virgil and other recent poets, a fact also alluded to by Domitius Marsus in the verse:

Epirota, fond nurse of fledgling bards.

XVII. Marcus Verrius Flaccus, a freedman, gained special fame by his method of teaching. For to stimulate the efforts of his pupils, he used to pit those of the same advancement against one another, not only setting the subject on which they were to write, but also offering a prize for the victor to carry off. This was some old book,

rarior. Quare ab Augusto quoque nepotibus eius praeceptor electus, transiit in Palatium cum tota schola,
verum ut ne quem[1] amplius posthac discipulum
reciperet; docuitque in atrio Catulinae[a] domus, quae pars
Palatii tunc erat, et centena sestertia in annum accepit.
Decessit aetatis exactae sub Tiberio. Statuam habet
Praeneste, in inferiore[2] fori parte contra[3] hemicyclium,[b]
in quo fastos a se ordinatos et marmoreo parieti incisos
publicarat.

XVIII. L. Crassicius, genere Tarentinus, ordinis liberti-
tini, cognomine Pasicles, mox Pansam se transnominavit.
Hic initio circa scenam versatus est, dum mimographos
adiuvat; deinde in pergula[4] docuit, donec commentario
"Zmyrnae" edito adeo inclaruit, ut haec de eo scriberen-
tur:

Uni Crassicio se credere Zmyrna probavit;
　　Desinite indocti coniugio hanc petere!
Soli Crassicio se dixit nubere velle,
　　Intima cui soli nota sua exstiterint.

Sed cum edoceret[5] iam multos ac nobiles, in iis Iullum[6]
Antonium, triumviri filium, ut Verrio quoque Flacco

[1] ne quem, *OW*; neque, *VLNGI.*

[2] inferiore, *VLW*; superiore, *NOGI.*

[3] contra, *NOI*; circa, *VLG*; *cf. Vahlen, Index Lectionum,
Berlin 1877.*　　[4] pergula, *Ven. ed. of 1474, Beroaldus*; percula,
OW; parcula, *VLNGI.*

[5] *The mss. have* et doceret, *except O, which omits* et; *W indicates a lacuna before* et.　　[6] Iulum, *OI*; Iulium, *VLNG.*

[a] Q. Lutatius Catulus; see chap. iii and Index.

[b] A semi-circular place for sitting; applied also by Vitruvius,
9. 9. 1, to a kind of sundial.

either beautiful or rare. He was therefore chosen by Augustus as the tutor of his grandsons and he moved to the Palace with his whole school, but with the understanding that he should admit no more pupils. He gave instruction in the hall of the house of Catulus,[a] which at that time formed part of the Palace, and was paid a hundred thousand sesterces a year. He died at an advanced age under Tiberius. His statue stands at Praeneste in the upper part of the forum near the hemicycle,[b] on which he exhibited the calendar[c] which he had arranged and inscribed upon its marble walls.

XVIII. Lucius Crassicius, a Tarentine by birth and a freedman by position, had the surname Pasicles, which he afterwards changed to Pansa. He was at first connected with the stage, as an assistant to the writers of farces; then he gave instruction in a school,[d] until he became so famous through the publication of his commentary on the "Zmyrna," that the following verses were written about him:

Zmyrna will trust her fate but to Crassicius;
   Cease then to woo her, ye unlettered throng.
She has declared none other will she wed,
   Since he alone her hidden charms doth know.[e]

But when he had already attracted many pupils of high rank, including Iullus Antonius, the triumvir's son, so that he was a rival even of Verrius Flaccus, he suddenly dis-

[c] The *Fasti Praenestini*, of which fragments have come down to us.   [d] A *pergula* was an upper floor or balcony on the front of a house; such balconies were used as shops, studios, schools, and the like; cf. *Aug.* xciv. 12.   [e] See Catullus 70 and 95.

compararetur, dimissa repente schola, transiit ad Q. Sexti
philosophi sectam.

XIX. Scribonius Aphrodisius, Orbilii servus atque dis-
cipulus, mox a Scribonia Libonis filia, quae prior Augusti
uxor fuerat, redemptus et manumissus, docuit quo Verrius tempore, cuius etiam libris "De Orthographia"
rescripsit, non sine insectatione studiorum morumque
eius.

XX. C. Iulius Hyginus, Augusti libertus, natione
Hispanus (nonnulli Alexandrinum putant et a Caesare
puerum Romam adductum Alexandria capta), studiose et
audiit et imitatus est Cornelium Alexandrum grammaticum Graecum, quem propter antiquitatis notitiam
Polyhistorem multi, quidam Historiam vocabant. Praefuit Palatinae bibliothecae, nec eo secius plurimos docuit;
fuitque familiarissimus Ovidio poetae et Clodio Licino[1]
consulari, historico, qui eum admodum pauperem deces-
sisse tradit et liberalitate sua, quoad vixerit, sustentatum.
Huius libertus fuit Iulius Modestus, in studiis atque doctrina vestigia patroni secutus.

XXI. C. Melissus, Spoleti natus ingenuus, sed ob dis-
cordiam parentum expositus, cura et industria educatoris
sui altiora studia percepit, ac Maecenati pro grammatico
muneri datus est. Cui cum se gratum et acceptum in
modum amici videret, quanquam asserente matre, permansit tamen in statu servitutis praesentemque condicionem verae origini anteposuit; quare cito manumissus,

---

[1] Licino, *Oudendorp, Bergk*; Licinio, *mss.*

[a] *Aug.* lxii. 2.
[b] *Aug.* xxix. 3.
[c] See note on *Tib.* vii. 2.

banded his school and became a disciple of the philosopher Quintus Sextius.

XIX. Scribonius Aphrodisius, slave and pupil of Orbilius, afterwards bought and set free by Scribonia, daughter of Libo, who had formerly been the wife of Augustus,[a] taught at the same time as Verrius. He wrote a critique of Verrius' "Orthography," at the same time attacking the author's scholarship and character.

XX. Gaius Julius Hyginus, a freedman of Augustus and a Spaniard by birth (some think that he was a native of Alexandria and was brought to Rome when a boy by Caesar after his capture of the city), was a zealous pupil and imitator of the Greek grammarian Cornelius Alexander, whom many called "Polyhistor" because of his knowledge of the past, and some "History." Hyginus was in charge of the Palatine Library,[b] but nevertheless took many pupils. He was an intimate friend of the poet Ovid and of Clodius Licinus the ex-consul and historian, who tells us that Hyginus died very poor after being supported as long as he lived by the writer's generosity. He had a freedman Julius Modestus, who followed in his patron's footsteps as student and scholar.

XXI. Gaius Melissus, a native of Spoletium, was freeborn, but was disowned[c] owing to a disagreement between his parents. Nevertheless through the care and devotion of the man who reared him, he received a superior education, and was presented to Maecenas as a grammarian. Finding that Maecenas appreciated him and treated him as a friend, although his mother claimed his freedom, he yet remained in a condition of slavery, since he preferred his present lot to that of his actual origin. In consequence he was soon set free, and even won the

Augusto etiam[1] insinuatus est. Quo delegante,[2] curam ordinandarum bibliothecarum in Octaviae porticu suscepit. Atque, ut ipse tradit, sexagesimum aetatis annum agens, libellos "Ineptiarum," qui nunc "Iocorum" inscribuntur, componere instituit, absolvitque C et L, quibus et alios diversi operis postea addidit. Fecit et novum genus togatarum inscripsitque trabeatas.

XXII. M. Pomponius Marcellus,[3] sermonis Latini exactor molestissimus, in advocatione quadam (nam interdum et causas agebat) soloecismum ab adversario factum usque adeo arguere perseveravit, quoad Cassius Severus, interpellatis iudicibus, dilationem petiit, ut litigator suus alium grammaticum adhiberet; quando non putat is cum adversario de iure sibi, sed de soloecismo controversiam futuram. Hic idem, cum ex oratione Tiberi verbum reprehendisset, affirmante Ateio Capitone, et esse illud Latinum, et si non esset, futurum certe iam inde: "Mentitur," inquit, "Capito; tu enim, Caesar, civitatem dare potes hominibus, verbo[4] non potes." Pugilem olim fuisse, Asinius Gallus hoc in eum epigrammate ostendit:

> Qui 'caput ad laevam' didicit, glossemata nobis
>   Praecipit; os nullum, vel potius pugilis!

[1] Augusto etiam, *NGOW*; Augusto et, *VLI*.
[2] quo delegante, *O*; quod elegantem, *VLNGIW*.
[3] Porcellus, *Kaster, perhaps rightly, cf. Sen. Suas.* 2. 12 f.
[4] verbo, *Roth*; verbis, *G. Faernus (Reiff.)*; verba, *mss.*

---

[a] See *Aug.* xxix. 4.   [b] The *fabulae togatae* presented scenes from Roman life, in contrast with the *fabulae palliatae*, or comedies adapted from the Greek.

[c] See note on *trabea*, Dom. xiv. 3. In the *trabeatae* the characters were knights or other wearers of the *trabea*.

favour of Augustus. At the emperor's appointment he undertook the task of arranging the library in the Colonnade of Octavia.[a] In his sixtieth year, as he himself writes, he began to compile his volumes of "Trifles," now entitled "Jests," of which he completed a hundred and fifty; and he later added other volumes of a different character. He likewise originated a new kind of *togatae*,[b] to which he gave the name of *trabeatae*.[c]

XXII. Marcus Pomponius Marcellus, a most pedantic critic of the Latin language, in one of his cases (for he sometimes acted as an advocate) was so persistent in criticizing an error in diction made by his opponent that Cassius Severus appealed to the judges and asked for a postponement, to enable his client to employ a grammarian in his stead: "For," said he, "he thinks that the contest with his opponent will not be on points of law, but of diction." When this same Marcellus had criticized a word in one of Tiberius' speeches, and Ateius Capito declared that it was good Latin, or if not, that it would surely be so from that time on, Marcellus answered: "Capito lies; for you, Caesar, can confer citizenship upon men, but not upon a word." That he had formerly been a boxer is shown by this epigram which Asinius Pollio made upon him:

He who learned 'Head to the left'[d] explains to us
        difficult language;
    Talent[e] indeed he has none, merely a pugilist's skill.

[d] To dodge a blow delivered with the right hand; cf. Virg. *Aen.* v. 428, *abduxere retro longe capita ardua ab ictu*; part of the instruction to a boxer.

[e] *Os* is of course used in a double sense, figuratively as above, and literally, of a pugilist's battered visage.

XXIII. Q. Remmius Palaemon, Vicetinus,[1] mulieris
verna, primo, ut ferunt, textrinum, deinde herilem filium
dum comitatur in scholam, litteras didicit. Postea
manumissus docuit Romae ac principem locum inter
grammaticos tenuit, quanquam infamis omnibus vitiis,
palamque et Tiberio et mox Claudio praedicantibus,
nemini minus institutionem puerorum vel iuvenum com-
mittendam. Sed capiebat homines cum memoria rerum,
tum facilitate sermonis; nec non etiam poemata faciebat
ex tempore. Scripsit vero variis, nec vulgaribus metris.
Arrogantia fuit tanta, ut M. Varronem porcum appellaret;
secum et natas et morituras litteras iactaret; nomen suum
in "Bucolicis" non temere positum, sed praesagante[2]
Vergilio, fore quandoque omnium poetarum ac poema-
tum Palaemonem iudicem. Gloriabatur etiam, latrones
quondam sibi propter nominis celebritatem pepercisse.[3]
Luxuriae ita indulsit, ut saepius in die lavaret, nec sufficeret sumptibus, quanquam ex schola quadringena annua
caperet, ac non multo minus ex re familiari; cuius diligen-
tissimus erat, cum et officinas promercalium vestium
exerceret, et agros adeo coleret, ut vitem manu eius insi-
tam satis constet CCCLXV dies[4] uvas edidisse. Sed
maxime flagrabat libidinibus in mulieres, usque ad infamiam oris; dicto quoque[5] non infaceto notatum ferunt
cuiusdam, qui cum[6] in turba osculum sibi ingerentem

---

[1] Vicetinus, *W*; *the other mss. have* Vicentinus (Vicc-, *G*).

[2] praesagante, *mss., Roth*; praesagiente, *Reiff.*

[3] pepercisse, *LO*: parsisse, *VG*.   [4] dies, *add. Murgia.*

[5] dicto quoque, *VLGO*; dictoque, *NI.*   [6] qui cum, *O*; qui
eum, *VNGI*; *omitted by L*; qui cum eum, *Reiff.*

---

[a] As *paedagogus*, cf. *Nero*, xxxvi. 2, etc.   [b] 3. 50 ff.

XXIII. Quintus Remmius Palaemon, of Vicetia, was the home-born slave of a woman. He first, they say, learned the weaver's trade, and then got an education by accompanying his master's son to school.[a] He was afterwards set free, and became a teacher at Rome, where he held a leading rank among the grammarians, in spite of the fact that he was notorious for every kind of vice, and that Tiberius and later Claudius openly declared that there was no one less fitted to be trusted with the education of boys or young men. But he caught men's fancy by his remarkable memory, as well as by his readiness of speech; for he even extemporized poems. He wrote too in various uncommon metres. He was so presumptuous that he called Marcus Varro "a hog"; declared that letters were born with him and would die with him; and that it was no accident that his name appeared in the "Bucolics,"[b] but because Virgil divined that one day a Palaemon would be judge of all poets and poems. He boasted too that brigands once spared him because of the celebrity of his name. He was so given to luxurious living that he went to the bath several times a day, and could not live within his income, although he received four hundred thousand sesterces a year from his school and almost as much from his private property. To the latter he gave great attention, keeping shops for the sale of ready made clothing and cultivating his fields with such care that it is common talk that a vine which he grafted himself yielded grapes every day of the year. But he was especially notorious for acts of licentiousness with women, which he carried to the pitch of shameful indecency; and they say that he was held up to scorn by the witty remark of a man who met him in a crowd and being unable to escape his kiss,

quanquam refugiens devitare non posset, "Vis tu," inquit,
"magister, quotiens festinantem aliquem vides, abli-
gurire?"

XXIV. M. Valerius Probus, Berytius, diu centuriatum
petiit, donec taedio ad studia se contulit. Legerat in
provincia quosdam veteres libellos apud grammatistam,
durante adhuc ibi antiquorum memoria, necdum omnino
abolita sicut Romae. Hos cum diligentius repeteret atque
alios deinceps cognoscere cuperet, quamvis omnes con-
temni magisque opprobrio legentibus quam gloriae et
fructui esse animadverteret, nihilo minus in proposito
mansit; multaque exemplaria contracta emendare ac distinguere et annotare curavit, soli huic nec ulli praeterea
grammatices parti deditus. Hic non tam discipulos quam
sectatores aliquot habuit. Nunquam enim ita docuit ut
magistri personam sustineret; unum et alterum, vel cum
plurimos tres aut quattuor postmeridianis horis admittere
solebat, cubansque inter longos ac vulgares sermones
legere quaedam idque perraro. Nimis pauca et exigua de
quibusdam minutis quaestiunculis edidit. Reliquit autem
non mediocrem "Silvam Observationum Sermonis
Antiqui."

although he tried to avoid it, cried: "Master, do you wish to mouth everyone whom you see in a hurry?"

XXIV. Marcus Valerius Probus of Berytus for a long time sought an appointment as centurion, finally grew tired of waiting, and devoted himself to study. He had read some early writers with an elementary teacher in one of the provinces; for the memory of those writers still lingers there and is not wholly lost, as it is in Rome. When he took these up again with greater care, and sought to extend his acquaintance to others of the same period, although he perceived that they were all held in contempt and brought rather reproach to those who read them than honour and profit, he nevertheless persisted in his purpose. After getting together a large number of copies, he gave his attention to correcting and punctuating them, and furnishing them with critical notes, devoting himself to this branch of grammar to the exclusion of all others. He had a few followers, rather than pupils; for he never taught in such a way as to assume the role of a master. He used to receive one or two, or at most three or four, in the afternoon hours, when he would lie upon a couch and in the course of long and general conversations[a] would read some few things, though very rarely. He published a few slight works on divers minute points, and also left a good sized "Grove[b] of Observations on our Early Language."

[a] Naturally, on literary and grammatical topics.

[b] See note on *Hyle*, chap. x.

DE RHETORIBUS

I (25). Rhetorica quoque apud nos perinde atque grammatica fere[1] recepta est, paululo[2] etiam difficilius, quippe quam constet nonnunquam etiam prohibitam exerceri. Quod ne cui dubium sit, vetus S. C.[3] item censorium edictum subiciam: "C.[4] Fannio Strabone M. Valerio Messala coss. M. Pomponius praetor senatum consuluit. Quod verba facta sunt de philosophis et rhetoribus, de ea re ita censuerunt, ut M. Pomponius praetor animadverteret curaretque, ut et[5] e re p. fideque sua videretur, uti Romae ne essent." De eisdem interiecto tempore Cn. Domitius Ahenobarbus, L. Licinius Crassus censores ita edixerunt: "Renuntiatum est nobis, esse homines qui novum genus disciplinae instituerunt, ad quos iuventus in ludum conveniat; eos sibi nomen imposuisse Latinos rhetoras; ibi homines adulescentulos dies totos desidere. Maiores nostri, quae liberos suos discere et quos in ludos

---

[1] fere, *VLNGI*; sero, *O, Beroaldus.*   [2] paululo, *VLGO*; paullo, *I*; paulo, *N.*   [3] S. C., *omitted by the mss.; inserted by Stephanus after, and by Lachmann before,* item; *O omits* item *also, marking a lacuna.*   [4] C., *added by Stephanus from Gell.* 15. 11. 1.   [5] ut ei, *OW* (*see Ihm, Rh. Mus.* 61. 552 *and cf. Gell.* 15. 11. 1); ut si ei, *edd.*

---

[a] The word *rhetor*, like *grammaticus*, had a different force

ON RHETORICIANS

I (25). The study of rhetoric[a] was introduced into our country in about the same way as that of grammar, but with somewhat greater difficulty, since, as is well known, its practice was at times actually prohibited. To remove any doubt on this point, I shall append an ancient decree of the senate, as well as an edict of the censors: "In the consulship[b] of Gaius Fannius Strabo and Marcus Valerius Messala the praetor Marcus Pomponius laid a proposition before the senate. As the result of a discussion about philosophers and rhetoricians, the senate decreed that Marcus Pomponius, the praetor, should take heed and provide, in whatever way seemed in accord with the interests of the State and his oath of office, that they be not allowed to live in Rome." Some time afterward the censors Gnaeus Domitius Ahenobarbus and Lucius Licinius Crassus[c] issued the following edict about the same class of men: "It has been reported to us that there be men who have introduced a new kind of training, and that our young men frequent their schools; that these men have assumed the title of Latin rhetoricians, and that young men spend whole days with them in idleness. Our forefathers determined what they wished their children to

from that of the corresponding English word; it meant a teacher of declamation and oratory.

[b] In 161 B.C.   [c] In 92 B.C.

413

itare vellent, instituerunt. Haec nova, quae praeter consuetudinem ac morem maiorum fiunt, neque placent
neque recta videntur. Quapropter et eis qui eos ludos
habent, et eis qui eo venire consuerunt, videtur faciun-
dum ut ostenderemus nostram sententiam, nobis non
placere."

Paulatim et ipsa utilis honestaque apparuit, multique
eam et praesidii causa et gloriae appetiverunt. Cicero ad
praeturam usque etiam Graece declamitavit, Latine vero
senior quoque et quidem cum consulibus Hirtio et Pansa,
quos discipulos et grandis praetextatos vocabat. Cn.
Pompeium quidam historici tradiderunt sub ipsum civile
bellum, quo facilius C. Curioni promptissimo iuveni,
causam Caesaris defendenti, contradiceret, repetisse
declamandi consuetudinem; M. Antonium, item Augustum ne Mutinensi quidem bello omisisse. Nero Caesar
primo imperii anno, publice quoque bis antea, decla-
mavit. Plerique autem oratorum etiam declamationes
ediderunt. Quare magno studio hominibus iniecto,
magna etiam professorum ac doctorum profluxit copia,
adeoque floruit, ut nonnulli ex infima fortuna in ordinem
senatorium atque ad summos honores processerint.

Sed ratio docendi nec una omnibus, nec singulis
eadem semper fuit, quando vario modo quisque discipulos exercuerunt. Nam et dicta praeclare per omnes figuras versare,[1] et apologos aliter atque aliter exponere, et

---

[1] versare, *Haupt*: per casus, *mss.*

---

[a] Cf. Seneca, *Controv.* 1, praef. 11 ff.
[b] Cf. *Aug.* lxxxiv. 1.

learn and what schools they desired them to attend. These innovations in the customs and principles of our forefathers do not please us nor seem proper. Therefore it appears necessary to make our opinion known, both to those who have such schools and to those who are in the habit of attending them, that they are displeasing to us."

By degrees rhetoric itself came to seem useful and honourable, and many devoted themselves to it as a defence and for glory. Cicero continued to declaim in Greek as well as Latin up to the time of his praetorship, and in Latin even when he was getting on in years; and that too in company with the future consuls Hirtius and Pansa, whom he calls "his pupils and his big boys."[a] Some historians assert that Gnaeus Pompeius resumed the practice of declaiming just before the civil war, that he might be the better able to argue against Gaius Curio, a young man of very ready tongue, who was espousing Caesar's cause; and that Marcus Antonius, and Augustus as well, did not give it up even during the war at Mutina.[b] The emperor Nero declaimed in the first year of his reign, and had also done so in public twice before. Furthermore, many of the orators also published declamations. In this way general enthusiasm was aroused, and a great number of masters and teachers flocked to Rome, where they were so well received that some advanced from the lowest estate to senatorial dignity and to the highest magistracies.

But they did not all follow the same method of teaching, and the individual teachers also varied in their practice, since each one trained his pupils in various ways. For they would give variety to fine stories by employing every figure of speech, recount fables now in one way and

415

narrationes cum breviter ac presse tum latius et uberius
explicare consuerant; interdum Graecorum scripta con-
vertere, ac viros illustres laudare vel vituperare; quaedam
etiam ad usum communis vitae instituta tum utilia et necessaria, tum perniciosa et supervacanea ostendere; saepe
fabulis fidem firmare aut demere, quod genus thesis et
anasceuas et catasceuas Graeci vocant; donec sensim haec
exoleverunt,[1] et ad controversiam ventum est.

Veteres controversiae aut ex historiis trahebantur,
sicut sane nonnullae usque adhuc, aut ex veritate ac re, si
qua forte recens accidisset; itaque locorum etiam appellationibus additis proponi solebant. Sic certe collectae edi-
taeque se habent, ex quibus non alienum fuerit unam et
alteram exempli causa ad verbum referre.

"Aestivo tempore adulescentes urbani cum Ostiam
venissent, litus ingressi, piscatores trahentes rete adierunt
et pepigerunt, bolum quanti emerent; nummos solverunt;
diu exspectaverunt, dum retia extraherentur; aliquando
extractis, piscis nullus affuit, sed sporta auri obsuta. Tum
emptores bolum suum aiunt, piscatores suum."

"Venalici cum Brundisi gregem venalium e navi educ-
erent, formoso et pretioso puero, quod portitores vere-
bantur, bullam et praetextam togam imposuerunt; facile
fallaciam celarunt. Romam venitur, res cognita est, peti-

---

[1] exoleverunt, *Beroaldus*; exoluerunt, *L* (*Pontanus*); exolu-
erint, *VOGI*; exsoluerint, *N*.

---

[a] They corresponded in general with the Roman *suasoriae*,
which with the *controversiae* formed the stock exercises of the
schools of rhetoric.

[b] The dress of a freeborn youth of good family; cf. *Jul.*
lxxxiv. 4. The *bulla* was also a badge of free birth.

now in another, and compose narratives sometimes in a condensed and brief form, again with greater detail and flow of words. Sometimes they would translate Greek works, and praise or censure distinguished men. They would show that some practices in everyday life were expedient and essential, others harmful and superfluous. Frequently they defended or assailed the credibility of myths, an exercise which the Greeks call "destructive" and "constructive" criticism. But finally all these exercises[a] went out of vogue and were succeeded by the debate.

The earlier debates were based either upon historical narrative, as indeed is sometimes the case at present, or upon some event of recent occurrence in real life. Accordingly they were usually presented with even the names of the localities included. At any rate that is the case with the published collections, from which it may be enlightening to give one or two specimens word for word.

"Some young men from the city went to Ostia in the summer season, and arriving at the shore, found some fishermen drawing in their nets. They made a bargain to give a certain sum for the haul. The money was paid and they waited for some time until the nets were drawn ashore. When they were at last hauled out, no fish was found in them, but a closed basket of gold. Then the purchasers said that the catch belonged to them, the fishermen that it was theirs."

"When some dealers were landing a cargo of slaves from a ship at Brundisium, they dressed a handsome and high-priced young slave in the amulet and fringed toga[b] for fear of the collectors of customs, and their fraud easily escaped detection. When they reached Rome, the case

417

tur puer, quod domini voluntate fuerit liber, in libertatem.[1]" Olim autem eas appellatione Graeca[2] ὑπο-θέσεις[3] vocabant; mox controversias quidem, sed aut fictas aut iudiciales.

Illustres professores, et quorum memoria aliqua exstet, non temere alii reperientur quam de quibus tradam.

II (26). L. Plotius Gallus. De hoc Cicero in epistula ad M. Titinnium sic refert: "Equidem memoria teneo, pueris nobis primum Latine docere coepisse Plotium quendam. Ad quem cum fieret concursus, quod studio-sissimus quisque apud eum exerceretur, dolebam mihi idem non licere. Continebar autem doctissimorum hominum auctoritate, qui existimabant Graecis exercita-tionibus ali melius ingenia posse." Hunc eundem (nam diutissime vixit) M. Caelius in oratione, quam pro se de vi habuit, significat[4] dictasse Atratino, accusatori suo, actionem; subtractoque nomine, hordearium eum rhetorem appellat, deridens ut inflatum ac levem et sor-didum.

III (27). M'. Otacilius[5] Pitholaus[6] servisse dicitur atque etiam ostiarius vetere more in catena fuisse, donec ob ingenium ac studium litterarum manumissus, accu-santi patrono subscripsit. Deinde rhetoricam professus,

[1] libertatem, *Vinetus*; libertate, *mss.*

[2] appellatione Graeca, *OI*; appellationes Graece, *VLW*; ap-pellationes Graeci, *NG*.

[3] ὑποθέσεις, *Wolf*: syn(*or* sin)taxis, syntasis, synthesis, *mss.*

[4] significat, *Muretus*; significabat, *mss.*   [5] M'. Otacilius, *R.G. Lewis* (*CR* 16 [1966] 271): L. Oltacilius, *mss.*

[6] Pitholaus, *Gyraldus*: Pilutus, *mss.*

was taken to court and a claim was made for the slave's
liberty, on the ground that his master had voluntarily
freed him." Such discussions they formerly called by
their Greek name of "hypotheses,"[a] but afterwards
"debates"; but they might be either fictitious or legal.

The eminent teachers of the subject, of whom any
account is to be found, are limited pretty closely to those
whom I shall mention.

II (26). Of Lucius Plotius Gallus, Cicero gives the following account in a letter to Marcus Titinnius:[b] "I well
remember that when we were boys a certain Plotius first
began to teach in Latin. When crowds flocked to him, for
all the most diligent students of the subject were trained
under him, I regretted not having the same privilege. But
I was deterred by the advice of certain men of wide experience, who believed that one's mind could better be
trained by exercises in Greek." Marcus Caelius, in a
speech in which he defended himself against a charge of
violence, implies that this same Plotius, for he lived to a
great age, supplied Caelius' accuser, Atratinus, with his
plea;[c] and without mentioning him by name, Caelius calls
him a "barley-bread rhetorician," mocking at him as
"puffy, light, and coarse."

III (27). Manius Otacilius Pitholaus is said to have
been a slave and even to have served as a doorkeeper in
chains, according to the ancient custom, until he was set
free because of his talent and interest in letters, and
helped his patron prepare his accusations. Then becom-

---

[a] ὑποθέσεις "subjects for debate" (*LSJ* s.v. II 1).

[b] The letter has not been preserved.

[c] That is, his speech in support of the charge against Caelius.

Cn. Pompeium Magnum docuit, patrisque eius res gestas, nec minus ipsius, compluribus libris exposuit; primus omnium libertinorum, ut Cornelius Nepos opinatur, scribere historiam orsus, nonnisi ab honestissimo quoque scribi solitam ad id tempus.

IV (28). M.[1] Epidius, calumnia notatus, ludum dicendi aperuit docuitque inter ceteros M. Antonium et Augustum; quibus quondam Ti.[2] Cannutius, obicientibus sibi quod in re p. administranda potissimum consularis Isaurici sectam sequeretur, malle respondit Isaurici esse discipulum quam Epidi calumniatoris. Hic Epidius ortum se a C. Epidio Nucerino praedicabat, quem ferunt olim praecipitatum in fontem fluminis Sarni, paulo post cum cornibus aureis[3] exstitisse, ac statim non comparuisse in numeroque deorum habitum.

V (29). Sextus Clodius, e Sicilia, Latinae simul Graecaeque eloquentiae professor, male oculatus et dicax, par oculorum in amicitia M. Antonii triumviri extrisse[4] se aiebat; eiusdem uxorem Fulviam, cui altera bucca inflatior erat, acumen stili tentare dixit, nec eo minus, immo vel magis ob hoc Antonio gratus. A quo mox consule ingens etiam congiarium accepit, ut ei in "Philippicis" Cicero obicit: "Adhibes[5] ioci causa magistrum, suffragio

---

[1] M., *added by Roth.*   [2] Ti., *Ernesti*: C, *mss.*

[3] aureis, *NO*: *om. others*: arietis, *Robinson.*

[4] extrisse, *Statius*; extricte, *mss.*

[5] adhibes, *Beroaldus from Cic.*; tibi et, *mss. except O, which omits, marking a lacuna.*

---

[a] Used in a double sense, implying that he had ruined his eyes by dissipation and late hours in Antony's company.

[b] Used in a double sense; she tempts me (1) to write a sharp epigram on her; (2) to lance her cheek.

ing a teacher of rhetoric, he had Gnaeus Pompeius the Great for a pupil, and wrote a history of the exploits of Pompey's father, as well as those of the son, in several volumes. In the opinion of Cornelius Nepos, he was the first of all freedmen to take up the writing of history, which up to that time had been confined to men of the highest position.

IV (28). Marcus Epidius, notorious as a blackmailer, opened a school of oratory and numbered among his pupils Mark Antony and Augustus; and when they once jeered at Tiberius Cannutius because he preferred to side with the political party of Isauricus, the ex-consul, Cannutius rejoined: "I would rather be a disciple of Isauricus than of a false accuser like Epidius." This Epidius claimed descent from Gaius Epidius of Nuceria, who, it is said, once threw himself into the source of the river Sarnus and came out shortly afterwards with golden horns on his head; then he at once disappeared and was reckoned among the number of the gods.

V (29). Sextus Clodius of Sicily, a teacher of both Greek and Latin oratory and a man with poor sight and a sharp tongue, used to say that he had worn out a pair of eyes[a] during his friendship with Mark Antony, the triumvir. He also said of the latter's wife, Fulvia, one of whose cheeks was somewhat swollen: "She tempts the point of my pen";[b] and by this witticism he rather gained than lost favour with Antony. When Antony presently became consul, Clodius received from him an enormous gift,[c] as Cicero charges against Antony in his "Philippics":[d] "For the sake of his jokes you employ a schoolmaster, elected

[c] See note on *Aug.* xli. 2.   [d] 2. 17. 42–43.

421

tuo et compotorum[1] tuorum rhetorem, cui concessisti ut
in te quae vellet diceret, salsum[2] omnino hominem, sed
materia facilis in te[3] et in tuos dicta[4] dicere. At quanta
merces rhetori est data! Audite, audite, P. C., et
cognoscite rei p. vulnera. Duo milia iugerum campi
Leontini Sex. Clodio rhetori assignasti et quidem immu-
nia, ut tanta mercede nihil sapere disceres."

VI (30). C. Albucius Silus, Novariensis, cum aedilitate
in patria fungeretur, cum[5] forte ius diceret, ab iis contra
quos pronuntiabat pedibus e tribunali detractus est.
Quod indigne ferens, statim contendit ad portam et inde
Romam, receptusque in Planci oratoris contubernium,
cui declamaturo mos erat prius aliquem qui ante diceret
excitare, suscepit eas partes, atque ita implevit ut Planco
silentium imponeret, non audenti in comparationem se
demittere.[6] Sed ex eo clarus, propria auditoria instituit,
solitus proposita controversia sedens incipere,[7] et calore
demum provectus consurgere ac perorare, declamare
autem genere[8] vario: modo splendide atque adornate,
tum, ne usque quaque scholasticus existimaretur, circum-
cise ac sordide et tantum non[9] trivialibus verbis. Egit et
causas, verum rarius, dum amplissimam quamque sec-

---

[1] compotorum, *Stephanus from Cic.*; competitorum, *mss.*
(compett-, *I*).

[2] salsum, *L* (*Pontanus*), *Beroaldus from Cic.*; *the other mss.
have* falsum. [3] in te, *omitted by VLNG.*

[4] dicta, *omitted by VLOGI.*

[5] cum, *mss.* (quom, *N*; eum, *V*); cumque, *Oudendorp, Reiff.*

[6] demittere, *J. Gronov*; dimittere, *mss.*

[7] incipere, *Faernus*; in opere, *mss.*

[8] autem genere, *Stephanus*; aut gemere, *mss.*

[9] tantum non, *VO*; tamen non, *L*; tantum modo, *NGI.*

a rhetorician by your vote and those of your pot-companions, and you have allowed him to say anything he likes about you; a witty fellow, no doubt, but it is not a hard matter to say clever things of you and your mates. But what pay does this rhetorician receive? Listen, senators, listen, and know the wounds which our country suffers. You made over to this rhetorician, Sextus Clodius, two thousand acres[a] of the Leontine territory, and free of taxes too, that at so great a price you might learn to know nothing."

VI (30). Gaius Albucius Silus of Novara, while he was holding the office of aedile in his native town and chanced to be sitting in judgment, was dragged by the feet from the tribunal by those against whom he was rendering a decision. Indignant at this, he at once made for the gate and went off to Rome. There he was admitted to the house of the orator Plancus, who had the habit, when he was going to declaim, of calling upon someone to speak before him. Albucius undertook that rôle, and filled it so effectively that he reduced Plancus to silence, since he did not venture to enter into competition. But when Albucius had thus become famous, he opened a lecture room of his own, where it was his habit after proposing a subject for a debate, to begin to speak from his seat, and then as he warmed up, to rise and make his peroration on his feet. He declaimed, too, in various manners, now in a brilliant and ornate style, and at another time, not to be thought invariably academic, speaking briefly, in everyday language and all but that of the streets. He also pleaded causes, but rather seldom, taking part only in those of

[a] The *iugerum* is literally about two-thirds of an acre.

423

tatur, nec alium in ulla locum quam perorandi. Postea
renuntiavit Foro partim pudore, partim metu; nam cum
in lite quadam centumvirali, adversario, quem ut impium
erga parentes incessebat, ius iurandum quasi per figuram
sic optulisset: "Iura per patris matrisque cineres, qui
inconditi iacent!" et alia in hunc modum, arripiente eo
condicionem, nec iudicibus aspernantibus, non sine
magna sui invidia negotium afflixit. Et rursus in cognitione caedis Mediolani apud L. Pisonem proconsulem
defendens reum, cum cohiberent lictores nimias laudan-
tium voces, et[1] ita excanduisset, ut deplorato Italiae statu,
quasi iterum in formam provinciae redigeretur, M. insuper Brutum, cuius statua in conspectu erat, invocaret
legum ac libertatis auctorem et vindicem, paene poenas
luit. Iam autem senior ob vitium vomicae Novariam
rediit, convocataque plebe causis, propter quas mori destinasset, diu ac more contionantis redditis, abstinuit cibo.

Fragmenta in Hieronymi Chronico servata

(31).   L. Cestius Pius, <Smyrnaeus rhetor, latine
Romae docuit [Ol.191.4]>.

---

[1] et, *added by Roth.*

---

[a] See note on *Aug.* xxxvi.   [b] The story is told in more
detail in Seneca, *Controv.* 7, Praef. 7. The defendant wished to
settle the case by taking oath to the truth of his contention, which
was permitted, provided the opposing counsel gave his consent.
Albucius said, "I consent, provided I may dictate the oath." But
when he challenged his opponent to swear by the ashes of his
father and mother who lay unburied, and the latter accepted the
condition, Albucius declared that he was speaking figuratively,
and had not intended to give his consent.

greatest importance, and even then confining himself to summing them up. Later he withdrew from the Forum, partly through shame and partly through fear. For in a case before the Hundred[a] he had offered his opponent, whom he was inveighing against as undutiful towards his parents, the privilege of taking oath but merely as a figure of speech, using the following language: "Swear by the ashes of your father and mother, who lie unburied"; and made other remarks in the same vein. His opponent accepted the challenge; and since the judges made no objection, Albucius lost his case to his great humiliation.[b] Again, when he was defending a client in a murder trial at Mediolanum before the proconsul Lucius Piso, and the lictors tried to suppress the immoderate applause,[c] he grew so angry that, lamenting the condition of Italy and saying that "it was being reduced once more to the form of a province," he called besides upon Marcus Brutus, whose statue was in sight, as "the founder and defender of our laws and liberties"; and for that he narrowly escaped punishment. When already well on in years, he returned to Novara because he was suffering from a tumour, called the people together and explained in a long set speech the reasons which led him to take his life, and then starved himself to death.

Fragments preserved in Jerome's Chronicle

(31). Lucius Cestius Pius,[d] <rhetorician from Smyrna, taught in Latin at Rome [13 B.C.]>.

[c] Pliny complains of this nuisance in *Epist.* 2. 14. 10 ff.
[d] Cf. Seneca the Elder *passim*; Quint. 10. 5. 20.

(32). M. Porcius Latro, <Latinus declamator, taedio duplicis quartanae semet interficit [Ol.194.1]>.

(33). Q. Curtius Rufus . . .

(34). L. Valerius Primanus . . .

(35). Verginius Flavus . . .

(36). L. Statius Ursulus, <Tolosensis, celeberrime in Gallia rhetoricam docet [Ol.209.1]>.

(37). P. Clodius Quirinalis, <rhetor Arelatensis, Romae insignissime docet [Ol.205.4]>.

(38). M. Antonius Liberalis, <Latinus rhetor, gravissimas inimicitias cum Palaemone exercet [Ol.206.4]>.

(39). Sex. Iulius Gabinianus, <celeberrimi nominis rhetor, in Gallia docuit [Ol.213.4]>.

(40). M. Fabius Quintilianus <Romam a Galba perducitur [Ol.211.4]> . . . <Quintilianus, ex Hispania Calagurritanus, primus Romae publicam scholam et salarium e fisco accepit et claruit [Ol.216.4]>.

(41). Iulius Tiro . . .

(32). Marcus Porcius Latro,[a] <Latin declaimer, commits suicide, unable to endure a double quartan fever [4 B.C.]>.

(33). Quintus Curtius Rufus[b] . . .

(34). Lucius Valerius Primanus[c] . . .

(35). Verginius Flavus[d] . . .

(36). Lucius Statius Ursulus,[c] <of Toulouse, acquires fame from teaching rhetoric in Gaul [A.D. 56]>.

(37). Publius Clodius Quirinalis,[c] <rhetorician from Arelate, teaches with distinction at Rome [A.D. 44]>.

(38). Marcus Antonius Liberalis,[c] <Latin rhetorician, engages in bitter feuding with Palaemon [A.D. 48]>.

(39). Sextus Iulius Gabinianus,[e] <a celebrated rhetorician, taught in Gaul [A.D. 76]>.

(40). Marcus Fabius Quintilianus[f] <is brought to Rome by Galba [A.D. 68]> . . . <Quintilian, from Calagurris in Spain, the first to receive a professorial appointment at Rome with a salary from the treasury, enjoyed fame [A.D. 88]>.

(41). Iulius Tiro[g] . . .

[a] Cf. Seneca the Elder *passim*; Pliny, *N.H.* 20. 160; Quint. 9. 2. 91; 10. 5. 18.

[b] Possibly the author of the *Historiae Alexandri Magni*.

[c] Otherwise unknown.

[d] A teacher of the poet Persius (*Vit. Pers.*).

[e] Mentioned with respect in Tacitus, *Dial.* 26. 8.

[f] Author of the *Institutio Oratoria*.

[g] Possibly Gaius Iulius Tiro Gaetulicus (*CIL* 2.3661).

DE POETIS

The following Index has been compiled from Jerome: L. Livius Andronicus, Cn. Naevius, T. Maccius Plautus, Q. Ennius, Statius Caecilius, P. Terentius Afer, M. Pacuvius, L. Accius, Sex. Turpilius, C. Lucilius, P. Quintius Atta, L. Afranius, L. Pomponius, T. Lucretius Carus, M. Furius Bibaculus, C. Valerius Catullus, P. Terentius Varro, D. Laberius, P. Publilius Lochius, Cornificius, M. Bavius, C. Cornelius Gallus, Aemilius Macer, Quintilius Varus, P. Vergilius Maro, Albius Tibullus, Sex. Propertius, Q. Horatius Flaccus, L. Varius Rufus, P. Ovidius Naso, Philistio, A. Persius Flaccus, M. Annaeus Lucanus.

The following Sigla are used:

For Terence: A = cod. Parisinus, 7920, eleventh century; B = cod. Parisinus, 7921; C = cod. Leidensis Vossianus, 186; D = cod. Dresdensis Elect. 539^b, Reg. D. 101; E = cod. Urbinas, 354; F = cod. Reginensis, 1496; G = cod. Neapolitanus, Mus. Borbon. 411 (all of the fifteenth century); Z = editio princeps of Donatus, Rome, 1472; Ald. = Aldine ed. of 1517; St. = ed. of Stephanus, Paris, 1529; Dz. = Dziatzko; Reiff. = Reifferscheid.

For Virgil: B = cod. Bernensis, 172, ninth or tenth century; G = cod. Sangallensis, 862, tenth century; P = cod. Parisinus Lat. 11308 (formerly Suppl. Lat. 1011), ninth

century; ᧣ = edition of Virgil by Heyne-Wagener, i. pp. lxxxi ff.

For Horace: V = cod. Blandinianus Vetustissimus; ϕ = cod. Parisinus, 7974, tenth century; ψ = cod. Parisinus, 7971, tenth century; F = ϕ and ψ; λ = Parisinus, 7972, tenth century; p = Parisinus Lat. 8214, twelfth century; ᧣ = mss. which contain the Life in an abridged form.

For Tibullus: A = cod. Ambrosianus, R 26 sup., fourteenth century; V = cod. Vaticanus, 3270; g = cod. Guelferbytanus, Ms. Aug. 82, 6 fol., both of the fifteenth century; ψ = other mss. or the Itali.

For Aulus Persius Flaccus: A = cod. Montepessulanus, 212, tenth century; B = cod. Vaticanus, tab. basil. Vat., H. 36, ninth century; P = cod. Montepessulanus, 125, formerly Pithoeanus.

For Lucan: M = cod. Montepessulanus, H. 113; B = cod. Bernensis, 45; P = cod. Parisinus, 7502, formerly Colbertinus, all of the tenth century.

DE POETIS

VITA TERENTI

I. Publius Terentius Afer, Karthagine natus, serviit Romae Terentio Lucano senatori, a quo ob ingenium et formam non institutus modo liberaliter sed et mature manumissus est. Quidam captum esse existimant, quod fieri nullo modo potuisse Fenestella docet, cum inter finem secundi Punici belli et initium tertii natus sit et[1] mortuus; nec si a Numidis et Gaetulis captus sit, ad ducem[2] Romanum pervenire potuisse, nullo commercio inter Italicos et Afros nisi post deletam Karthaginem coepto. Hic cum multis nobilibus familiariter vixit, sed maxime cum Scipione Africano et C.[3] Laelio. Quibus etiam corporis gratia conciliatus existimatur, quod et ipsum Fenestella arguit, contendens utroque maiorem natu fuisse, quamvis et Nepos aequales omnes fuisse tradat et Porcius suspicionem de consuetudine per haec faciat:

Source of text: Donatus' *Commentary on Terence.* Suetonian authorship: attested by Donatus.

[1] natus sit et, *Ald.*; et natus sit et, *Ritschl*; natus est et, *mss.*

[2] ad ducem, *mss.*; ad dominum, *J. Gronov. (Reiff., Dz.).*

[3] C., *AF; the other mss. have* cum.

ON POETS

THE LIFE OF TERENCE

I. Publius Terentius Afer, born at Carthage, was the slave at Rome of Terentius Lucanus, a senator, who because of the young man's talent and good looks not only gave him a liberal education, but soon set him free. Some think that he was taken in war, but Fenestella shows that that could not possibly be, since Terence was born and died between the end of the second Punic war and the beginning of the third;[a] and even if he had been taken by the Numidians and Gaetulians, he could not have come into the hands of a Roman general, since commerce between the Italic and the African races did not begin until after the destruction of Carthage.[b] He lived on intimate terms with many men of high rank, in particular with Scipio Africanus and Gaius Laelius. It is even thought that he won the favour of these two men by his youthful beauty, but Fenestella denies this too, maintaining that he was older than either of them. Nepos, however, writes that they were all three of an age, and Porcius rouses a suspicion of too great intimacy in the following words:

[a] Between 201 and 149 B.C.
[b] In 146 B.C.

431

Dum lasciviam nobilium et laudes fucosas petit,
Dum Africani vocem divinam inhiat[1] avidis auribus,
Dum ad Philum[2] se cenitare et Laelium pulchrum
    putat,
Dum in Albanum crebro rapitur[3] ob florem aetatis
    suae:
Post sublatis rebus ad summam inopiam redactus est.
Itaque e conspectu omnium abit Graeciam in terram
    ultimam,
Mortuos Stymphalist,[4] Arcadiae in[5] oppido. Nil
    Publius[6]
Scipio profuit, nil illi Laelius, nil Furius,
Tres per id tempus qui agitabant nobiles facillime.
Eorum ille opera ne domum quidem habuit conducti-
    ciam,
Saltem ut esset quo referret obitum domini servulus.

II. Scripsit comoedias sex, ex quibus primam
"Andriam" cum aedilibus daret, iussus ante Caecilio[7]
recitare, ad cenantem cum venisset, dictus est initium
quidem fabulae, quod erat contemptiore vestitu, subsellio
iuxta lectulum residens legisse, post paucos vero versus
invitatus ut accumberet cenasse una, dein cetera percu-
currisse non sine magna Caecilii[8] admiratione. Et hanc

---

[1] vocem divinam inhiat, *Muretus*; vocē dum et inhuius et, *A*;
the other mss. have voce divina inhiat.   [2] Philum, *Roth*; fixu,
A; *the other mss. have* furium.   [3] *The reading of Ritschl*; *A*
has dum se amari ab his credat crebro in Albanum rapitur; *the*
other mss., dum ... credit ... rapi.   [4] Stymphali, *Ritschl*;
mortuus est in falo, *A, with similar readings in the other mss.*;
Stymphalo, *Roth*.   [5] in, *added by Roth*.   [6] Publio, *E*
(*Ritschl*).   [7] caerio, *AB*; cenam, *G*; *the other mss. have* cerio.

[8] caerii, *A*; eorum, *G*; *the other mss. have* cerii (cerrii, cerei).

Though he courted the wantonness of great men and their counterfeit[a] praise, though with greedy ears he drank in the divine voice of Africanus, though he thought it fine to frequent the tables of Philus and Laelius, though he was often taken to the Alban villa because of his youthful charms, he later found himself stripped of his all and reduced to utmost want. So he withdrew from the sight of men to a remote part of Greece and died at Stymphalus, a town of Arcady. Naught availed him Publius Scipio, naught Laelius, naught Furius, the three wealthiest[b] nobles of that time. Their help did not give him even a rented house, to provide at least a place where his slave might announce his master's death.

II. He wrote six comedies, and when he offered the first of these, the "Andria," to the aediles, they bade him first read it to Caecilius. Having come to the poet's house when he was dining, and being meanly clad, Terence is said to have read the beginning of his play sitting on a bench near the great man's couch. But after a few lines he was invited to take his place at table, and after dining with Caecilius, he ran through the rest to his host's great

---

[a] Cf. Hor. *Epist.* 1. 10. 26 ff.: *Non qui Sidonio contendere callidus ostro Nescit Aquinatem potantia vellera fucum, Certius accipiet damnum propiusve medullis, Quam qui non poterit vero distinguere falsum.*

[b] *facillime agitare* means "to live most comfortably," or, "most free from care"; cf. Ter. *Adelph.* 501, and the Greek ῥεῖα ζῶντες. In an opposite sense we have *difficultate nummaria, Tib.* xlviii. 1.

autem et quinque reliquas aequaliter populo probavit,
quamvis Vulcatius in dinumeratione omnium ita scribat:

Sumetur Hecyra sexta ex his fabula.

"Eunuchus" quidem bis die acta est meruitque pretium
quantum nulla antea cuiusquam comoedia, id est octo
milia nummorum; propterea summa quoque titulo
ascribitur. Nam "Adelphorum" principium Varro etiam
praefert principio Menandri.

III. Non obscura fama est adiutum Terentium in
scriptis a Laelio et Scipione, eamque ipse auxit numquam
nisi leviter refutare[1] conatus, ut in prologo "Adelphorum":

> Nam quod isti dicunt malevoli, homines nobiles
> Hunc adiutare assidueque una scribere;
> Quod illi maledictum vehemens esse existumant,
> Eam laudem hic ducit maxumam, quom illis placet
> Qui vobis univorsis et populo placent,
> Quorum opera in bello, in otio, in negotio
> Suo quisque tempore usus est sine superbia.

Videtur autem se levius defendisse, quia sciebat et Laelio
et Scipioni non ingratam esse hanc opinionem; quae
tamen magis et usque ad posteriora tempora valuit. C.
Memmius in oratione pro se ait: "P. Africanus, qui a Terentio personam mutuatus, quae domi luserat ipse,
nomine illius in scaenam detulit." Nepos auctore certo

---

[1] refutare, A; *the other mss. have* se tutare (tutari, F).

---

[a] Text and meaning are uncertain. Dziatzko suggested *sub-maeret (poeta) Hecyra sexta exclusa fabula.*
[b] The *didascalia.*   [c] That is, presumably, the beginning of
the play of Menander on which the *Adelphoe* is based.

admiration. Moreover, this play and the five others were equally pleasing to the people, although Vulcatius, in enumerating them all, writes thus:

> The sixth play, the 'Hecyra,' will not be included.[a]

The "Eunuch" was even acted twice in the same day and earned more money than any previous comedy of any writer, namely eight thousand sesterces; and for this reason the sum is included in the title-page.[b] Indeed Varro rates the beginning of the "Adelphoe" above that of Menander.[c]

III. It is common gossip that Scipio and Laelius aided Terence in his writings, and he himself lent colour to this by never attempting to refute it, except in a half-hearted way, as in the prologue to the "Adelphoe":

> For as to what those malicious critics say, that men of rank aid your poet and constantly write in concert with him; what they regard as a grievous slander, he considers the highest praise, to please those who please you all and all the people, whose timely help everyone has used without shame in war, in leisure, in business.

Now he seems to have made but a lame defence, because he knew that the report did not displease Laelius and Scipio; and it gained ground in spite of all and came down even to later times. Gaius Memmius in a speech in his own defence says: "Publius Africanus, who borrowed a mask from Terence, and put upon the stage under his name what he had written himself for his own amusement at home." Nepos says that he learned from a trustworthy

comperisse se ait, C. Laelium quondam in Puteolano Kal. Martiis admonitum ab uxore temperius ut discumberet petisse ab ea ne interpellaret,[1] seroque tandem ingressum triclinium dixisse, non saepe in scribendo magis sibi successisse; deinde rogatum ut scripta illa proferret pronuntiasse versus qui sunt in "Heautontimorumeno":

Satis pol proterve me Syri promissa huc induxerunt.

IV. Santra Terentium existimat, si modo in scribendo adiutoribus indiguerit, non tam Scipione et Laelio uti potuisse, qui tunc adulescentuli fuerunt, quam C. Sulpicio Gallo, homine docto et cuius consularibus[2] ludis initium fabularum dandarum fecerit, vel Q. Fabio Labeone et M. Popillio, consulari utroque ac poeta; ideo ipsum non iuvenes designare qui se adiuvare dicantur,[3] sed viros "quorum operam et in bello et in otio et in negotio" populus sit expertus.

Post editas comoedias nondum quintum atque vicesimum egressus annum,[4] causa vitandae opinionis qua videbatur aliena pro suis edere, seu percipiendi Graecorum instituta moresque, quos non perinde exprimeret in scriptis, egressus[5] est neque amplius rediit. De morte eius Vulcatius sic tradit:

Sed ut Afer populo sex dedit comoedias,

[1] interpellaret, *A*; interpolleretur, *F*; *the other mss. have* interpellaretur.

[2] et cuius consularibus, *A*; et consularibus, *D*; *the other mss. have* et qui consularibus; quo consule Megalensibus, *Ritschl*.

[3] dicantur, *Roth*; dicuntur, *A*; designarentur, *D*; *the other mss. have* dicerentur.

[4] annum animi, *A*; animi causa seu, *Dz.* (aut, *Bährens*).

[5] egressus urbe, *Muretus*; urbem, *St.*

source that once at his villa at Puteoli Gaius Laelius was urged by his wife to come to dinner on the Kalends of March[a] at an earlier hour than common, but begged her not to interrupt him. When he at last entered the dining-room at a late hour, he said that he had seldom written more to his own satisfaction; and on being asked to read what he had written, he declaimed the lines of the "Heau-tontimorumenos," beginning:

Impudently enough, by Heaven, has Syrus lured me here by promises.

IV. Santra thinks that if Terence had really needed help in his writing, he would not have been so likely to resort to Scipio and Laelius, who were then mere youths, as to Gaius Sulpicius Gallus, a scholarly man, at whose consular games he brought out his first play, or to Quintus Fabius Labeo and Marcus Popillius, both of whom were ex-consuls and poets; and that it was for that reason that he spoke, not of "young men" who were said to help him, but "men whose mettle the people had tried in war, in leisure, in business."

After publishing these comedies before he had passed his twenty-fifth year, either to escape from the gossip about publishing the work of others as his own, or else to become versed in Greek manners and customs, which he felt that he had not been wholly successful in depicting in his plays, he left Rome and never returned. Of his death Vulcatius writes in these words:

But when Afer had presented six comedies to the

[a] See note c on *Vesp.* xix. 1.

Iter hinc in Asiam fecit, et[1] navem ut semel
Conscendit, visus numquam est; sic vita vacat.

V. Q. Cosconius redeuntem e Graecia perisse in mari
dicit cum C et VIII[2] fabulis conversis a Menandro.
Ceteri mortuum esse in Arcadia Stymphali[3] sive
Leucadiae[4] tradunt Cn. Cornelio Dolabella M. Fulvio
Nobiliore consulibus, morbo implicitum[5] ex dolore ac
taedio amissarum sarcinarum,[6] quas in nave praemiserat,
ac simul fabularum, quas novas fecerat.

Fuisse dicitur mediocri statura, gracili corpore, colore
fusco. Reliquit filiam, quae post equiti Romano nupsit;
item hortulos XX iugerum via Appia ad Martis villam.
Quo magis miror Porcium scribere:

Scipio nihil profuit, nihil Laelius, nihil Furius,
Tres per id tempus qui agitabant nobiles facillime;
Eorum ille opera ne domum quidem habuit conducti-
ciam,
Saltem ut esset quo referret obitum domini servu-
lus.[7]

Hunc Afranius quidem omnibus comicis praefert
scribens in "Compitalibus":

Terenti non similem dicas[8] quempiam.

---

[1] et, *added by Roth*; navem autem, *Ritschl*.   [2] C et VIII,
omitted by Ritschl, Dz.   [3] *Omitted as interpolation by
Ritschl, Reiff.*   [4] sive Leucadiae, *A; the other mss. have* sinu
Leucadiae; sinu Leucadiae *after* mari, *Dz.*; Leucadia, *Erasmus.*

[5] implicita ac, *A; the other mss. have* implicitum acri.

[6] sarcinarum, *A; the other mss. have* fabularum.

[7] *The last two lines are regarded as an interpolation by
Ritschl, Reiff.*   [8] dicas, *Ritschl:* dicens, *mss.*

people, he journeyed from here to Asia, but from the time he embarked was never seen again; thus he vanished from life.

V. Quintus Cosconius writes that he was lost at sea as he was returning from Greece with one hundred and eight plays adapted from Menander; the rest of our authorities declare that he died at Stymphalus in Arcadia, or at Leucadia, in the consulship[a] of Gnaeus Cornelius Dolabella and Marcus Fulvius Nobilior, having fallen ill from grief and annoyance at losing his baggage, which he had sent on to the ship, and with it the new plays which he had written.

He is said to have been of moderate height, slender and of dark complexion. He left a daughter, who afterwards became the wife of a Roman knight; also gardens twenty acres[b] in extent on the Appian Way, near the villa of Mars. This makes me feel the more surprised that Porcius should write:

Naught availed him Scipio, naught Laelius, naught Furius, the three wealthiest nobles of that time. Their aid did not even give him a rented house, to provide at least a place where his slave might announce his master's death.

Afranius ranks Terence above all other writers of comedy, writing in his "Compitalia":

You would not call anyone the equal of Terence.

[a] In 159 B.C.
[b] See note on *Rhet.* v.

Vulcatius autem non solum Naevio et Plauto et Caecilio, sed Licinio quoque et Atilio postponit. Cicero in "Limone" hactenus laudat:

> Tu quoque, qui solus lecto sermone, Terenti,
> Conversum expressumque Latina voce Menandrum
> In medium nobis sedatis vocibus[1] effers,
> Quiddam come loquens atque omnia dulcia dicens.

Item C. Caesar:

> Tu quoque, tu in summis, o dimidiate Menander,
> Poneris, et merito, puri sermonis amator.
> Lenibus atque utinam scriptis adiuncta foret vis,
> Comica ut aequato virtus polleret honore
> Cum Graecis neve[2] hac despectus parte iaceres!
> Unum hoc maceror ac doleo tibi desse,[3] Terenti.

Haec Suetonius Tranquillus.

---

[1] vocibus, *mss.*; motibus, *Ritschl.*
[2] neve, *Roth*; neque, *mss.*
[3] desse, *Ritschl*; deesse, *mss.* (derē, A).

But Vulcatius[a] puts him not only below Naevius, Plautus, and Caecilius, but even below Licinius and Atilius. Cicero in his "Limo"[b] gives him this much praise:

> Thou, Terence, who alone dost reclothe Menander in choice speech, and rendering him into the Latin tongue, dost present him with thy quiet utterance[c] on our public stage, speaking with a certain graciousness and with sweetness in every word.

Also Gaius Caesar:[d]

> Thou too, even thou, art ranked among the highest, thou half-Menander, and justly, thou lover of language undefiled. But would that thy graceful verses had force as well, so that thy comic power might have equal honour with that of the Greeks, and thou mightest not be scorned in this regard and neglected. It hurts and pains me, my Terence, that thou lackest this one quality.

So the account of Suetonius Tranquillus.

[a] In his celebrated "canon," Gell. 15. 24.

[b] "Meadow," a fanciful title for a book of miscellaneous contents, like the "Silvae" of Statius, the "Pratum" of Suetonius, and the like.

[c] Perhaps, "amid a hush of silence" in the audience. Because of the awkwardness of *voce . . . vocibus* Ritschl preferred *motibus* (*animi*).

[d] Referring to Julius Caesar.

VITA VERGILI

1   P. Vergilius Maro Mantuanus parentibus modicis fuit
ac praecipue patre, quem quidam opificem figulum,
plures Magi cuiusdam viatoris initio mercennarium, mox
ob industriam generum tradiderunt, egregieque substan-
tiae silvis coemendis et apibus curandis auxisse reculam.
2   Natus est Cn. Pompeio Magno M. Licinio Crasso primum
coss. Iduum Octobrium die in pago qui Andes dicitur et
3   abest a Mantua non procul. Praegnans eo mater somniavit enixam se laureum ramum, quem contactu terrae
coaluisse et excrevisse ilico in speciem maturae arboris
refertaeque variis pomis et floribus, ac sequenti luce cum
marito rus propinquum petens ex itinere devertit atque in
4   subiecta fossa partu levata est. Ferunt infantem ut sit editus neque vagisse et adeo miti vultu fuisse, ut haud
5   dubiam spem prosperioris geniturae iam tum daret. Et
accessit aliud praesagium, siquidem virga populea more
regionis in puerperiis eodem statim loco depacta ita brevi
evaluit tempore, ut multo ante satas populos adaequavis-
set, quae arbor Vergilii ex eo dicta atque etiam consecrata
est summa gravidarum ac fetarum religione suscipien-
tium ibi et solventium vota.
6   Initia aetatis Cremonae egit usque ad virilem togam,
quam XV.[1] anno natali suo accepit iisdem illis consulibus

Source of text: preface of Virgil mss., written by Donatus.
Suetonian authorship: assured.

[1] XVII, *BP*; VII, *G*.

---

[a] Oct. 15, 70 B.C.   [b] In 55 B.C.

THE LIFE OF VIRGIL

Publius Vergilius Maro, a native of Mantua, had parents of humble origin, especially his father, who according to some was a potter, although the general opinion is that he was at first the hired man of a certain Magus, an attendant on the magistrates, later became his son-in-law because of his diligence, and greatly increased his little property by buying up woodlands and raising bees. He was born in the first consulship of Gnaeus Pompeius the Great and Marcus Licinius Crassus, on the Ides of October,[a] in a district called Andes, not far distant from Mantua. While he was in his mother's womb, she dreamt that she gave birth to a laurel-branch, which on touching the earth took root and grew at once to the size of a full-grown tree, covered with fruits and flowers of various kinds; and on the following day, when she was on the way to a neighbouring part of the country with her husband, she turned aside and gave birth to her child in a ditch beside the road. They say that the infant did not cry at its birth, and had such a gentle expression as even then to give assurance of an unusually happy destiny. There was added another omen; for a poplar branch, which, as was usual in that region on such occasions, was at once planted where the birth occurred, grew so fast in a short time that it equalled in size poplars planted long before. It was called from him "Virgil's tree" and was besides worshipped with great veneration by pregnant and newly delivered women, who made and paid vows beneath it.

Virgil spent his early life at Cremona until he assumed the gown of manhood, upon his fifteenth birthday, in the consulship[b] of the same two men who had been consuls

iterum duobus,[1] quibus erat natus, evenitque ut eo ipso
7 die Lucretius poeta decederet. Sed Vergilius a Cremona
8 Mediolanum et inde paulo post transiit in urbem.
Corpore et statura fuit grandi, aquilo colore, facie rusti-
cana, valetudine varia; nam plerumque a stomacho et a
faucibus ac dolore capitis laborabat, sanguinem etiam
9 saepe reiecit. Cibi vinique minimi; libidinis in pueros
pronioris,[2] quorum maxime dilexit Cebetem et Alexandrum, quem secunda "Bucolicorum" ecloga Aleximᵃ
appellat, donatum sibi ab Asinio Pollione, utrumque non
ineruditum, Cebetem vero et poetam. Vulgatum est con-
10 suesse eum et cum Plotia Hieria. Sed Asconius Pedianus
adfirmat, ipsam postea maiorem natu narrare solitam,
invitatum quidem a Vario ad communionem sui, verum
11 pertinacissime recusasse. Cetera sane vitae et ore et
animo tam probum constat, ut Neapoli Parthenias vulgo
appellatus sit, ac si quando Romae, quo rarissime commeabat, viseretur in publico, sectantis demonstrantisque se
12 subterfugeret[3] in proximum tectum. Bona autem cuiusdam exsulantis offerente Augusto non sustinuit accipere.
13 Possedit prope centiens sestertium ex liberalitatibus amicorum habuitque domum Romae Esquiliis iuxta hortos
Maecenatianos, quamquam secessu Campaniae Sicili-
aeque plurimum uteretur.
14 Parentes iam grandis amisit, ex quibus patrem captum
oculis, et duos fratres germanos, Silonem inpuberem,

---

[1] duobus, *omitted by G.*

[2] promoris, *G*; pronior his, *BP.*

[3] subter fugere, *G*; subterfugere solitum, *ᛉ*; suffugere, *BP*;
suffugeret, *Reiff.*

ᵃ "The Maiden."

444

the year he was born; and it chanced that the poet Lucretius died that very same day. Virgil, however, moved from Cremona to Mediolanum, and shortly afterwards from there to Rome. He was tall and of full habit, with a dark complexion and a rustic appearance. His health was variable; for he very often suffered from stomach and throat troubles, as well as with headache; and he also had frequent haemorrhages. He ate and drank but little. He was especially given to passions for boys, and his special favourites were Cebes and Alexander, whom he calls Alexis in the second poem of his "Bucolics." This boy was given him by Asinius Pollio, and both his favourites had some education, while Cebes was even a poet. It is common report that he also had an intrigue with Plotia Hieria. But Asconius Pedianus declares that she herself used to say afterwards, when she was getting old, that Virgil was invited by Varius to associate with her, but obstinately refused. Certain it is that for the rest of his life he was so modest in speech and thought, that at Naples he was commonly called "Parthenias,"[a] and that whenever he appeared in public in Rome, where he very rarely went, he would take refuge in the nearest house, to avoid those who followed and pointed him out. Moreover, when Augustus offered him the property of a man who had been exiled, he could not bring himself to accept it. He possessed nearly ten million sesterces from the generous gifts of friends, and he had a house at Rome on the Esquiline, near the gardens of Maecenas, although he usually lived in retirement in Campania and in Sicily.

He was already grown up when he lost his parents, of whom his father previously went blind, and two full brothers: Silo, who died in childhood, and Flaccus, who

445

Flaccum iam adultum, cuius exitum sub nomine Daphnidis deflet.

15 Inter cetera studia medicinae quoque ac maxime mathematicae operam dedit. Egit et causam apud
16 iudices unam omnino nec amplius quam semel; nam et in sermone tardissimum eum ac paene indocto similem fuisse Melissus tradidit.

17 Poeticam puer adhuc auspicatus in Ballistam ludi magistrum ob infamiam latrociniorum coopertum lapidibus distichon fecit:

> Monte sub hoc lapidum tegitur Ballista sepultus;
> Nocte die tutum carpe, viator, iter.

Deinde "Catalepton"[1] et "Priapea" et "Epigrammata" et "Diras," item "Cirim" et "Culicem," cum esset annorum XVI. Cuius materia talis est. Pastor fatigatus aestu
18 cum sub arbore condormisset et serpens ad eum proreperet,[2] e palude culex provolavit atque inter duo tempora aculeum fixit pastori. At ille continuo culicem contrivit[3] et serpentem interemit ac sepulchrum culici statuit et distichon fecit:

> Parve culex, pecudum custos tibi tale merenti
> Funeris officium vitae pro munere reddit.

19 Scripsit etiam de qua ambigitur "Aetnam." Mox cum res Romanas incohasset, offensus materia ad "Bucolica"

---

[1] *The mss. have* catalecton.
[2] proriperet, *B*[1]*P*; praereperet, *G*.
[3] attrivit (adt-), *BP*.

---

[a] *Ecl.* 5. 20.　　[b] *Culex*, 413 f.

lived to grow up, and whose death he laments under the name of Daphnis.[a]

Among other studies he gave attention also to medicine and in particular to mathematics. He pleaded one single case in court too, but no more; for, as Melissus has told us, he spoke very slowly and almost like an uneducated man.

He made his first attempt at poetry when he was still a boy, composing the following couplet on a schoolmaster called Ballista, who was stoned to death because of his evil reputation for brigandage:

> Under this mountain of stones Ballista is covered
>   and buried;
>   Wayfarer, now night and day follow your course
>   without fear.

Then he wrote the "Catalepton," "Priapea," "Epigrams" and the "Dirae," as well as the "Ciris" and the "Culex," when he was sixteen years old. The story of the "Culex" is this. When a shepherd, exhausted by the heat, had fallen asleep under a tree, and a snake was creeping upon him, a gnat flew from a marsh and stung the shepherd between his two temples; he at once crushed the gnat and killed the snake; then he made a tomb for the insect, inscribed with this couplet:

> Thee, tiny gnat, well deserving, the flock's grateful
>   keeper now offers
> For the gift of his life due funeral rites in requital.[b]

He also wrote the "Aetna," though its authorship is disputed. Presently he began to write of Roman history,

transiit, maxime ut Asinium Pollionem, Alfenum Varum et Cornelium Gallum celebraret, quia in distributione agrorum, qui post Philippensem victoriam veteranis triumvirorum iussu trans Padum dividebantur, indem-

20 nem se praestitissent. Deinde scripsit "Georgica" in honorem Maecenatis, qui sibi mediocriter adhuc noto opem tulisset adversus veterani cuiusdam violentiam, a quo in altercatione litis agrariae paulum afuit quin occideretur.

21 Novissime "Aeneidem" incohavit, argumentum varium ac multiplex et quasi amborum Homeri carminum instar, praeterea nominibus ac rebus Graecis Latinisque commune, et in quo, quod maxime studebat, Romanae simul

22 urbis et Augusti origo contineretur. Cum "Georgica" scriberet, traditur cotidie meditatos mane plurimos versus dictare solitus ac per totum diem retractando ad paucissimos redigere, non absurde carmen se more ursae

23 parere dicens et lambendo demum effingere. "Aeneida" prosa prius oratione formatam digestamque in XII libros particulatim componere instituit, prout liberet quidque,

24 et nihil in ordinem arripiens. Ac[1] ne quid impetum moraretur, quaedam inperfecta transmisit, alia levissimis verbis veluti fulsit, quae per iocum pro tibicinibus interponi aiebat ad sustinendum opus, donec solidae columnae advenirent.

25   "Bucolica" triennio, "Georgica" VII, "Aeneida" XI

---

[1] ac, *G*; ut, *BP*.

but thinking himself unequal to the subject turned to the "Bucolics," especially in order to sing the praises of Asinius Pollio, Alfenus Varus, and Cornelius Gallus, because at the time of the assignment of the lands beyond the Po, which were divided among the veterans by order of the triumvirs after the victory at Philippi, these men had saved him from ruin. Then he wrote the "Georgics" in honour of Maecenas, because he had rendered him aid, when the poet was still but little known, against the violence of one of the veterans, from whom Virgil narrowly escaped death in a quarrel about his farm. Last of all he began the "Aeneid," a varied and complicated theme, and as it were a mirror of both the poems of Homer; moreover it treated Greek and Latin personages and affairs in common, and contained at the same time an account of the origin of the city of Rome and of Augustus, which was the poet's special aim. When he was writing the "Georgics," it is said to have been his custom to dictate each day a large number of verses which he had composed in the morning, and then to spend the rest of the day in reducing them to a very small number, wittily remarking that he fashioned his poem after the manner of a she-bear, and gradually licked it into shape. In the case of the "Aeneid," after writing a first draft in prose and dividing it into twelve books, he proceeded to turn into verse one part after another, taking them up just as he fancied, in no particular order. And that he might not check the flow of his thought, he left some things unfinished, and, so to speak, bolstered others up with very slight words, which, as he jocosely used to say, were put in like props, to support the structure until the solid columns should arrive.

The "Bucolics" he finished in three years, the "Geor-

26   perfecit annis. "Bucolica" eo successu edidit, ut in
scaena[1] quoque per cantores crebro pronuntiarentur.
27   "Georgica" reverso post Actiacam victoriam Augusto
atque Atellae reficiendarum faucium causa commoranti
per continuum quadriduum legit, suscipiente Maecenate
legendi vicem, quotiens interpellaretur ipse vocis offen-
28   sione. Pronuntiabat autem cum suavitate et[2] lenociniis
29   miris. Ac[3] Seneca tradidit, Iulium Montanum poetam
solitum dicere, involaturum se Vergilio quaedam, si et
vocem posset et os et hypocrisin; eosdem enim versus
ipso pronuntiante bene sonare, sine illo inanes esse
30   mutosque. "Aeneidos" vixdum coeptae tanta exstitit
fama, ut Sextus Propertius non dubitaverit sic praedicare:

> Cedite, Romani scriptores, cedite Grai:
>   Nescio quid maius nascitur Iliade.

31   Augustus vero—nam forte expeditione Cantabrica
aberat—supplicibus atque etiam minacibus per iocum litteris efflagitarat, ut "sibi de 'Aeneide,'" ut ipsius verba
sunt, "vel prima carminis ὑπογραφὴ vel quodlibet κῶλον
32   mitteretur." Cui tamen multo post perfectaque demum
materia tres omnino libros recitavit, primum,[4] quartum
et sextum, sed hunc notabili Octaviae adfectione, quae
cum recitationi interesset, ad illos de filio suo versus, "tu
Marcellus eris," defecisse fertur atque aegre focilata.
33   Recitavit et pluribus, sed neque frequenter et ea fere

---

[1] scenam, *BP*; sena, *G*.   [2] suavitate et, ᔑ; suavitate cum,
BP; suavitatem, *G*.   [3] ac, *Hagen*; et, *Reiff.*; ut, *mss.*
[4] primum, *Ribbeck, Murgia*: secundum, *mss.*

---

[a] 2. 34. 65 f.   [b] *Aen.* 6. 884 f.

gics" in seven, the "Aeneid" in eleven. The success of the
"Bucolics" on their first appearance was such that they
were even frequently rendered by singers on the stage.
When Augustus was returning after his victory at Actium
and lingered at Atella to treat his throat, Virgil read the
"Georgics" to him for four days in succession, Maecenas
taking his turn at the reading whenever the poet was
interrupted by the failure of his voice. His own delivery,
however, was sweet and wonderfully effective. In fact,
Seneca has said that the poet Julius Montanus used to
declare that he would have purloined some of Virgil's
work, if he could also have stolen his voice, expression,
and dramatic power; for the same verses sounded well
when Virgil read them, which on another's lips were flat
and toneless. Hardly was the "Aeneid" begun, when its
repute became so great that Sextus Propertius[a] did not
hesitate to declare:

> Yield, ye Roman writers; yield, ye Greeks;
>   A greater than the Iliad is born.

Augustus indeed (for it chanced that he was away on
his Cantabrian campaign) demanded in entreating and
even jocosely threatening letters that Virgil send him
"something from the 'Aeneid'"; to use his own words,
"either the first draft of the poem or any section of it that
he pleased." But it was not until long afterwards, when
the material was at last in shape, that Virgil read to him
three books in all, the first, fourth, and sixth. The last of
these produced a remarkable effect on Octavia, who was
present at the reading; for it is said that when he reached
the verses about her son, "Thou shalt be Marcellus,"[b] she
fainted and was with difficulty revived. He gave readings

451

de quibus ambigebat, quo magis iudicium hominum
34 experiretur. Erotem librarium et libertum eius exactae
iam senectutis tradunt referre solitum, quondam eum in
recitando duos dimidiatos versus complesse ex tempore.
Nam cum hactenus haberet: "Misenum Aeoliden"
adiecisse: "quo non praestantior alter," item huic: "aere
ciere viros," simili calore iactatum subiunxisse: "Martemque accendere cantu," statimque sibi imperasse ut utrumque volumini ascriberet.

35   Anno aetatis quinquagesimo secundo inpositurus
"Aeneidi" summam manum statuit in Graeciam et in
Asiam secedere triennioque continuo nihil amplius quam
emendare, ut reliqua vita tantum philosophiae vacaret.
Sed cum ingressus iter Athenis occurrisset Augusto ab
Oriente Romam revertenti destinaretque non absistere
atque etiam una redire, dum Megara vicinum oppidum
ferventissimo sole cognoscit, languorem nactus est
eumque non intermissa navigatione auxit ita ut gravior[1]
aliquanto Brundisium appelleret, ubi diebus paucis obiit
36 XI. Kal. Octobr. Cn. Sentio Q. Lucretio coss. Ossa eius
Neapolim translata sunt tumuloque condita qui est via
Puteolana intra lapidem secundum, in quo distichon fecit
tale:

Mantua me genuit, Calabri rapuere, tenet nunc
    .Parthenope; cecini pascua rura duces.

---

[1] gravior, *mss.*; aegrior, *Hagen.*

[a] *Aen.* 6. 164.
[b] *Aen.* 6. 165.
[c] Sept. 21, 19 B.C.

also to various others, but never before a large company, selecting for the most part passages about which he was in doubt, in order to get the benefit of criticism. They say that Eros, his amanuensis and freedman, used to report, when he was an old man, that Virgil once completed two half-verses off-hand in the course of a reading. For having before him merely the words "Misenum Aeoliden," he added "quo non praestantior alter,"[a] and again to "aere ciere viros" he joined "Martemque accendere cantu,"[b] thrown off with like inspiration, and he immediately ordered Eros to add both half-lines to his manuscript.

In the fifty-second year of his age, wishing to give the final touch to the "Aeneid," he determined to go away to Greece and Asia, and after devoting three entire years to the sole work of improving his poem, to give up the rest of his life wholly to philosophy. But having begun his journey, and at Athens meeting Augustus, who was on his way back to Rome from the Orient, he resolved not to part from the emperor and even to return with him; but in the course of a visit to the neighbouring town of Megara in a very hot sun, he was taken with a fever, and added to his disorder by continuing his journey; hence on his arrival at Brundisium he was considerably worse, and died there on the eleventh day before the Kalends of October, in the consulship of Gnaeus Sentius and Quintus Lucretius.[c] His ashes were taken to Naples and laid to rest on the via Puteolana less than two miles from the city, in a tomb for which he himself composed this couplet:

Mantua gave me the light, Calabria slew me; now holds me
    Parthenope. I have sung shepherds, the country, and wars.

37 Heredes fecit ex dimidia parte Valerium Proculum fratrem alio patre, ex quarta Augustum, ex duodecima Maecenatem, ex reliqua L. Varium et Plotium Tuccam, qui eius "Aeneida" post obitum iussu Caesaris emendav-

38 erunt. De qua re Sulpicii Carthaginiensis exstant huius-modi versus:

> Iusserat haec rapidis aboleri carmina flammis
> Vergilius, Phrygium quae cecinere ducem.
> Tucca vetat Variusque; simul tu, maxime Caesar,
> Non sinis et Latiae consulis historiae.
> Infelix gemino cecidit prope Pergamon igni,
> Et paene est alio Troia cremata[1] rogo.

39 Egerat cum Vario, priusquam Italia decederet, ut si-quid sibi accidisset, "Aeneida" combureret; at is[2] ita fac-turum se pernegarat; igitur in extrema valetudine assidue scrinia desideravit, crematurus ipse; verum nemine of-

40 ferente nihil quidem nominatim de ea cavit. Ceterum eidem Vario ac simul Tuccae scripta sua sub ea condi-cione legavit, ne quid ederent, quod non a se editum

41 esset. Edidit autem auctore Augusto Varius, sed summa-tim emendata, ut qui versus etiam inperfectos sicut[3]

---

[1] cremata sepulta, *G*; sepulta, *Hagen*.
[2] at is, *Hagen*; sed is, *Reiff.*; et is, *BP*; *omitted* (Italia . . . at is) *by G.*
[3] sicut, *Gronov*; si qui, *mss.*

---

[a] Cf. *Aug.* ci. 3.

He named as his heirs Valerius Proculus, his half-brother, to one-half of his estate, Augustus to one-fourth, Maecenas to one-twelfth; the rest he left to Lucius Varius and Plotius Tucca, who revised the "Aeneid" after his death by order of Augustus. With regard to this matter we have the following verses of Sulpicius of Carthage:

> Virgil had bidden these songs by swift flame be
> turned into ashes,
> Songs which sang of thy fates, Phrygia's leader
> renowned.
> Varius and Tucca forbade, and thou, too, greatest of
> Caesars,
> Adding your veto to theirs, Latium's story
> preserved.
> All but twice in the flames unhappy Pergamum
> perished
> Troy on a second pyre narrowly failed of her
> doom.

He had arranged with Varius, before leaving Italy, that if anything befell him[a] his friend should burn the "Aeneid"; but Varius had emphatically declared that he would do no such thing. Therefore in his mortal illness Virgil constantly called for his book-boxes, intending to burn the poem himself; but when no one brought them to him, he made no specific request about the matter, but left his writings jointly to the above mentioned Varius and to Tucca, with the stipulation that they should publish nothing which he himself would not have given to the world. However, Varius published the "Aeneid" at Augustus' request, making only a few slight corrections, and even leaving the incomplete lines just as they were.

erant reliquerit; quos multi mox supplere conati non
perinde valuerunt ob difficultatem, quod omnia fere apud
eum hemistichia absoluto perfectoque sunt sensu,
42 praeter illud: "quem tibi iam Troia." Nisus grammaticus
audisse se a senioribus aiebat, Varium duorum librorum
ordinem commutasse, et qui nunc secundus sit in tertium
locum transtulisse, etiam primi libri correxisse principium, his versibus demptis:

> Ille ego qui quondam gracili modulatus avena
> Carmina et egressus silvis vicina coegi,
> Ut quamvis avido parerent arva colono,
> Gratum opus agricolis, at nunc horrentia Martis—
> Arma virumque cano.

43 Obtrectatores Vergilio numquam defuerunt, nec
mirum; nam nec Homero quidem. Prolatis "Bucolicis"
Numitorius quidam rescripsit "Antibucolica," duas modo
eclogas, sed insulsissime παρῳδήσας quarum prioris initium est:

> Tityre, si toga calda tibi est, quo 'tegmine fagi'?

sequentis:

> Dic mihi Damoeta: 'cuium pecus' anne Latinum?
> Non, verum Aegonis nostri; sic rure loquuntur.

---

[a] *Aen.* 3. 340.
[b] I.e., the original order was 3, 1, and 2.

These last many afterwards tried to finish, but failed
owing to the difficulty that nearly all the half-lines in Virgil are complete in sense and meaning, the sole exception
being "quem tibi iam Troia."[a] The grammarian Nisus
used to say that he had heard from older men that Varius
changed the order of two of the books and made what is
now the second book the third;[b] also that he emended the
beginning of the first book by striking out the lines:

> I who on slender reed once rustic numbers did
>   render,
> Parting then from the groves, commanded the
>   neighbouring fallows
> Tribute to pay to their lords, however much they
>   exacted,
> Task hailed with joy by farmers; but now dread
>   deeds of the war-god,
> Arms and the hero I sing.

Virgil never lacked detractors, which is not strange; for
neither did Homer. When the "Bucolics" appeared, a certain Numitorius wrote "Anti-bucolics," consisting of but
two poems, which were a very insipid parody. The first
began as follows:

> Tityrus, if a warm toga you have, why then a beech
>   mantle?

The second:

> Tell me, Damoetas, I pray, is 'cuium pecus' really
>   good Latin?
> Nay, but our Aegon's way, and thus men talk in the
>   country.

Alius recitante eo ex "Georgicis": "nudus ara, sere nudus"
44 subiecit: "habebis frigore febrem." Est et adversus
"Aeneida" liber Carvili Pictoris, titulo "Aeneomastix." M.
Vipsanius a Maecenate eum suppositum appellabat novae
cacozeliae repertore, non tumidae nec exilis, sed ex com-
munibus verbis, atque ideo latentis. Herennius tantum
45 vitia eius, Perellius Faustus furta contraxit. Sed et Q.
Octavi Aviti Ὁμοιοτήτων octo volumina quos et unde
46 versus transtulerit continent. Asconius Pedianus libro,
quem "Contra obtrectatores Vergilii" scripsit, pauca
admodum obiecta ei proponit eaque circa historiam fere
et quod pleraque ab Homero sumpsisset; sed hoc ipsum
crimen sic defendere adsuetum ait: cur non illi quoque
eadem furta temptarent? Verum intellecturos facilius
esse Herculi clavam quam Homero versum subripere. Et
tamen destinasse secedere ut omnia ad satietatem
malevolorum decideret.

Another man, when Virgil recited from his "Georgics,"
"nudus ara, sere nudus,"[a] added "habebis frigore
febrem."[b] There is also a book in criticism of the "Aeneid"
by Carvilius Pictor, called "Aeneomastix."[c] Marcus Vipsanius called Virgil a supposititious child of Maecenas, that
inventor of a new kind of affected language,[d] neither
bombastic nor of studied simplicity, but in ordinary words
and hence less obvious. Herennius made selections confined to his defects, and Perellius Fausta to his pilferings.
More than that, the eight volumes of Quintus Octavius
Avitus, entitled "Resemblances," contain the verses which
he borrowed, with their sources. Asconius Pedianus, in a
book which he wrote "Against the Detractors of Virgil,"
sets forth a very few of the charges against him, and those
for the most part dealing with history and with the accusation that he borrowed a great deal from Homer; but he
says that Virgil used to meet this latter accusation with
these words: "Why don't my critics also attempt the same
thefts? If they do, they will realize that it is easier to filch
his club from Hercules than a line from Homer." Yet
Asconius says that Vergil had intended to go into retirement, in order to prune down everything to the satisfaction of carping critics.

[a] "Plough naked, naked sow."
[b] "A chill will give you the fever."
[c] The scourge of Aeneas.
[d] See *Aug.* lxxxvi. 2.

VITA HORATI

Q. Horatius Flaccus, Venusinus, patre ut ipse tradit libertino et exactionum coactore (ut vero[1] creditum est salsamentario, cum illi quidam in altercatione exprobrasset[2]: "Quotiens ego vidi patrem tuum brachio se emungentem!") bello Philippensi excitus a Marco Bruto imperatore, tribunus militum meruit; victisque partibus venia impetrata scriptum quaestorium comparavit. Ac primo Maecenati, mox Augusto insinuatus non mediocrem in amborum amicitia locum tenuit. Maecenas quantopere eum dilexerit[3] satis testatur[4] illo epigrammate:

Ni te visceribus meis, Horati,
Plus iam diligo, tu tuum sodalem
Ninnio[5] videas strigosiorem;

sed multo magis extremis iudiciis tali ad Augustum elogio: "Horati Flacci ut mei esto memor." Augustus[6] epistularum quoque ei officium optulit, ut[7] hoc ad Maecenatem scripto significat: "Ante ipse sufficiebam scribendis epistulis amicorum, nunc occupatissimus et infirmus Horatium nostrum a[8] te cupio abducere. Veniet

Source of text: scholia to Horace, *Epist.* 2. 1. 1. Suetonian authorship: assured.

[1] vero, *Muretus*; vere, *mss.*; fere, *Casaubon.*
[2] exprobasset, *Fλ.*   [3] dilexerit, ς; *the other mss. have* dilexit.   [4] testatur, *Fλp*; monstratur, *V.*
[5] nimio, *mss.* (ninio, *φ*); Ninnio, *P. Pithoeus*; hinnulo, *Oudendorp*; hinno me, *Lambinus*; simio, *Sudhaus.*
[6] Augustus . . . tua tempora, Caesar" (p. 464), *omitted in* ς.
[7] ut, *added by Lambinus.*   [8] a, *added by Nannius.*

THE LIFE OF HORACE

Quintus Horatius Flaccus of Venusia had for a father, as he himself writes, a freedman who was a collector of money at auctions; but it is believed that he was a dealer in salted provisions, for a certain man in a quarrel thus taunted Horace: "How often have I seen your father wiping his nose with his arm!" Horace served as tribune of the soldiers in the war of Philippi, at the instance of Marcus Brutus, one of the leaders in that war. When his party was vanquished, he was pardoned and purchased the position of a quaestor's clerk. Then contriving to win the favour, first of Maecenas and later of Augustus, he held a prominent place among the friends of both. How fond Maecenas was of him is evident enough from the well known epigram:

> If that I do not love you, my own Horace, more
> than life itself, behold your comrade scraggier than
> a rag doll.[a]

But he expressed himself much more strongly in his last will and testament in this brief remark to Augustus: "Be as mindful of Horatius Flaccus as of myself." Augustus offered him the post of secretary, as appears in this letter of his to Maecenas: "Before this I was able to write my letters to my friends with my own hand; now overwhelmed with work and in poor health, I desire to take our friend Horace from you. He will come then from that

---

[a] Taking *ninnio* as a common noun, cf. Fraenkel, *Horace* (Oxford 1957), p. 16, n. 4.

461

ergo ab ista parasitica mensa ad hanc regiam, et nos in epistulis scribendis iuvabit." Ac ne recusanti quidem aut suscensuit quicquam aut amicitiam suam ingerere desiit. Exstant epistulae, e quibus argumenti gratia pauca subieci: "Sume tibi aliquid iuris apud me, tamquam si convictor mihi fueris; recte enim et non temere feceris, quoniam id usus mihi tecum esse volui, si per valitudinem tuam fieri possit." Et rursus: "Tui qualem habeam memoriam, poteris ex Septimio quoque nostro audire; nam incidit ut illo coram fieret a me tui mentio. Neque enim si tu superbus amicitiam nostram sprevisti, ideo nos quoque ἀνθυπερηφανοῦμεν."[1] Praeterea saepe eum inter alios iocos "purissimum penem"[2] et "homuncionem lepidissimum" appellat, unaque et altera liberalitate locupletavit. Scripta quidem eius usque adeo probavit mansuraque perpetuo[3] opinatus est, ut non modo Saeculare carmen componendum iniunxerit sed et Vindelicam victoriam Tiberii Drusique, privignorum suorum, eumque coegerit propter hoc tribus Carminum libris ex longo intervallo quartum addere; post Sermones vero quosdam lectos nullam sui mentionem habitam ita sit questus: "Irasci me tibi scito, quod non in plerisque eius modi scriptis mecum potissimum loquaris; an vereris ne apud posteros infame tibi sit, quod videaris familiaris nobis esse?" Expressitque eclogam ad se, cuius initium est:

[1] *Casaubon.*   [2] penem, *Muretus*; pene, *mss.*
[3] perpetuo, *V*; *the other mss. have* perpetua.

---

[a] It seems probable that there is a word-play on the double sense of *rex*, "king" and "wealthy patron," since Augustus would hardly use *regiam* literally of his table. The meaning would then be "let the parasite change tables (and patrons)."

[b] See Th. Birt, Müller's *Handbuch*, I[3]. 3. 166.

parasitic table of yours to my imperial board, and help me write my letters."[a] Even when Horace declined, Augustus showed no resentment at all, and did not cease his efforts to gain his friendship. We have letters from which I append a few extracts by way of proof: "Enjoy any privilege at my house, as if you were making your home there; for it will be quite right and proper for you to do so, inasmuch as that was the relation which I wished to have with you, if your health had permitted." And again, "How mindful I am of you our friend Septimius can also tell you; for it chanced that I spoke of you in his presence. Even if you were so proud as to scorn my friendship, I do not therefore return your disdain." Besides this, among other pleasantries, he often calls him "a most immaculate libertine"[b] and "his charming little man," and he made him well to do by more than one act of generosity. As to his writings, Augustus rated them so high, and was so convinced that they would be immortal, that he not only appointed him to write the Secular Hymn, but also bade him celebrate the victory of his stepsons Tiberius and Drusus over the Vindelici, and so compelled him to add a fourth to his three books of lyrics after a long silence. Furthermore, after reading several of his "Talks,"[c] the Emperor thus expressed his pique that no mention was made of him: "You must know that I am not pleased with you, that in your numerous writings of this kind you do not talk with me, rather than with others. Are you afraid that your reputation with posterity will suffer because it appears that you were my friend?" In this way he forced from Horace the selection which begins with these words:

[c] *Sermones* was apparently the title which Horace gave his "Satires"; the term *saturae* is broader and covers the Epistles as well; see p. 464, note *b*.

Cum tot sustineas et tanta negotia solus,
Res Italas armis tuteris, moribus ornes,
Legibus emendes: in publica commoda peccem,
Si longo sermone morer tua tempora, Caesar.

Habitu corporis fuit brevis atque obesus, qualis et a semet ipso in saturis describitur et ab Augusto hac epistula: "Pertulit ad me Onysius libellum tuum, quem ego ut excusantem,[1] quantuluscumque est, boni consulo. Vereri autem mihi videris ne maiores libelli tui sint, quam ipse es; sed tibi statura deest, corpusculum non deest. Itaque licebit in sextariolo scribas, quo[2] circuitus voluminis tui sit ὀγκωδέστατος, sicut est ventriculi tui."

Ad res Venerias intemperantior traditur; nam speculato cubiculo scorta dicitur habuisse disposita, ut quocumque respexisset ibi ei imago coitus referretur. Vixit plurimum in secessu ruris sui Sabini aut Tiburtini, domusque ostenditur circa Tiburni luculum. * * * *[3] Venerunt in manus meas et elegi sub titulo eius et epistula prosa oratione quasi commendantis se Maecenati, sed utraque falsa puto; nam elegi vulgares, epistula etiam obscura, quo vitio minime tenebatur.

Natus est VI. Idus Decembris L. Cotta et L. Torquato consulibus, decessit V. Kal. Decembris C. Marcio[4] Censorino et C. Asinio Gallo consulibus post nonum et quin-

---

[1] accusantem, *mss.*; excusantem, *Reiff.*; ut accusem te, *Bentley.*   [2] quo, *Salmasius*: cum, *mss.*
[3] *O. Jahn indicated a lacuna; there is no mention of Horace's genuine works.*   [4] Marcio, *Bongars*; mario, *mss.*

---

[a] *Epist.* 2. 1. 1 ff.   [b] *Epist.* 1. 4. 15; 1. 20. 24; see note on p. 463.   [c] Dec. 8, 65 B.C.

Seeing that single-handed thou dost bear the burden of tasks so many and so great, protecting Italy's realm with arms, providing it with morals, reforming it by laws, I should sin against the public weal, Caesar, if I wasted thy time with long discourse.[a]

In person he was short and fat, as he is described with his own pen in his satires[b] and by Augustus in the following letter: "Onysius has brought me your little volume, and I accept it, small as it is, in good part, as an apology. But you seem to me to be afraid that your books may be bigger than you are yourself; but it is only stature that you lack, not girth. So you may write on a pint pot, that the circumference of your volume may be well rounded out, like that of your own belly."

It is said that he was immoderately lustful; for it is reported that in a room lined with mirrors he had harlots so arranged that whichever way he looked, he saw a reflection of venery. He lived for the most part in the country on his Sabine or Tiburtine estate, and his house is pointed out near the little grove of Tiburnus. * * * I possess some elegies attributed to his pen and a letter in prose, supposed to be a recommendation of himself to Maecenas, but I think that both are spurious; for the elegies are commonplace and the letter is besides obscure, which was by no means one of his faults.

He was born on the sixth day before the Ides of December in the consulate of Lucius Cotta and Lucius Torquatus,[c] and died on the fifth day before the Kalends of the same month in the consulship of Gaius Marcius Censorinus and Gaius Asinius Gallus, fifty-nine days after

quagesimum diem quam Maecenas obierat, aetatis agens septimum et quinquagesimum[1] annum, herede Augusto palam nuncupato, cum urgente vi valitudinis non sufficeret ad obsignandas testamenti tabulas. Humatus et conditus est extremis Esquiliis iuxta Maecenatis tumulum.

[1] diem . . . quinquagesimum, *supplied by Vahlen; see Hermes*, 33, 245.

the death of Maecenas, in his fifty-seventh year.[a] He named Augustus as his heir by word of mouth, since he could not make and sign a will because of the sudden violence of his ailment. He was buried and laid to rest near the tomb of Maecenas on the farther part of the Esquiline Hill.

[a] Nov. 27, 8 B.C.

VITA TIBULLI

Te quoque Vergilio comitem non aequa, Tibulle,
  Mors iuvenem campos misit ad Elysios,
Ne foret, aut elegis molles qui fleret amores
  Aut caneret forti regia bella pede.

Albius Tibullus eques Romanus,[1] insignis forma
cultuque corporis observabilis, ante alios Corvinum Mes-
salam oratorem[2] dilexit, cuius etiam contubernalis Aqui-
tanico bello militaribus donis donatus est. Hic multorum
iudicio principem inter elegiographos obtinet locum.
Epistolae quoque eius amatoriae, quamquam breves,
omnino utiles sunt. Obiit adulescens, ut indicat epi-
gramma supra scriptum.

Source of text: mss. of Tibullus. Suetonian authorship: most
improbable.

[1] eques Romanus, ψ; eques Regalis, A; eques R(omanus) e
Gabiis *Bährens.*

[2] oratorem, ψ; originem, A.

THE LIFE OF TIBULLUS

Thee too, Tibullus, companion of Virgil, envious death sent in youth to the Elysian fields, that there might be no one to mourn tender loves in elegy, or sing the wars of kings in heroic verse.[a]

Albius Tibullus, a Roman knight, remarkable for his good looks and conspicuous for his personal elegance, was devoted above all others to Messala Corvinus the orator. He was his tent companion[b] in the war in Aquitania[c] and was given military prizes.[d] In the judgment of many men he holds the first place among writers of elegy. His amatory letters, too, though short are very useful.[e] He died in youth, as is indicated by the epigram written above.

[a] Written by Domitius Marsus.

[b] Cf. *Jul.* ii.

[c] Messala was sent to Aquitania soon after the battle of Actium (App. *B.C.* 4. 38); he celebrated his triumph in 27 B.C.

[d] See *Aug.* xxv. 3.

[e] This is quite meaningless, so far as anything we know of Tibullus is concerned.

VITA AULIS PERSI FLACCI

Aules[1] Persius Flaccus natus est pridie Nonas Decembris Fabio Persico L. Vitellio coss., decessit VIII. Kalendas Decembris P. Mario Afinio[2] Gallo coss. Natus in Etruria Volaterris, eques Romanus, sanguine et affinitate primi ordinis viris coniunctus. Decessit ad octavum miliarium via Appia in praediis suis.

Pater eum Flaccus pupillum reliquit moriens annorum fere sex. Fulvia Sisennia mater eius[3] nupsit postea Fusio[4] equiti Romano et eum quoque extulit intra paucos annos.

Studuit Flaccus usque ad annum XII. aetatis suae Volaterris, inde Romae apud grammaticum Remmium Palaemonem et apud rhetorem Verginium Flavum. Cum esset annorum XVI, amicitia coepit uti Annaei Cornuti ita ut nusquam ab eo discederet; a quo inductus aliquatenus in philosophiam est.

Amicos habuit a prima adulescentia Caesium Bassum poetam et Calpurnium Staturam, qui vivo eo iuvenis decessit. Coluit ut[5] patrem Servilium Nonianum. Cognovit per Cornutum etiam Annaeum Lucanum aequaevum auditorem Cornuti.[6] Lucanus mirabatur adeo

Source of text: mss. of Persius, attributed to Valerius Probus. Suetonian authorship: doubtful.

[1] Aules, *mss.*, an Etruscan form of the Latin Aulus.

[2] Asinio, *mss.*; *cf.* Tac. *Ann.* 14. 48.

[3] mater eius, *omitted by some mss.*

[4] Fuscio *or* Ruscio, *mss.*   [5] ut, *omitted by the mss.*

[6] *After* Cornuti *the mss. have* Nam Cornutus illo tempore tragicus (grammaticus, *Martinius*) sectae poeticae (stoicae, *Pithoeus*), qui libros philosophiae reliquit. Sed . . .

THE LIFE OF
AULES PERSIUS FLACCUS

Aules Persius Flaccus was born the day before the Nones of December in the consulshp of Fabius Persicus and Lucius Vitellius,[a] and died on the eighth day before the Kalends of December, when Publius Marius and Afinius Gallus were consuls.[b] He was born at Volaterrae in Etruria, was a Roman knight, but was connected by blood and by marriage with men of the senatorial order. He died on his estate near the eighth milestone of the Appian Way.

His father Flaccus died when his son was about six years old, leaving him to the care of a guardian. His mother, Fulvia Sisennia, afterwards married a Roman knight named Fusius, but buried him also within a few years.

Flaccus studied until the twelfth year of his age at Volaterrae, and then at Rome with the grammarian Remmius Palaemon[c] and the rhetorician Verginius Flavus. When he was sixteen years old he became so intimate a friend of Annaeus Cornutus that he never left his side; and from him he obtained some knowledge of philosophy.

From early youth he enjoyed the friendship of Caesius Bassus, the poet, and of Calpurnius Statura, who died in youth, while Persius still lived. Servilius Nonianus he revered as a father. Through Cornutus he came to know Annaeus Lucanus also, a pupil of Cornutus and of the same age as himself. Lucan so admired the writings of

---

[a] Dec. 4, A.D. 34.   [b] Nov. 24, A.D. 62.
[c] See *Gram.* xxiii.

471

scripta Flacci, ut vix se retineret recitantem a clamore quae illius essent vera esse poemata, se ludos facere.[1] Sero cognovit et Senecam, sed non ut caperetur eius ingenio. Usus est apud Cornutum duorum convictu doctissimorum et sanctissimorum virorum acriter tunc philosophantium, Claudi Agathurni medici Lacedaemonii et Petroni Aristocratis Magnetis, quos unice miratus est et aemulatus, cum aequales essent Cornuti, minor esset ipse.[2]

Idem decem fere annis summe dilectus a Paeto Thrasea est ita ut peregrinaretur quoque cum eo aliquando, cognatam eius Arriam uxorem habente.

Fuit morum lenissimorum, verecundiae virginalis, formae pulchrae, pietatis erga matrem et sororem et amitam[a] exemplo sufficientis.

Fuit frugi, pudicus.

Reliquit circa HS viciens matri et sorori scriptis tantum ad matrem codicillis. Cornuto rogavit ut daret sestertia, ut quidam dicunt, C, ut alii, L et argenti facti pondo viginti et libros circa septingentos Chrysippi sive bibliothecam suam omnem. Verum a Cornuto sublatis libris pecunia sororibus, quas heredes frater fecerat, relicta est.[3]

Scriptitavit et raro et tarde. Hunc ipsum librum imperfectum reliquit. Versus aliqui dempti[4] sunt ultimo

---

[1] suo ludo faceret, *mss.; corr. Villeneuve.*

[2] minores ipse, *mss.;* minor esset ipse, *Owen.*

[3] pecuniam . . . reliquit et, *mss.*

[4] *Owen suggests* additi.

---

[a] There is clearly something wrong here; elsewhere but one sister is mentioned.

Flaccus that, when he read them, he could hardly refrain from crying out that Flaccus' were real poems, but that he was merely playing. Towards the end of his life he made the acquaintance also of Seneca, but was not impressed by his talents. At the house of Cornutus he enjoyed the society of two learned and venerable men, who were then eagerly pursuing philosophical studies: Claudius Agathurnus, a physician of Lacedaemon, and Petronius Aristocrates of Magnesia, whom he admired exceedingly and emulated, although they were of the same age as Cornutus, while he was a younger man.

He was also for nearly ten years so great a favourite of Paetus Thrasea that he sometimes even travelled abroad with him; and Paetus's wife, Arria, was a relative of his.

He was very gentle in manner, of virginal modesty and very handsome; and he showed an exemplary devotion to his mother, sister, and aunt.

He was good and pure.

He left about two million sesterces to his mother and sister, and a letter addressed only to his mother. He requested her to give Cornutus a hundred thousand, as some say, or according to others, fifty thousand sesterces, and twenty pounds of silver plate, besides about seven hundred volumes of Chrysippus or his entire library. But Cornutus, while accepting the books, turned over the money to the sisters[a] whom their brother had made his heirs.

He wrote rarely and slowly. This very volume[b] he left unfinished, and some verses were taken from the last

[b] The collection of six satires, for which this Life was used as an introduction.

libro, ut quasi finitus esset. Leviter correxit[1] Cornutus et Caesio Basso petenti, ut ipse ederet, tradidit edendum.

Scripserat in pueritia Flaccus etiam praetextam et hodoeporicon librum unum et paucos in socrum[2] Thraseae[3] versus, quae se ante virum occiderat. Omnia ea auctor fuit Cornutus matri eius ut aboleret.

Editum librum continuo mirari homines et diripere coeperunt.

Decessit autem vitio stomachi anno aetatis XXX.[4]

Sed mox ut a schola magistrisque devertit, lecto Lucili libro decimo vehementer saturas componere studuit. Cuius libri principium imitatus est sibi primo, mox omnibus detrectaturus cum tanta recentium poetarum et oratorum insectatione, ut etiam Neronem principem illius temporis inculpaverit. Cuius versus in Neronem cum ita se haberet "auriculas asini Mida rex habet," in eum modum a Cornuto ipso tantum nomine mutato est emendatus "auriculas asini quis non habet?" ne hoc in se Nero dictum arbitraretur.

---

[1] correxit, *Laurentianus*; contraxit *or* recitavit, *mss.*

[2] in socrum, *Casaubon*; sororum, *mss.*

[3] *After* Thraseae *the mss. have* in Arriam matrem.

[4] XXIIX, *Reizius.*

book, that it might have the appearance of completion. Cornutus made some slight corrections, and on the request of Caesius Bassus that he might publish it, turned it over to him for that purpose.

In his boyhood Flaccus had written a *praetexta*,[a] one book describing his travels, and a few verses on the mother-in-law of Thrasea,[b] who had killed herself before her husband. All these Cornutus advised the poet's mother to destroy.

As soon as his book appeared, men began to admire it and to buy it up rapidly.

He died of a stomach trouble in the thirtieth year of his age.

As soon as he left school and his teachers, he conceived a strong desire to write satires from reading the tenth book of Lucilius. The beginning of this he imitated with the intention at first of criticizing himself: but presently turning to general criticism,[c] he so assailed the poets and orators of his day that he even attacked Nero, who was at that time emperor. His verse on Nero read as follows: "King Midas has ass's ears," but Cornutus by merely changing the name, and writing "Who has not an ass's ears?" so altered it that Nero might not think that it was said of him.

[a] A Roman tragedy.
[b] The elder Arria.
[c] Text and meaning are uncertain; see Marx, *Lucilius*, 2, p. 145.

VITA LUCANI

M. Annaeus Lucanus Cordubensis[1] prima ingenii experimenta in "Neronis laudibus" dedit quinquennali certamine, dein[2] "Civile Bellum," quod a[3] Pompeio et Caesare gestum est, recitavit,[4] ut praefatione quadam aetatem et initia sua cum Vergilio comparans ausus sit dicere:

> et quantum mihi restat
> Ad Culicem?

Hic initio adolescentiae, cum ob infestum matrimonium patrem suum ruri agere longissime cognovisset * * * Revocatus Athenis a Nerone cohortique amicorum additus atque etiam quaestura honoratus, non tamen permansit in gratia. Siquidem aegre ferens, recitante[5] se subito ac nulla nisi refrigerandi sui causa indicto senatu recessisse,[6] neque verbis adversus principem neque factis exstantibus[7] post haec temperavit, adeo ut quondam in latrinis publicis clariore cum strepitu[8] ventris emissi[9] hemistichium Neronis magna consessorum fuga pronuntiarit:

Source of text: mss. of Lucan. Suetonian authorship: probable.
[1] M.... Cordubensis, *MB*; *omitted by P.*   [2] *Hosius indicates a lacuna after* dein.   [3] a, *Baumgarten-Crusius;* cum, *mss.*   [4] *Hosius indicates a lacuna after* recitavit; *the codex Berolinensis*, 35 *has* sub tantae levitatis et immoderatae linguae fuit.   [5] *Reiff. and Hosius insert* quod Nero se *before* recitante.   [6] recessisset, *MP (Reiff., Hosius).*   [7] exstantibus, *M*; excitantibus, *Jahn, Hosius.*   [8] strepitu, *B*; crepitu, *P*; trepitu, *M.*   [9] *Regarded by Reiff. as due to dittography.*

THE LIFE OF LUCAN

Marcus Annaeus Lucanus of Corduba made his first appearance as a poet with a "Eulogy of Nero" at the emperor's Quinquennial Contests,[a] and then gave a public reading of his poem on the "Civil War" waged between Pompey and Caesar. In a kind of introduction to the latter, comparing his time of life and his first essays with those of Virgil, he had the audacity to ask:

How far, pray, do I fall short of the Culex?[b]

In his early youth, learning that his father was living in the remote country districts because of an unhappy marriage.... He was recalled from Athens by Nero and made one of his intimate friends, besides being honoured with the quaestorship; but he could not keep the emperor's favour. For piqued because Nero had suddenly called a meeting of the senate and gone out when he was giving a reading, with no other motive than to throw cold water on the performance,[c] he afterwards did not refrain from words and acts of hostility to the prince, which are still notorious. Once for example in a public privy, when he relieved his bowels with an uncommonly loud noise, he shouted out this half line of the emperor's, while those who were there for the same purpose took to their heels:

[a] See *Nero*, xii. 3. [b] Or perhaps, "How much younger am I than the author of the Culex?" Lucan compares his great epic, written at an earlier age, with Virgil's early work. Cf. Stat. *Silv.* 2. 7. 73, *haec* (= Pharsaliam) *primo iuvenis canes sub aevo, Ante annos culicis Maroniani.* [c] Cf. *Claud.* xli. 1.

Sub terris tonuisse putes.

Sed et famoso carmine cum ipsum tum potentissimos amicorum gravissime proscidit. Ad extremum paene signifer Pisonianae coniurationis exstitit, multus[1] in gloria tyrannicidarum palam praedicanda[2] ac plenus minarum, usque eo intemperans ut Caesaris caput[3] proximo cuique iactaret. Verum detecta coniuratione nequaquam parem animi constantiam praestitit; facile enim confessus et[4] ad humillimas devolutus preces matrem quoque innoxiam inter socios nominavit, sperans impietatem sibi apud parricidam principem profuturam. Impetrato autem mortis arbitrio libero codicillos ad patrem corrigendis quibusdam versibus suis exaravit, epulatusque largiter brachia ad secandas venas praebuit medico. Poemata eius etiam praelegi memini, confici vero ac proponi venalia non tantum operose et diligenter sed inepte quoque.

[1] multus, *Omnibonus*; multis, *mss.*
[2] praedicanda, *some late mss.*; praedicenda, *MBP.*
[3] *Genthe marks a lacuna; so Francken.*
[4] ut, *MP*; *omitted by B.*

You might suppose it thundered 'neath the earth.

He also tongue-lashed not only the emperor but also his most powerful friends in a scurrilous poem. Finally he came out almost as the ringleader[a] in the conspiracy of Piso, publicly making great talk about the glory of tyrannicides, and full of threats, even going to the length of offering Caesar's head to all his friends. But when the conspiracy was detected, he showed by no means equal firmness of purpose; for he was easily forced to a confession, descended to the most abject entreaties, and even named his own mother among the guilty parties, although she was innocent, in hopes that this lack of filial devotion would win him favour with a parricidal prince. But when he was allowed free choice of the manner of his death, he wrote a letter to his father, containing corrections for some of his verses, and after eating heartily, offered his arms to a physician, to cut his veins. I recall that his poems were even read in public,[b] while they were published and offered for sale by editors lacking in taste, as well as by some who were painstaking and careful.

[a] Literally, standard-bearer.
[b] That is, lectured on by grammarians; see *Gram.* i.

VITA PLINII SECUNDI

Plinius Secundus Novocomensis equestribus militiis industrie functus procurationes quoque splendidissimas et continuas summa integritate administravit, et tamen liberalibus studiis tantam operam dedit, ut non temere quis plura in otio scripserit. Itaque bella omnia, quae unquam[1] cum Germanis gesta sunt, XX[2] voluminibus comprehendit, itemque "Naturalis Historiae" XXXVII libros absolvit. Periit clade[3] Campaniae; cum enim Misenensi classi praeesset et flagrante Vesuvio ad explorandas propius causas liburnica[4] pertendisset,[5] nec adversantibus ventis remeare posset, vi pulveris ac favillae oppressus est, vel ut quidam existimant a servo suo occisus, quem aestu deficiens ut necem sibi maturaret oraverat.[6]

Source of text: mss. of Pliny. Suetonian authorship: possible. Mss.: various manuscripts of Pliny, dating from the eleventh to the fifteenth century. V = cod. Vaticanus, 1951, fifteenth century; T = cod. Toletanus, thirteenth century.

[1] umquam] undique, *V.*

[2] XX], *the mss. have* XXXVII.

[3] clade, *Hermolaus Barbarus;* gades (gadis, *V*) *or* grades, *mss.*

[4] laburnica, *T; the other mss. have* liburnicas (*V*) *or* liburnicam.

[5] pertendisset, *Burmann;* praetendisset, *mss.*

[6] oraverat, *mss.;* oraverit, *Vinetus.*

THE LIFE OF PLINY THE ELDER

Plinius Secundus of Novum Comum, after performing with energy the military service required of members of the equestrian order, administered several important stewardships in succession with the utmost justice. Yet he gave so much attention to liberal studies that hardly anyone who had complete leisure wrote more than he. For instance, he gave an account in twenty volumes of all the wars which were ever carried on with Germany, besides completing the thirty-seven books of his "Natural History." He lost his life[a] in the disaster in Campania. He was commanding the fleet at Misenum, and setting out in a Liburnian galley[b] during the eruption of Vesuvius to investigate the causes of the phenomenon from nearer at hand, he was unable to return because of head winds. He was suffocated by the shower of dust and ashes, although some think that he was killed by a slave, whom he begged to hasten his end when he was overcome by the intense heat.

[a] In A.D. 79.
[b] See *Calig.* xxxvii. 2.

VITA PASSIENI CRISPI

Passienus[1] Crispus, municeps Viselliensis,[2] tirocinio suo in senatu ita coepit: "Patres conscripti et tu Caesar!" propter quod simulata oratione[3] plenissime a Tiberio conlaudatus est.[4] Plurimas sponte causas apud centumviros egit, pro qua re in basilica Iulia eius statua posita est. Consulatus duos gessit. Uxores habuit duas, primam Domitiam, deinde Agrippinam, illam amitam, hanc matrem Neronis Caesaris. Possedit bis milies sestertium. Omnium principum gratiam adpetivit, sed praecipue C.[5] Caesaris, quem iter facientem secutus est pedibus. Hic nullo audiente ab eodem[6] interrogatus, haberetne sicut ipse cum sorore germana consuetudinem, "Nondum" inquit, quantumvis decenter et caute, ne aut negando[7] eum argueret aut adsentiendo[8] semet mendacio dehonestaret. Periit per fraudem Agrippinae, quam heredem reliquerat, et funere publico elatus est.

Source of text: scholia to Juvenal, 4. 81. Suetonian authorship: possible. Sigla: P = cod. Montepessulanus, 125, formerly Pithoeanus, ninth century; S = cod. Sangallensis, 870, ninth century.

[1] Passienus, *added by Reiff.*

[2] municeps Viselliensis, *omitted by Reiff.*

[3] simulata oratione, *Jahn*; simuloratione, *PS*; simulatione, *Pithoeus.*

[4] est, *added by Jahn.*

[5] C., *added by Lipsius.*

[6] eodem, *Valla*: Nerone, *PS.*

[7] negando, *Lipsius*; negantem, *PS*: negans, *Pithoeus.*

[8] adsentiendo, *Lipsius*; adsentientem, *PS*; adsentiens, *Pithoeus.*

THE LIFE OF PASSIENUS CRISPUS

Passienus Crispus, a native of Visellium, began his first speech in the senate with these words: "Conscript fathers and you, Caesar," and was in consequence highly commended by Tiberius, though not sincerely. He voluntarily pleaded a number of cases in the court of the Hundred,[a] and therefore his statue was set up in the Basilica Julia.[b] He was twice consul. He married twice: first Domitia and then Agrippina, respectively the aunt and the mother of the emperor Nero. He possessed an estate of two hundred million sesterces. He tried to gain favour with all the emperors, but especially with Gaius Caesar, whom he attended on foot when the emperor made a journey. When he was asked by Gaius in a private conversation whether he had commerce with his own sister, as the emperor had with his, he replied "Not yet"; a very fitting and cautious answer, neither accusing the emperor by denying the allegation, nor dishonouring himself with a lie by admitting it. He was slain by the treachery of Agrippina, whom he had made his heir, and was honoured with a public funeral.

[a] See note on *Aug.* xxxvi.
[b] In the Roman Forum.

INDEX

Besides proper names, the Index includes the Latin words which are taken over into the translation, and a few others which seem to require explanation. The references are to chapter and section. The following abbreviations are used: A., *Augustus*; Cal., *Caligula*; Cl., *Claudius*; D., *Domitian*; G., *Galba*; J., *Julius* (*Caesar*); N., *Nero*; O., *Otho*; T., *Tiberius*; Tit., *Titus*; V., *Vespasian*; Vit., *Vitellius*; Gr., *De Grammaticis*; Rh., *De Rhetoribus*; Ter., *Life of Terence*; Virg., *Life of Virgil*; Hor., *Life of Horace*; Tibull., *Life of Tibullus*; Luc., *Life of Lucan*; Pers., *Life of Persius*; Plin., *Life of Pliny*; Pass., *Life of Passienus Crispus*.

people of ancient Latium, dwelling east of Rome on both banks of the Anio.

Aesculapius, A. LIX. (*signum*); Cl. XXV. 2 (*insula*). Latin form of Asclepios, the Greek god of healing and medicine. His temple was on the Island in the Tiber, which was therefore sometimes called the Island of Aesculapius.

Aeserninus, A. XLIII. 2. Grandson of Asinius Pollio.

Aesius Proculus, Cal. XXXV. 2.

Aethiopes, Cal. LVII. 4. The people of Aethiopia.

Aethiopia, J. LII. 1. A country in the interior of Africa.

Aetna, Virg. 19. The name of a poem.

Aetnaeus, -a, -um, *adj.* from Aetna, the volcano in western Sicily: *vertex*, Cal. LI. 1.

Aetolia, A. XVII. 3. A district in the western part of central Greece.

Afer, *see* Tedius *and* Terentius.

Afer, -ra, -rum, *adj.* meaning African: *generis*, A. IV. 2; *pugiles*, Cal. XVIII. 1. *See* Afri.

Afinius Gallus, Pers.

Afranius (L.), N. XI. 2; Ter. V. A Roman writer of *fabulae togatae*, or plays based upon Italic life. He lived in the latter part of the second century B.C.

Afranius, L., J. XXXIV. 2, LXXV. 2, 3. One of Pompey's generals.

Afri, Ter. I.

Africa, J. XXXV. 2, XXXVI., LIX., LXX. (*bis*); A. XVI. 4, XLVII.; T. XXXI. 2; N. XXXI. 4; G. VII. 1, VIII. 1, XI.; O. I. 2; Vit. V.; V. III., IV. 3. Usually applied to the Roman province.

Africanus, -a, -um, *adj.* from Africa: *triumphus*, J. XXXVII. 1, A. VIII. 1; as subst., *Africanae* (*sc. bestiae*), Cal. XVIII. 3; Cl. XXI. 3. Panthers or leopards.

Africanus, *see* Fabius *and* Scipio.

Africus, -a, -um, *adj.* to Africa: *bellum*, J. LVI. 1.

Agamemnon, T. LXI. 3.

Agathurnus, *see* Claudius.

Agermus, L., N. XXXIV. 3.

Agrippa, M., A. XVI. 2, XXV. 3, XXIX. 5, XXXV. 1, XLII. 1, LXIII. 1 (*bis*), LXIV. 1 (*bis*), LXVI. 3, XCIV. 12, XCVII. 1; T. VII. 2, X. 1; Cal. VII., XXIII. 1; Gr. XVI.

Agrippa Postumus, M., A. XIX. 2, LI. 1, .LXIV. 1, LXV. 1, 4; T. XV. 2 (*bis*), XXII., XXV. 1. Son of the preceding and grandson of Augustus.

Agrippina, T. VII. 2, 3 (*bis*). Granddaughter of Atticus.

Agrippina, A. LXIV. 1 (*bis*), LXXVI. 3; T. LIII. 1; Cal. VII., VIII. 1, 3, 4 (*bis*). Granddaughter of Augustus and wife of Germanicus, known as "the elder Agrippina."

Agrippina, Cal. VII.; Cl. XXVI. 3 (*bis*), XXIX. 2, XXXIX. 2, XLIII., XLIV. 1, 2; N. V. 2, VI. 1, 2, XXVIII. 2, XXXIX. 3; G., V. 1; V., IV. 2,

town of Latium on the Appian Way, at the beginning of the Pomptine Marshes.

Appia via, T. LXXII. 1; Cal. XIX. 1; Cl. I. 3; N. V. 1; Ter. V; Pers. The most famous of Roman roads, leading south-east to Capua, and later to Beneventum and Brundisium.

Appius, *see* Claudius *and* Iunius.

Appuleius, L., Gr. III.

Appuleius, Sex., A. C. 1. Consul in A.D. 14.

Apragopolis, A. XCVIII. 4; *see* note.

Aprilis, N. LV.

Apulia, Vit. I. 3. A district in the south-eastern part of Italy.

Aquila, *see* Pontius.

Aquileia, A. XX.; T. VII. 3; V. VI. 2. A town of northern Italy at the head of the Adriatic.

Aquilius Niger, A. XI.

Aquitania, A. XXI. 1; G. VI. 1, IX. 2. A district and province of south-eastern Gaul.

Aquitanicus, -a, -um, *adj.* from Aquitania: *bello*, Tibull.

Arcadia, V. VII. 3; Ter. I., V. A district in the central part of the Peloponnesus.

Archelaus, T. VIII., XXXVII. 4. A king of Cappadocia.

Archelaus, *see* Laelius.

Arelate, T. IV. 1. A town of southern Gaul on the Rhone, modern Arles.

Areus, A. LXXXIX. 1. A philosopher.

Argivus, G. XX. 2.

Aricia, A. IV. 2 (*bis*). An ancient town of Latium on the Appian Way, sixteen miles south-east of Rome.

Aricinus, -a, -um, *adj.* from Aricia: A. IV. 1.

Ariminum, A. XXX. 1. A town of Umbria on the Adriatic, modern Rimini.

Aristarchus, Gr. II., XIV. The famous Alexandrian grammarian and critic (c. 217–c. 145 B.C.).

Aristocrates, Petronius, Pers. A philosopher of Magnesia.

Armenia, J. XLIV. 3 (minor); A. XXI. 3; T. IX. 1, XI. 1, XLI.; Cal. I. 2; N. XIII. 1, XXXIX. 1, XL. 2. A large country east of Asia Minor and Cappadocia, divided into Armenia Major and Armenia Minor.

Armenii, Cl. XXV. 4. The people of Armenia.

Arrecina Tertulla, Tit. IV. 2. Wife of Titus.

Arrecinus Clemens, M., D. XI. 1.

Arria, Pers. Wife of Caecina Paetus. When her husband was ordered by Claudius to take his own life in A.D. 42 and hesitated to do so, she stabbed herself and handed the dagger to her husband, saying: "Paetus, it does not pain me."

Arria, Pers. Daughter of the preceding and wife of Thrasea.

Arruntius, *see* Furius.

INDEX

Artabanus, T. LXVI.; Cal. XIV. 3; Vit. II. 4. A king of the Parthians.

Arverni, N. II. 1. A tribe of south-eastern Gaul.

Asclepiades, A. XCIV. 4. A philosopher of Mendes, a town of Egypt.

Ascletario, D. XV. 3. An astrologer.

Asconius Pedianus, Virg. 10, 46.

Asellius Sabinus, T. XLII. 2.

Asia, J. II.; IV. 2, XXII. 2, XXVIII. 1, XXXIX. 1, LXIII.; A. III. 2, XVII. 3, XXVI. 3; T. XLVIII. 2; Cal. LVII. 3, LVIII. 1; V. I. 2; D. X. 2; Gr. VI.; Ter. IV.; Virg. 35.

Asiaticus, -a, -um, *adj.* from Asia: *oratores*, A. LXXXVI. 3.

Asiaticus, Vit. XII.

Asillius, Cal. VIII. 4.

Asinius Epicadus, Cl. XIX. 1, 2.

Asinius Gallus, C., Cl. XLI. 3; Gr. XXII., Hor. Son of Asinius Pollio and consul in 9 B.C.

Asinius Gallus, C., Cl. XIII. 2. Grandson of Asinius Pollio.

Asinius Marcellus, Cl. XLV. Consul in A.D. 54.

Asinius Pollio, J. XXX. 4, LV. 4, LVI. 4; A. XXIX. 5, XLIII. 2; Cl. XIII. 2; Gr. X. (*ter*); Virg. 9, 19. A celebrated orator, soldier, statesman and patron of literature. Author of a history of the war between Pompey and Caesar, and of tragedies mentioned by Hor. *Odes*, 2, 1.

Asprenas, *see* Nonius.

Astici ludi, T. VI. 4 (*see* note); Cal. XX.

Astura, A. XCVII. 3; T. LXXII. 2; A small island off the coast of Latium near Antium, where many distinguished Romans had villas; later joined to the mainland by a causeway; modern Astura (Torre d'Astura).

asturco, N. XLVI. 1. A horse from Asturia in Hispania Tarraconensis.

Atalanta, T. XLIV. 2. Daughter of Iasius of Arcadia, beloved by Meleager.

Ateius Capito, Gr. X., XXII. (*bis*).

Ateius Praetextatus Philologus, L., Gr. VII., X. (*bis*).

Atella, T. LXXV. 3; Virg. 27. An Oscan town in Campania, north of Naples; *see* Atellana.

Atellana (fabula), Cl. XXVII. 4; N. XXXIX. 3. A farce of Oscan origin named from Atella, and representing scenes from everyday life by stock characters. In later times such farces were sometimes given after a tragedy and called *Atellanica exodia*.

Atellanicus, -a, -um, *adj.* from Atella: *exodium*, T. XLV.

Atellanus, -a, -um, *adj.* from Atella: *actor*, G. XIII.

Athenae, A. LX., XCIII.; Gr. X., XV.; Virg. 35; Luc.

Athenodorus, Cl. IV. 5.

Atia, A. IV. 1 (*bis*), XCIV. 4 (*ter*). Mother of Augustus.

Atilius (C), J. LXXXIV. 2 (*see* note on text); Ter. V. An early

492

INDEX

Caligula, *see* Gaius

Callippides, T. xxxviii (*see* note).

Calpenus, Q., J. xxxix. 1.

Calpurnia, J. xxi., lxxxi. 3. Daughter of L. Piso and third wife of Julius Caesar.

Calpurnius Piso (C.), Cal. xxv. 1 (*bis*). Husband of Livia Orestilla and leader of a conspiracy against Nero in 62; *see* Pisonianus.

(Calpurnius) Piso, Cn., J. ix. 3 (*bis*).

(Calpurnius) Piso (Cn.), T. lii. 3; Cal. ii., iii. 3; Vit. ii. 3. Governor of Syria.

(Calpurnius) Piso, L., J. xxi., lxxxiii. 1. Father of Caesar's wife Calpurnia.

(Calpurnius) Piso, L., T. xlii. 1; Rh. vi.

(Calpurnius) Piso Frugi Licinianus, G. xvii.; O. v. 1, vi. 3.

Calpurnius Statura, Pers.

Calvina, *see* Iunia.

Calvini, N. i. 1.

Calvinus, *see* Eficius.

Calvus, *see* Licinius.

Camerinus, *see* Sulpicius.

Camilla, *see* Livia Medullina.

Camillus, *see* Furius.

Campania, A. lxxii. 2, xcviii. 1; T. xi. 1, xxxix., xl., lxxii. 2; Cal. xiv. 2, xxiv. 2, xxxvii. 2; Cl. v.; Vit. xvi.; V. xxiv.; Tit. viii. 3, 4; Virg. 13; Plin.

Campanus, -a, -um, *adj.* to Campania: *ager*, J. xx. 3; A. iv. 2; *pugiles*, Cal. xviii. 1; *via*,

A. xciv. 7 (*see* note).

Campus, *see* Martius, Esquilinus, Leontinus, Stellas.

Canace, N. xxi. 3. Daughter of Aeolus. She had several children by Poseidon and was killed by her father because of her guilty passion for her brother. She was the subject of a tragedy sung by Nero.

Caninius Rebilus, N. xv. 2; cf. J. lxxvi. 2. Appointed consul for a single day by Julius Caesar.

Cannutius, Ti., Rh. iv.

Cantabria, A. xxi. 1, lxxxi. 1; G. viii. 2. A district in the northern part of Spain.

Cantabricus, -a, -um, *adj.* from Cantabria: *bellum*, A. xx., lxxxv. 1; *expeditio*, A. xxix. 3; T. ix. 1; Virg. 31.

Canus, G. xii. 3.

Capella, *see* Statilius.

Capita Bubula, *see* Bubula.

Capito, *see* Ateius *and* Fonteius.

Capitolinus, -a, -um, *adj.* from Capitolium: *area*, Cal. xxii. 4, xxxiv. 1; *certamen*, D. xiii. 1. *See also* Catulus, Iuppiter, Venus.

Capitolium, J. x. 1, xv., xxxvii. 2, liv. 3, lxxix. 2; A. xxix. 1, lvii. 1, lix., xci. 2, xciv. 8, 9 (*bis*); T. i. 2, ii. 4, iii. 2, xx.; Cal. vi. 1, xvi. 4, xxii. 4, xlvi., lx.; Cl. ii. 2, x. 3, xxii., xxiv. 3; N. xii. 4, xiii. 2, xlvi. 2; Vit. xv. 3; V. viii. 5, xviii.; D. i. 2, v. (*bis*), xiii. 2, xv. 2, xxiii. 2. The temple of

497

INDEX

Jupiter Optimus Maximus, with Juno and Minerva, on the Capitoline hill. Also applied to the whole of that summit of the hill and to temples to the same triad of gods in other cities of Italy: Beneventi, Gr. IX.; Capuae, T. XL.; Cal. LVII. 2.

Cappadocia, Cal. I. 2; V. VIII. 4. A country in the eastern part of Asia Minor.

Cappadox, *adj.* to Cappadocia: T. XXXVII. 4.

Capreae, A. LXXII. 3, XCII. 2, XCVIII. 1, 3, 4; T. XL., LX., LXII. 2, LXXIII. 1, LXXIV; Cal. X. 1; Vit. III. 2; cf. T. XLV. An island near Naples, modern Capri.

Caprensis, -e, *adj.* from Capreae: *secessus*, T. XLIII. 1.

Capricornus, A. XCIV. 12. One of the signs of the Zodiac.

Caprineus, T. XLIII. 2.

Capua, J. LXXXI. 1 (*bis*); T. XL.; Cal. LVII. 2. An ancient city of Campania.

Capys, J. LXXXI. 1 (*bis*). Founder and king of Capua.

Carchedoniaca, Cl. XLII. 2 (*bis*). A History of Carthage, by the emperor Claudius, from Καρχηδών, the Greek name of the city.

Carinae, T. XV. 1 (*see* note); Gr. XV.

Carmelus, V. V. 6. The god of Mount Carmel in Phoenicia.

Carnulus, T. LXI. 5 (*bis*).

Carthago, Ter. I. (*bis*).

Carthago Nova, G. IX. 2. A seaport of south-eastern Spain; modern Cartagena.

Carthaginiensis, -e, *adj.* from Carthago: *see* Sulpicius.

Carvilius Pictor, Virg. 44.

Cascae, J. LXXXII 1, 2. Two brothers, members of the conspiracy against Julius Caesar.

Caspiae Portae, N. XIX. 2. A pass through the range of mountains south-east of the Caspian Sea.

Cassiope, N. XXII. 3. A town of Corcyra (modern Corfu).

Cassius, N. XXII. 3. An epithet applied to Jupiter as the tutelary divinity of Cassiope.

Cassius, Cal. LVII. 1.

Cassius, C., J. LXXX. 4, LXXXV.; A. IX., X. 1; T. LXI. 3; N. III. 1, XXXVII. 1; G. III. 2; O. X. 1; Gr. XIII. Leader with M. Brutus of the conspiracy against Julius Caesar.

Cassius, L., J. LXIII.; Gr. XIII.

Cassius Chaerea, Cal. LVI. 2, LVII. 3, LVIII. 2 (*bis*).

Cassius Longinus, L., Cal. XXIV. 1, LVII. 3. Consul in A.D. 30.

Cassius Longinus, N. XXXVII. 1.

Cassius Parmensis, A. IV. 2. A poet, who was one of the murderers of Julius Caesar; cf. Hor. *Epist.* 1. 4. 3.

Cassius Patavinus, A. LI. 1.

Cassius Scaeva, J. LXVIII. 4 (*bis*). One of Caesar's centurions.

Cassius Severus, A. LVI. 3;

498

INDEX

Compitales Lares, in the early part of January.

Comum, *see* Novum Comum.

Concordia, T. XX.; Vit. XV. 4. A Roman goddess with a temple at the western end of the Forum, at the foot of the Capitoline hill. A title given to Vitellius, Vit. XV. 4 (*bis*).

Confluentes, Cal. VIII. 1. A town at the confluence of the Moselle and the Rhine, modern Coblenz.

Cordubensis, -e, *adj.* from Corduba, a city of southern Spain, modern Cordova: A. LI. 2; Luc.

Cordus, *see* Cremutius.

Corfinium, J. XXXIV. 1; N. II. 2. A city of the Paeligni in central Italy, modern Pelino.

Corinthiarius, A. LXX. 2; *see* note.

Corinthius, -a, -um, *adj.* from Corinthus: *vasa*, A. LXX. 2 (*bis*); T. XXXIV. 1. Vessels made of Corinthian bronze and highly prized.

Corinthus, G., III. 4.

Cornelia, J. I. 1, VI. 1, 2. First wife of Julius Caesar.

Cornelia, D. VIII. 4. A chief Vestal.

Cornelii, J. LIX.

Cornelius, A. XXVI. 1; *see also* Scipio *and* Sulla.

Cornelius, -a, -um, *adj.* to Cornelius: *legibus*, J. XI.; *lege*, A. XXXIII. 2.

Cornelius Alexander, surnamed Polyhistor and Historia, Gr. XX.

Cornelius Balbus, J. LXXVIII. 1, LXXXI. 2; A. XXIX. 5.

(Cornelius) Cinna (L.), J. I. 1. Consul with Marius.

(Cornelius) Cinna, L., J. V. Son of the preceding.

Cornelius Cinna, J. LXXXV.

(Cornelius) Dolabella, J. IV. 1, XLIX. 1 (*bis*), LV. 1.

Cornelius Dolabella, Cn., Ter. V.

(Cornelius) Dolabella, Cn., G. XII. 2.

(Cornelius) Dolabella, P., J. XXXVI.

(Cornelius) Dolabella (P.), Gr. XIV. Son-in-law of Cicero.

Cornelius Epicadus, Gr. XII.

Cornelius Fuscus, D. VI. 1. Prefect of the praetorian guard.

Cornelius Gallus, A. LXVI. 1, 2; Gr. XVI. (*ter*); Virg. 19. The elegiac poet.

Cornelius Laco, G. XIV. 2. Prefect of the praetorian guard.

Cornelius Nepos, J. LV. 1; A. LXXVI.; Gr. IV.; Rh. III.; Ter. I., III. The well-known Roman writer (99–24 B.C.).

Cornelius Phagita, J. LXXIV. 1.

Cornelius Sabinus, Cal. LVIII. 2 (*bis*).

Cornificius, L., A. XXIX. 5.

Cornutus, L. Annaeus, Pers. (*deciens*).

Corvinus, *see* Statilius *and* Valerius.

Cosanus, -a, -um, *adj.* from Cosa, a city of Etruria, modern Ansedonia: *praedia*, V. II. 1.

507

INDEX

Flavius, -a, -um, *adj.* to Flavius,
Flavii: *gens*, V. I. 1; *gentis templum*, D. I. 1, V., XV. 2, XVII. 3;
generis origo, V. XII.

Flavius Clemens, D. XV. 1.
Cousin of Domitian.

Flavius Liberalis, V. III. Father-
in-law of Vespasian.

Flavius Petro, T., V. I. 2, 4.

Flavius Sabinus, V. I. 2, V. 2. Son
of Flavius Petro and father of
Vespasian.

Flavius Sabinus, Vit. XV. 2, 3; V. I.
3; D. I. 2. Brother of Vespasian.

Flavius Sabinus, D. X. 4. Cousin
of Domitian.

Flavus, *see* Verginius *and* Sulpicius.

Florales ludi, G. VI. 1. Games on
the Floralia, the festival of
Flora, goddess of flowers,
held April 28.

Florus (Flaurus), *see* Mestrius.

Fonteius Capito, C., Cal. VIII. 1.
Consul in A.D. 12.

Fonteius Capito (L.), G. XI.
Consul in A.D. 59.

Formiani, Vit. VII. 2. The people
of Formiae, a town of south-
eastern Latium on the Appian
Way.

Fortuna, A. LXV. 1; N. XXIII. 3; G.
IV. 3, XVIII. 2 (*bis*); *Praenestina*,
D. XV. 2; *Fortunae Antiatinae*,
Cal. LVII. 3.

Forum Appi, T. II. 2. A small
town of Latium south-east
of Rome on the Appian Way,
at the beginning of the

Pomptine Marshes.

Frugi, *see* Calpurnius *and*
Licinius.

Fucinus lacus, J. XLIV. 3; Cl. XX. 1,
2, XXI. 6, XXXII. A lake in the
country of the Marsi, east
of Rome, drained by
Claudius.

Fulvia, A. XVII. 5, LXII. 1 (*bis*);
Rh. V. Wife of Mark Antony.

Fulvia Sisennia, Pers.

Fulvius Nobilior, M., Ter. V.
Consul in 159 B.C.

Fundanus, -a, -um, *adj.* from
Fundi, T. V.; *decurione*, Cal.
XXIII. 2; *see also* Galeria.

Fundi, T. V.; G. IV. 1, VIII. 1. A
town of Latium on the Appian
Way.

Furiae, N. XXXIV. 4. The Furies,
the Greek Eumenides.

Furius, Ter., I. V.

Furius Bibaculus, Gr. IV., IX., XI.
A Roman poet born 103 B.C.,
parodied by Horace, *Serm.* 2.
5. 39 ff.

(Furius) Camillus, T. III. 2, Cl.
XXVI. 1. Dictator in 396 B.C.

(Furius) Camillus Arruntius, O.
II. 1. Consul in A.D. 32.

Furius Camillus Scribonianus,
Cl. XIII. 2, XXXV. 2; O. I. 2.

Furius Leptinus, J. XXXIX. 1.

Furnilla, *see* Marcia.

Fuscus, *see* Cornelius.

Fusius, Pers.

Gabinius, A., J. L. 1.

Gabinius Secundus Cauchius
(P.), Cl. XXIV. 3.

INDEX

Suetonius:

essedarii, who fought from Gallic chariots (*essedae*): Cal. XXXV. 3; Cl. XXI. 5.

meridiani, *see* note on Cl. XXXIV. 2.

murmillones, who fought with the *Thraeces* and with the *retiarii*. They derived their name from a kind of fish (μορμύρος or μορμύλος), an image of which they wore as a device on their helmets. Little or nothing is known about their armour: Cal. XXXII. 2, LV. 2; N. XXX. 2; D. X. 1.

oplomachi, heavy armed gladiators; according to Lipsius, a later name for the Samnites, derived from their large shield (ὅπλον): Cal. XXXV. 2.

paegniarii, Cal. XXVI. 5 (*see* note).

retiarii, "net-fighters," who were lightly armed and fought with uncovered heads. They carried a net, in which they tried to entangle their opponents, and a trident and dagger, with which they slew them, if successful: Cal. XXX. 3; Cl. XXXIV. 1.

secutores, the usual opponents of the *retiarii*. They were armed with a sword, a shield, one greave, and a visored helmet: Cal. XXX. 3.

Thraeces, heavily armed gladiators, but distinguished from the *oplomachi* by the small Thracian buckler (*parma*) in place of the large shield. They wore greaves on both legs, a visored helmet, and a sleeve on the right arm, and carried a short curved or bent sword (*sica*). They fought with one another, with the *oplomachi*, and with the *murmillones*: Cal. XXXV. 2, LIV. 1, LV. 2; Tit. VIII. 2; D. X. 1.

Glycias, T. II. 2.

Glyco, A. XI. A physician.

Gnipho, *see* Antonius.

Gracchi, T. III. 2. The celebrated tribunes, Tiberius and Gaius Gracchus.

Graecanicus, -a, -um, *adj.* from Graecia: *toga*, D. IV. 4.

Graece, *adv.* from Graecus: T. LXXI.; Cal. XXXIX. 1, XLII. 1; N. VII. 2, XXXIX. 2; Tit. III. 2; D. IV. 4, XIII. 2; Gr. VII.; Rh. I.

Graecia, J. XXVIII. 1; T. XLIX. 2; Cal. XXII. 2; Cl. XVI. 2 (*provincia*); N. XXV. 1, XXVIII. 2, XXXIV. 4, LIII.; Ter. I., III., V.; Virg. 35.

Graeci, J. LII. 2, LXVIII. 4; A. XCVIII. 3; T. XLVI.; Cal. XXIX. 2; N. XXII. 3; Gr. I., IV. (*bis*); Rh. I. (*bis*); Ter. IV., V.; *semigraeci*, Gr. IV.

Graeculi, T. XI. 1, LVII.; *sing.*, Cl. XV. 4. Diminutive of Graecus, with a contemptuous or patronizing force.

INDEX

the Lupercal, the cave at the south-west corner of the Palatine hill, and with a mythical Lupercus, but the god in whose honour it was celebrated was unknown to the Romans themselves. As a part of the ceremony the Luperci, girt with the skins of sacrificed goats and with strips of the skins in their hands, ran about the base of the Palatine, striking the women whom they met, or who put themselves in their way, that they might "shake off their sterile curse" (Shakes., *Julius Caesar*, 1. 2. 9).

Luperci, J. LXXVI. 1. Two colleges of priests for the celebration of the Lupercalia, *q.v.*

Lurco, *see* Aufidius.

Luscio, D. I. 1. The name of a poem of Nero.

Lusitani, J. LIV. 1; G. III. 2. The people of Lusitania.

Lusitania, O. III. 2. A country in the western part of the Spanish peninsula, modern Portugal.

Lutatius Daphnis, Gr. III.

Lycia, A. LXV. 1; V. VIII. 4. A district of south-western Asia Minor.

Lycii, Cl. XXV. 3. The inhabitants of Lycia.

Lycius, A. XLIII. 3.

Lydia, Gr. XI. (*ter*). A poem of Valerius Cato.

Macedones, Cal. LVII. 4. The people of Macedonia.

Macedonia, J. XXXV. 1; A. III. 1, IV. 1; T. XIV. 3, XVI. 2; Cl. XXV. 3; Gr. IX. A country north of Greece, at the north-eastern end of the Aegean Sea.

Macer, *see* Clodius *and* Pompeius.

Macro, Cal. XII. 2 (*bis*), XXIII. 2, XXVI. 1. Prefect of the praetorian guard.

Maecenas, A. LXVI. 3, LXXII. 2, LXXXVI. 2; Gr. XXI.; Hor. (*sexies*); Virg. 20, 27, 37, 44.

Maecenatianus, -a, -um, *adj.* from Maecenas: *hortos*, T. XV. 1; Virg. 13; *turre*, N. XXXVIII. 2 (*see* note).

Maecius, D. XX.

Maenianum, Cal. XVIII. 3. The projecting balcony of a house, named from its originator, one Maenius; commonly used in the plural.

Magi, N. XXXIV. 4. A body of learned men among the Persians; also used generally in the sense of "magicians."

Magnes, Pers., of Magnesia, a city in western Asia Minor (Lydia), on the river Hermus.

Magnus, *see* Alexander, Mithridates, Pompeius.

Mago, D. X. 3. The name of a brother of Hannibal, applied to a slave.

Magus, Virg. 1.

Mallia, A. LXX. 1 (*see* note).

Mallonia, T. XLV.

521

INDEX

(Munatius) Plancus, L., A. CI. 1.
Consul in A.D. 13.

Munda, A. XCIV. 11. A town of
Spain, the scene of Caesar's
final victory in the Civil War.

Mundensis, -e, *adj.* from
Munda; *proelium*, J. LVI. 5.

Murena, *see* Varro.

murmillo, *see* gladiator.

Musa, *see* Antonius.

Musae, Gr. VI.; *see* also Hercules.

Musium (Museum), Cl. XLII. 2.
An institution at Alexandria
for the advancement of learning and the support of scholars, containing a lecture hall,
a common dining-room, clois-
ters, etc.

Mutina, A. X. 2, LXXVII. A city
of Cisalpine Gaul; modern
Modena.

Mutinensis, -e, *adj.* from
Mutina: *acies*, A. XII.; *bellum*,
A. IX. 1, LXXXIV. 1; Rh. I.

Mylae, A. XVI. 1. A promontory
and town in the north-eastern
part of Sicily, not far from
Messana.

Mytilenae, J. II.; A. LXVI. 3; T. X.
1. The chief city of Lesbos, a
large island off the western
coast of Asia Minor.

Naevia, *see* Ennia.

Naevius (Cn.), Gr. II.; Ter. V. The
early Roman epic and dra-
matic poet (269–199 B.C.).

Nais, *see* Servilia.

Narbo, T. IV. 1. A city of

southern Gaul; modern
Narbonne.

Narcissus, Cl. XXVIII., XXXVII. 2;
Vit. II. 5; V. IV. 1, 2; Tit. II.
Freedman of Claudius.

Naso, *see* Actorius.

Naturalis Historia, Plin.

Naulochus, A. XVI. 1. A town in
the north-eastern part of
Sicily, near Mylae.

Nauplius, N. XXXIX. 3. Nauplius,
king of Euboea and father of
Palamedes. To avenge the
unjust execution of his son
before Troy, he caused the
wreck of the returning Greek
ships by false beacons.

Neapolis, A. XCVIII. 5; T. IV. 2, VI.
2; N. XX. 2, 3; XXV. 1, XL. 4; Virg.
11, 36. Modern Naples.

Neapolitani, A. XCII. 2. The
inhabitants of Neapolis
(Naples).

Neapolitanus, -a, -um, *adj.* from
Neapolis: *certamen*, Cl. XI. 2.

Nemausenses, T. XIII. 1. The
inhabitants of Nemausus, a
city of southern Gaul; modern
Nîmes.

Nemorensis, -e, *adj.* from
nemus, "grove," applied to the
grove of Diana at Aricia, J.
XLVI.; *rex*, Cal. XXXV. 3. The
priest of Diana of Aricia (*see*
note).

Neoptolemus, Cal. LVII. 4. A
tragic actor.

Nepos, *see* Cornelius.

Neptunus, A. XVI. 2, XVIII. 2. The
Italic god identified with the

524

INDEX

Nonnius, Hor.

Norbanus Flaccus, Vit. III. 2. Consul in A.D. 15.

Noricum regnum, T. XVI. 2. A country of central Europe, between Cisalpine Gaul and the upper course of the Danube.

Novaria, Rh. VI. A town of Transpadane Gaul.

Novariensis, -e, *adj.* from Novaria: Rh. VI.

Novatus, *see* Iunius.

November mensis, J. XL. 2; A. XXXII. 3.

Novius Niger, J. XVII. 1, 2.

Novocomensis, -e, *adj.* from Novum Comum: Plin.

Novum Comum, J. XXVIII. 3. A town of Cisalpine Gaul on lacus Larius (the Lake of Como); modern Como.

Nuceria, Vit. I. 3, II. 2. A residence of the Vitellii, probably the town in Campania, southeast of Naples.

Nucerinus, -a, -um, *adj.* from Nuceria: Rh. IV.

Numidae, Ter. I. The people of Numidia in northern Africa.

numidicae (*sc. aves*), Cal. XXII. 3. A kind of guinea-fowl.

Numidicus, *see* Caecilius.

Numidicus, -a, -um, *adj.* from Numidia: *lapis*, J. LXXXV. A handsome yellow marble from Numidia, giallo antico.

Numitorius, Virg. 43.

Nursia, V. I. 3 (*bis*). A town in the Sabine country, north-east of Rome on the Nar.

Nursini, A. XII. The people of Nursia.

Nymphae, T. XLIII. 2.

Nymphidius Sabinus, G. XI., XVI. 1. Prefect of the Praetorian Guard.

Nysa, J. XLIX. 3. Daughter of Nicomedes.

Oceanus, Cal. XLVI. (*bis*), XLVII.; Cl. I. 2; *septemtrionalis*, Cl. XVII. 3.

Ocellare cognomen, G. IV. 1.

Ocellina, *see* Livia.

Octavia, maior, A. IV. 1. Sister of Augustus.

Octavia, minor, J. XXVII. 1; A. IV. 1, XXIX. 4, LXI. 2, LXIII. 1; T. VI. 4; Virg. 32. Sister of Augustus.

Octavia, Cl. XXVII. 1, 2; N. VII. 2, XXXV. 1 (*bis*), 3, XLVI. 1, LVII. 1. Daughter of the Emperor Claudius.

Octaviae porticus, A. XXIX. 4; Gr. XXI. A colonnade between the circus Flaminius and the theatre of Marcellus, built by Augustus in place of the porticus Metelli, and named from his younger sister Octavia.

Octavii, A. I., II. 2, 3.

Octavius, -a, -um, *adj.* to Octavius: *gens*, A. I.; *vicus*, A. I. A street of Velitrae.

Octavius, A. I. A general of Velitrae.

Octavius, *see* Augustus.

Octavius, J. XLIX. 2.

INDEX

Otacilius, *see* Pitholaus.

Otho, *see* Salvius.

Ovidius (Naso, P.), Gr. xx. The famous Roman poet, 43 B.C. to A.D. 17.

Pacis templum, V. IX. 1. Begun by Vespasian in A.D. 71, and completed four years later. It lay behind the basilica Aemilia and south-east of the forum of Augustus.

Paconius, M., T. LXI. 6 (*bis*).

Pacuvius, M., J. LXXXIV. 2. An early Roman writer of tragedies (220–132 B.C.), a nephew of Ennius.

Padus, Virg. 19.

Paean, N. XXXIX. 2. An epithet of Apollo as the Healer.

paegniarius, *see* gladiator.

Paetina, *see* Aelia.

Paetus Thrasea, N. XXXVII. 1; D. X. 3; Pers. (*bis*).

Palaemon, *see* Remmius.

Palatinus, -a, -um, *adj.* from Palatium: *Apollo, see* Apollo; *atriensis*, Cal. LVII. 3; *biblio-theca*, Gr. II., xx.; *domus*, A. XXIX. 3, LVII. 2; Cl. XVII. 3; V. XXV.; D. XV. 2; *ludi*, Cal. LVI. 2.

Palatium, A. v., XXIX. 1, LXXII. 1; T. v., LIV. 2; Cal. XIV. 2, XXII. 2, 4, XLI. 1, XLVI., LIV. 2; Cl. XVIII. 2; N. VIII., xxv. 2, XXXI. 1, XXXIV. 1; G. XIV. 2, XVIII. 1; O. I. 3, VI. 1, 2, VII. 1, VIII. 2; Vit. XV. 2, XVI.; Tit. II.; Gr. II., XVII. (*bis*) The Palatine hill; applied also to the Palace of the

Caesars on that hill; cf. *Palatina domus*.

Palfurius Sura, D. XIII. 1.

Pallas, Cl. XXVIII.; V. II. 5. A freedman of Claudius.

Palumbus, Cl. XXI. 5. A gladiator.

Pan, Gr. III. The Greek god of flocks and shepherds.

Pandataria (Pandateria), T. LIII. 2; Cal. XV. 1. A small island off the coast of Latium, used as a place of imprisonment.

Paneros, N. xxx. 2.

Panisci, T. XLIII. 2. Diminutive of Pan; rural gods.

Pannonia, A. XXI. 1; O. IX. 3; Vit. XV. 1. A country north of Illyricum.

Pannonicus, -a, -um, *adj.* from Pannonia: T. XVII. 2; *bellum*, T. IX. 1, 2; *bella*, A. xx.

Pannonii, T. XVII. 1. The people of Pannonia.

Pannonius, -a, -um, *adj.* to Pannonia: *ducem*, T. xx.

Pansa, A. X. 3, XI. (*bis*); T. v.; Rh. I.; *see also* Crassicius.

Paphia, Tit. v. 1. A surname of Venus, from her temple at Paphos in western Cyprus.

Papia Poppaea lex, Cl. XIX., XXIII. 1; N. x. 1. A law passed by the consuls M. Papius Mutilus and Q. Poppaeus Secundus (A.D. 9), regulating the relations of the sexes.

Papus, *see* Aemilius.

Parilia, Cal. XVI. 4. The festival of Pales on April 21, also the

528

535

and writer, consul in 105 B.C.

Sabbata, A. LXXVI. 2; T. XXXII. 2 (*see* note). The Sabbath of the Jews; the seventh day of the week, Saturday.

Sabina, *see* Poppaea.

Sabini, T. I. 1; Vit. I. 2; V. I. 4, II. 1; Tit. X. 1. The Sabines, a people of central Italy, dwelling in the region north-east of Rome.

Sabinus, -a, -um, *adj.* from Sabini: *lingua*, T. I. 2; *ruris*, Hor.

Sabinus, *see* Asellius, Cornelius, Flavius, Nymphidius, Oppius, Poppaeus.

Sabratensis, -e, *adj.* from Sabrata, a town of northern Africa, south-west of Carthage: V. III.

Sacra via, J. XLVI., LXXX. 4; Vit. XVII. 1. The oldest and most famous street of Rome, running from the Colosseum valley to the summit of the Velia (marked by the arch of Titus), and thence across the Forum to the temple of Saturn and the beginning of the clivus Capitolinus.

Saeculare carmen, Hor. An ode written by Horace for the Saeculares ludi of Augustus.

Saeculares ludi, A. XXXI. 4 (*bis*); Cl. XXI. 2; Vit. II. 5; D. IV. 3. Sacrifices to the gods of the Lower World, made in the Tarentum, a part of the

campus Martius near the Tiber. In the year 249 B.C. they were made a national festival, to be celebrated every one hundred years. Augustus celebrated them in 17 B.C., Claudius in A.D. 47 and Domitian in A.D. 88.

Saepta, A. XLIII. 1, 4; T. XVII. 2 (*see* note); Cal. XVIII. 1, XXI.; Cl. XXI. 4; N. XII. 4. A large enclosure in the campus Martius, divided into smaller sections, where the comitia centuriata voted.

Salaria via, N. XLVIII. 1; V. XII. The road leading from Rome north-east to the Sabine territory. It derived its name from the trade in salt.

Salassi, A. XXI. 1. A people dwelling in the western part of Transpadane Gaul.

Salii, Cl. XXXIII. 1 (*see* note). An ancient college of priests who in the early part of March made solemn processions in honour of Mars, in which they danced, sang a hymn, and carried the sacred shields (*ancilia*); cf. O. VIII. 3.

Salinator, *see* Livius.

Sallustius Crispus (C.), A. LXXXVI. 3; Gr. X. (*quater*), XV. The famous Roman historian (86–34 B.C.).

Sallustius Lucullus, D. X. 3; cf. Luculleus.

Salus, A. XXXI. 4. Safety, worshipped as a goddess. The

537

538

INDEX

XVIII. 1; N. XXXV. 1. One of the generals of Augustus, who in 30 B.C. built the first permanent amphitheatre at Rome. It was in the campus Martius and was the only amphitheatre in the city until the building of the Colosseum.

Statura, *see* Calpurnius.

Stellatis campus, J. XX. 3. A district of northern Campania.

Stephanio, A. XLV. 4.

Stephanus, D. XVII. 1, 2.

Stilo, *see* Aelius.

Stoechades, Cl. XVII. 2. Islands on the southern coast of Gaul, near Massilia (Marseilles).

Strabo, *see* Fannius.

Strabo, Caesar, J. LV. 2. An orator and writer of tragedies, who died in 87 B.C.

Stymphalus, Ter. I., V. A town of Arcadia, near a mountain and lake of the same name.

Subura, J. XLVI. A street in Rome, in the valley formed by the Quirinal, Viminal, and Oppian (Esquiline) hills.

Suebi, A. XXI. 1. A nation of north-eastern Germany.

Suetonius Laetus, O. X. 1. The father of C. Suetonius Tranquillus.

Sulla, Cal. LVII. 2. An astrologer.

Sulla, Faustus, J. XXVII. 1, LXXV. 3; Gr. XII. Son of the dictator.

Sulla, Faustus, Cl. XXVII. 2.

Sulla Felix, L. Cornelius, the Dictator, J. I. 1, 2, III., V., XI., XLV. 3, LXXII. 1, LXXV. 4, LXXVII.;

T. LIX. 2; Gr. XII. (*bis*).

Sulla, P., J. IX. 1 (*bis*).

Sullanus, -a, -um, *adj.* from Sulla, referring to the Dictator: *temporis*, Gr. XI.; *temporibus*, Gr. XIII.

Sulpicii (Galbae), G. III. 1 (III. 3).

Sulpicius, Cl. IV. 5.

Sulpicius, Ser., J. XXIX. 1, L. 1.

Sulpicius Camerinus, Q., V. II. 1. Consul in A.D. 9.

Sulpicius Carthaginiensis, Virg. 38.

Sulpicius Flavus, Cl. XLI. 1.

Sulpicius Galba, G. III. 1. The first of the name, consul in 144 B.C.

(Sulpicius) Galba, C., G. III. 4 (*bis*). Brother of the emperor Galba.

(Sulpicius) Galba, Ser., G. III. 2. Great-grandfather of the emperor Galba.

Sulpicius Galba, Ser., the Emperor: *Ser. Galba imperator*, G. IV. 1; *Servius*, G. III. 4, IV. 1; *Caesar*, G. XI.; O. V. 2; *L. Livius Ocella*, G. IV. 1; *Galba*, N. XXXII. 4, XL. 3, XLII. 1, XLVII. 2, XLVIII. 2, XLIX. 3; G. II., III. 3, IV. 2, V. 1, VI. 2, XX. 2; O. IV. 1, V. 1, VI. 1, 2, 3, VII. 2, X. 1, XII. 2; Vit. VII. 1, VIII. 2, IX., X. 1; V. V. 1, 7, VI. 2, XVI. 1; Tit. V. 1; *Galba Cupido*, G. XX. 2.

Sulpicius Gallus, C., Ter. IV.

Superum mare, J. XXXIV. 1, XLIV. 3, A. XLIX. 1. "The Upper Sea," a name applied to the Adriatic; cf. Inferum mare.

INDEX

Sura, *see* Palfurius.

Suria, *see* Syria.

Surrentum, A. LXV. 1. A town at the southern end of the Bay of Naples, modern Sorrento.

Syracusae, T. LXXIV.; Cal. XX., XXI., XXIV. 2. The celebrated city of eastern Sicily; applied by Augustus to his study, A. LXXII. 2.

Syria (Suria), J. XXII. 2 (Suria), XXXV. 2; A. XVII. 3; T. XIV. 3, XXXIX., XLI., XLII. 1, XLIX., 2, LII. 3; Cal. II.; N. XXXIX. 1; Vit. II. 4, 5; V. IV. 5, VI. 3, XV.

Syria dea, N. LVI. (dea Syria); *see* note.

Syriacus, -a, -um *adj.* from Syria: *legionibus*, T. XLVIII. 2; *expeditione*, Cal. X. 1; *exercitum*, V. VI. 4.

Syriaticus, -a, -um, *adj.* from Syria: *exercitus*, Vit. XV. 1.

Syrus, -a, -um, *adj.* meaning "Syrian": Gr. VIII.; *pueri*, A. LXXXIII.

Syrus, Ter. III.

Talarius, Cal. VIII. 4.

Talentum, J. IV. A Greek weight and sum of money. The latter varied according to whether it was of gold or silver, as well as in different states of Greece. The Attic talent, which is most frequently meant, contained 6000 *drachmae*.

Tanusius Geminus, J. IX. 2 (*bis*). A writer of history and the author of an epic poem (*Annales*), slightingly referred to by Seneca (*Epist.* 93. 9).

Tarentinus, -a, -um, *adj.* from Tarentum, the city of southern Italy: Gr. XVIII.

Tarichaeae. Tit. IV. 3 (*see* note).

Tarpeius, -a, -um, *adj.* from Tarpeia, who betrayed the Roman citadel to the Sabines: *monti*, J. XLIV. 1; *culmine*, D. XXIII. 2. Applied to the Capitoline hill and to the temple of Jupiter Capitolinus.

Tarquinius Priscus, A. II. 1. The fifth king of Rome.

Tarracina, T. XXXIX.; G. IV. 1. A town of Latium on the via Appia, modern Terracina.

Tarraco, A. XXVI. 3. A town of north-eastern Spain, modern Tarragona.

Tarraconenses, G. XII. 1. The people of Tarraco.

Tarraconensis, -e, *adj.* from Tarraco: *Hispania*, G. VIII. 1, one of the provinces into which Spain was divided under the empire.

Tarsensis, -e, *adj.* from Tarsus, a city of Cilicia: D. X. 1.

Tatius, T. I. 1. A Sabine king who, according to tradition, shared the throne with Romulus.

Taurus, *see* Statilius.

Tedius Afer, A. XXVII. 3.

Tegea, V. VII. 3. A city of Arcadia.

Telegenius, Cl. XL. 3 (*see* note).

Telephus, A. XIX. 1, 2.

INDEX